The Legacy of the German Refugee Intellectuals

The Legacy of the German Refugee Intellectuals

edited by
Robert Boyers

SCHOCKEN BOOKS • NEW YORK

First SCHOCKEN edition 1972

Copyright © 1969 by Skidmore College

Library of Congress Catalog Card No. 73–185326

Manufactured in the United States of America

CONTENTS

The Legacy of the German Refugee Intellectuals

PREFACE*

BY ROBERT BOYERS

THE SPECIAL issue of SALMAGUNDI on German refugee intellectuals grew out of a number of discussions I have had over the years with Henry Pachter. From the very first, I think he understood a good deal better than I how difficult, if not impossible, the project would be to assemble. For one thing, there was simply so much ground to cover, and unless we were prepared to publish a multi-volume work, we would have to select rather narrowly. Neither of us quite knew what criteria were available to guide such a selection. Were we to omit Brecht because his relation to this country has been discussed before, though never exhaustively? Since we would have no room for all, or even for most of the artists, were we to leave them out completely? Would our readership appreciate a close examination of distinguished contributions by emigre scientists and mathematicians?

Finally, I suppose, I decided on the basis of my own inclinations, my own sense of what is at once crucially important and crucially interesting, both for me and for that ideal reader through whose hands I always imagine SALMAGUNDI passing. I cannot, then, defend what we have done in definitive terms, but I can recommend this collection as having great interest for anyone who would see more clearly the relations between the emigre generation that left Germany in the thirties and the broader culture of the west that nurtured, appropriated, or rejected them. Some of the articles in this collection deal specifically with the problem of exile, and with the ramifications of cross-fertilizing influences. Others deal more with the intrinsic questions raised by a particular body of work that has been insufficiently understood in our country, as in the case of Herbert Marcuse. A couple consider figures who never even emigrated, for one reason or another, but who are nonetheless significantly a part of the emigre generation. These include Walter Benjamin and Karl Kraus.

*Written for the Fall 1969–Winter 1970 issue of SALMAGUNDI magazine, of which this volume is a reprint.

Though more might be said in explanation, of course, I think I should permit the volume to speak for itself, to stand on its merits, and to provoke the criticism it deserves. If it succeeds in illuminating some of our recent cultural and political history so that they seem a bit more accessible than before, I shall consider its value confirmed. For what else can one hope, unless of course we might wish that the breath of another age, another generation, do more than simply touch us, that it move us and quicken us, and make us better men. Perhaps.

My gratitude to all those who have contributed articles to this volume is very great indeed, but I must thank in particular Fredric Jameson and Henry Pachter, without whose encouragement and help this volume would not have been possible.

ROBERT BOYERS

July 1969

Six Portraits by Michael Dolen

Hermann Broch   Dolan 69

Hannah Arendt   David Levine 69

Brecht   Dolan 169

T. Mann

Herbert Marcuse

poku 169

Freud   DOk 169

On Being an Exile

An Old-Timer's Personal and Political Memoir

BY HENRY PACHTER

I

WHEN TWO comrades of our group had been arrested I decided it was time for me to leave Berlin. My fiancee also had been detained, but thanks to her father's connections she had been released. She had been fortunate, too, in that it was not the S.A. but the police who came to her house; on the way to police headquarters the evidence somehow was lost. In 1933 one still could rely on the Berlin police.

But it was no longer advisable to print our little pamphlets in anyone's house. Most of us were too well known in the district; to my greatest disgust I learned one day that good people were speaking highly of me, crediting me with things I did not care to have advertised. On a beautiful afternoon I noticed Vera in the street, an old friend who belonged to a very conspirational group. She hissed something like "Evaporate, please!" and I had no choice but to act as though I had made a pass and she had given me the brush-off. I also ran into Wendt, a former president of the Communist Students' club; though I had been expelled from the Communist Youth many years earlier, I had occasionally written for his paper. He had always been very open-minded, so I talked to him frankly about the situation, indicating how one might perhaps coordinate underground work. He answered rather curtly — the next week someone told me that Wendt had gone over to the Nazis. I felt like the horseman who had crossed the frozen lake; but to my knowledge Wendt made no use of what I had told him. Should he be alive, I wish to thank him publicly.

However, that revelation did it for me. I had to get out of Berlin;

anyway since I looked too Jewish I was a danger to any friend I visited, and all friends were comrades who in one way or another, more or less, for this or for that group, were involved in underground work. By November 1933 I was tired of sleeping in a different bed every night.

But where should I go? It was not easy for a Jew to find a job anywhere in Germany. Besides, by December 1933 I had become convinced that Hitler was neither ephemeral nor temporary. I was not looking for a hiding place over a short period. The Nazis were going to last at least five years; they were not ruining themselves ("abwirtschaften") to make place for a communist comeback, as the Stalinists thought. I knew that the communist apparatus was in shatters. Desperately, some brave militants kept painting hammer-and-sickle signs on walls and chimneys; but they could not indefinitely prolong the optical illusion that the CP was alive outside the concentration camps. Their leaders, however, continued to send these young comrades into the arms of the police, ruthlessly exploiting their blind faith in early victory. It was criminal to continue such revolutionary gymnastics; but the Stalinist bosses could not admit that their party had been beaten.

The Social-Democratic Party's presidium had already gone to Prague. To the most militant among us it appeared that the old parties of the Left were dead and that a new movement would have to be built — inside Germany by small circles which would meet very quietly, avoiding any foolish action for action's sake; outside Germany by those who were able to formulate the new ideas and to publicize them. It was also clear to me that the place where new ideas would crystallize out of this ferment must be Paris, the birthplace of all European radicalism, every European's second capital, the probable center of any international action against Hitler. I knew that I would have to go to Paris to explain to the comrades my four conclusions: that we had been beaten; that Hitler would last all of five years; that Hitler would not be removed by the old parties; and that the birth of a new movement depended on a frank admission of these propositions. A further consequence was that Hitler could not be beaten by the German opposition alone but only in conjunction with foreign governments; but it took some more time to recognize what that meant for the movement and for me.

Before I left Berlin I explained to my comrades why I thought this was necessary, and they agreed. I also told them that it would be better for them to survive than to perish as unsung heroes. I sug-

gested that they use every available device to camouflage themselves
and I encouraged the workers among them to join the Nazi shop
organization (NSBO). Idiots among the American occupation authorities later screened people for their "affiliation with Nazi organizations;" little did they know, or even imagine, what life was like in
a totalitarian environment. Bertolt Brecht has written a beautiful
poem about the brave men whose names and faces nobody ever knew;
after it was all over, we unquestionable anti-Nazis must have given
hundreds, or thousands, of affidavits of good faith to people of whom
we had no first-hand knowledge but whom we felt we would have
trusted under the trying conditions of the Third Reich. Still later
we met people whom we would not have trusted at first: Prussian
aristocrats and conservative churchmen who became disgusted with
Hitler only when he revealed himself. One of them was my father-in-
law, a Lutheran pastor who had looked upon the Nazis as, at worst,
misbehaved patriots but, at best, helpers against godless communists;
on April 1, 1933, the day they boycotted Jewish shops, he wrote me
a letter saying he had been wrong. Under the dictatorship, no one
knew how many of his kind were lingering inside Nazi Germany as
"internal exiles."

The experience of the Third Reich has made me more tolerant —
or better: more than tolerant. The great discovery of the 'thirties
was that the dividing line is not between Left and Right but between
decent people and political gangsters, between tolerant people and
totalitarians. Not between those who stayed in Germany (and per-
force had to be involved in the daily life of the Third Reich) and
those who emigrated for whatever reason, but between those who
enjoyed the atmosphere of the Third Reich and profited from it, and
those who lived as aliens either in their own country or in another.

My own emigration was, of course, determined by the accident of
my birth — which turned out to be a help in one respect: "Aryans"
who had to flee from Hitler's jailers were suspects in the eyes of the
French authorities. These political refugees, simple members of the
Republican Defense League, the Social-Democratic or the Communist Party, were not welcome in the country of liberty. Those of us
who hoped that the French would consider us as allies were sadly
mistaken. To the French authorities the German Left was at least
as dangerous as Hitler. Like Professor A. J. P. Taylor they thought
of Hitler as just a less polished edition of Stresemann. It was quite
a surprise to me that even French liberals showed a profound distrust
of everything German and had little knowledge (and less appreciation)

of the heroic efforts our republican governments had made to pay Germany's war debts and to become reconciled to the West. It never dawned on the French that a more generous policy toward the Weimar Republic might have saved us and them from Hitler.

Later, during the war, they interned in camps all those who technically still were German citizens — Jews and anti-Nazi militants together with Nazis who happened to be in France when the war broke out, as well as discharged members of the Foreign Legion, real toughs who often were Nazis, too. When we tried to explain to our commanding officer that this created precarious, perhaps even dangerous situations, he answered: "Some of you may not be *Boches* but you are still *Allemands.*" A staunch French royalist, he had utter contempt for "Germans" who tried to make him believe that they were on the side of France in this war. After the defeat I told this story to a friendly farmer who had allowed me to hide in his barn; he looked at me without any sign of sympathy and said: "Sure, it's suspicious if a man denies his fatherland." This simple man did not expect me to side with his country but with mine; and yet he sheltered me!

Try as I might, I never succeeded in being accepted. Yet I still consider France my second fatherland. I was poor there most of the time and I had to accept the oddest jobs, but I enjoyed every day of my seven years in France. I liked the people and I fell in love with the language; I began writing in French, too, and I even got involved in French politics. Nevertheless, it must be stated that in France I remained an alien in more than a technical sense.

In the beginning this was quite natural; one does not shed an underground existence so easily. I lived and worked for the day when we would all return openly. It is true that I had come to explain that that day was not going to dawn as early as the refugee colony in Paris thought; but in the beginning I made no arrangements to stay longer, and it did not matter that the French authorities did not even recognize my existence.

How strange is it to be a person without a passport! I soon had to fight very hard to obtain from the Paris police an expulsion order, for to be expelled meant to be recognized, and in the process of protesting the injustice one gradually acquired legal status until one eventually wrangled a permit to stay. To achieve this, one had to learn the art of bribery. In a country that is largely governed by corruption, to know whom to pay for administrative services is really a sign that one has become acclimatized. The experience shattered both my Hegelian ideas of the dignity of the state and my liberal prejudices about France. As I said, our guerilla warfare with the French authorities ended in our internment on the day the war broke out. The ghastly routine of evading the police and dealing with it prepared us for the Kafkaesque world which we finally came to recognize as ours.

II

Being an exile is not a matter of needing a passport; it is a state of mind. I discovered this but gradually. In the beginning I did not experience exile as a universal mode of existence. I still attributed my stance entirely to the specific and, so it seemed, transitory phenomenon of Hitler. We all felt that Hitler was something extra-ordinary, irregular, unforeseeable and, if rightly considered, impossible. According to the German philosophy which still was most commonly accepted and to which the Marxists also paid their tribute, this unthinkable phenomenon had no right to, and therefore did not, exist. Not really. Ernst Cassirer, the philosopher who was to be my neighbor in New York, once expressed it in a classical way which I repeat every year for my undergraduates' edification: "You know, Mr. Pachter, this Hitler is an error (Irrtum) of History; he does not belong in German history at all. And therefore he will perish." This is what all decent people felt at the time. But History cared not for human decency — or German philosophy for that matter.

While I still felt that History owed us a rectification of her mistakes — a faith on which hinged our confidence in the eventual triumph of anti-Fascism — yet I delivered my message that Hitler would last five years and that the condition of our rebirth was recognition of our defeat. They almost lynched me. Bertolt Brecht said: "How can you maintain that we suffered a defeat when we did not even fight?" He was capable of such sophistries on behalf of the Party, and I never found out whether he believed them or whether he really was an unpolitical person. But other comrades' answers were no better; all the has-beens expressed the fervent belief that nothing had happened to debunk their prophets. None of the political groups that met in somber backrooms of a brasserie or bistro to deliberate the fate of the world knew its own fate yet. Each was trying to prove to the others that its special brand of Marxism should have been followed and that others should not have betrayed the cause. There is nothing as inconsequential as émigré *querelles,* and in the midst of all that activity I soon felt more isolated than I had been in Nazi

Berlin. I formed an alliance with Arkadj Gurland, who also had managed to be alienated from all groups and who was prepared to start thinking anew — that is if he was not reading whodunits, which he considered an appropriate occupation for us.

Many of us, indeed, fell silent. The myth that exile produces Dantes, Marxes, Bartoks and Avicennas certainly is not justified in the mass. More often exile destroys talent, or it means the loss of the environment that nourished the talent morally, socially and physically. Even the musicians, whose idiom one might suppose is both personal and international, were surprised to find out how little their values were appreciated in a culture just next door. Only the few who already had world-famous names were able to carry on — living on reduced royalties, but not reduced to starting from scratch; yet, even in this category we have Thomas Mann's comically pathetic complaint that he had to live in a hotel room! Lucky also were those young enough to claim that their studies had been interrupted: benevolent committees provided the means for them to complete their education, and some endured hunger for the opportunity of a new start in intellectual life. But for most of us a new country meant more than a new language. Few found jobs in their field, and most not even jobs that might be termed tolerable. No one had a working permit, and the kind of work one could do illegally was poorly paid, never steady, and often demeaning. The more pleasant opportunities were "nègre" (ghosting), i.e. a dentist, lawyer, engineering consultant, research chemist etc. did the job of a Frenchman who lent his name and took most of the pay. Many of the jobs I had were fraudulent, ridiculous or repulsive. Having been taught by my puritanical father that work ennobles, I now learned that work can be more degrading than anything else. People who once had taken money for granted shared my feelings. One day Rudolf Hilferding, former Finance Minister and author of *Das Finanzkapital,* asked me with a sigh: "Did you ever have to work for a living?"

Each of us solved this problem in his own way, and not all did so honorably. Many had to rely on their wives, who could always find maids' jobs; but over this, many marriages broke. Others made an art of persuading backers and committees that we had a claim on their respect and money: even those of us who had not produced a line yet represented that thin veneer of culture which stood between Western civilization and the new barbarians. Our physical and moral survival depended on this high-class form of extortion, and the piratical attitude we developed toward moneyed institutions prepared us for the games we later had to play with American foundations. We may even have helped to develop the art of thinking up research projects and writing outlines which has now become the mark of the academic operator in the Western world. (I suspect this because the percentage of German problems in American research, notably in the 'forties and 'fifties, far exceeded our share in the academic population.) While one could not beat the Nazis one could still analyze them — hoping in one act to keep the question of the century before the public eye and to justify one's existence.

It is no exaggeration to say that at that time we needed the Nazis as our *raison d'être*. They had become our obsession. Their omnipotence could not be illustrated more poignantly than by the way Nazism or Fascism affected our professional careers. Erich Fromm, a psychologist, wrote *Escape from Freedom;* Theodor Adorno, who had sparked the modern interest in Kierkegaard and was interested in the sociology of music, instead studied *The Authoritarian Personality;* Hannah Arendt, a gifted philosopher with little talent for politics, gave us the book on the origins of totalitarianism; Ernst Kris, Freud's co-editor of *Imago,* studied Nazi propaganda; Ernst Cassirer, who detested the entire area of politics and statecraft, nevertheless had to write *The Myth of the State.* Remote fields like philology were raked over in efforts to discover strands of Nazi ideology in early German literature or in the structure of the German language. Having published an analysis of Nazi grammar, I was deeply touched when after the war I discovered that two scholars inside Germany had collected evidence of totalitarian corruption of the German language — a handsome example of parallel ideas among internal and external exiles. (How even the purest of sciences had been affected became apparent only much later when it was revealed that Einstein, Meitner, Bohr, Bethe and other pacifists had contributed to the development of the atomic bomb.)

Unfortunately, the Nazis were not alone in debasing the German language. We the pure ones, the bearers and preservers of German culture, became guilty of something worse: our language froze at the point of emigration, or it even became poorer for want of a dialogue with the people who create and develop speech every day. The sweet preciousness of the past which some of the famous among us cultivated was no substitute for living communion. By observing my Russian and Italian friends I had seen what happens to people who are reduced to in-breeding as émigrés. (The Russian newspaper in Paris even refused to use the simplified spelling the Bolsheviks had introduced.) Were we similarly dated? We were writing about ghosts, writing for ghosts, and gradually becoming ghosts.

It was even worse when one decided to abandon German. Working in a language which is not the language of one's dreams is to miss many over- and undertones, ambiguities and poetic notions, the spontaneousness and even the silences. Dimensions of thought and feeling must be replaced by a technique of significations, using spoken words in prefabricated, studied sequences which threaten to impoverish that which they ought to enrich. Few succeeded in becoming creative writers in their second language, though they learned to express their ideas precisely in a technical Esperanto.

Observation: uneducated people quickly learn to make small talk in canned phrases. Intellectuals learn slowly and tend to speak "translatese," painfully aware that it is one flight below the level they would like to inhabit intellectually.

III

The exile literature of those days is deeply steeped in the experience of defeat, of emigration, of the breakdown of hope. Alfred Döblin's *Babylonische Wanderung*, Thomas Mann's *Joseph*, Anna Segher's *Seventh Cross*, Ernst Glaeser's *Last Civilian*, Erich Maria Remarque's *Three Comrades* (as well as his later *Arch of Triumph* and Franz Werfel's *Jacobowsky and the Colonel*) offer glimpses of the new outlook. Thomas Mann probably was unaffected in his Olympian serenity; he continued to write for an imaginary cosmopolitan audience. Anna Seghers on her part knew others for whom she wrote: the comrades of the Communist International. But Döblin told me that he did not know his audience any longer and was afraid his art might suffer from it; he then made a deliberate effort to find an audience: he wrote a Rosa Luxemburg trilogy. Brecht, likewise, gave me a long, angry and didactic speech on the necessity for the writer to be in good standing with the Party. "Stalin?" he exclaimed contemptuously in answer to my objection; "fifty years from now the communists will have forgotten who Stalin was. But I want them to read and produce Brecht; therefore I must not alienate myself from the Party now."

It was, of course, not a question of having a publisher (which Brecht ironically called "the inner question") but of knowing that one was writing for a culture with a future; that no matter how gloomy its present content, one's play or novel would hold out hope for those to whom it addressed itself. Writers who had lost this faith, or no longer believed that their audience shared their faith, foundered and their style deteriorated. Some of the older writers who no longer knew which values they defended fell silent. Some younger ones who had given promises were stopped in their tracks for want of an audience or a sympathetic environment. The only German writer to achieve world stature in exile was Hermann Broch; most of those who had gained it before failed to sustain their excellence. But we shall never know how many good writers were broken by the shattering experience of loneliness. No unpublished masterworks emerged from secret drawers after the fall of the Third Reich. Joseph Roth died of drinking absinthe. Ernst Glaeser broke down and returned to Nazi Germany (where he became a hack, and after the war drank himself to death). In a moving letter to Walter Hasenclever, Kurt Tucholsky relates how someone asked Nitti, whose cabinet Mussolini overthrew: "What are you doing in Paris?" He answered: "I am waiting." Tucholsky comments: "I would not want to be like him." Both Tucholsky and Hasenclever took their lives. The same sense of futility caused the suicides of Stefan Zweig, Walter Benjamin, Klaus Mann, Ernst Weiss and Ernst Toller.

Many who tried to avoid failure met regularly in the German Exile Writers' Club and assured each other that German culture was where they were and that Hitler could not suppress German literature. Other writers, we heard, had little circles in Prague, at the Cote d'Azur, in London, in New York and even in Hollywood — though it also was reported that in this latter place they were unhappy or ineffective and received stipends rather than remuneration for services rendered. In Paris, at least, the indignities of our miserable life were compensated by the knowledge that our exile had significance. The closeness of refugee circles might give us a rather dim view of our leaders' human qualities; but as carriers of the great European heritage we saw ourselves, ten feet tall, bestriding the theatre of history.

This sense of our mission received an enormous boost when the Communist International held its Seventh World Congress in 1934. After a long period of sterility, Stalin — for his own reasons, of course — returned to the humanistic and democratic wellsprings of Marxism. As he sought a rapprochement with the Western powers, he launched the Popular Front slogan and issued the "Trojan Horse" directive: his propagandists engaged in a vast campaign of cultural mobilization, organized writers' congresses against Fascism, created magazines and promoted fellow-traveling enterprises. Reputable publishing houses which previously had been denounced as purveyors of mass deception now were infiltrated as vehicles of mass enlightenment; bourgeois culture, which so far had been an object for derision, now became the heritage which the proletariat was to bring to new flowering. The refugee writers, more dependent and more malleable, eagerly seized the opportunities this well-heeled conspiracy opened to them and, knowingly or unknowingly, provided the core of the alliance whose outer fringes encompassed Aldous Huxley and Julien Benda. In these circles it was easy to meet André Gide, Aragon, Malraux, Nizan, Georges Friedman and others. Though Gide was soon to voice his disappointment with the Soviet Union, it is fair to say that staying close to the Communist Party did no harm to some lesser literary reputations at that time.

The German writers, indoctrinated and disciplined by our club, constituted a sort of cadre for this campaign. Our meetings were graced by appearances of Heinrich Mann, Arthur Koestler, Erich Reger and Alfred Döblin; but our discussions were dominated by the commissars and conducted in the style of the Moscow Writers' Club. Manes Sperper — then an editor of Gallimard publishers and now an important figure in Paris literary circles — bravely tried to stem the tide of party literature by emphasizing that art must speak to the deeper emotions too; but Alfred Kantorowicz remained plagued by the knowledge that his mediocrity condemned him to remain a partisan writer and a liar.* After the war he acted as East Germany's literary pope for a while, but eventually he had to seek asylum in the West.

Another staunch defender of the party line was then Arthur Koestler. Later he boasted that he had an anti-Soviet play hidden in his desk; but at that time his job and his fame depended on the party, and the only time we met we clashed rather vehemently. Despite his "Spanish Testament," which at the time was a deeply moving document, I still think that he is no more than an intelligent reporter. After he broke with the Communists, he found a comfortable niche in the liberal establishment and retired to his private ivory tower. But his later writings betray an acute awareness of the problem with which I am concerned here: what it means to be a refugee cannot be described in the simple terms of finding a job and adjusting to foreign

* When he came to New York, he was a frequent guest of Gerhart Eisler and took part in many private conferences of Communist writers; yet in his memoirs he pretends that he did not know who Eisler was. Even as an outsider I knew, and I know that many others of Kantorowicz's acquaintances knew, that Eisler was the secret director of the Communist Party in the U.S. Kantorowicz has also written that the Spanish Trotskyites had poisoned the wells, and he never retracted even after his eyes were opened about his sources.

customs. It is a way of being, constantly lingering between arrival
and departure. No one has told it better than Koestler.

It would be tempting to describe here the intellectual excitement
of the Popular Front in France and in Spain. I never felt so close
to the masses; I never experienced a similar unity of thought and
action. Here was the great cause that allied the future of the European
culture, the achievement of social justice, the rise of the masses to
a share in power, and the fight against the abominable dictators and
usurpers. My own monument to this episode is *España Crisol Politico*
— a book that tells of our hopes and how they were shattered by
our friends.

This is not the place to repeat the story of Léon Blum's weakness,
of Chamberlain's betrayal, of Stalin's gangsterism; I am concerned
here with the consequences for our mission. The Spanish Civil War
offered the last chance for the peoples to fight the dictators in a
revolutionary way; thereafter, the European intelligentsia could hope
to fight Hitler only with the great powers' help. Since many of us
were pacifists, this meant a split after the day of Munich: a split
that rent parties, families, and even individual consciences down the
middle.

IV.

I sided with those who would have defended Czechoslovakia, and
so did most Jewish refugees. But that placed us at odds with many
of our friends in the British Labour Party and among the French
Socialists as well as many intellectuals. I did not know then, of
course, that the "internal exiles" hoped the Western nations would
resist and thereby give them a chance to get rid of Hitler; but I felt
that Munich made World War II inevitable. Only the Communists
understood this too; but ten months later they drew the conclusion —
quite natural for them — that it was better to be allied with Hitler
than opposed to him, and resumed their attacks on the democracies.

These developments left a small number of us alone between two
hostile groups of friends: those who stood on their pacifist principles
even if that meant a victory of Hitler, and those who wanted victory
over Hitler even if that meant war. War destroys principles and
shakes men into alignments. Soon the hour was to strike when men
would have to choose their comrades. Hate of Hitler, bitterness over
the defeat of Spain, desire to avenge the rape of Czechoslovakia converted most emigrants into unquestioning patriots of their host countries or of any country that would join the alliance. (One did not

mention the Moscow trials as long as Stalin seemed to hate Hitler as badly as we did.) They became super-patriots and worked for agencies from which the liberal intellectual naturally shrinks, such as the Deuxième Bureau in France or the F.B.I. in the United States, even the G.P.U. Some, like Karl August Wittfogel, Stefan Possony and others, later forgot their native liberalism so far as to support Joseph McCarthy.

A few of us, however, did not see things that simply. Cosmopolitans and liberals, we could not turn into chauvinists and militarists, and we doubted whether we had a right to shed French blood to redeem our defeat in Germany; we wondered: did we have a right to appeal, in France, to the same patriotic instincts which we had condemned in Germany, from which we had fled and which we pretended to fight in the name of civilization?

Nor was Western civilization any longer as self-evident a value as we would have liked to think. In France we had become familiar with a new literature which ran counter to our notions of criticism: starting from Rimbaud, a series of poètes maudits had rejected that civilization wholesale; the line ended with Montherlant and Céline in France, with T. S. Eliot in U.S.A., with D. H. Lawrence in England. After Nietzsche, Germany too had produced a similar revolution against intellectualism, but we had dismissed its symptoms as a peculiar German disease. The same disease now stared us in the face as a European phenomenon. Our cherished culture was sick, and whether Céline was right or was merely a symptom, his immediate success was proof that the enemy was not only on the other side of the Rhine. Moreover, some of these writers, like the revered Hamsun, the mad Ezra Pound (himself a voluntary exile), Céline, openly sympathized with Fascism and were rabid anti-Semites. Worse still, the disease was not confined to the Right. Sartre, who passed for a man of the Left, published the deeply pessimistic "Nausea," a sort of manifesto of despair. Western letters suffered from a failure of nerve. Though their mainstream was still represented by Jules Romains *(Men of Good Will)* and Galsworthy *(The Forsythe Saga)*, the new and incisive literature tended towards totalitarian ideas and anti-democratic instincts. Were we fighting a rearguard action? Was Fascism the wave of the future? Hemingway — whom the Left claimed because of *A Farewell to Arms* — seemed to preach a vision of the hero which Mussolini must have liked. Would we be exiles from the age of liberalism in a coming age of beehive states that was dawning in all countries alike?

As Aldous Huxley and George Orwell in England and Harold
Lasswell in this country drew the caricature of the "garrison state,"
inside Germany the expressionist poet Gottfried Benn,[1] so we found
later, had given this age the name of "Quartär," quartary, following
the tertiary order: the age where gigantic apparatuses would manip-
ulate and dominate the minds of amorphous masses. Visions of 1984
were anticipated in a curious book, *La bureaucratisation du monde*
by B. Riccio, and Rudolf Hilferding, the well-known Marxist, specu-
lated in a Russian émigré paper about the possibilities of a totalitarian
economy free of unemployment and crises.

These discoveries posed a special problem for two kinds of intellectuals who otherwise have little in common: the Marxists and the
Bohemians. Neither can bear the thought of being out of step. The
Bohemians are constantly keeping up with the newest literary or
artistic fashion, and the Marxists must be careful not to fall off the
escalator of "Progress." The literatti no longer were content with
l'art pour l'art against society; they were graduating to l'art contre
l'art and against all values. The Marxists always hailed the "next
stage" and confused post hoc with supra hoc. Walter Benjamin already saw that the common interpretation of "historical materialism"
needed a serious revision, no matter what Marx had "really" meant.
In the current version Fascism was a "higher" form of capitalism, as
the purges were a "higher" form of socialism and the literary mob
was a "higher" form of criticism. Hannah Arendt soon was to describe
totalitarianism as the action of lumpen-bourgeoisie, lumpen-proletar-
iat, and lumpen-literatti — all hell-bent on destroying the values of
Western civilization. It required the stamina of an exile not to surrender to these dark forces of man's tribal past which had unleashed
their fury in the name of progress, truth and nature.

No; this war was not being waged between a more perfect and a
less perfect totalitarianism but between a world that feared it might
lose its humanism and one that was rushing to erase all vestiges of
humanism. I had no doubt that among my allies in this war there
were many traditionalists and reactionaries, and many who discovered
too late that in the end the totalitarians must persecute them too.

To have such allies is not easy; especially if one lives in a French
internment camp and the only way to get out is by joining the Foreign
Legion. Not even those whose citizenship Hitler had revoked were

---

[1] Though Benn was quite aware of the meaning of Hitler's dictatorship, he
tried to idealize it as "expressionist politics"; after the war he ungraciously attacked
the exiles for having spent the bad times abroad in luxury hotels. Another parlour
Nazi, Ernst Jünger, also turned up on our side, surprisingly.

allowed to join the regular French Army, or were promised French citizenship at the end of their service in the Foreign Legion.

In the camp I met Heinrich Blücher, a friend of Walter Benjamin and Hannah Arendt's second husband, who now is educational director of Bard College. He had been a movie writer and he used his enforced leisure to read Kant. He also gave a test to his fellow inmates: those who liked Brecht's ballad on the origin of the Tao-tze-king were invited to further confidences. Since I found the poem particularly apposite to the exile situation, we quickly developed an understanding on the character of the near future and on the values to be preserved for a farther-off day.

The Blüchers have helped many other refugees, and it might even be said that they made a fetish of the exile condition. When I met them again in New York, they were spending a fortune to live in an uncomfortable hotel because they felt it was unbecoming for people like us to have an apartment with furniture of our own. When I bought a second-hand car, they remonstrated as though I had betrayed them. In Paris I had only garden furniture which could be abandoned without loss, and even now some of my New York furnishings have an air of the provisional. I suppose I shall never own the heavy oak table and chairs my parents had in their dining room. Contempt of the settled, bourgeois style of life is common to artists and to the exiled, as I have observed in my Russian and Italian friends too, and along with it goes a generous desire to help others who are in similar conditions of poverty and solitude.

Solidarity was the redeeming experience in the defeat of France, the details of which I must skip here. It may sound strange, but the months of insecurity in a little hiding place in southern France belong to the happiest of my life. Everybody was hungry, everybody was fleeing somewhere, everybody shared what we had, everybody felt like everybody's brother. We did not have much hope but we developed a "nerve of failure," a dogged conviction that, even should the Nazis win, life would go on and there would be new generations. Soon many thousand Frenchmen would be exiles in their own country. Hitler was converting all Europe into a refugee camp. Most of those who became martyrs had not chosen to be heroes; history had thrown them into a role they had not been prepared to play. It was natural that they could not be sustained by the positive faith of those who deliberately had chosen to resist evil or who resisted in order to promote their own cause. They found comfort and strength, however, in the new philosophy of existentialism which — strangely, again

— Sartre had introduced from Germany and developed into a philosophy of desperate affirmation. The myth of Sisyphus, as re-interpreted by Camus, taught them to return to the stone of history even as it had rolled downhill, and to begin again. In my only interview with Camus, after the war, he also said that the greatest problem for man was solitude.

I was tempted to place as a motto over this section of the essay a verse by Max Hermann-Neisse (made significant by Oskar Kokoschka's portrait for those, too, who don't read German poetry):

> "Nun scheint mir alles, was ich schatzte, nichtig.
> Der Nebel draussen hüllt die Scham nicht ein.
> Ich weiss, ich lebte meine Zeit nicht richtig
> Und muss mein Leben lang erfolglos sein."

(Now all I valued highly seems futile. The fog outside cannot cloak the shame. I know I failed to live with my age and I must be a failure as long as I live.)

V. — An Excursus

I must confess that I was also a little annoyed by the new philosophy whose adepts proclaimed with sectarian zeal the new gospel of commitment — engagement, Sartre called it — as though no philosophy ever before had taught man to act in response to the needs of his fellow men. Kant's categorical imperative in effect says nothing else; Hegel had developed the full dialectics of human interaction, and Marx's epistemology started out from the explicit assumption that social action is the only *human* way to know others; Marx concluded with his own categorical imperative: that man must join the action that leads to the liberation of all mankind. These activist, dialectical traits in Marx's thinking had been brought out by Lukacs and Korsch even before J. P. Mayer published the "early manuscripts" which contained these ideas in so many words. Erich Fromm now has given these ideas wide circulation.

In his own way, Sidney Hook, with whom I had been in Korsch's course, had found a convergence of these ideas with Dewey's logic of action. The dialectics, after all, is nothing but the recognition that in the humanities and social sciences the observer is always part of the scene he observes. Involvement, therefore, was nothing new to us, and we hailed "engagement" as a more poignant word, also for the possibilities of future development it seemed to open. Unfortun-

ately the word remained barren. Sartre just assumed that "engagement" always meant engagement on our side; he never showed why
this was so and why one could not be engaged on the other side as
well. In fact, most of the earlier existentialists were engaged on the
other side. There is nothing especially "Left" in St. Exupéry, and it
would not be difficult to make out Mussolini as an existentialist
politician.

It has often been said that the same act done by a different person
becomes a different act. It is just as true that the same act done by
the same person at a different time is a different act. When the
refugees introduced existentialism in America it already had become
a fad, an empty attitude. Soon courses were held and systems were
studied; every society lady could repeat the banality that existence
came before essence, or find everything "absurd." Likewise, Hannah
Arendt had the unfortunate intuition that America needed Kafka, and
people who lived quite comfortably in the world he had scorned,
assured each other gleefully that they were living in a Kafkaesque
world. Surrealism became the "in" thing and Dali made a fortune.
To be accepted in the American literary establishment one had to
mention Anxiety. A thread to which desperate people had clung in
their great distress thus became the plaything of a literary game. In
the context of the American society which we tried to enter by converting it, existentialism became, in Adorno's words, the last form
of conformism. It was particularly suited to a society which no longer
knew what it wished to conform to; perhaps it was meant to épatez
les bourgeois, but it only tickled them.

I am, of course, not referring here to existentialism as a technique
of philosophical inquiry or of psycho-therapeutical intuition, but as
"Lebensanschauung" or "Weltanschauung." This aspect of it fulfilled a need in times of great ambiguity; but it could never be a
revolutionary philosophy capable of guiding the perplexed out of their
condition. After the war existentialism blossomed out into a full-
fledged system, with various sub-schools — Marxist, atheist, Christian,
humanist — fighting for precedence. Since this development must be
considered a gigantic failure and existentialism was an exile philosophy
more than anything else, we have to confess that philosophically the
war-time emigration remained sterile. We produced no basically new
idea and, in contrast to the Italians, no new political movement
either.

At that time Paris was swarming with refugees from many countries,
and in 1938 they were joined by a wave of Spaniards. I had many

friends among the two older emigrations that had preceded us in Paris: the Russians and the Italians. Their life was tragic. It seemed to me that the length of their exile had hardened rather than mellowed their sectarianism; especially the Russians had learned little and forgotten even less. Their attitude to the Soviet State did not change until Stalin called on their patriotic feelings, and then many thought of going back — precisely at the moment when the dictatorship exhibited its ugliest features.

A new attitude was struck by the brothers Rosselli and their group "Giustizia e Libertà." When they were murdered by Mussolini's agents 200,000 of us marched behind their biers to Père Lachaise Cemetery, where so many of the earlier *fuorusciti* lie buried. Giustizia e Libertà was neither pre-Fascist nor Marxist; it prepared a new humanist leadership for the post-Fascist era. Ignazio Silone (and, as we found out much later, Carlo Levi) had a similar vision of Man in rebellion against the Fascist state.

Since the Fascist state was more porous than the Nazi state, it was possible for the fuorusciti to remain in contact with their homeland; but they could do little to organize an opposition inside the country. It was not until the war had brought disaster rather than glory to Italy that new groupings arose and the partisans started looking for a new politics. Professor Parri's Action Party and the men of Giustizia e Libertà then tried to lead this movement towards a democratic and socialist revolution; but they were small in number, and the revolution was betrayed by the big parties. A similar fate befell the Rassemblement which emerged in France after the war. Inspired by Sartre, Roussel and other intellectuals, it remained without influence on the masses. All practical politics quickly was taken over by the big parties and the traditional organizations. There was no European revolution after Hitler, and the Jacobin intellectuals remained exiles from the political process even in the democracies.

VI.

I have to skip the adventurous story of our flight from France and arrival in the U.S. But I cannot deny myself a note of gratitude to the International Rescue Committee, founded by Lovestone, and the Emergency Rescue Committee, called into being by Paul Hagen, both of which were most active in rescuing people and securing visas for them. The Jewish committees helped Jewish refugees once they were here, but they were more interested in promoting Zionism than in opening the United States to immigration. Secretary of the Interior Harald Ickes at one point suggested settlements in Alaska, but the Zionists exploited the plight of the refugees for their political purposes. They wagered the lives of many thousands whom Hitler had doomed to die, in order to force the opening of Palestine. Fortunately, in times of emergency the American Government has always overcome the resistance of anti-immigration lobbies and obtained from Congress the power to grant visas outside the regular quota.

Going to America was in itself an admission of defeat; but we were fortunate in preserving our lives, and we were glad that so many of us were able to escape from the destruction of Europe. Many had preceded us to these shores and prepared the mold for a different kind of émigré existence: here one tried to find a place in a society that was prepared to accept the immigrant. One had the right to work and no need to feel excluded. Moreover, American society was engaged in a great revolution which seemed to continue where the Popular Front in France had failed, and that revolution offered the progressive intellectual a special opportunity to experiment with Utopias. An enlightened government was transforming the Republic into a social democracy whose ideology was at the opposite pole from Hitler's and Stalin's.

At the same time, America was on the verge of a great reorientation in her foreign policy. She had been isolationist and secure in her own strength between two oceans. But F.D.R.'s vision, combined with the shock of the fall of France, gradually produced the change which we refugees — perhaps erroneously — interpreted as a conversion of America to our political philosophy. We felt that anti-Fascism and international security were really two facets of one policy and that we were able to explain her mission to America while helping F.D.R. to educate his country for this new responsibility.

But to do this we also had to learn and to unlearn a lot. Americans did not react to the same appeals that could move us. Americans do not easily respond to abstract ideas. They don't admire a man for what he proposes but for the way he carries it out. They are forever trying out something new but are careful to keep it in the framework of old institutions which, however, are capable of infinite re-interpretation. They think that the term "pragmatic" implies something honorable and laudable and they conceive of their laws as of mere guidelines that one circumvents, modifies, disregards or adapts to. To a European mind all of this can be exasperating, most of all the ambiguity of that experimenting and temporizing: one never can tell whether "flexibility" will lead to utter corruption or to greater efficiency. Americans are gamblers, and to provide some European solidity for our program we had to gamble too.

The immigrants tried their best to understand this climate of general permissiveness and to blend into it, to prosper in it personally and to gain profit from it for their special cause. To enlist our new country in the service of humanity (and its good war) we were able to appeal to its own ideals, which we embraced ardently; but we also had to overlook some of its glaring blemishes and crying injustices. (Few of us then were aware of the full depth of the Negro problem.) To exploit the political naiveté of America, we had to flatter its consciousness of history which we knew it did not have. But we loved America for its promises, its youthfulness, its strength, and also because it was different from Europe in one important respect: America allows the individual to retreat from society and to have ties to various associations and bodies in many different ways; Europe always assumes that one is part of a social group whose every attitude and opinion one shares. In America a religious crisis does not entail a political collapse; an economic depression may leave the social structure intact; a revolution at the universities need not involve other strata. A man may be a racist and yet support the welfare state, or he may be a civil rights fighter and yet hate labor unions. This was almost incomprehensible to me in the beginning. Later I found that herein lies the true secret of America's domestic security: each group is revolutionary in its own field at one time; no convergence toward a total revolution ever threatens the system as a whole. Since the refugees had no desire to be revolutionary in America, they thankfully embraced this system which permitted them to be dynamic reformers each in his own field. They accepted the so-called conformism which sits so lightly on most Americans' shoulders — precisely because it never seems to affect vital interests of the individual; politics does not involve Americans with the totalitarian intensity of European party life. In the beginning of this century, European socialism immigrated into New York's sweat shops with the immigrants. The refugees of the 'thirties and 'forties by contrast, had no quarrel with the American government; it had saved them from destruction and, they hoped, would help to defeat their enemies — first Hitler, then Stalin. Eagerly they absorbed the gospel of opportunity. Many went into business or found positions that might not have been open to them in their old countries. In that respect they were no different from earlier waves of immigrants, except that their rise to prosperity was steeper and faster.*

Beyond these purely personal and mundane reasons, however, the American creed held the promise of another mission for us especially: we would return to post-war Europe as apostles of a global new deal. For once it was possible to identify with a living state, and we gladly exchanged European ideologies for the absorbing and fascinating adventure of American pragmatism. I don't know what would have happened if we had arrived here under Hoover. But F.D.R. and after him Truman persuaded us that our fight and America's were one, not only against Hitler but against all forms of totalitarianism, against hunger and backwardness, against colonialism and power politics.

During the war I worked for intelligence — no cloak-and-dagger operations but desk work, which is 95% of the job — and later found employment in market research. In contrast to many intellectuals I know a little about American business, but though I was a pretty good economist I found economics less and less rewarding, the people I met positively boring, their manners appalling and their outlook distressing. I had considerable difficulty in getting "adjusted" — an American word which had not been in my vocabulary before; but this hardly was America's fault. My upbringing and experience probably would have made it hard for me to adjust to any business community or to live by business-oriented values in any country. Yet America seems to have developed the purest strain of that culture, unadulterated by aristocratic or intellectual impurities. To make things worse, whiskey does not agree with me, I loathe loud noise, television and cocktail parties where one has to shout over the din of other people's chatter. I find baseball the most boring of sports to look at. I agree with Brecht and Sarte that the consumer culture of the American middle class represents a low point in taste and "engagement." Had my naturalization depended on my acceptance of the

* Unlike the Irish and Puerto Ricans, we did not have to start from the bottom and work our way up. Thanks to benevolent committees, general prosperity and the war, many of us were able to join the social class we had left in Europe. This was particularly true of intellectuals. In the beginning, many of us had to take positions that might be described as "academic proletariat;" but eventually, many reached positions they might not have obtained in the old country. "Upward social mobility" is no myth, and despite a few cases of failure the percentage of successful careers is truly astounding. Even my friend W. J., whose charms are not of the kind that goes with efficiency and whose academic credentials are doubtful, achieved tenure. — Observation: one could be very poor and yet be sure that upward mobility exists for us; one might also be quite sensitive to discrimination and yet not be aware of the absolute limits to the social mobility of negroes.

"American way," I would scarcely have passed. The same is true of some of my friends, though others have mastered the arts of socializing in this country.

When I turned to teaching, my worries were not over. American students were not used to the freedom that was the pride of European universities. They were poorly informed, provincial, grade-conscious and difficult to interest in problems of universal significance. When our daughter went to school, however, I began to understand why American education fails to stimulate and to slake the thirst for knowledge. What is wrong with the college in the United States is the American high school and elementary school. My idea of education was based on the European model of élite culture to which, one hopes, the masses can be lifted up. American education seems to strive for an optimum which neither develops the highest cultural potential for the élite nor the maximum useful and relevant knowledge for the masses. The result is that the cultural avant-garde moves in a vacuum, unrelated to yesterday's cultures which may or may not be taught in the schools and colleges, unrelated also to itself. I did not find in the U.S., as in other countries, a cultural capital where a constant circle of conversation is spinning a web of intellectual relations. There were no coffee-houses — and college cafeterias are notoriously unconducive to talk. Writers in this country don't seem to congregate; they emerge from their respective farms or college-residences with a book every two or three years, and then disappear from public view, except on speaking tours for enormous fees. Academic departments, of course, congregate; but not with each other. They hardly mix for lunch.

I also found it difficult to land a desirable position because I do not fit into any of the approved slots; I have written on Fascism, on Renaissance medicine, on foreign policy, on propaganda — which makes people uneasy. I am no culture snob, but I find myself saying "we" when I am referring to Europeans of the period I happen to teach, and my students have learned to accept me as a witness or as an exhibit of what I am trying to demonstrate. Friends and other refugee scholars who have written memoirs report similar experiences, and unless those who are well adjusted are not talking, the Americanization of refugee intellectuals seems far less perfect than their outward success. Yet, this is not the whole story —

How much of an American one has become he notices only on his first return "home," where everything now appears so small, so petty, so mean, so over-sophisticated, that one is prepared to praise everything American, even the shortcomings; I took offense at the servility, the class spirit, the maid's constant "Ja, Herr Doktor," the chauffeur's heel-clicking, the over-correctness of officials and the air of importance in every business executive's ante-room. No matter how heavy the cultural heritage one carries on his back, "you can't go home again." No matter how close the friends to whom you return, you come home as a stranger, or at least as a different person. Back in Europe, I loved America's freedom.

As a result, I found myself constantly caught between two camps — explaining Europe to Americans and explaining America to Europeans. I am writing for European papers and I am teaching in America. Carl Friedrich and Hans Rothfels are in a similar position, holding chairs in this country and in Germany. Others who have permanent positions at American universities like to spend a summer semester or a year at some European academy. Still more make it a habit to go to Europe at least for their vacation, or even own a house in the Alps — not to speak of the conferences and congresses they have to attend in Europe. This jetting about seems to indicate, not that European scholars have caught the American virus of restlessness but that they still live in two worlds. Despite success and adjustment, they seem to need a yearly replenishment with their previous cultural resources even while they have elected to stay in this country.

In discussing this strange paradox of outstanding successes in American academic life despite a nostalgic attachment to European culture, one easily comes upon two interconnected observations: perhaps we can be better Europeans in the United States than anywhere in Europe — unencumbered by special interests —, and perhaps precisely this purity of our European idealism makes us marketable in the United States. Both sides of this equation are also related to my earlier remark on the permissiveness of American society and government: America does not either absorb or reject a person but allows many hundred flowers to bloom in its garden. Divergency, dissent, even strangeness can be allowed to produce the sweet poison from which this enormously resourceful society may yet distill some useful drug.

VII.

The situation I have described was institutionalized at the New School for Social Research in New York. Alvin Johnson had invited a dozen great scholars from Germany to form a graduate faculty.

There were — besides some Social-Democratic secretaries of state, — Lowe, Köhler, Wertheimer, Lederer, Speyer, Kahler, Kris, Schütz, Salomon. Then came the French and Italians: Ascoli, Pekelis, Gourvitch, Mirkine-Guetzevitch. Many others taught in the Adult Education division, which after the war developed a B.A. program. The school was different from anything that existed in America — a true window to Europe. You had the impression that a correct English pronunciation would be conspicuous or improper, and when I first entered my lecture room, unknown to the students, I heard a woman ask: "Does the teacher speak English?" Having mastered the language, many teachers went from the New School to richer, more American and more normal institutions. I stayed for fifteen years in various capacities, as research fellow, lecturer, visiting professor at the Graduate Faculty, and acting dean, until a new administration decided to commercialize and Americanize the place — just at a time when American education was experiencing a deep crisis and other institutions began to imitate our methods. Already the Middle States Association had given us its accreditation and we were able to guarantee the points which our students earned in unorthodox ways. [Up to then, the Ivy League universities had accepted our students, but some southern State University might reject them. I admit that they were taking a chance, for we might have spoiled the students for the American educational system, and this was worse than any "pink" opinion they might have picked up in class.]

The New School was a place of constant experimentation and of complete freedom for teachers and students. I am tempted to say that a place so European is possible "only in America"; it was endowed with the best of Europe without any of the drawbacks and reservations. The advantage of maintaining an exile situation is precisely that you can reject compromises — provided you are satisfied with low pay or even no pay. The school, by the way, was not half as pink as its reputation. To be sure, we always had a house communist or even a martyr who had been in trouble with HUAC; but we also had a house reactionary — Ernst van den Haag, who likes to clown, played that role handsomely —, a house mystic — Alan Watt —, and several other oddballs. But on the whole the complexion of the faculty was social democratic and New Dealish. During the McCarthy period the subversive Orozco murals in the old cafeteria were hidden by a curtain (which could be opened on request, however!), and the New School had a loyalty oath, affirming allegiance to democratic institutions, before anyone else. What mattered, however, was the classroom situation, and there our audiences expected us to be left-of-center in domestic affairs and critical of the government in foreign affairs. Debate was essential, and the communists paid me the special respect of always sending a heckler into my class. In the 'sixties they also got a strong hold on the students' club until the Maoists took it away from them.

The New School used to have some links with the New York Labor scene, and some of the older students in the adult education courses may still be coming because of a sentimental attachment to the causes of the thirties of which the school retains a flavor. But the majority now come simply for the opportunities it presents: it is relatively inexpensive, it has a liberal admissions policy, and it is especially kind to older students who had to interrupt their curriculum for some reason or who cannot stand the spoon-feeding methods elsewhere. In the 'forties and 'fifties, however, students came to the Graduate Faculty because nowhere else could one get genuine Max Weber, genuine *Gestalt,* genuine Phenomenology, or as close a reading of Plato as Leo Strauss taught his admiring followers.

The principal difference between New School teaching and the methods of traditional American colleges, however, was our higher degree of conceptualization. We taught that science is not a collection of more or less true facts but the crystallizing of ideas from facts. We were less interested in methods and more in ideas. More than any particular attitude to current questions, I think that this insistence on concepts constituted one of the time bombs which we placed on the American intellectual scene. In fact, the school should have been extraterritorial in New York: it was pinkish and foreign. Nevertheless, Leo Strauss's students now occupy important chairs across the country, Gerhard Colm was a member of the President's Council of Economic Advisers, Max Weber has become an oracle for American sociologists, and Schütz left behind a great number of graduates when he died.

Meanwhile, another group of refugee scholars had established itself uptown and solved its problem of exterritoriality in quite an ingenious way. The once-famous Institute for Social Research of Frankfurt, then the only Marxist academy west of Minsk, had transferred its headquarters first to Paris and Geneva, then to New York and, more specifically, to West 117th Street. Its letterhead ostentatiously announced that its telephone ran through the Columbia University switchboard, and thanks to the salesmanship of Max Horkheimer or to the constellation of the war, its members eventually succeeded in teaching courses at Columbia. They also served in war agencies of the U.S. Government. Franz Neumann and Herbert Marcuse there bombarded Secretary of War Stimson with plans for a postwar Germany that would give democratic socialism a chance; they probably prevented the worst stupidities an occupation régime is capable of. Neumann wrote what to this day is the best analysis of the Nazi régime, stressing its nihilistic attack on all the values inherent in the Western conception of State. Other members used this terminology to plant more ideological time bombs: since Marx and Marxism could not be mentioned, they used Hegel or "German idealism" as code words. They said alienation when they meant capitalism, reason when they meant revolution, and Eros when they meant proletariat. In this way they hoped to assure Marxist philosophy an underground survival during the McCarthy episode. Fortunately their precautions proved to be unnecessary, and their "Aesopian" language became the fashion.

When the success story of the word "alienation" in America is written, the contribution of the Institute people will receive its due acknowledgment. In other respects too the Institute planted seeds. Adorno's Studies on the Authoritarian Personality are now a classic. Erich Fromm and Siegfried Kracauer, who originally were members but struck out independently in this country, became famous in their fields. After the war, Franz Neumann attracted many gifted students who now grace important chairs of history and government. He taught a Jacobin philosophy of politics, while his friend Marcuse went back to Rousseau or worse, preaching the return to paradise tomorrow. This won him the acclaim of students who do not understand the seriousness of his philosophy, and his latest development confirms the suspicion that he never had contact with any real society.

With *Eros and Civilization* Marcuse was ten years ahead of the Hippie revolution. But he was lagging ten years behind another German writer who combined Marx with Freud and preached the gospel of total gratification: Wilhelm Reich. A genius and a sort of racketeer, he died in solitude after having infected America with the "sexual revolution."

VIII.

Horkheimer and Adorno went back to Germany after a stint in California. As a gesture of moral restitution, Chancellor Adenauer made Horkheimer the first "rector" of the re-built University of Frankfurt. Adorno continued to be productive and influential in esoteric European circles until his recent death. Fromm has exiled himself to

Mexico but continues to come to the U.S. as a highly respected psychologist, as an influential participant of the peace movement, as a widely revered writer on sane man in a sane society.

Post-war, post-Hitler Germany offered many interesting jobs to returning exiles. But going back had to be a political decision. It was natural for Erich Ollenhauer, Willi Eichler, Ernst Reuter and Willy Brandt — representing four distinct groups which now joined in the social-democratic party — that they should return to redeem their exile image: they had to prove that one could continue where the Weimar Republic had left off. This was not so natural for me; one cannot step in the same river twice. Unless there was a really new beginning in Europe, a revolution in whatever form, I knew that the old powers would come back and Europe's tragedy would be repeated. In France one could discern the beginnings of such a revolution, but the Communists quickly stifled it. In Germany, on the contrary, no one even gave a thought to a "new" beginning. The Russians imported and imposed their systems in the East, and the Western powers revived the old parties in their occupation zone. Karl Frank (Paul Hagen), whose group "New Beginning" had prepared itself for just such a situation, did not go to Germany but became a psychoanalyst in New York. Some members of this group with excellent American and British contacts, however, infiltrated the Military Government and (I note this here as a footnote to history because the fact has nowhere else been recorded) helped prevent the merger of the Social-Democratic Party with the Communists in Berlin and saved the city from a Russian take-over. Two prominent members of the group, Richard Lowenthal and Paul Herz, became influential in Berlin. (This is not to diminish the importance of the Luxemburgist Left and of the religious socialists who also contributed to the revival of the social-democratic party; but they were less strongly represented among the exiles.)

The head of the party came from the religious socialists. Kurt Schumacher represented the best of the internal emigration. He emerged from the concentration camp warped in body and soul; but his cadaverous appearance and the mystical glimmer in his eye made him a charismatic leader who could decide to take his flock through the wilderness of opposition policies. He was an exile by choice, capable of neither revolution nor construction, and he staked his party's political fortunes on a Utopian nationalism.

Since I had concluded that neither Stalin and his successors nor the Western powers and their allies would allow Germany's reunification, I could see no place for me in a Socialist party that pursued this chimera. The Christian-Democratic Party was more realistic; but like its French and Italian sister parties it had subdued its left wing so quickly that today hardly anyone remembers the possibilities of a political realignment in Europe during the late 'forties. Adenauer's Restoration régime would not have deterred me, but neither did it inspire me, and as to its only redeeming aspiration — though I deeply care for a United Europe, there was little I could do for it.

Some five years ago Hermann Kesten published a curious book with two dozen answers to the question: "Why I don't live in the Federal Republic." German writers here explain their resentments against Germans and their disgust with the middle-class Bonn Republic; but none of them mentions the reasons I just cited. Looking up a review of that book which I published at the time, I find that I did not cite these reasons either but frankly stated: These writers, including myself, have become so accustomed to the condition of exile that they are loath to abandon it. Writers do not communicate readily with real people, and while they are extraordinarily "engaged" with their desk, with words and ideas, their actual involvement with the sordid details of political life is minimal. In exile one can project this alienation into the evasive dimension of linguistic and cultural differentials; but this differential, I confessed at the time, also serves as a protective fence. It disengages me from other people and their worries in a way that might be impossible in a country whose most intimate fears and passions I had absorbed with its nursery rhymes. The nursery rhymes our daughter learned in America gave me clues to the mind of friends I had made in the new country; but there is a difference between learning them at the age of 3 or of 33. In his own autobiography, *Les Mots,* Sartre suggests that words separate people as much as they help them communicate. Action alone, concrete engagement unites people and constitutes reality. I think that for many the exile situation suspends the need to engage in action.

I wrote: "Once upon a time we were engaged too deeply; we dreamed that the intellectual's alienation can be overcome by political action. The error was costly. The punishment has left scars. Now we shun the fire that has burned us once." Perhaps that suggestion is being confirmed by the observation that some staunch German patriots such as Otto Strasser and Hermann Rauschning, after first returning to Germany, later came back into their American exile because the old fatherland refused to adopt their particular brand of patriotism. Karl Mannheim (who died in London in his second exile) developed the idea of the "freely hovering (socially unattached) intellectual" in his first exile, Germany. His one-time friend, George Lukacs, who in the 'twenties gave us the deepest interpretation of Marxism, thereafter sacrificed his intellectual powers because he could not bear to live without a spiritual home. Utopia is forever the locus where the intellectual must take his stand.

Paradoxically, therefore, my decision to stay in the United States was not a sign of my greater attachment to this country than to my country of birth but, on the contrary, a sign that I could be less involved here and need not identify with the burning issues of national politics to the extent one does in Europe. There one can hardly avoid taking sides and one is quickly isolated if he is consistently on the "wrong" side of every issue, as I was likely to be. In the United States the fringe area of possible dissent is so wide and the variety of eccentric circles so great that one can maintain his autonomy even while participating.

IX

This is perhaps a left-handed compliment to the United States and its pluralistic democracy. The convenience of the arrangement, however, helped us over the shock of Hiroshima. I opposed the use of the A-bomb and even wrote to several scientists asking them to declare a strike; but I am sure that my opposition would have taken more violent forms had a European government dropped the bomb. Then Joseph McCarthy's investigations put my admiration of America to a severe test; but meanwhile the cold war — the first rape of Czechoslovakia, the Berlin blockade, the Korean war — had forced us to identify American power with the cause of liberty. More importantly, we now identified ourselves closely with those American friends who were defending the cause of freedom abroad simultaneously with the American Constitution. These same friends assured us that McCarthy was no Hitler — as we feared from analogy — but an ephemeral phenomenon. They were right; in America, democracy provides a favorable fighting arena for democrats — in Europe it often does for its enemies.

Largely in this spirit Erich Fromm, Lewis Coser and I took a hand in founding DISSENT magazine. Its editors then included Norman Mailer, Meyer Schapiro, A. J. Muste, Michael Harrington, Norman Thomas and George Woodcock. They were a dedicated group of radicals, mostly ex-Marxists, led by Irving Howe, who were striving for a democratic socialism and an undogmatic approach to politics. The words radical and politics may not go well together, but I suspect that Irving Howe would like to combine them. In practice, however, DISSENT has been an ideological gadfly rather than a political animal, and to that extent I am engaged in American politics. Insofar as we are an opposition that "engages" the Establishment, we "are engaged" with it in a dialectical relationship. The editors of *Dissent,* of course, are mostly college professors and thus beneficiaries of the establishment they criticize and attack. I do not deny that it would be possible to assemble a similar group of people with a similarly ambivalent attitude in Germany; but they are not active there and leave the field to the sterile "extra-parliamentary opposition" — or consume abroad the rich royalties German publishers pay to leftist terrorists. *Dissent* has been a frequent outlet for Günter Grass, but not for Hans Magnus Enzensberger.

We also published Norman Mailer's "White Negro," which is now — like many other pieces we first discovered — part of every anthology; but we did not dig Eldridge Cleaver. We gave Franz Fanon and Malcolm X. respectful but not very sympathetic reviews; and though we have published plans to redistribute the world's wealth, we have condemned Che Guevara and other self-styled leaders of the "Third World." We are hopelessly committed to "old Left" internationalism and do not agree with those who equate socialism with the humiliation of the United States by small-time dictators. While some of us have been closely identified with the peace movement, we have not concluded that we must identify with the other side in the cold war. My own awareness of the long history of European imperialism and my studies of Soviet imperialism may have helped my friends to correct their own gut reaction to the power play of the post-war years — for American populists and radicals have a provincial preconception that their own government must be to blame for whatever wrong happens in the world; whatever sins of the past they may be atoning for, I cannot conceive that they can obtain forgiveness by groveling before the destructive forces of black, yellow and red nationalism. Having fought German, Jewish, American, Spanish and French nationalism, I fail to appreciate how the cause of liberty, equality, justice and abundance for all can be advanced by the victory of their s-o-b's over our s-o-b's. For that attitude I have been attacked from two sides — the New Left thinks that one cannot be sincerely radical without being anti-American, and the F.B.I. seems to agree with that reasoning. I must confess that the incomprehension on my Left was less expected and more painful; that on my right was more annoying in practical ways: it cost me two jobs.

Writers who decided to stay and work in the United States are not, for that reason, necessarily apologists for its government. On the contrary, it is possible to make such a decision without even trying to relate to the American scene. Such is the case of two friends who should have gone back by every criterion in the book. Karl O. Paetel often tells his friends with a mixture of irony and glee that a Nazi book on race includes his photo as the prototype of the Nordic. When I met him, way back at the Berlin University, he was a sort of Nazi Trotskyite, a national-revolutionary with his own brand of socialism who, however, had exposed Hitler's double-dealings, had denounced his anti-Semitism and criticized his movement's middle-class attitudes. Paetel has published extensively on the German Youth Movement (Wandervogel) which he knew intimately. One should have thought that the ambiguous post-war situation, with Germany being exploited by her conquerors, offered attractive opportunities for a national-revolutionary leader. Yet Paetel resumed his personal contacts with no thought of reviving his old politics. Instead, he published a "Beat anthology," became briefly a devotee of Stevenson and the Kennedys, but now has returned to his youthful romanticism as a partisan of the Hippies.

The other case is even stranger. Oskar Maria Graf, a Bavarian poet and novelist, was as German — or, to be precise, as Bavarian — as a beer mug both in appearance and speech. His politics had been slightly leftish, but since the Nazis had a hang-up on regional, peasant and dialect writers, they did not bother him. On the day of the book-burning, therefore, Graf published a powerful "Open Letter" to the German Government, calling it an insult that he had been excluded from the distinguished company of Thomas Mann, Brecht etc., and ending with a strident plea: Please burn me, too! He did not learn a word of Czech in his Prague exile and he lived for over twenty years in New York without learning any English. He despised German middle class culture and stayed in New York in order to avoid any contact with the German establishment; as to its American counterpart, he was so happily ignorant of it that he could ignore it. He was committed to a Germany that exists only in literature and he has written movingly about the influence which W. Whitman, Hemingway and other American writers have exercised on him though he could read them only in translations. He loved the freedom of America, the circle of square emigrants who admired him and his own "Way down into Mediocrity" as his autobiography is entitled. The city of Munich has provided for his ashes a resting place more dignified than he had ever had in life.

By contrast, one cannot imagine a writer less Bavarian than Ludwig Marcuse, a cosmopolitan Jew, an urbane rationalist who first emigrated to southern France and later taught philosophy at UCLA. Yet after the war he bought a farm at Miesbach, of all places. To be sure, it is a beautiful spot at the foot of the Alps, but it also is the town where the Nazis had published their first daily paper! Other writers, like Hans Habe, also live in the Alps, but on the Swiss side. I suggest that alienation is equally comfortable on both sides of the Alps. As a German satirist said: "It's nice to grumble bravely from afar."

A small group of activists who wished to be both aloof and committed found shelter in the United Nations — a little society of international civil servants capable of maintaining their own standards independent of any particular nation. I regret very much that latterly a quota system has given their jobs to people who represent their respective governments and don't care for internationalism.

The greatest opportunity for combining freedom with security is still provided in the American academy. It permits a certain detachment or even dissociation from the Establishment without destroying the dialectical relationship between society and its critic. No doubt many who seem to be dissenters merely feel that, in a country where every disgruntled general grabs the nearest microphone, they would be ungrateful if they withheld their own dissent, which anyway is offered for love of the country. They represent, with many of their native-born colleagues, what Hegel called "the unhappy consciousness" — awareness of unfulfilled ideals, the powerless attempt to pit the American dream against the American reality. More than any European institution, the American academy allows the scholar to be an outsider with respect to the mainstream yet at the same time an insider with respect to itself. Success and failure can be combined almost seamlessly.

This does not completely explain yet why unorthodox scholars and teachers of foreign birth, expressing themselves in clumsy English and using as their frame of reference examples which were not within the experience of their audience, could have had such outstanding success in America. Hajo Holborn — the distinguished Harvard historian, a disciple of Meinecke — already has suggested that all this might not have happened had it happened 20 years earlier. In the 'thirties and 'forties, the exiles achieved their stature not in spite of their alienation but because of it. America, deeply shaken by the Great Depression, was passing through a moral and cultural crisis. With intellectuals now the "in" thing is to be "out," and conformism now expresses itself in conforming with the non-conformists. In such a situation the ideal-type exile can be very effective as a model; he represents alienation in his person and he describes it in his work. But a deep misunderstanding occurs here. To him, dissent from society is radical and total; to his audience, dissent is only partial. The American society is porous and multi-directional; even radical dissent in one sector does not affect the whole, and the meaning of alienation has become so fuzzy that the final effect of so much pseudo-alienation is no alienation at all. This misunderstanding has caused considerable shock when people discovered what Marcuse really meant.

X.

Let me turn now to another category of refugee scholars, a group situated on the other end of the alienation scale: those who have experienced no problem of adjustment but, on the contrary, are swimming happily in the mainstream of American life and politics. They are consultants of the government or of institutions; they fly from conference to congress to convention as veritable jet-profs, and they are part of the new power complex of industry, military and intelligentsia. This is true whether they are Republicans like Professor Kissinger or Vietnam dissenters like Professor Morgenthau: both have introduced a generation of American poli-scientists to the Metternichian and Bismarckian principles of cold power politics. But they have shown how conservatism can develop intelligently, provided it is not weighted down with nativist ideologies. In these cases, being foreign-born has an advantage which American government can turn to good account. In the economics field, Mr. Peter Drucker has made a similar contribution to the development of a progressive conservatism.

One assumes wrongly that refugees ought to be liberals; (this is not necessarily so.) I have before me a leaflet in support of Dr. Hayakawa, supposedly a cause as conservative as one can find these days in the American academy. Among the signers I find 5-10% foreign-born professors. I might also refer to Professors Hayek and Mises in economics, leaders of the Adam Smith-Robert Taft school of thought; to Professors Possony and Strausz-Hupé, two outspoken advocates of the cold war; I might refer to the role Dr. Teller played in the development of the H-bomb and in the Oppenheimer affair. Like most Irish who came to identify with America 100 per cent, German-born Jews have embraced their new fatherland fervently and are angry at those who doubt its righteousness or would like to soften its power. Professor Karl August Wittfogel — not a Jew, but once the China expert of the German Communist Party — went so far as to inform on his American sponsor to the McCarthy Committee.

As the refugee generation grows older, it may develop a natural inclination to grow conservative, either by comparison with the new student generation, which has overtaken their old-fashioned liberalism, or in reaction to its rebellion. The black revolution also has passed us by on the Left, and those of us who do not feel as guilt-ridden as Mr. Hechinger of the New York Times are apt to tell the Negroes that they must do like other minorities — smugly: Look at us! — and conquer a place in the American mainstream. Such arguments, of course, are ridiculous when coming from Jews who are Zionists or support segregated schools for their own group.

In this connection I remember my first meeting with America as it is, as opposed to the myth we had learned from our school textbooks. We had arrived in April 1941, and from habit I went to watch the May Day demonstration. I was shocked to see the ILGWU parading with posters demanding Palestine for the Jews, independence for the Puerto Ricans, colonies for the Italians; there were no Labor demands and no Negro demands. The melting pot apparently had not done much melting in the ILGWU yet! Only gradually did I learn that America is not a unified society but a multi-dimensional jig-saw puzzle: its national, racial, religious, regional, social-cultural divisions seem to be more important than the class divisions and the nation-to-nation divisions we accept in Europe. Many who came to this country with a European idea of what makes a country and how a society is structured were bewildered when they saw the American model of a pluralistic society.

Europeans usually complain that children here have no respect for their parents and teachers, employees have no respect for their superiors, thieves have no respect for the police, the uneducated have no respect for the educated. This last disregard hurts most, and a certain Matthias even has published a book saying that America is doomed because it is a society without ranks. Those who recommend European models to the Americans, however, merely prove how little they know about the society they criticize. By European standards American society may be both compartmentalized and amorphous; but it is not unstructured. Peer groups and functional élites (a term I borrow from the Vienna-born sociologist, Suzanne Keller) here are just as jealous in defending their privileges against outsiders and intruders as are classes in Europe. Most of us who have struggled to achieve status in American society know the power of "in" groups; but that which one is in or out of is not the same thing here and in Europe. I always tell European visitors here that they should not be misled by the white skin and English (or semblance of it) language of the Americans they meet; they will not understand America until they pretend that all people here have green hair and are playing a game the rules of which the observer is supposed to guess.

Part of this culture, two Britishers, Evelyn Waugh and Jessica Mitford, have told us, is a ritualistic refusal to recognize death. Every educated European will tell you at the drop of a hat that Americans lack "depth" because they evade the question that puts every human being in his place. Personally, I think that this is nonsense and that Europeans too would be much better off if they could get rid of the notion that death is accompanying them wherever they go. However, the myth of death evokes, for us, two important categories of thought: tragedy and history. Americans tend to feel frustrated when a problem does not yield to analysis, manipulation and engineering; Europeans experience failure as proof of the final futility of all human endeavor and they positively resent a people that refuses to admit that some problems cannot be solved. We wallow in history while Americans are notoriously anti-historical. At best, they can be induced to admit that history can teach some lessons; but they see their own history as a success story, not as conflict and tragedy.

American literature has produced few great tragedies, and it does not deal with fate. Europeans believe that their tragic understanding of human life can add a missing dimension to the American dream — notably by liberating it from the "shallow" notion of Progress and of the good-guy-bad-guy dichotomy. Hannah Arendt stirred America by stating the obvious: that evil is deeply embedded in every man's banal existence. Nor is it an accident that Lewis Coser introduced into American sociology "conflict" as a prime mover rather than an impediment to progress. Perhaps it would be fairer to state these contributions in a more modest way: it was a fortunate coincidence that precisely at the moment when America had lost her innocent faith in everlasting harmony and progress she became host to people whose nations had a longer memory of tragedy and whose

personal experiences had made them singularly sensitive to the crisis
of the Western mind. We often catch ourselves saying: Such and such
event reminds me of the German Youth Movement or of some other
feature of recent European history. Our sense of *"déjà-vu"* sometimes
tempts us to affect a slightly ironical stance vis-à-vis "one-dimensional" citizens. I don't suppose that such impolite display of superiority must be attributed to any feeling of a cultural differential. At
best, it is the irony of wisdom such as we find in the multi-refractory
style of Thomas Mann: a little tired, a little ashamed to reveal the
truth without devaluating its relevance, somewhat decadent or at
least aged, reflecting a knowledge that action may be necessary but
not expecting that it will solve the problem for good or avoid creating
new problems. Perhaps such a Brahmin attitude — that nerve of
failure — was a necessary counterpoise for America at the moment
when she was ready to make the century hers; indeed, some refugees
are proud to be citizens of this new Roman Empire provided they
can be its Athenian teachers.

XI.

An ancient Chinese manuscript, I am told, divides the animal
kingdom into those animals drawn on paper, those belonging to the
Emperor, those crowing in the morning, and all others. My listing
of refugee scholars must be similarly arbitrary, if for no other reason
than because some are mentioned in existing bibliographies and others
are not,[2] or because social scientists and psychologists research themselves better than others, or because atomic physicists, painters and
musicians blend better into an international pattern than stage actors,
poets and philosophers. To my knowledge, there are no statistics dividing the Jewish from the non-Jewish immigrants or those who came
from Germany directly from those who came after a stop in another
country, or from that country directly, or for whom Germany already
had been a country of asylum. In the latter category belong the
Russian Mensheviks and the Hungarian Communists. Later, America
also received refugees from Austria, Hungary, Czechoslovakia and
other countries where another totalitarian government was killing
freedom, or refugees who did not want to go back to Soviet Russia.
Add to this the Spanish Civil War refugees, and the political gamut
runs from anarchists to persons far on the Right; the motivations for
seeking asylum vary from the purely personal to the intensely political;

---

[2] One, published in vol. X and XI of *Fahrbuch Für Amerika-Studien* (Heidelberg 1965, 1966), is extremely skimpy. See my review in *Aufbau* Sept. 9, 1966.

the immediate occasions for emigrating from dire fear for one's life to rank opportunism. It is obvious that besides Freiheer von Braun many others must be counted as immigrants but not as refugees.

There are still other distinctions the statistics suggest: between those who came as established scholars, writers or artists and those who began their career in exile, like Peter Weiss in Sweden; between those who succeeded and those who, tragically, had to exchange the gown for some other trade. The most important distinction, however, must be made between those who returned to their country of origin after the war, and those who remained in their adopted country to become immigrants.

The National Refugee Service listed 7622 professional and academic immigrants between 1933 and 1945. A bio-bibliography of exile literature published in 1963 by Professor Wilhelm Sternfeld contains the names of 1,513 writers. Only a fifth of these returned to Germany or Austria, mostly from other European countries. As early as in 1936 a list of emigrated scientists carried 1,652 names. An exhibition of books, pamphlets and magazines published by exiles between 1933 and 1945 contained 900 names of authors, 100 magazines and newspapers, 150 organizations, and 120 publishers. As we might expect, exile literature proper is more concerned with the condition of Germany and of Europe between 1933 and 1945, whereas immigrant literature later-on shows increasing concern with and adjustment to the conditions of the host country, as well as a widening spread among the various sciences and arts. This is quite natural, despite notable exceptions such as Peter Gay's sudden return to the Weimar Republic after a brilliant career in the field of French Enlightenment.

The case of Peter Gay suggests an entire class of refugee scholars who arrived here young enough to attend an American university and to rise through the regular mill of an academic career. Refugee scholars proper had to break in from outside if they wished a status commensurate with their age and previous achievements. In some areas this proved more difficult than coming in on the ground floor. Some scholars and scientists (like Einstein, Köhler, Bethe, Panofsky, Schumpeter, Liebert, Röpke, Freud or Ernst Cassirer) had been world-famous before the 'thirties and merely took asylum in the United States, continuing the work they had been forced to interrupt. Others had been well-known in their home country but rose to world fame only through their work in exile. In this group belong Paul Tillich, Bruno Bettelheim, Erich Fromm, Karl Mannheim, Theodor W. Adorno, Franz Borkenau, Eduard Heimann, etc. Some younger authors also continued the work which they had begun before Hitler cut off their careers in Germany, and they went on to complete this same career in this country, publishing works which could have been written had their authors never heard of Hitler or left Germany. The Renaissance historians, Hans Baron and Paul Kristeller, are distinguished examples of such rigid separation between private experience and academic ambitions. Similar observations apply to historians like Felix Gilbert, Hans Kohn, Ernst Kantorowicz, E. Vagts, to art historians such as Panofsky and literary critics like Auerbach who introduced the methods of the Warburg Institute to America. Nor was the service some of us rendered to American scholarship lessened by the fact that it was first of all one of transferring and teaching a skill we had learned in the old country. American mathematics was never the same after Courant settled at New York University, and American musicology had almost not existed before we came, to name only two fields where the dispersion of ideas might have taken longer without personal contact.

I think we can name four fields where the influx of European scholars accelerated a movement which might well have been under way but took shape only after their arrival. One is the philosophy of logical empiricism, which was greatly stimulated when Carnap founded the Encyclopedia of Unified Science. At the other end of the scale we might place the enormous influence of the "theology without God" which Tillich introduced at Union Theological Seminar. Thirdly, it may not be just an accident that refugee scholars have been so much concerned with the philosophy of history (Meyerhoff here is a link to the Neo-Kantians, Hempel to the Viennese school, Lowith to Existentialism, Stern to Ranke, Kahler and Heilbronner to neo-Marxian conceptions) and with the history of ideas as represented by the brilliant circle that edits the Journal for the History of Ideas. (The method of the History of Ideas also has its drawbacks; it can show by documents, for instance, that Max Weber and Karl Mannheim had been known to American sociologists long before C. Wright Mills struck his alliance with Hans Gerth. But can anyone seriously deny that the European sociologists hit the American universities with an impact comparable to the invasion of classical studies by Greek scholars after 1453?)

The case of the psychologists and psychoanalysts is quite different. When the Viennese doctors arrived, America had been well advanced into the age of psychologizing. Freud, Jung and Rorschach were well established not only in scholarly circles but in the public mind. It is not surprising, therefore, that the red carpet was out for European psychologists of all schools and that all flourished under the warm sun of increasing public interest: the father of child psychology, William Stern, and the founder of Individualpsychologie, Alfred Adler; the teachers of the Gestalt school, Koffka, Koehler and Wertheimer; the neurologist Kurt Goldstein, psychoanalysts like Otto Fenichel, Ernst Kris, Frieda Fromm-Reichmann, Theodor Reik, Otto Rank; independents such as the Brunswicks and the Buehlers were able to continue their own work in new surroundings. There were others, however, who opened new frontiers. Though still European in their thinking, they nevertheless conquered problems which either were posed by the new environment or suggested by the methods and facilities it placed at the disposal of research. Thus each in his or her own way, Karen Horney, Erich Fromm, Ernest Schachtel, Bruno Bettelheim, Rudolph Arnheim and others transcended the schools from which they had come. The most interesting case, perhaps, was that of Kurt Lewin; originally a Gestalt psychologist, he quickly adopted the experimental methods of American psychology, made important contributions towards its conceptualization, proved with experiments on children that democracy is superior to dictatorship and left, at his early death, an intellectual heritage which still bears interest.

With this observation we come to the fields where the influence probably worked in reverse: the refugee scholars who made themselves a name in political science and government had more to learn from their new environment than they could teach it. Whether profound or superficial, their studies in the mechanics of government or the laws of political behavior are more American than their authors probably would like to admit. That is true even of highly original works like Karl Deutsch's application of Cybernetics to the art of government and Hannah Arendt's controversial book on Eichmann, which originally appeared in the "Reporter at Large" column of the New Yorker magazine. It is obviously true of studies whose subject matter is American or whose train of thought was inspired by American problems, like Hannah Arendt's *On Revolution* or Richard Neustadt's *Presidential Power*. Arnold Brecht's *Political Theory* certainly is more "American" in its relativistic attitude than David Easton's, and it points to at least one of the reasons why Europeans have become so well equipped to explain America not only to Europeans but to Americans, too — they have indeed found much to admire and much to learn. They experience their American horizon as more than

50 HENRY PACHTER

an addition to their European horizon: as a veritable new dimension which includes and comprises their old horizon. Moreover, the interesting observation has been made that many of the European scholars now teaching political science in the United States originally came from some other field. They had been open to new experiences, and when they had to organize that new experience into a framework of thought, they obviously could not use the bankrupt systems from which they had fled.

All of this naturally applies even more to the scientists. The style of research in this country is so tempting that European universities now are complaining about the "brain drain." There are obvious dangers in this migration. Many scientists are being lured away, from subjects which might be of greater scientific value, to projects which are of interest to American corporations or to the American government. Science is no longer "free"; it is highly influenced and directed by state interests, and many physicists, obviously, might not be doing the work they are doing now in the United States had they remained in Europe under pre-war conditions. But I understand that personally, the European scientists here are happy not only with the conditions of life they can afford, but above all with the research facilities and the professional prospects.

One more observation: science now has become a highly international venture, and discoveries made in one country can be duplicated in others at will. Moreover, scientific research and technological invention has now become so factory-like that we can speak of inventioneering: discovery and invention are functions of input. Any government willing to pay the price can now order any tailor-made material or device within definite time limits. Since America has the monetary resources she can invite foreign scientists and inventors to use her laboratories and other facilities. American science thus has become the meeting ground of an international community with little consciousness of citizenship.

Furthermore, international corporations now are spreading know-how across the globe while engineers and researchers merge with financial and commercial families to form one big international manager-class.

As a group, scientists probably are the most widely traveled elite next to the jet set with the most frequent changes of citizenship. Fulbright grants, international conventions, sabbaticals abroad and service in United Nations organizations have made them into an international community where everybody is losing his ties to native country and national government.

XII.

I have not spoken of artists, musicians, entertainers and other fellow sufferers. Their statistics are less reassuring. Many have not been able to catch the American bus; as against a few outstanding successes — a Lindner, a Martha Schlamme — we can cite sad instances of failure which cannot even be recorded by statistics because the contestant did not cross the threshold of the arena in the first place. With few exceptions, the present volume does not deal with poets, artists and novelists either; it would be dealing with buried hopes.

Ludwig Marcuse has said that Hollywood's cemeteries are the resting places of many Weimar personalities: the great director Leopold Jessner; at least five great actors and actresses; Heinrich Mann, Franz Werfel, Bruno Frank, Lion Feuchtwanger. He could have added that Hollywood also became the graveyard of many emigrant illusions: Alfred Döblin, Leonhard Frank, Alfred Polgar, Walter Mehring were unable to return the host country's hospitality. Many of those who have not made an impact on their adopted country nevertheless deserve to be remembered. They were sacrificed in the slaughterhouse of history; but the present volume, for all the arbitrariness of its selection, bears witness to the possibility of posthumous discovery, as in the strange case of Walter Benjamin.

There will be, in each of us, a little of Ahasuerus and also a little of the Trojan Aeneas who became the ancestor of Romulus. The experience of exile has been summed up by Bertolt Brecht in a quatrain which he set as a preface before some unpublished poems:

> "Dies ist nun alles und ist nicht genug.
> Doch sagt es euch vielleicht, ich bin noch da.
> Dem gleich ich, der den Backstein in mit sich trug,
> Der Welt zu zeigen, wie sein Haus aussah."

(This is now all and is not enough. Yet perhaps it will tell you that I am still there. I'm like the man who carried the brick with him to show the world what his house had been like.)

Walter Benjamin, * or Nostalgia

BY FREDRIC JAMESON

> Every feeling is attached to an a priori object, and the presentation of the latter is the phenomenology of the former.
> — *Ursprung des deutschen Trauerspiels*

So THE melancholy that speaks from the pages of Benjamin's essays — private depressions, professional discouragement, the dejection of the outsider, the distress in the face of a political and historical nightmare — searches the past for an adequate object, for some emblem or image at which, as in religious meditation, the mind can stare itself out, into which it can discharge its morbid humors and know momentary, if only an esthetic, relief. It finds it: in the Germany of the thirty years war, in the Paris of the late nineteenth century ("Paris — the capitol of the nineteenth century"). For they are both — the baroque and the modern — in their very essence allegorical, and they match the thought process of the theorist of allegory, which, disembodied intention searching for some external object in which to take shape, is itself already allegorical *avant la lettre*.

Indeed, it seems to me that Walter Benjamin's thought is best grasped as an allegorical one, as a set of parallel, discontinuous levels of meditation which is not without resemblance to that ultimate model of allegorical composition described by Dante in his letter to Can Grande della Scala, where he speaks of the four dimensions of his

---

* Walter Benjamin was born in 1892 of a wealthy Jewish family in Berlin. Unfit for service in World War I, he studied for a time in Bern, and returning to Berlin in 1920 tried unsuccessfully to found a literary review there, before turning to academic life as a career. His *Origins of German Tragedy* was however refused as a Ph.D. thesis at the University of Frankfurt in 1925. Meanwhile, he had begun to translate Proust, and, under the influence of Lukacs' *History and Class Consciousness*, became a Marxist, visiting Moscow in 1926-27. After 1933, he emigrated to Paris and pursued work on his unfinished project *Paris: Capitol of the Nineteenth Century*. He committed suicide at the Spanish border after an unsuccessful attempt to flee occupied France in 1940. He numbered among close friends and intellectual acquaintances, at various moments of his life, Ernst Bloch, Gershom Scholem, T. W. Adorno, and Bert Brecht.

poem: the literal (his hero's earthly destinies), the allegorical (the fate of his soul), the moral (in which the encounters of the main character resume one aspect or another of the life of Christ), and the anagogical (where the individual drama of Dante foreshadows the progress of the human race towards the Last Judgement)*. It will not be hard to adapt this scheme to twentieth century reality, if for literal we read simply *psychological,* and for allegorical *ethical;* if for the dominant archetypal pattern of the life of Christ we substitute some more modern one (and for myself, replacing religion with the religion of art, this will be the coming into being of the work of art itself, the incarnation of meaning in Language); if finally we replace theology with politics, and make of Dante's eschatology an earthly one, where the human race finds its salvation, not in eternity, but in History itself.

Benjamin's work seems to me to be marked by a painful straining towards a wholeness or unity of experience which the historical situation threatens to shatter at every turn. A vision of a world of ruins and fragments, an ancient chaos of whatever nature on the point of overwhelming consciousness — these are some of the images that seem to recur, either in Benjamin himself or in your own mind as you read him. The idea of wholeness or of unity is of course not original with him: how many modern philosophers have described the "damaged existence" we lead in modern society, the psychological impairment of the division of labor and of specialization, the general alienation and dehumanization of modern life and the specific forms such alienation takes? Yet for the most part these analyses remain abstract; and through them speaks the resignation of the intellectual specialist to his own maimed present; the dream of wholeness, where it persists, attaches itself to someone else's future. Benjamin is unique among these thinkers in that he wants to save his own life as well: hence the peculiar fascination of his writings, incomparable not only for their dialectical intelligence, nor even for the poetic sensibility they express, but above all, perhaps, for the manner in which the autobiographical part of his mind finds symbolic satisfaction in the shape of ideas abstractly, in objective guises, expressed.

Psychologically, the drive towards unity takes the form of an obsession with the past and with memory. Genuine memory determines

---

* It is, at least, a more familiar and less intimidating model than that proposed by Benjamin himself, in a letter to Max Rychner: "I have never been able to inquire and think otherwise than, if I may so put it, in a theological sense — namely in conformity with the Talmudic prescription regarding the forty-nine levels of meaning in every passage of the Torah."

"whether the individual can have a picture of himself, whether he
can master his own experience." "Every passion borders on chaos,
but the passion of the collector borders on the chaos of memory" (and
it was in the image of the collector that Benjamin found one of his
most comfortable identities). "Memory forges the chain of tradition
that passes events on from generation to generation." Strange reflexions, these — strange subjects of reflexion for a Marxist (one thinks
of Sartre's acid comment on his orthodox Marxist contemporaries:
"materialism is the subjectivity of those who are ashamed of their own
subjectivity"). Yet Benjamin kept faith with Proust, whom he translated, long after his own discovery of communism; like Proust also, he
saw in his favorite poet Baudelaire an analogous obsession with rem-
iniscence and involuntary memory; and he followed his literary master
in the fragmentary evocation of his own childhood called *Berliner
Kindheit um 1900;* he also began the task of recovering his own
existence with short essayistic sketches, records of dreams, of isolated
impressions and experiences, which however he was unable to carry
to the greater writer's ultimate narrative unity.

He was perhaps more conscious of what prevents us from assimilating our life experience than of the form such a perfected life would
take: fascinated, for example, with Freud's distinction between unconscious memory and the conscious act of recollection, which was for
Freud basically a way of destroying or eradicating what the former
was designed to preserve: "consciousness appears in the system of
perception *in place* of the memory traces . . . consciousness and the
leaving behind of a memory trace are within the same system mutually
incompatible." For Freud, the function of consciousness is the defense
of the organism against shocks from the external environment: in this
sense traumas, hysterical repetitions, dreams, are ways in which the
incompletely assimilated shock attempts to make its way through to
consciousness and hence to ultimate appeasement. In Benjamin's
hands, this idea becomes an instrument of historical description, a
way of showing how in modern society, perhaps on account of the
increasing quantity of shocks of all kinds to which the organism is
henceforth subjected, these defense mechanisms are no longer personal
ones: a whole series of mechanical substitutes intervenes between
consciousness and its objects shielding us perhaps, yet at the same
time depriving us of any way of assimilating what happens to us or
to any genuinely personal experience. Thus, to give only one example,
the newspaper stands as a shock-absorber of novelty, numbing us to
what might perhaps otherwise overwhelm us, but at the same time

rendering its events neutral and impersonal, making of them what by definition has no common denominator with our private existences.

Experience is moreover socially conditioned in that it depends on a certain rhythm of recurrences and similarities, on certain categories of likeness in events which are properly cultural in origin. Thus even in Proust and Baudelaire, who lived in relatively fragmented societies, ritualistic devices, often unconscious, are primary elements in the construction of form: we recognize them in the "vie anterieure" and the correspondences of Baudelaire, in the ceremonies of salon life in Proust. And where the modern writer tries to create a perpetual present — as in Kafka — the mystery inherent in the events seems to result not so much from their novelty as from the feeling that they have merely been forgotten, that they are in some sense "familiar," in the haunting significance which Baudelaire lent that word. Yet as society increasingly decays, such rhythms of experience are less and less available.

At this point, however, psychological description seems to pass over insensibly into moral judgement, into a vision of the reconciliation of past and present which is somehow an ethical one. But for the western reader the whole ethical dimension of Benjamin's work is likely to be perplexing, incorporating as it does a kind of ethical psychology which, codified by Goethe, has become traditional in Germany and deeply rooted in the German language, but for which we have no equivalent. This *Lebensweisheit* is indeed a kind of halfway house between the classical idea of a fixed human nature, with its psychology of the humors, passions, sins or character types; and the modern idea of pure historicity, of the determining influence of the situation or environment. As a compromise in the domain of the individual personality, it is not unlike the compromise of Hegel in the realm of history itself: and where for the latter a general meaning was immanent to the particular moment of history, for Goethe in some sense the overall goal of the personality and of its development is built into the particular emotion in question, or latent in the particular stage in the individual's growth. For the system is based on a vision of the full development of the personality (a writer like Gide, deeply influenced by Goethe, gives but a pale and narcissistic reflexion of this ethic, which expressed middle class individualism at the moment of its historic triumph); it neither aims to bend the personality to some purely external standard of discipline, as is the case with Christianity, nor to abandon it to the meaningless accidents of empirical psychology, as is the case with most modern ethics, but rather sees the individual psychological experience as something which includes within itself seeds of development, something in which ethical growth is inherent as a kind of interiorized Providence. So, for example, the closing lines of *Wilhelm Meister:* "You make me think of Saul, the son of Kish, who went forth to seek his father's asses and found, instead, a kingdom!"

It is however characteristic of Benjamin that in his most complete expression of this Goethean ethic, the long essay on *Elective Affinities,* he should lay more stress on the dangers that menace the personality than on the picture of its ultimate development. For this essay, which speaks the language of Goethean life-psychology, is at the same time a critique of the reactionary forces in German society which made this psychology their own: working with the concept of myth, it is at the same time an attack on the obscurantist ideologies which made the notion of myth their rallying cry. In this, the polemic posture of Benjamin can be instructive for all those of us who, undialectically, are tempted simply to reject the concept of myth altogether, on account of the ideological uses to which it is ordinarily put; for whom this concept, like related ones of magic or charisma, seems not to aim at a rational analysis of the irrational but rather at a consecration of it through language.

But for Benjamin *Elective Affinities* may be considered a mythical work, on condition we understand myth as that element from which the work seeks to free itself: as some earlier chaos of instinctual forces, inchoate, natural, pre-individualistic, as that which is destructive of genuine individuality, that which consciousness must overcome if it is to attain any real autonomy of its own, if it is to accede to any properly human level of existence. Is it far-fetched to see in this opposition between mythical forces and the individual spirit a disguised expression of Benjamin's thoughts about past and present, an image of the way in which a remembering consciousness masters its past and brings to light what would otherwise be lost in the prehistory of the organism? Nor should we forget that the essay on *Elective Affinities* is itself a way of recovering the past, this time a cultural past, one given over to the dark mythical forces of a proto-fascist tradition.

Benjamin's dialectical skill can be seen in the way this idea of myth is expressed through attention to the form of Goethe's novel, no doubt one of the most eccentric of Western literature, in its combination of an eighteenth century ceremoniousness with symbols of a strangely artificial, allegorical quality: objects which appear in the blankness of the non-visual narrative style as though isolated against a void, as though fateful with a kind of geometrical meaning — cautiously selected detail of landscape, too symmetrical not to have significance, analogies, such as the chemical one that gives the novel its title, too amply developed not to be emblematic. The reader is of course familiar with symbolism everywhere in the modern novel; but in general the symbolism is built into the work, like a sheet of instructions supplied inside the box along with the puzzle pieces. Here we feel the burden of guilt laid upon us as readers, that we lack what strikes us almost as a culturally inherited mode of thinking, accessible only to those who are that culture's members: and no doubt the Goethean system does project itself in some such way, in its claim to universality.

The originality of Benjamin is to cut across the sterile opposition between the arbitrary interpretations of the symbol on the one hand, and the blank failure to see what it means on the other: *Elective Affinities* is to be read, not as a novel by a symbolic writer, but as a novel *about* symbolism. If objects of a symbolic nature loom large in this work, it is not because they were chosen to underline the theme of adultery in some decorative manner, but rather because the real underlying subject is precisely the surrender over into the power of symbols of people who have lost their autonomy as human beings. "When people sink to this level, even the life of apparently lifeless things grows strong. Gundolf quite rightly underlined the crucial role of objects in this story. Yet the intrusion of the thing-like into human life is precisely a criterion of the mythical universe." We are required to read these symbolic objects to the second power: not so much directly to decipher a one-to-one meaning from them, as to sense that of which the very fact of symbolism is itself symptomatic.

And as with the objects, so also with the characters: it has for example often been remarked that the figure of Ottilie, the rather saintly young woman around whom the drama turns, is somehow different in its mode of characterization from the other, more realistically and psychologically drawn characters. For Benjamin however this is not so much a flaw, or an inconsistency, as a clue: Ottilie is not reality but appearance, and it is this which the rather external and visual mode of characterization conveys. "It is clear that these Goethean characters come before us not so much as figures shaped from external models, nor wholly imaginary in their invention, but rather entranced somehow, as though under a spell. Hence a kind of obscurity about them which is foreign to the purely visual, to painting for instance, and which is characteristic only of that whose very essence is pure appearance. For appearance is in this work not so much presented as a theme as it is rather implicit in the very nature and mode of the presentation itself."

This moral dimension of Benjamin's work, like Goethe's own, clearly represents an uneasy balance, a transitional moment between the psychological on the one hand, and the esthetic or the historical on the other. The mind cannot long be satisfied with this purely ethical description of the events of the book as the triumph of fateful, mythical forces; it strains for historical and social explanation, and at length Benjamin himself is forced to express the conclusion "that the writer shrouds in silence: namely, that passion loses all its rights, under the laws of genuine human morality, when it seeks to make a pact with wealthy middle-class security." But in Benjamin's work, this inevitable slippage of morality into history and politics, characteristic of all modern thought, is mediated by esthetics, is revealed by attention to the qualities of the work of art, just as the above conclusion was articulated by the analysis of those aspects of *Elective Affinities* that might best have been described as allegorical rather than symbolic.

For in one sense Benjamin's life work can be seen as a kind of vast museum, a passionate collection, of all shapes and varieties of allegorical objects; and his most substantial work centers on that enormous studio of allegorical decoration which is the Baroque.

The Origins — not so much of German *tragedy* ("Tragödie") — as of German *Trauerspiel:* the distinction, for which English has no equivalent, is crucial to Benjamin's interpretation. For "tragedy," which he limits to ancient Greece as a phenomenon, is a sacrificial drama in which the hero is offered up to the Gods for atonement. *Trauerspiel,* on the other hand, which encompasses the baroque generally, Elizabethans and Calderon as well as the 17th century German playwrights, is something that might best be initially characterized as a pageant: a funereal pageant — so might the word be most adequately rendered.

As a form it reflects the baroque vision of history as chronicle, as the relentless turning of the wheel of fortune, a ceaseless succession across the stage of the world's mighty, princes, popes, empresses in their splendid costumes, courtiers, maskeraders and poisoners, — a dance of death produced with all the finery of a Renaissance triumph. For chronicle is not yet historicity in the modern sense: "No matter how deeply the baroque intention penetrates the detail of history, its microscopic analysis never ceases to search painstakingly for political calculation in a substance seen as pure intrigue. Baroque drama knows historical events only as the depraved activity of conspirators. Not a breath of genuine revolutionary conviction in any of the countless rebels who appear before the baroque sovereign, himself immobilized in the posture of a Christian martyr. Discontent — such is the classic motive for action." And such historical time, mere succession without development, is in reality secretly spatial, and takes the court (and the stage) as its privileged spatial embodiment.

At first glance, it would appear that this vision of life as chronicle is in *The Origins of German Tragedy,* a pre-Marxist work, accounted for in an idealistic manner: as Lutherans, Benjamin says, the German baroque playwrights knew a world in which belief was utterly separate from works, in which not even the Calvinistic preordained harmony intervenes to restore a little meaning to the succession of empty acts that make up human life, the world thus remaining as a body without a soul, as the shell of an object divested of any visible function. Yet it is at least ambiguous whether this intellectual and metaphysical position causes the psychological experience that is at the heart of baroque tragedy, or whether it is not itself merely one of the various expressions, relatively abstract, through which an acute and concrete emotion tries to manifest itself. For the key to the latter is the central enigmatic figure of the prince himself, halfway between a tyrant justly assassinated and a martyr suffering his passion: interpreted allegorically, he stands as the embodiment of Melancholy in a stricken world, and Hamlet is his most complete expression. This interpretation of the funereal pageant as a basic expression of pathological melancholy has the advantage of accounting both for form and content at the same time.

Content in the sense of the characters' motivations: "The indecision of the prince is nothing but saturnine *acedia.* The influence of Saturn makes people 'apathetic, indecisive, slow.' The tyrant falls on account of the sluggishness of his emotions. In the same fashion, the character of the courtier is marked by faithlessness — another trait of the predominance of Saturn. The courtier's mind, as portrayed in these tragedies, is fluctuation itself: betrayal is his very element. It is to be attributed neither to hastiness of composition nor to insufficient characterization that the parasites in these plays scarcely need any time for reflection at all before betraying their lords and going over to the enemy. Rather, the lack of character evident in their actions, partly conscious Machiavellianism to be sure, reflects an inconsolable, despondent surrender to an impenetrable conjunction of baleful constellations, a conjunction that seems to have taken on a massive, almost thing-like character. Crown, royal purple, scepter, all are in the last analysis the properties of the tragedy of fate, and they carry about them an aura of destiny to which the courtier is the first to submit as to some portent of disaster. His faithlessness to his fellow men corresponds to the deeper, more contemplative faith he keeps with these material emblems."

Once again Benjamin's sensitivity is for those moments in which human beings find themselves given over into the power of things; and the familiar content of baroque tragedy — that melancholy which we recognize from *Hamlet* — those vices of melancholy — lust, treason, sadism — so predominant in the lesser Elizabethans, in Webster for instance — veers about slowly into a question of form, into the problem of objects, which is to say of allegory itself. For allegory is precisely the dominant mode of expression of a world in which things have been for whatever reason utterly sundered from meanings, from spirit, from genuine human existence.

And in the light of this new examination of the baroque from the point of view of form rather than of content, little by little the brooding melancholy figure at the center of the play himself alters in focus, the hero of the funereal pageant little by little becomes transformed into the baroque playwright himself, the allegorist par excellence, in Benjamin's terminology the *Grübler:* that superstitious, overparticular reader of omens who returns in a more nervous, modern guise in the hysterical heroes of Poe and Baudelaire. "Allegories are in the realm of thoughts what ruins are in the realm of things"; and it is clear that Benjamin is himself first and foremost among these depressed and hyperconscious visionaries who people his pages. "Once the object has beneath the brooding look of Melancholy become allegorical, once life has flowed out of it, the object itself remains behind, dead, yet preserved for all eternity; it lies before the allegorist, given over to him utterly, for good or ill. In other words, the object itself is henceforth incapable of projecting any meaning on its own; it can only take on that meaning which the allegorist wishes to lend it. He instills it with his own meaning, himself descends to inhabit it: and this must be understood not psychologically but in an ontological sense. In his hands the thing in question becomes something else, speaks of something else, becomes for him the key to some realm of hidden knowledge, as whose emblem he honors it. This is what constitutes the nature of allegory as script."

Script rather than language, the letter rather than the spirit; into this the baroque world shatters, strangely legible signs and emblems nagging at the too curious mind, a procession moving slowly across a stage, laden with occult significance. In this sense, for the first time it seems to me that allegory is restored to us — not as a gothic monstrosity of purely historical interest, nor as in C. S. Lewis a sign of the medieval health of the (religious) spirit, but rather as a pathology with which in the modern world we are only too familiar. The tendency of our own criticism has been to exalt symbol at the expense of allegory (even though the privileged objects proposed by that criticism — English mannerism and Dante — are more properly allegorical in nature; in this, as in other aspects of his sensibility, Benjamin has much in common with a writer like T. S. Eliot). It is, perhaps, the expression of a value rather than a description of existing poetic phenomena: for the distinction between symbol and allegory is that between a complete reconciliation between object and spirit and a mere will to such reconciliation. The usefulness of Benjamin's analysis lies however in his insistence on a temporal distinction as well: the symbol is the instantaneous, the lyrical, the single moment in time; and this temporal limitation expresses perhaps the historical impossibility in the modern world for genuine reconciliation to last in time, to be anything more than a lyrical, accidental present. Allegory is on the contrary the privileged mode of our own life in time, a clumsy deciphering of meaning from moment to moment, the painful attempt to restore a continuity to heterogeneous, disconnected instants. "Where the symbol as it fades shows the face of Nature in the light of salvation, in allegory it is the *facies hippocratica* of history that lies like a frozen landscape before the eye of the beholder. History in everything that it has of unseasonable, painful, abortive, expresses itself in that face — nay rather in that death's head. And as true as it may be that such an allegorical mode is utterly lacking in any 'symbolic' freedom of expression, in any classical harmony of feature, in anything human — what is expressed here portentously in the form of a riddle is not only the nature of human life in general, but also the biographical historicity of the individual in its most natural and organically corrupted form. This — the baroque, earthbound exposition of history as the story of the world's suffering — is the very essence of allegorical perception; history takes on meaning only in the stations of its agony and decay. The amount of meaning is in exact proportion to the presence of death and the power of decay, since death is that which traces the surest line between Physis and meaning."

And what marks baroque allegory holds for the allegory of modern times, for Baudelaire as well: only in the latter it is interiorized: "Baroque allegory saw the corpse from the outside only. Baudelaire sees it from within." Or again: "Commemoration [Andenken] is the secularized version of the adoration of holy relics . . . Commemoration is the complement to experience. In commemoration there finds expression the increasing alienation of human beings, who take inventories of their past as of lifeless merchandise. In the nineteenth century allegory abandons the outside world, only to colonize the inner. Relics come from the corpse, commemoration from the dead occurrences of the past which are euphemistically known as experience."

Yet in these late essays on modern literature a new preoccupation appears, which signals the passage in Benjamin from the predominantly esthetic to the historical and political dimension itself. This is the attention to machines, to mechanical inventions, which characteristically first appears in the realm of esthetics itself in the study of the movies ("The Reproduceable Work of Art") and only later is extended to the study of history in general (as in the essay "Paris — Capitol of the 19th Century," in which the feeling of life in this period is conveyed by a description of the new objects and inventions characteristic of it — the passageways, the use of cast iron, the Daguerrotype and the panorama, the expositions, advertising). It is important to point out that however materialistic such an approach to history may seem, nothing is farther from Marxism than the stress on invention and technique as the primary cause of historical change. Indeed it seems to me that such theories (of the kind for which the steam engine is the cause of the industrial revolution, and which have recently been rehearsed yet again, in streamlined modernistic form in the works of Marshall McLuhan) function as a substitute for Marxist historiography in the way in which they offer a feeling of concreteness comparable to economic subject matter, at the same time that they dispense with any consideration of the human factors of classes and of the social organization of production.

Benjamin's fascination with the role of inventions in history seems to me most comprehensible in psychological or esthetic terms. If we follow, for instance, his meditation on the role of the passerby and the crowd in Baudelaire, we find that after the evocation of Baudelaire's physical and stylistic characteristics, after the discussion of shock and organic defenses outlined earlier in this essay, the inner logic of Benjamin's material leads him to material invention: "Comfort isolates. And at the same time it shifts its possessor closer to the power of physical mechanisms. With the invention of matches around the middle of the century, there begins a whole series of novelties which have this in common that they replace a complicated set of operations with a single stroke of the hand. This development goes on in many different spheres at the same time: it is evident among others in the telephone, where in place of the continuous movement with which the crank of the older model had to be turned a single lifting of the receiver now suffices. Among the various elaborate gestures required to prepare the photographic apparatus, that of 'snapping' the photograph was particularly consequential. Pressing the finger once is enough to freeze an event for unlimited time. The apparatus lends the instant a posthumous shock, so to speak. And beside tactile experiences of this kind we find optical ones as well, such as the classified ads in a newspaper, or the traffic in a big city. To move through the latter involves a whole series of shocks and collisions. At dangerous intersections, impulses crisscross the pedestrian like charges in a battery. Baudelaire describes the man who plunges into the crowd as a reservoir of electrical energy. Thereupon he calls him, thus singling out the experience of shock, 'a kaleidoscope endowed with consciousness'." And Benjamin goes on to complete this catalogue with a description of the worker and his psychological subjection to the operation of the machine in the factory. Yet it seems to me that alongside the value of this passage as an analysis of the psychological effect of machinery, it has for Benjamin a secondary intention, it satisfies a deeper psychological requirement perhaps in some ways even more important than the official intellectual one; and that is to serve as a concrete embodiment for the state of mind of Baudelaire. The essay indeed begins with a relatively disembodied psychological state: the poet faced with the new condition of language in modern times, faced with the debasement of journalism, the inhabitant of the great city faced with the increasing shocks and perceptual numbness of daily life. These phenomena are intensely familiar to Benjamin, but somehow he seems to feel them as insufficiently "rendered": he cannot possess them spiritually, he cannot express them adequately, until he finds some sharper and more concrete physical image in which to embody them. The machine, the list of inventions, is precisely such an image; and it will be clear to the reader that we consider such a passage, in appearance a historical analysis, as in reality an exercise in allegorical meditation, in the locating of some fitting emblem in which to anchor the peculiar and nervous modern state of mind which was his subject-matter.

For this reason the preoccupation with machines and inventions in Benjamin does not lead to a theory of historical causality; rather it finds its completion elsewhere, in a theory of the modern object, in the notion of "aura." Aura for Benjamin is the equivalent in the modern world, where it still persists, for what anthropologists call the "sacred" in primitive societies; it is in the world of things what "mystery" is in the world of human events, what "charisma" is in the world of human beings. In a secularized universe it is perhaps easier to locate at the moment of its disappearance, the cause of which is in general technical invention, the replacement of human perception with those substitutes for and mechanical extensions of perception which are machines. Thus it is easy to see how in the movies, in the "reproduceable work of art," that aura which originally resulted from the physical presence of actors in the here-and-now of the theater is short-circuited by the new technical advance (and then replaced, in genuine Freudian symptom-formation, by the attempt to endow the stars with a new kind of personal aura of their own off the screen).

Yet in the world of objects, this intensity of physical presence which constitutes the aura of something can perhaps best be expressed by the image of the look, the intelligence returned: "The experience of aura is based on the transposition of a social reaction onto the relationship of the lifeless or of nature to man. The person we look at, the person who believes himself looked at, looks back at us in return. To experience the aura of a phenomenon means to endow it with the power to look back in return."

And elsewhere he defines aura thus: "The single, unrepeatable experience of distance, no matter how close it may be. While resting on a summer afternoon, to follow the outline of a mountain against the horizon, or of a branch that casts its shadow on the viewer, means to breath the aura of the mountain, of the branch." Aura is thus in a sense the opposite of allegorical perception, in that in it a mysterious wholeness of objects becomes visible. And where the broken fragments of allegory represented a thing-world of destructive forces in which human autonomy was drowned, the objects of aura represent perhaps the setting of a kind of utopia, a utopian present, not shorn of the past but having absorbed it, a kind of plenitude of existence in the world of things, if only for the briefest instant. Yet this utopian component of Benjamin's thought, put to flight as it is by the mechanized present of history, is available to the thinker only in a simpler cultural past.

Thus it is his one evocation of a non-allegorical art, his essay on Nikolai Leskow, "The Teller of Tales," which is perhaps his masterpiece. As with actors faced with the technical advance of the reproduceable art-work, so also with the tale in the face of modern communications systems, and in particular of the newspaper. The function of the newspapers is to absorb the shocks of novelty, and by numbing the organism to them to sap their intensity. Yet the tale, always constructed around some novelty, was designed on the contrary to preserve its force; where the mechanical form "exhausts" ever increasing quantities of new material, the older word-of-mouth communication is that which recommends itself to memory. Its reproduceability is not mechanical, but natural to consciousness; indeed, that which allows the story to be remembered, to seem "memorable" is at the same time the means of its assimilation to the personal experience of the listeners as well.

It is instructive to compare this analysis by Benjamin of the tale (and its implied distinction from the novel) with that of Sartre, so similar in some ways, and yet so different in its ultimate emphasis. For both, the two forms are opposed not only in their social origins — the tale springing from collective life, the novel from solitude — and not only in their raw material — the tale using what everyone can recognize as common experience, the novel that which is uncommon and highly individualistic — but also and primarily in the relationship to death and to eternity. Benjamin quotes Valéry: "It is almost as though the disappearance of the idea of eternity were related to the increasing distaste for any kind of work of long duration in time." Concurrent with the disappearance of the genuine story is the increasing concealment of death and dying in our society: for the authority of the story ultimately derives from the authority of death, which lends every event a once-and-for-all uniqueness. "A man who died at the age of thirty-five is at every point in his life a man who is going to die at the age of thirty-five": so Benjamin describes our apprehension of characters in the tale, as the anti-psychological, the simplified representatives of their own destinies. But what appeals to his sensitivity to the archaic is precisely what Sartre condemns as inauthentic: namely the violence to genuine lived human experience, which never in the freedom of its own present feels itself as fate, for which fate and destiny are always characteristic of other people's experience, seen from the outside as something closed and thing-like. For this reason Sartre opposes the tale (it is true that he is thinking of the late-nineteenth century well-made story, which catered to a middle-class audience, rather than to the relatively anonymous folk product of which Benjamin speaks) to the novel, whose task is precisely to render this open experience of consciousness in the present, of freedom, rather than the optical illusion of fate.

There can be no doubt that this opposition corresponds to a historical experience: the older tale, indeed the classical nineteenth century novel as well, expressed a social life in which the individual faced single-shot, irreparable chances and opportunities, in which he had to play everything on a single roll of the dice, in which his life did therefore properly tend to take on the appearance of fate or destiny, of a story that can be told. Whereas in the modern world (which is to say, in Western Europe and the United States), economic prosperity is such that nothing is ever really irrevocable in this sense: hence the philosophy of freedom, hence the modernistic literature of consciousness of which Sartre is here a theorist: hence also, the decay of plot, for where nothing is irrevocable (in the absence of death in Benjamin's sense) there is no story to tell either, there is only a series of experiences of equal weight whose order is indiscriminately reversible.

Benjamin is as aware as Sartre of the way in which the tale, with its appearance of destiny, does violence to our lived experience in the present: but for him it does justice to our experience of the past. Its "inauthenticity" is to be seen as a mode of commemoration, so that it does not really matter any longer whether the young man dead in his prime was aware of his own lived experience as fate: for us, henceforth remembering him, we always think of him, at the various stages of his life, as one about to become this destiny, and the tale thus gives us " the hope of warming our own chilly existence upon a death about which we read."

The tale is not only a psychological mode of relating to the past, of commemorating it: it is for Benjamin also a mode of contact with a vanished form of social and historical existence as well; and it is in this correlation between the activity of story-telling and the concrete form of a certain historically determinate mode of production that Benjamin can serve as a model of Marxist literary criticism at its most revealing. The twin sources of story-telling find their archaic embodiment in "the settled cultivator on the one hand and the seafaring merchant on the other. Both forms of life have in fact produced their own characteristic type of story-teller . . . A genuine extension of the possibilities of story-telling to its greatest historical range is however not possible without the most thorough-going fusion of the two archaic types. Such a fusion was realized during the middle ages in the artisanal associations and guilds. The sedentary master and the wandering apprentices worked together in the same room; indeed, every master had himself been a wandering apprentice before settling down at home or in some foreign city. If peasants and sailors were the inventors of story-telling, the guild system proved to be the place of its highest development." The tale is thus the product of an artisan culture, a hand-made product, like a cobbler's shoe or a pot; and like such a hand-made object, "the touch of the story-teller clings to it like the trace of the potter's hand on the glazed surface."

In his ultimate statement of the relationship of literature to politics, Benjamin seems to have tried to bring to bear on the problems of the present this method, which had known success in dealing with the objects of the past. Yet the transposition is not without its difficulties, and Benjamin's conclusions remain problematical, particularly in his unresolved, ambiguous attitude towards modern industrial civilization, which fascinated him as much as it seems to have depressed him. The problem of propaganda in art can be solved, he maintains, by attention, not so much to the content of the work of art, as to its form: a progressive work of art is one which utilizes the most advanced artistic techniques, one in which therefore the artist lives his activity as a technician, and through this technical work finds a unity of purpose with the industrial worker. "The solidarity of the specialist with the proletariat . . . can never be anything but a mediated one." This communist "politicalisation of art," which he opposed to the fascist "estheticalisation of the machine," was designed to harness to the cause of revolution that modernism to which other Marxist critics (Lukacs, for instance) were hostile. And there can be no doubt that Benjamin first came to a radical politics through his experience as a specialist: through his growing awareness, within the domain of his own specialized artistic activity, of the crucial influence on the work of art of changes in the public, in technique, in short of History itself. But although in the realm of the history of art the historian can no doubt show a parallelism between specific technical advances in a given art and the general development of the economy as a whole, it is difficult to see how a technically advanced and difficult work of art can have anything but a "mediated" effect politically. Benjamin was of course lucky in the artistic example which lay before him: for he illustrates his thesis with the epic theater of Brecht, perhaps indeed the only modern artistic innovation that *has* had direct and revolutionary political impact. But even here the situation is ambiguous: an astute critic (Rolf Tiedemann) has pointed out the secret relationship between Benjamin's fondness for Brecht on the one hand and "his lifelong fascination with children's books" on the other (children's books: hieroglyphs: simplified allegorical emblems and riddles). Thus, where we thought to emerge into the historical present, in reality we plunge again into the distant past of psychological obsession.

But if nostalgia as a political motivation is most frequently associated with fascism, there is no reason why a nostalgia conscious of itself, a lucid and remorseless dissatisfaction with the present on the grounds of some remembered plenitude, cannot furnish as adequate a revolutionary stimulus as any other: the example of Benjamin is there to prove it. He himself, however, preferred to contemplate his destiny in religious imagery, as in the following paragraph, according to Gershom Scholem the last he ever wrote: "Surely Time was felt neither as empty nor as homogeneous by the soothsayers who inquired for what it hid in its womb. Whoever keeps this in mind is in a position to grasp just how past time is experienced in commemoration: in just exactly the same way. As is well known, the Jews were forbidden to search into the future. On the contrary, the Thora and the act of prayer instruct them in commemoration of the past. So for them, the future, to which the clientele of soothsayers remains in thrall, is divested of its sacred power. Yet it does not for all that become simply empty and homogeneous time in their eyes. For every second of the future bears within it that little door through which Messiah may enter."

Angelus novus: Benjamin's favorite image of the angel that exists only to sing its hymn of praise before the face of God, to give voice, and then at once to vanish back into uncreated nothingness. So at its most poignant Benjamin's experience of time: a pure present, on the threshold of the future honoring it by averted eyes in meditation on the past.

The Reception of Existentialism in the United States

BY WALTER KAUFMANN

IT IS DIFFICULT to deal briefly with the reception of existentialism in the United States. The response to even one or two of the writers who are often lumped together as "existentialists" could easily be made the subject of a monograph, and to deal adequately with about ten writers in a single essay is impossible. Broad generalizations about "existentialism," on the other hand, are bound to be of very dubious value if it is not clear to whom precisely they apply. What is needed is a combination of generalizations with attention to the individual "existentialists."

I shall first attempt a sketch in very broad strokes of the influence of European on American philosophy before 1930. Next I shall ask what existentialism is, and offer first an ostensive, historical definition and then a more analytical answer that brings out what the so-called existentialists have in common. After that I shall briefly consider the reception of the major figures, one by one;[1] and in the end I

---

[1] Comprehensive bibliographies of their writings, including English translations, are included in the following volumes: *The Philosophy of Martin Buber*, ed. Paul Arthur Schilpp and Maurice Friedman (1967); *The Philosophy of Karl Jaspers*, ed. Paul Arthur Schilpp (1957); and *Religion and Culture: Essays in Honor of Paul Tillich*, ed. Walter Leibrecht (1959). William J. Richardson, S.J., *Heidegger* (1963), lists Heidegger's lectures and seminars, 1915-58, on pp. 663-71, his writings in order of publication, 1912-62, on pp. 675-78, and in order of composition, pp. 678-80, while English translations are listed on p. 688. The bibliography in Walter Kaufmann, *Nietzsche* (3d rev. ed., 1968) includes Nietzsche's writings, collected editions, and translations, as well as studies of his thought by over one hundred writers.

In the following pages I shall not attempt any philosophical criticism, as I have done that elsewhere. Critical essays on Kierkegaard, Jaspers, and Heidegger are included in my *From Shakespeare to Existentialism* (1959; rev. ed., 1960), and critical discussions of Tillich in my *Critique of Religion and Philosophy* (1958), secs. 50, 53, and 57 and *The Faith of a Heretic* (1961), secs. 32-34; the chapters on commitment and death also deal with Heidegger, Sartre, and Camus; and Sartre's attempt to offer an ethic is criticized in section 86. My estimate of "Buber's Religious Significance" is included in *The Philosophy of Martin Buber*.

shall offer some systematic conclusions about the impact of existentialism in the United States.

I

Only three or four peoples have produced more than three or four truly original philosophers whose impact has been widely felt beyond the languages in which they wrote: the Greeks, the British, the Germans, and perhaps also the French. American philosophy may turn out to be comparable to Roman philosophy: mainly derivative. There is no Washington or Lincoln in American philosophy; unlike American history, American philosophy cannot boast of figures that can hold their own against the best men anywhere.

Philosophy is altogether unlike history or literature or sculpture; it is more like tragedy. All of Western philosophy has its origin in Greek philosophy, and all Western philosophers to this day share an international European tradition. Within this tradition, the British were the first in modern times who developed a distinctive strain of their own, beginning with Bacon and Hobbes, Locke, Berkeley, and Hume. When Hume died in 1776, no other people since the Greeks could point to such a subtradition. The other giants of modern philosophy were loners: Descartes, Spinoza (whose genius was not widely recognized until the end of the century), and Leibniz.

The French *philosophes*, of whom there were many, did not attain to the first rank, except for Voltaire and Rousseau (both died in 1778) who dwelt on the margins of philosophy in the rich border land of literature. Soon Rousseau became the second French philosopher to influence the course of European philosophy; like Spinoza, he was embraced by nascent German philosophy.

The influence of Greek and British philosophy on American philosophy does not need to be stressed. All modern European philosophy is based on that of the Greeks, and the British influence on American institutions, literature, and thought is obvious and not surprising, given a common language. But in 1781 German philosophy came into its own with the publication of Kant's *Critique of Pure Reason*, and since the early nineteenth century the German impact on American philosophy has been immense. The pattern has remained remarkably constant down to our own time.

As soon as Kant's influence in Germany had given way to Hegel's, Kantianism arrived in England; when Hegel went into eclipse in Germany, Hegelianism came to dominate British philosophy; and both times it took a little longer for German thought to cross the

Atlantic Ocean. But eventually the influence on American thought was at least as great as it had ever been in England.

The reception of existentialism in the United States should be considered against this background and compared with the impact of other contemporary philosophies, such as logical positivism, phenomenology, and neo-Thomism. The spread of all four in the United States was helped by the arrival of refugees, but there is no reason for doubting that all four would have won some popularity in America even without any such assistance, allowing only for the usual time lag.

This is not to say that Nazi persecution made no difference at all to American philosophy. At the very least it changed the timeable by forcing postivism into eclipse in the thirties, while Heidegger was discredited in Germany in 1945 when the Nazi state collapsed. It might be supposed further that by expelling some philosophers who subsequently found a home in the United States, the process was speeded up, as it did not have to move by way of England. But this is more doubtful, although positivism was the last European philosophy that reached America via England.

The case of positivism was unusual in at least two ways. First, Ludwig Wittgenstein (1889-1951) left his native Austria for England long before 1930, and at Cambridge he became a teacher of exceptional intensity and passion. Thus his influence was naturally felt in England long before it reached the United States. Seocndly, Wittgenstein went to Cambridge because he felt some affinity for G. E. Moore and Bertrand Russell; and the various philosophies that are sometimes collectively called positivism were in many ways congenial to the British tradition, all the way back to David Hume. Existentialism, on the other hand, was and is profoundly uncongenial to the British philosophers. That it did not come to the United States by way of England was not due to the direct migration of Central European philosophers to America. Existentialism never found a home in England. After World War II communication between the two continents was greatly speeded up, owing to technological advances; and it was only after 1945 that existentialism really impinged on the American consciousness.[2]

II

What is existentialism? The question can be answered in two ways: ostensively, by naming the writers meant, or analytically, by char-

[2] Thus *Partisan Review* devoted its spring 1946 issue to "New French Writing" and in 1947 published William Barrett's "What is Existentialism?"

acterizing the movement and its tenets or characteristic tendencies. To begin with such an analysis is methodologically unsound; that way there is no guard against arbitrariness, and different analysts come up with different descriptions. Some writers who are generally identified as existentialists may turn out in the light of such analyses, not to be existentialists at all, while someone else whom the analyst happens to fancy — or dislike — becomes the paradigm. We ought to keep in mind in all such cases that the writers come first and the label afterwards, as part of an attempt to group some men together.

Descartes, Spinoza, and Leibniz *are* "the continental rationalists," and it makes good sense to study them together, not because they shared the same philosophy but rather because Spinoza set himself the task of correcting what he considered Descartes' errors; and Leibniz, although he found fault with both, tried to integrate their valid insights. Those who wish to devote a course, anthology, or study to these three men often find it useful to have a single label — and that is the primary meaning of "continental rationalism." What the three continental rationalists have in common is a question that arises only after that.

The situation is precisely the same with British empiricism. Primarily, that means Locke, Berkeley, and Hume. But once a tradition has been identified, we can meaningfully ask whether John Stuart Mill or Bertrand Russell was a British empiricist, too. Nothing much depends on the answer: the question is one not of fact but of convenience, although it is interesting to point out what marginal figures have in common with the Big Three and to what extent they differ.

The term *Existenzphilosophie* seems to have been introduced in 1929 by Fritz Heinemann, then a Privatdozent at the University of Frankfurt, in a book entitled *Neue Wege der Philosophie: Geist/Leben/Existenz: Eine Einführung in die Philosophie der Gegenwart* (New paths of philosophy: spirit/life/existence: an introduction to contemporary philosophy). The book begins with "A Postscript as a Preface" in which it is suggested that the antithesis of "spirit" and "life" is overcome by "existence" — the new principle of a number of new, existential philosophies: *das neue Prinzip einer Reihe von Philosophien, der Existenzphilosophien.*[3]

Around 1800, "the *Geistphilosphien* of European rationalism" gave way to "the principle of life in Herder, Hamann, and Jacobi," while Goethe and Humboldt championed *Existenz*. Similarly, in the nineteenth century, "the rationalism of German idealism gave way to the

[3] Heinemann, *Neue Wege,* p. xviii.

Lebensphilosophie of romanticism, and this in turn to the *Existenz-philosophie* of Marx, Feuerbach, and Kierkegaard."

Finally, these three principles succeeded each other in the development of the phenomenological school, in which Edmund Husserl, according to Heinemann, represents *Geist,* Max Scheler *Leben,* and Martin Heidegger *Existenz.*[4]

Heinemann's book does not seem to have been widely read or discussed, but the term *Existenzphilosophie* stuck, and his use of it prevailed. The notion that it is in Kierkegaard that we find "the first beginnings of an *Existenzphilosophie* that fits thinking again into the inviolable unity of man, that makes philosophizing a communication of existence,"[5] the suggestion that some earlier movements might also be called existential, and the point that the principle of existence was also championed by Karl Barth, Martin Buber, Franz Rosenzweig, and several others[6] — all this and much else, including the long appreciation of Heidegger and the passing references to Jaspers, has been repeated again and again by others after World War II, without any reference to Heinemann or any clear awareness of the time lag of which we spoke earlier.

Heinemann himself participated in the migration of the thirties, went to England, and eventually published *Existenzphilosophie Lebendig oder Tot?* (1954), as well as an expanded English version, *Existentialism and the Modern Predicament* (1958). Although both appeared in prestigious paperback series[7] and called attention to the 1929 book, I cannot recall ever having seen that book discussed in the mushrooming literature on existentialism. Heinemann's stress on *Existenz* was clearly derived from Heidegger's *Sein und Zeit* (1927, Being and Time), in which that term had been invested with a new significance, suggested much earlier by Soren Kierkegaard, especially in his *Concluding Unscientific Postscript* (1846). But neither Kierkegaard nor Heidegger had spoken of *Existenzphilosophie,* and Heinemann's use of that term was very casual; he did not call attention to it as a coinage. Perhaps the term had even been used orally by others before it turned up in Heinemann's book.

We find it next in Jaspers' little volume, *Die geistige Situation der Zeit* (1931), which appeared in a popular hardcover pocketbook series (Sammlung Göschen, vol. 1000) and reached a very large audience. In 1933, English, Spanish, and Japanese translations ap-

[4] Ibid., p. xxi.
[5] Ibid., p. 54.
[6] Ibid., p. xx.
[7] Urban-Bücher in Stuttgart and Harper Torchbooks in New York.

peared, the first under the title *Man in the Modern Age*. The first French version appeared in Louvain in 1951 and in Paris in 1952; and in 1954 another Japanese translation appeared. The fifth of the six chapters was entitled "How Being Human is Comprehended Today," and was divided into two parts: "(1) Sciences of Man: Sociology — Psychology — Anthropology" and "(2) *Existenzphilosophie*." Rather oddly, the last-named section, comprising four pages, reported on *Existenzphilosophie* as if it were a well-known feature of the contemporary situation, but what Jaspers actually offered was a miniature summary of his own *Philosophie*, which appeared in three volumes the following year. Indeed, following the last page there was an announcement of this work, complete with the titles of the three volumes which coincided with the three phases of *Existenzphilosophie* as described in the summary.[8] Jaspers gave credit to Kierkegaard, Schelling, and Nietzsche but did not mention Heidegger, and in effect gave the impression that the only contemporary philosophy that contributed to the comprehension of man was his own.

In his *Philosophie* (1932), *Existenz* is a key concept, and the second volume bears the title *Existenzerhellung* (Illumination of existence); but the term *Existenzphilosophie* occurs only a couple of times near the end of volume 3.[9] It thus seems highly likely that Jaspers picked up this label from Heinemann, although he does not mention him and may have come by the word indirectly, without any awareness of Heinemann. He may even have thought it was his own coinage. At any rate, he henceforth appropriated the term for *his* philosophy, without, however, looking on his own philosophy as merely one among others. There is more than a suggestion that he shared the conviction classically formulated by Hegel "Philosophy is its age comprehended in thought."[10]

In Jaspers' three-volume *Philosophie* no other philosopher is referred to anywhere near so much as Kant and Hegel; Schelling and Kierkegaard are the runners-up, mentioned less than half as often; Nietzsche is cited a few times, Heidegger once, and no other living philosopher more than once. The footnote reference to Heidegger reads in full: "About being in the world and about *Dasein* and historicity M. *Heidegger* (*Sein und Zeit*, Halle 1927) has said things of significance."[11] In *Sein und Zeit*, Jaspers' *Psychologie der Weltanschauungen* (1919) was cited in three footnotes that were

[10] *Philosophie des Rechts* (1821), pp. xxi-xxii.
[8] P. 145.
[9] Pp. 215, 217.

almost equally insignificant. [12] Jaspers and Heidegger have never dealt with each other's ideas in print, although it is no secret that they were friends for a while before the Nazis came to power and that they have not been on speaking terms since then.

In his "Philosophical autobiography"[13] Jaspers discusses many minor figures and devotes a whole section to Heinrich Rickert, but one looks in vain for a single mention of Heidegger — or of Dilthey.

In 1935 Jaspers published a volume of five-lectures, *Vernunft und Existenz* (Reason and existence), of which one was devoted to "The historical significance of Kierkegaard and Nietzsche." [14] The following year, he published a full-length interpretation of Nietzsche,[15] and in 1938 a book consisting of three lectures, which he called *Existenzphilosophie.*

The term "existentialism" (or *Existentialismus*) was not yet in use at that time, and *Existenzphilosophie* brought to mind Kierkegaard, Heidegger, and Jaspers. It was understood that Nietzsche was a precursor of twentieth-century *Existenzphilosophie,* though that label did not fit his philosophy. Not only Jaspers kept stressing Nietzsche's significance; Heidegger did, too, and eventually, after World War II, published several essays as well as a two-volume work on him.[16] By that time, Jaspers had come more and more to prefer Kierkegaard to Nietzsche, although he had published much more about Nietzsche,[17] while Heidegger openly disparaged Kierkegaard, whom he had cited with respect in *Sein und Zeit,* and proclaimed Nietzsche as a world-historical figure. (It is arguable that Heidegger owes as much to Kierkegaard as he does to Nietzsche — and that his originality is widely overestimated.)

It was further understood that *Existenzphilosophie* was not merely a name for the philosophies of Jaspers and Heidegger, which had roots in Nietzsche, Kierkegaard, and the late Schelling (Jaspers' *Schelling* appeared in 1955), but that it signified a way of thinking

[11] 1: 66n.

[12] In sections 49, 60, and 68.

[13] In *The Philosophy of Karl Jaspers,* ed. Paul Arthur Schilpp (1957), pp. 5–94.

[14] English translation by William Earle in *Reason and Existenz* (1955), reprinted in *Existentialism from Dostoevsky to Sartre,* ed. Walter Kaufmann (1956).

[15] English translation of *Nietzsche* by Charles F. Wallraff and Frederick J. Schmitz (1965).

[16] "Nietzsches Wort 'Gott ist tot' " in *Holzwege* (1950); "Wer ist Nietzsches Zarathustra?" in *Vorträge und Aufsätze* (1954), English translation by Bernd Magnus in *Lectures and Addresses* (1967); and *Nietzsche,* 2 vols. (1961).

[17] In addition to the works named, most notably a short book, *Nietzsche und das Christentum* (n.d. [1946]), English translation by E. B. Ashton, *Nietzsche and Christianity* (1961).

to which some other contemporary writers, including Martin Buber
and Franz Rosenzweig, were also close.

During the war, Jaspers was not allowed by the Nazis to teach
or publish, and Heidegger published nothing except his collected
Erläuterungen zo Hölderlins Dichtung (1944, Elucidations of Hölderlin's poetry). In 1945, when the Nazi state collapsed, Heidegger was
temporarily discredited while Jaspers resumed his chair at Heidelberg and began to publish again; but at that point Jean-Paul Sartre,
who called his own philosophy *existentialisme*, made existentialism
the most widely discussed philosophy of our time. Even in Germany
it was he who redirected attention to Heidegger; and in the United
States and elsewhere the sudden interest in the so-called existentialists was created largely by Sartre's works.

We are now ready to give our first answer to the question, What
is existentialism? When we speak of the continental rationalists or
the British empiricists, we do not imply that the men concerned
welcomed, or would have welcomed, this label. If this is firmly kept
in mind, we may call Kierkegaard, Jaspers, Heidegger, and Sartre
the Big Four existentialists. We shall have to deal briefly with the
reception of all four and of Nietzsche, before we consider some
other writers who have often been lumped with the existentialists,
notably Tillich and Buber. But before we consider these men one at
a time, we must attempt a nonostensive, analytical answer to the
question of what existentialism is.

III

"Existentialism" is not merely a label that happens to have been
applied to the philosophies of several men; it represents an attempt
to call attention to the fact that they have something in common.
To list affinities and get involved in the crisscross of family resemblances — these two share this feature, and one of them shares that
trait with those two — would serve little purpose. Let us be bold
and suggest a fundamental conviction common to all: philosophy
should begin neither with axioms nor with doctrines, neither with
ideas nor with sense impressions, but with experiences that involve
the whole individual.

In his *Psychologie der Weltanschauungen* (1919), Jaspers called
them *Grenzsituationen* (border situations) and paid particular attention to four: struggle, death, accident (*Zufall*), and guilt. In his
Philosophie (1932) he changed the sequence and substituted suffering for accident. Toward the middle of the nineteenth century,

Kierkegaard had written books on dread, fear and trembling, and the sickness unto death which is despair. Heidegger, in *Sein und Zeit* (1927), dealt at length with care *(Sorge)*, dread, and attitudes toward one's own death. In Sartre's literature even more than in his philosophy, the experience of one's own impending violent death is again and again central, as it is also in both *The Stranger* and *The Plague* by Camus. Camus' third and last novel, *The Fall*, like Sartre's *Flies*, deals centrally with guilt feelings, and both works are very close to Nietzsche in their strong opposition to guilt feelings and in linking them with Christianity. The twentieth-century existentialists also stress our always being in situations, and Sartre, following Kierkegaard, the dread-full dizziness of freedom that typically accompanies crucial decisions. Martin Buber is most interested in genuine dialogue that involves the whole person. Buber calls this *Zwiesprache* or *Dialog*, Jaspers, *Kommunikation*. Buber also wrote a book on guilt and guilt feelings *(Schuld und Schuldgefühle*, 1958), and so (in 1912) did Tillich.[18]

When we call these men existentialists we do not imply that they are all very fond of each other or that they share a common philosophy. What they have in common is a notion about how philosophers might fruitfully *begin*. This may seem little enough, especially if one keeps in mind how much these men disagree about ever so much else, but it is enough to distinguish them from the continental rationalists and the British empiricists, Kant and Hegel, Bertrand Russell and G. E. Moore, as well as positivists and analytical philosophers. Moreover, close family resemblances are never any warrant that those who look similar to outsiders are pleased to hear how much they look alike or get along well with each other. As we have seen, the continental rationalists defined their own contributions in terms of their differences, and the same is true of the British empiricists.

The notion that philosophy is, and ought to remain, closer to literature than to the sciences, and the active interest many of the existentialists have taken in literature are corollaries of their common starting point; for our "ultimate" experiences have long been a staple of great literature and especially of tragedy. The widespread assumption that the existentialists stay closer to real life and are less academic than other philosophers is belied by the scholasticism of so many existentialist tomes, but is due to their commmon starting point.

Sartre's passing suggestion in one of the most widely read lectures

---

[18] See n. 22 below.

of all time that there are two kinds of existentialists, Christian and atheist, has been parroted *ad nauseam,* but would be unhelpful even if he had not falsely classified Jaspers as a Catholic.[19] You might as well say that there were three kinds of continental rationalists — Catholic (Descartes), Jewish (Spinoza), and Protestant (Leibniz); or two kinds — theist and atheist (or pantheist). And there were also three kinds of British empiricists: unitarian or deist (Locke), Christian or theist (Berkeley), and atheist or agnostic (Hume). And American pragmatism can be divided the same way: theist (Peirce), agnostic or believer in a finite god (James), and atheist (Dewey).

In other words, none of these convenient labels justifies the notion that those grouped together agreed on essentials or that they would have been happy to be lumped together. The opposite was true in every case, and existentialism is not singular in this respect. What is unusual is that historical self-consciousness has become so acute that men are labeled, pigeonholed, and all but embalmed while still alive and vigorous, and hence have ample opportunity to explicitly repudiate the ways in which others would classify them.

No sooner had Sartre called his philosophy *existentialisme* and a form of *humanisme* than Heidegger and Jaspers sought to dissociate themselves both from him and from each other; and eventually even Sartre grew tired of existentialism and pronounced it a parasitic growth on the margins of Marxism, which he proclaimed the philosophy of our age.[20]

IV

Turning now to the reception of existentialism in the United States, let us consider the major writers, one at a time, before attempting some generalizations in the end. We shall begin with the two nineteenth-century thinkers.

Before World War II, Kierkegaard was not widely known in the United States, but David Swenson and Walter Lowrie had begun their translations of his books; and by 1945 most of them, including all the major works, were available in English along with two biographies by Lowrie, one long and one short. This tremendous labor had been independent both of the migrations prompted by

---

[19] *L'existentialisme est un humanisme* (1946). Philip Mairet's translation, originally entitled *Existentialism and Humanism,* is included, under the title *Existentialism is a Humanism,* in *Existentialism from Dostoevsky to Sartre,* ed. Walter Kaufmann (1956). See p. 289.

[20] *Search for a Method,* translated by Hazel E. Barnes (1963), p. 8. *"Question de méthode"* is the prefatory essay in Sartre's *Critique de la raison dialectique* (1960).

the Nazis and of the sudden explosion of interest in existentialism after the war, which vastly increased the audience for this literature and in time led to some new translations from the Danish as well as a large secondary literature.

For almost a hundred years, Kierkegaard's books had had to wait to be translated into English. Untimely when they were written, they were not yet timely when they were first translated. In Germany translations had begun to appear before the end of the nineteenth century, but it was only after World War I that Kierkegaard became popular, as dread and despair became common concerns. Before the war one had not spoken of such things. Now one spoke of little else, and here was a writer who had devoted whole books to these extreme experiences. Jaspers and Karl Barth discovered him before the war was over, Heidegger and the general public a little later. But in the United States widespread interest in Kierkegaard, and in existentialism generally, was aroused only after World War II, by Jean-Paul Sartre. Thus American interest in Kierkegaard owes little or nothing to the migration from Central Europe.

Nietzsche was well known but little understood in the United States since at least 1900, and unreliable translations of all of his works appeared before World War I. Many writers paid tribute to him, but when George Allen Morgan, Jr., published *What Nietzsche Means* in 1941, hardly any American philosophers were as yet taking Nietzsche seriously; and Morgan, who did, promptly left academic life, went into the Department of State, and ceased publishing philosophical books or articles.

Nietzsche's reception in the United States does owe something to the expulsion of the Jews from Germany. In 1950 the first edition of my *Nietzsche: Philosopher, Psychologist, Antichrist* appeared. I had left Germany in 1939, studied at Williams College and Harvard University, and started teaching at Princeton in 1947. In 1954 I published new translations of four of Nietzsche's books, as well as selections from his other works, his notes, and his letters (*The Portable Nietzsche*), and in 1966-67 translations with commentaries of five more books (collected in one Modern Library Giant, *Basic Writings of Nietzsche*, in 1968) and also of *The Will to Power*. In 1968, a third, revised and greatly expanded, edition of my *Nietzsche* appeared. In the late forties some American academicians were still astonished that a young man should be working on a book on Nietzsche, and the incredulous remark "I thought Nietzsche was dead as a doornail" voiced a common feeling. Twenty years later the same remark would only suggest that the speaker was wholly out of touch with the American scene.

I presented Nietzsche neither as an existentialist nor in the perspective of existentialism. While Nietzsche is now often studied as a precursor of existentialism, he has been linked even more often with other movements and currents; and earlier generations associated him with Darwin and evolutionary ethics, with Freud and psychoanalysis, with Schopenhauer or Spengler, Shaw or Gide, or Mussolini and Hitler; and in the mid-sixties the "death of God" theologians drew inspiration from him while some philosophers began to claim him as a precursor of analytic philosophy. It seems safe to predict that interest in Nietzsche will outlast the fashionable concern with existentialism. To what extent the fact that large numbers of young American philosophers have begun to read Nitzsche will affect American philosophy, it is too early to say. The effect on American theologians, on the other hand, is palpable and would have distressed Nietzsche.

V

American interest in Jaspers and Heidegger is largely due to Sartre although — indeed in part because — neither of them admires Sartre. In the United States, as elsewhere, it was not the philosophical community that discovered Sartre. *The Flies* and *No Exit, Nausea,* his short stories, and his later plays and novels won a large audience before *Being and Nothingness* appeared in English, and they are still incomparably more widely read than any of his philosophical essays. Only his lecture *Existentialism is a Humanism* is anywhere near so well known. But from the start of his international popularity it was common knowledge that Sartre was also a philosopher and that his *Being and Nothingness* owed something to Heidegger's *Being and Time;* also that the concern with nothingness could be traced back to Heidegger, and that Heidegger and Jaspers were full-fledged professors of philosophy who taught at old universities and did not spend much of their time in cafés or on fiction. Thus one read Sartre's literary works and his famous lecture but for the most part not *Being and Nothingness,* and one talked knowingly of Heidegger, often by way of suggesting that his *Being and Time,* which one had not read either, was of course incomparably more profound than Sartre's philosophy.

Even if it was not the professional philosophers that started these rumors, they had to reckon with them; and gradually the demand for English translations of Heidegger mounted. As enough translations became available, many departments of philosophy introduced courses in which they were studied.

With the exception of Descartes, French philosophers of note have tended not to be "pure" philosophers. Few are the philosophy courses at American colleges and universities in which Montaigne, Montesquieu, or Voltaire are discussed at all, and Comte and Bergson fare little better. Rousseau and Sartre *are* studied, but not by themselves. Rousseau may be linked with other social contract theorists; Sartre is lumped with Heidegger and other "existentialists" or — the new wave of the late sixties — whit phenomenology. The refugee phenomenologists had never succeeded in creating any wide interest in phenomenology, but Sartre has.

Interest in Jaspers is not at all keen among American philosophers; there is a little but not much more of it at theological seminaries. That his three-volume *Philosophie* of 1932 had not yet appeared in English thirty-five years later, any more than his *Psychologie der Weltanschauungen* (1919) and his *Von der Wahrheit* (1947, On truth), is surely due to this fact, not the other way around. All this is the more remarkable when one consders that not one avowed Heidegger disciple emigrated to the United States, while Jaspers' most famous student, Hannah Arendt, made her home in the United States and acquired considerable influence. Yet her labors on behalf of Jaspers have not won for him the recognition Heidegger enjoys even among many philosophers who feel uncomfortable about his Nazi past.

The major translators of Jaspers, Heidegger, and Sartre are not immigrants; nor have studies by refugees helped notably to acclimatize these three writers. Although many students have approached the subject by way of my own *Existentialism from Dostoevsky to Sartre* (1956), which includes a long introduction as well as essays by Jaspers and Heidegger that had not been done into English before, I have never published any study of Sartre, and my essays on Jaspers and Heidegger are sharply critical.

Of course, several studies of Sartre and of existentialism generally have been contributed by American scholars born in Europe, but they were published to meet an existing demand that none of them affected significantly. And *Being and Nothingness* was translated by Hazel Barnes (1956), *Being and Time* by Edward Robinson and John MacQuarrie (1962), the first two born in the United States, the last in Scotland.

In the sum, the American reception of Jaspers, Heidegger, and Sartre owes little to the migrations set in motion by the Nazis. We may add that the differences between the reactions to Jaspers and to Heidegger parallel their reception in their native land. There, too, Jaspers' many popular books reach a wider audience than any of Heidegger's volumes, while professional philosophers have manifested far more interest in Heidegger, especially in *Sein und Zeit*. Ever since that book first appeared in 1927, Heidegger has attracted a much larger following and elicited far more discussion among professors and professors-to-be than Jaspers ever did. There are several reasons for this.

The first involves the personalities of the two men. Philosophers hesitate to touch upon such points because it seems indelicate and they are taught that *ad hominem* arguments are fallacious, but historians cannot always avoid personalities, seeing how often influence and success depend on them. To understand the different receptions with which Jaspers' and Heidegger's philosophies have met from the start, we must discuss their personalities, if only briefly. The basis for my juxtaposition is threefold: the printed record, which includes their writings and some essays about them; conversations with scholars who studied under them; and my personal impressions during the years 1946 to 1956. The picture that emerges from these sources is remarkably consistent.

Heidegger, a short man vibrant with energy and a demonic touch, may put one in mind of Napoleon. There was something electric about him, and he generated a sense of excitement. Whether in conversation — "under four eyes," as the Germans say — or in a huge auditorium, lecturing to thousands, he created the expectation that something of the first importance was at stake and on the verge of discovery. When he entered the lecture hall, the atmosphere was charged, and though his large audience soon got lost and many people went literally to sleep, he always managed to regain their attention before he concluded with some intimation that, although everything was dark now, next time a great revelation was to be expected. And most of the audience always blamed itself for its failure to understand what he had said, and came back. Some professors who were his students before 1933 and felt appalled by his quick embrace of Nazism still felt a quarter of a century later that he was the greatest teacher they had ever had, especially in seminars.

Jaspers, very tall and pale, tried to keep students and colleagues at a distance; having a hole in one lung, he had to guard against catching cold. His life was spent largely at his desk, writing, not in seminars or in discussion. His aristocratic reserve appealed to many who like to listen to one or two lecture courses in philosophy, not to many professors-to-be.

Jaspers' second handicap was much less important but still deserves mention. Between 1923 and 1931 he published nothing, and his major philosophic work, his three-volume *Philosophie*, appeared less than a year before the Nazis came to power. Had this effort appeared five years earlier, the year *Sein und Zeit* was published, it would obviously have had more time to gain a hearing before World War II. But this point was not crucial.

The third point was much more decisive. Jaspers was more interested in *philosophieren*, philosophizing — or as one now says, in *doing* philosophy — than he was in offering doctrines; but unlike Wittgenstein, of whom the same could be said, Jaspers neither taught nor even seemed to teach a method. He was not primarily a teacher, he did not *desire* disciples, and he did not offer what professional students of philosophy, hoping to become professors, were looking for. His books do not lend themselves as well to endless discussions in seminars as does *Sein und Zeit*. Jaspers' works have the hortatory quality of Kierkegaard's and Nietzsche's, but without their literary grace, passion, and wit.

Heidegger's fame depends almost entirely on *Sein und Zeit* which, though long-winded and repetitious, is much less so than Jaspers' three-volume magnum opus, not to speak of *Von der Wahrheit* (1947; xxiii plus 1,103 pages). A hostile critic might say that Heidegger's forbidding jargon strikes many philosophers as an uncomfortable challenge and that, having figured out how many pages that at first reading made little sense could be interpreted, one can then teach a seminar. But there is more to it than that, and it is noteworthy that Sartre, who never had the least liking for Nazism, discovered Heidegger after 1933 and was fascinated by his thought, while Jaspers, from whom Sartre also accepted important ideas, never appealed much to him, although Jaspers, devoted to his Jewish wife, never became a Nazi.

Sartre lacks the professorial bearing of both men and plainly does not desire disciples. Though he owes much to both, he is in many ways closer to Kierkegaard and Nietzsche. His versatility, his restless brilliance, and his literary gifts exert a fascination that few writers can match. Both the popular image of, and the wide interest in, existentialism are inseparable from these qualities. The spell Sartre has cast over generations of American students, beginning right after the war, has created an almost unique interest that courses in philosophy, religion, literature departments, and humanities have been designed to satisfy or to exploit. Jaspers and Heidegger have been among the major beneficiaries. But this is not merely an American phenomenon.

Even in Germany it was the French who permitted Heidegger to teach again at Freiburg, after he had first been retired in 1945. And the Germans, having little to boast of at that time, even culturally, were persuaded by Sartre that at least they had a great philosopher of international repute. Jaspers' decision in 1948 to leave Heidelberg, where he had resumed teaching in 1945, to accept a call to Basel certainly did not increase his influence in postwar Germany; nor did he acquire any influence in Switzerland.

That Sartre's impact in the United States has been so much greater than either Jaspers' or Heidegger's is less a function of his philosophy than of his literature. His lecture *Existentialism is a Humanism* (1946) along with his two plays, *No Exit* and *The Flies* and some awareness of his major philosophic work, *Being and Nothingness* — all three published during the war in occupied Paris — hit the American consciousness and much of the rest of the world all at once; and while *Being and Nothingness* alone might not have attracted very much more attention than the tomes of the German existentialists, the knowledge that there was a philosophy behind the plays, the novels, and the short stories unquestionably added a great deal to their attraction. That existentialism elicits greater interest in the United States than any previous philosophic movement is almost entirely due to Jean-Paul Sartre.

VI

Several other wrters have often been called existentialists. Dostoevsky and Tolstoy, Rilke and Kafka, though dead before anyone had ever heard of "existentialism" or *Existenzphilosophie*, profoundly influenced Jaspers, Heidegger, and Sartre;[21] but judicious writers are agreed that these four men, like Nietzsche, ought not to be called existentialists.

[21] Kafka may not have influenced Jaspers and Heidegger; his influence on Camus was formative.

The central section on death in *Sein und Zeit* is plainly inspired by Tolstoy's *The Death of Ivan Ilyitch* (1886). For Tolstoy's concern with self-deception, one of the major themes of Sartre's philosophy and fiction, see Walter Kaufmann, *Religion from Tolstoy to Camus* (1961, rev. ed., 1964), pp. 2–8.

Dostoevsky, like Nietzsche, exerted a decisive influence on the whole climate of thought, especially after World War I.

Of Rilke's *Aufzeichnungen des Malte Laurids Brigge* (1910, The notes of M.L.B.) one feels reminded especially by Sartre's *La Nausée* (1938, Nausea). See also Heidegger's essay on Rilke in *Holzwege* (1952).

Given our account of existentialism, we can readily see why this should be so. These men, being novelists or poets, were not especially concerned with the proper starting point for philosophy. They were profoundly concerned with extreme situations, but so were Shakespeare and the Greek tragic poets, Heinrich von Kleist and Georg Büchner, the Buddha and the prophets. These experiences have always been close to the heart of religion and of tragic literature, and to call dozens of poets and religious figures of all ages existentialists would be exceedingly unhelpful.

In any case, these four writers do not owe their richly deserved fame in the English-speaking world to refugees. Dostoevsky's and Tolstoy's works had been translated and their reputations were secure long before 1930. Rilke was the greatest German poet since Goethe's death. And Kafka was one of the most original novelists of all time.

Kafka was a Jew, and it might be supposed that his vast reputation and influence in the United States did owe something to the exodus of Jews from Germany. He died in 1924, and his unfinished novel, *Der Prozess* (*The Trial*) was published by his friend, Max Brod, the following year, although Kafka had asked him to destroy the manuscript. In 1926 Brod published *Das Schloss* (*The Castle*), and in 1927 *Amerika*, both also against the author's express desire and unfinished. When the Nazis came to power, Brod, long a Zionist, went to Palestine. His editorial labors on his friend's behalf continued, and he also wrote a biography of Kafka. Other refugees did their share, but it does not appear that the expulsion of so many intellectuals from Central Europe made any decisive difference to Kafka's reception abroad. Willa and Edwin Muir, who were not refugees, translated *The Castle* in 1930, *The Trial* in 1937, and *Amerika* in 1938; and as Kafka's visions turned into reality, his fame spread.

The most important way in which the Nazi regime promoted existentialism and the literature associated with it was not by compelling many people to emigrate but rather by killing so many more. As fear and trembling, dread and despair, and the vivid anticipation of one's own death ceased to be primarily literary experiences and, like the absurd visions of Kafka, turned into the stuff of everyday life, the originally untimely Kafka and Kierkegaard became popular along with Jaspers and Heidegger, Sartre and Camus, who were fashionable from the first; and Dostoevsky, Tolstoy, and Nietzsche, whose fame was long established, suddenly appeared in a new light.

The case of Camus may seem different because for a while he was Sartre's friend, before their political differences estranged them; and, like Sartre, he tried to write philosophy as well as plays, novels, short stories, and journalism. But his philosophical efforts were so feeble that it makes more sense to see him as a literary figure whose reputation depends on his three novels and, to a lesser extent, on his plays and short stories. His *Myth of Sisyphus* and *The Rebel* have been highly successful with American undergraduates but have been almost wholly ignored by philosophers. For good measure, Camus disdained the label of existentialism (this in itself would not be decisive); and his American reception owes nothing to the mid-century migrations.

VII

It might be argued that Paul Tillich and Martin Buber, who were above all religious writers, should be left out of account here; but we shall consider both. Tillich's case is relevant and instructive because in 1933 he left Germany for the United States; because after the war he often called himself an existentialist; and because he saw himself, and others came to see him, as a philosopher-theologian who to some extent transformed both disciplines by infusing existentialist ideas into them.

While Sartre moved from existentialism to Marxism, Tillich traveled in the opposite direction, from Marxism to existentialism. He had been a Christian socialist in Germany in the 1920's and, far from trying to recant his Marxist past when the Nazis came to power, accepted an invitation to teach at Union Theological Seminary in New York although he was unable as yet to speak English. He had the vitalitiy to begin a new life at the age of forty-six, soon lectured in English, then began to write in English, and eventually, after World War II, became incomparably more influential in the New World than he had ever been in the Old. As existentialism became popular, Tillich, by now in his sixties, identified with it — he liked to say that he was an existentialist when he asked questions and a theologian when he gave answers — and he quickly became the most widely acclaimed Protestant theologian in the United States, far outstripping his only rival, Reinhold Niebuhr. (The competition in this field is not as keen as in nuclear physics.)

An admirer might say that quality gains recognition, even if it takes time, while a cynic might suggest that Tillich offered the latest intellectual fashions and Christianity, too. There is a good deal of truth in both points. Most theologians pour new wine into old skins, and that Tillich's impact became so much greater than that of the others was due partly to the quality of what he had to offer, though it also owed something to the unusual vigor and charm of his personality.

His frequent use in the 1950's of the term "existentialism" was unquestionably opportune and shrewd, but Tillich's ideas were not improvised to meet a new demand. His dissertations had been on Schelling;[22] Nietzsche's influence on Tillich had been formative; and Tillich's interest in Freud long antedated Sartre's. He was a contemporary of Jaspers and Heidegger, between them in age, shaped by similar reading and experiences — an authentic exemplar of that German philosophical tradition to which a new generation was suddenly seeking an indirect approach by way of Sartre. Unlike all the others, Tillich was in the United States, writing and teaching and preaching in English, and available for lectures and symposia.

Even so, his popularity also exemplified the time lag of which we have spoken. For Tillich's thought always remained closer in essentials to Schelling than to Sartre, and what he brought to Union Theological Seminary and then, after his retirement, even more obviously to Harvard, and eventually, during his last years, to the University of Chicago, was not so much a new wave as the final ripple of German idealism and romanticism.

At the University of Berlin, the old Schelling had replaced Hegel in 1841, ten years after Hegel's death. The king of Prussia had called him there expressly to root out 'the dragon seed of the Hegelian pantheism." [23] Schelling in his last years characterized Hegel's philosophy along with his own early efforts as merely negative philosophy and demanded a new positive philosophy. Hegel was, first according to Schelling and then also in the writings of Kierkegaard, who heard the old Schelling lecture in Berlin, a mere conceptmonger, while what truly mattered was genuine existence and eternal happiness. In the later nineteenth century, Protestant theology became more modest. While Hegelianism lost its hold on German philosophy it found a new home not only in British and American philosophy but also in German Protestant theology. What had struck king Frederick William IV as "pantheism" now passed for liberalism. And the revival of philosophical interest in Hegel was spearheaded by the fine

[22] *Die religionsgeschichtliche Konstruktion in Schellings positiver Philosophie* (The construction of the history of religion in Schelling's positive philosophy) . . . : *Inaugural-Dissertation zur Erlangung der philosophischen Doktorwürde . . . Breslau* (1910) and *Mystik und Schuldbewusstsein in Schellings philosophischer Entwicklung* (Mysticism and the consciousness of guilt in Schelling's philosophical development): *Inaugural-Dissertation zur Erlangung der Lizentiatenwürde der hochwürdigen theologischen Fakultät Halle-Wittenberg, in Beitrage zur Förderung christlicher Theologie,* 16:1 (1912).

new editions of his *Encyclopädie* (1905) and *Phänomenologie* (1907)
that were produced by Georg Lasson, a Protestant pastor whose father,
Adolf Lasson (originally, Ahron Lazarussohn), had championed
Hegel's philosophy at the University of Berlin. The revival of Hegel
in Germany also owed a great deal to Wilhelm Dilthey's study of the
young Hegel (1906); and Dilthey's own "philosophy of life" and his
concern with *Weltanschauungen* left their mark on German
existentialism.[24]

While in many ways close to the old Schelling, Tillich was far from
merely trying to bring back a system that was a hundred years old,
and even further from Schelling's pathetic resentment against his
erstwhile friend Hegel, whose fame had long exceeded his own; nor
was Tillich up in arms against the dragon seed of pantheism. He had
himself come out of that liberal Protestantism which was permeated
by Hegelianism; he had been a student when Dilthey's *Jugend-
geschichte Hegels* appeared in 1906, followed the next year by the first
publication of *Hegels theologische Jugenschriften* — his early, really
rather antitheological, fragments on Christianity, written during the
last decade of the eighteenth century. And Tillich liked to say that
Marx, Nietzsche, and Freud had been the greatest Protestants of the
past hundred years.

Philosophical idealism in America had had a definitely Protestant
tinge, and the many theologians and the few philosophers who still
looked back nostalgically to Josiah Royce and idealism were not ready
to take the leap to Barth or Kierkegaard. Tillich met their needs
perfectly. He did not propose a renaissance of idealism; he combined
Schelling and Hegel with the most modern movements, spoke approvingly of everything that was avant garde, and, while acclaimed
as an existentialist like Kierkegaard, excelled in the art of obviating
any either-or.

Only a few years earlier, being *au courant* with Kierkegaard had
meant being neo-orthodox, contemptuous of liberalism, and exposed
to the charge of fundamentalism. Tillich was liberalism incarnate.

A mere two years after his death, any appraisal of the extent of
Tillich's influence on American Protestant theology must be hedged
with doubt, but it seems safe to say that his influence will be confined

---

[23] See Kaufmann, *Hegel* (1965), secs. 68 and 70.
[24] See, e.g., Jaspers, *Psychologie der Weltanschauungen;* Heidegger, *Sein und
Zeit*, pp. 46–47, 205n., 209–10, 249n., 376–77, 385n., and 397–404; and Buber's
occasional references to Dilthey as "my teacher" (once even as "my master") — but
see also Buber's protest in *The Philosophy of Martin Buber*, ed. Paul Schilpp and
Maurice Friedman (1967), p. 702.

to theology. His *Systematic Theology* has little competition. No other American theologian of comparable *niveau* has written a systematic theology in this century. Hence Tillich's may well continue to be studied in seminaries. And some of his many short and relatively popular books will, no doubt, continue to find readers. As far as new directions in Protestant theology are concerned, the much publicized death-of-God theology may be seen as an attempt to push beyond Tillich. While he unquestionably paved the way for it, he is obviously not responsible for the fact that it is more notable for the headlines it has produced than it is for thoughtful or substantial writings.

In sum, Tillich took existentialism away from Barth and the neo-orthodox and used its popular appeal to liberalize American Protestantism and to animate it with more interest in German philosophy — including Nietzsche — as well as doubts about God. Incidentally he proved that all this can command the widest popular interest and even, as long as it is fused with homage to Christ, the covers of the slickest news magazines. This lesson was not lost.

VIII

Martin Buber left Germany for Jerusalem in 1938. His *Ich und Du* (1923) appeared in English in 1937 and in French the following year. *I and Thou* was translated by Ronald Gregor Smith and published in Edinburgh. With the exception of *Jewish Mysticism and the Legends of the Baal-Shem,* which appeared in London and Toronto in 1931, it was until 1945 the only one of Buber's many books available in English. Considering the migration of so many Jews from Central Europe, this is a remarkable fact; for among the German-speaking Jews who fled from the Nazi terror Buber's prestige was immense. But when the war ended, interest in his ideas was still largely confined to Christian theologians who considered *I and Thou* a seminal work.

Buber had long been a Zionist, and it was thus no mere accident that he went to the Hebrew University; and he would never have wished to teach at a theological seminary. But if he had taught in the United States, beginning in 1933 or 1938, and learned to write and publish in English — as he did learn to write and publish in Hebrew — his impact would surely have been far greater than it has been in fact. Whether this would have made any very great difference to long-range currents of thought is another question. By the time he died in 1965 — the same year Tillich died — most of his books were available in American paperbacks.

Tillich is the only influential American writer who is regularly classified as, and who frequently labeled himself, an existentialist; and Buber's belated arrival in the United States coincided with the arrival of existentialism, and was understood in this context. Tillich is the only so-called existentialist whose reception was facilitated by his immigration, and it is instructive to juxtapose Tllich and Buber.

Buber's acceptance was also facilitated by his many visits to the United States after World War II; but these cannot be accounted part of the large-scale migrations from Central Europe. Rudolf Bultmann weathered the war in Germany, as a Protestant theologian, and also visited the United States after the war, although, lacking Buber's charisma, his personal appearances had relatively little to do with the spread of interest in his program of demythologizing the New Testament. But if he had taught here for a quarter century, or if Karl Barth, who went to Basel after the Nazis came to power, had done so, there would unquestionably be large numbers of American preachers and professors now who could be classified as their disciples. It is different with Buber.

In spite of his charisma, Buber did not develop disciples any more than he developed doctrines. If one accepted the notion that existentialism, unlike other philosophies, sticks to experience instead of becoming preoccupied with concepts and doctrines — that the existentialists deal with existence, while other philosophers deal with essences — then the men we have discussed are not really existentialists, excepting only Buber.

This may be a reduction to the absurd of the popular notion of existentialism, and it shows that our earlier suggestion that it is only the common starting point in our extreme experiences that sets off the existentialists is more judicious. Yet our account of the reception of existentialism would be grossly misleading if we ignored one of the most crucial facts. The insistence that philosophy is, or ought to be, closer to literature than to science and that we must begin with our most intense experiences has been the bait that has led thousands to swallow some new scholasticism that differs from one fisher of men to another. Not only do the concepts and the doctrines furnish meat for seminars and the backbone of solid respectability, the jargon is part of the bait. The neophyte knows that once he has mastered that, he is "in," he belongs, and he has a spiritual home. This is the central irony of existentialism: the jargon of anguish, solitude, and authenticity allays anguish, liberates from solitude, and facilitates inauthenticity. One sneers at the anonymous "one," chatters about mere "chatter," is curious about the latest diatribes against "curiosity," and feels superior.

Buber never fitted into this pattern. He did not only begin with experience, he stayed with it. His greatest achievements were literary — notably his collection of *Tales of the Hasidim*,[25] his translation of the Hebrew Bible into German,[26] and his novel [27] — and his own prose always remained literary and never degenerated into jargon. His rhapsodic *Ich und Du* is no exception, although English-speaking theologians soon derived from it "a Thou," "a Thou-relationship," and a few other phrases one could juggle somewhat like Sartre's *en-soi* and *pour-soi*. Buber's stance did not only forestall disciples, it also went so much against the grain of organized religion in America, and of the universities as well, that, his prestige notwithstanding, his approach was little understood or appreciated. What he offered was neither theology nor philosophy, and least of all fundamentalism or revivalism. It was a highly literate and somewhat literary experience of religion as a dialogue.

The single person who did the most to popularize Buber in America was Maurice Friedman, born in Oklahoma, who wrote a book and innumerable articles on Buber while also translating him tirelessly. The migration from Central Europe affected Buber's reception scarcely at all, and when he died his personal prestige was ever so much greater than his actual influence. No doubt he has begun to reach single individuals here and there; but whether his books will give either American Judaism or American philosophy new directions remains to be seen.

IX

Existentialism developed in at least three stages: Danish, German, and French. The first stage was represented by a single writer who rightly saw himself as an exception. He bucked the currents of the early Victorian era and projected his own extraordinary sensibility in a highly original and eccentric series of books. He deliberately remained outside every establishment — church, state, and university — countered

[25] 2 vols., translated by Olga Marx, 1947-48. *Die Erzählungen der Chassidim* (1950), Manesse-Bibliothek der Weltliteratur, is the definitive edition of the original.
[26] Definitive edition in 4 vols., *Die Schrift*, 1954, 1955, 1958, 1962. The enterprise was understaken jointly with Franz Rosenzweig, in the 1920's, and the books of the Bible appeared one at a time.
[27] *Gog and Magog* (1949); English translation by Ludwig Lewisohn, *For the Sake of Heaven* (1945).

a favorable notice in the press by declaring his contempt for the journal in which it had appeared, and added that in that publication he would prefer to be pilloried — which he promptly was.

The second stage is represented by two German professors. Both began to publish over half a century after Kierkegaard's death, rose to the top of their profession, and attracted some notice, but no more than several of their colleagues who did philosophy in a different key; for example, Edmund Husserl, Max Scheler, Nicolai Hartmann, Ernst Cassirer, and Rudolf Carnap.

Then Jean-Paul Sartre captured the imagination of the Western world with *his* version of existentialism. His plays and fiction were unusually philosophical, his academic philosophic volumes were enlivened by a wealth of vivid unacademic examples, his political and critical journalism was tireless, and his autobiography a masterpiece. He did not only get himself read all over the world; he also created international interest in German existentialism; and he led large numbers to study Kierkegaard and Nietzsche as forerunners of existentialism, and Camus, Buber, and Tillich as existentialists. Initially, it was fashionable to see him as a mere journalist without genuine depth or genius. What a few saw soon was so plain twenty years after the end of the war that he was named winner of the Nobel Prize for literature although he had let it be known that he would not accept the prize — a gesture that shows how much closer he is in some ways to Kierkegaard than to the German existentialists. He wears the mantle of Voltaire and Rousseau, and the subtitle of Iris Murdoch's *Sartre* (1953) may show how he does have ties to both: *Romantic Rationalist*.

Indeed, we may speak of a fourth stage in the development of existentialism. After the arrival of Sartre, a number of other writers who had not called themselves existentialists or been so labeled before 1945 became identified with this label and triumphed *in hoc signo* We can also distinguish four levels in the *reception* of existentialism. The first is the stage of fashion, chatter, and journalism. This phase is not over yet, either in the United States or in Europe, although in France and Germany anthropology and sociology have begun to replace existentialism, also at the second level, which is that of research, seminars, and scholasticism. In the United States, the second phase, unlike the first, has not yet reached its high point, although it is well along its way. By the time it reaches its climax, existentialism will probably be in eclipse in the countries of its origin.

The third phase eludes easy observation and remains a subject for conjecture, but in the case of existentialism we must also ask to what extent the writers mentioned have had the impact they explicitly desired, changing the quality of men's lives. This level cannot be inferred from the first two. On the contrary, insofar as the journalistic and the scholastic reception permit any inference about it, they give the impression that there has been very little of this and that both the popular and the academic approach have, each in its own way, pulled the fangs of existentialism and made it innocuous. This, of course, does not preclude that here and there an individual's life may have been changed by reading one or another of these writers. I have no doubt even so that on this level the impact of Jaspers and Heidegger, Sartre, Tillich, and Buber is not remotely comparable to that of Tolstoy, Nietzsche, and Kafka.

This may seem no more than a surmise, but an examination of the fourth and final level bears it out. What has been the impact of the writers whom we have considered on those individuals who have in turn become influential writers? Nietzsche's influence on all the writers we have been considering, excepting only the three who belonged to an earlier generation, is as obvious as his impact on Thomas Mann and Hermann Hesse, André Gide and André Malraux, Shaw and Yeats and O'Neill, Freud and Adler and Jung, Stefan George and Gottfried Benn, Max Scheler and Nicolai Hartmann, and any number of others. That this became evident only after his death is irrelevant, considering that he died early. His impact on these men was plain as soon as they had read him, and he had left a decisive mark on world literature and philosophy well before he would have been eighty. When we ask about the impact of existentialism in the United States in *this* sense, we find that as yet there is no evidence that the writers here discussed have changed the quality of American philosophy or poetry, drama or fiction, or our intellectual life. Nor are there signs as yet that many American philosophers have been persuaded that our extreme experiences furnish a fruitful starting point for philosophical reflection. Insofar as such experiences are mentioned at all, the question discussed is usually what Heidegger may have meant when he said this or that. In our philosophical community, existentialism is acquiring some respectablity only in its scholastic form.

There is one exception. One idea that is widely associated with existentialism is making some headway among professional philosophers: *engagement*. In the civil rights movement and the protests against the Vietnam war, many professors of philosophy have followed Sartre's lead in committing themselves publicly. Unlike Sartre, however, they do this, as it were, after hours, without claiming any close connection between such activities and their philosophies. Moreover, it might be questioned whether *engagement* is really a part of existentialism or merely a notion that Sartre, with his experience of the resistance during World War II, has championed all along. To be sure, *engagement* was never that central in Heidegger's philosophy, and his brief flirtation with political commitment is humiliating to recall.[28] But not only has the later Jaspers written several books in

[28] See above all Heidegger's *Die Selbstbehauptung der deutschen Universität* (1933).

which he adopts stands on questions of the day, but Sartre's message and the popular image of existentialism were from the beginning associated with *engagement*. Here, if anywhere, the impact of existentialism on American intellectuals is striking. Or is this a case of *post hoc ergo propter hoc*? Is there after all no causal link?

I cannot prove here that there is a link, but I believe there is. In support of this surmise one might adduce these points. The impetus for commitment has come largely from students and younger faculty, as well as some of the younger clergy — the generation that grew up reading Sartre. Then, Sartre's protests against the Algerian war have left a deep impression on American intellectuals and persuaded many that an intellectual minority can have an influence on stopping what is felt to be an unjust and immoral war. Finally, Sartre's protests against the Vietnam war have helped to rouse the conscience of large numbers of Americans. But this impact of existentialism on the American conscience owes little to the migration of intellectuals during the Nazi period, even though some refugees have greatly welcomed this development.

X

The most surprising result of our study is surely that the migration of so many Central European intellectuals to the United States has had so little impact on the spread of existentialism in America. Almost all of the major translations were done by native English speakers, and few refugees published pioneering studies of the so-called existentialists. Only Nietzsche's influence was decisively advanced by an immigrant, but then Nietzsche was not really an existentialist. Sartre and Camus, Kierkegaard, Buber and Heidegger, owe little or nothing to the migration; and although Jaspers' favorite student has gained some influence in her own right, few American philosophers are particularly interested in him.

Only Tillich's impact on the American scene is almost wholly due to the migrations set in motion by the Nazis. Had he stayed in the Old World, writing his later works in German, Swedish, or Hebrew, Americans would hardly speak of 'ultimate concern" and "being-itself." Clearly, intellectual fashions would be different. And had Karl Barth come here instead of Tillich, it is even possible that the history of Protestant theology in the United States would have proceeded differently. American theology is even more derivative than is American philosophy.

The main reason why existentialism has not had more effect on American philosophy is that some other Central European philosophers have been so much more influential: to some extent, Rudolf Carnap, Herbert Feigl, and C. G. Hempel; to an even far greater extent Ludwig Wittgenstein. For this there are many reasons.

The first three came to the United States and taught and wrote in English. Their ideas were highly teachable and discussable, admirably precise, and congenial to students brought up on a high regard for the exact sciences. Teaching at different universities, they all attracted excellent students who then became teachers and attracted students of their own. Wittgenstein also taught in English and showed his students a highly contagious way of doing philosophy that, while not so scientific, did fit in with contemporary tendencies not only at his own Cambridge but also at Oxford.

Since World War I, competence in foreign languages has been a rarity among American graduate students in philosophy, and many of the most promising young philosophers have had difficulty in satisfying such requirements as showing the ability to translate one printed page of German philosophy in an hour, with a dictionary. Few indeed know German well enough to be able to read untranslated books by Hegel, Dilthey, Heidegger, or Jaspers. The best students and young professors, given a chance to spend a year abroad on some fellowship, have for the most part gone to England, both because there are more bright philosophers at Oxford than at any other European university and because they did not have sufficient competence in any foreign language. As a result, ties between British and American philosophy have been very greatly strengthened, and most of the best British philosophers have also been invited to American universities — once, twice, three times, or permanently — while few continental European philosophers have taught at American institutions.

It would be an egregious error to think of contemporary American philosophers as merely an offshoot of British philosophy. Besides the Central Europeans mentioned above, there is also Sir Karl Popper, born in Vienna, who turns out disciples at the London School of Economics. But it would be entirely fair to say that philosophy nowadays is wholly tied to our universities, that professors are trained in graduate schools, and that our graduate programs are built around the general examinations which, at least in most of the best departments, stress logic, theory of knowledge, the philosophy of science, meta-ethics, and the way philosophy is done in our journals, à la Oxford. Those who have no stomach for all this tend to go into other fields, such as literature or religion. The Nazis kept Heidegger and drove out the positivists; but in the United States "The stone which the builders rejected has become the chief cornerstone."

Max Wertheimer and Gestalt Psychology

BY RUDOLF ARNHEIM

MAX WERTHEIMER arrived on the scene of American psychology in the early thirties as a conspicuous and disquieting figure. It was a time at which a fundamental change of attitude and outlook became apparent in the new generation of scientists. Reassured by the precision of their equipment, their measurements, and formulae, many of these new practitioners of the sciences seemed not particularly impressed by the endlessness of their task, the complexity of nature, the delicacy of organic functioning, the awesome recesses of the mind. Business-like and matter-of-fact, they were trained to go about their work by asking some particular question, selected in such a way as to fit the measurable dimensions of controllable situations; they made the experiments, calculated the results, published them, and proceeded to the next job. Not that they were insensitive to the charm and fascination of the oldtimers, whose faces were engraved with the haunting awareness of the unfathomable. They saw the quiet smile that greeted their confident assertions, and they listened, as children will to fairy tales, when the head of the department quoted from the classics. They sensed that here was something strangely beautiful, but related to their own work only in an outdated, quaint fashion, something they were deprived of but that had to be saved for a hobby after retirement.

Hence the powerful effect of Max Wertheimer on the few hundred students and colleagues who, during the decade of his American years, came in direct contact with him. Here was a man who called for a fuller vision and less mechanical procedure not as a dream but as a technical research requirement, to be applied immediately and in practice. Romantic and frail, with the Nietzsche moustache of non-conformity, Wertheimer lectured in his improvised English at the Graduate Faculty of the New School for Social Research. He described aspects of the mind which gave the shock of recognition to his listeners but seemed beyond the grasp of accepted procedure. And while the vision was humane and gentle, its application demanded an unexpected discipline, a stringency of argument and proof for which the students were not trained. Hence their devotion, irritation, despair.

Wertheimer was one of the three principal proponents of gestalt psychology, who had come to the United States. Owing to their presence in this country, the strange-sounding name of the new doctrine became familiar to American psychologists; but to what extent were theory and practice influenced by the new ideas? Wolfgang Köhler, who went to Swarthmore, was well known for his experiments on the intelligence of chimpanzees. But while his results were recognized as substantial, his explanatory concepts — "insight," for example — seemed uncomfortable to the touch, and there was little realization that this special study in the psychology of problem solving belonged in the framework of a totally new and comprehensive approach to psychology in general. Köhler's early book on gestalten in physics has never been translated, and his later experiments on the figural after-effect in visual perception were again received as an interesting specialty without broader implications. The third man of the gestalt triumvirate, Kurt Koffka, at Smith College, wrote the representative treatise on gestalt psychology, a book densely packed with valuable facts and ideas, but so hard on the reader that it served philosophers better than psychologists.

What do the textbooks of psychology say about gestalt psychology, about Wertheimer? Students learn that, according to gestalt theory, a whole is more than or different from the sum of its parts — an innocuous-sounding statement, unlikely to impress them as revolutionary or practically relevant. Of Wertheimer they hear that he performed early experiments on illusory movement and on the perception of visual shape. But again, as in the case of Köhler, the connection of these studies with the basic gestalt thesis will seem to them by no means obvious.

The textbook describes Wertheimer's rules of perceptual grouping: when a person looks at an assortment of shapes, these elements will be seen as related to each other if they are similar in size or shape or color or some other perceptual trait. Now such a combination of pieces does not look like an example of a gestalt process, and in fact the rules of grouping constitute only the first part of a paper in which Wertheimer moved from a more traditional approach to the revolutionary switch, showing that a perceptual pattern cannot be accounted for merely *from below,* that is, by tracing the relations among the elements, but requires an approach *from above*. Only by describing the overall structure of the pattern can one determine the place and function of each part and the nature of its relations to other parts. This reversal of the customary scientific approach, calling for totally different methods, is generally omitted from the report a student receives about Wertheimer's study of shape perception.

However, piecemeal and preliminary though the rules of perceptual grouping are, they can be shown to involve the basic characteristic of the gestalt attitude, namely, a respect for the inherent nature of the situation confronting the observer. In Wertheimer's view, the rules of grouping are not arbitrarily imposed by the perceiver upon an incoherent collection of pieces. Rather the constellation of the elements themselves, their own objective properties, steer the groupings performed by the observer's mind.

This respect for the structure of the physical world as it impinges upon the nervous system has been stressed by gestalt psychologists in conscious opposition to the subjectivism of British empiricist philosophy, on which the training of most American psychologists is based. According to that tradition, the sensory stimulus material, by which a human being or animal is informed about the outer world, is in itself amorphous, an accumulation of elements; and it is the recipient mind that ties them together by connections established in the past. In consequence, association by frequent coincidence in subjective time and space became the dominant explanatory principle of experimental psychology in this country.

Needless to say, the two antagonistic theories were based on opposing world views: the one, proudly asserting the dominion of the individual's views and judgments over the environment, the other, distinctly irritated by such egocentrism and affirming that it was man's task to find his own humble place within the world and to take the cues for his conduct and comprehension from the order of that world. Equally, gestalt theory demanded of the individual citizen that he derive his rights and duties from the objectively ascertained functions and needs of society. Here, then, the deeply ingrained individualism of the Anglo-Saxon tradition, the suspicion against central power and planning from above, was challenged implicitly by a scientific approach, which, in moments of bad temper, was even accused of totalitarianism.

One of Wertheimer's favorite epithets of defiance was the word "blind." It referred to self-centered, prejudiced, insensitive behavior, a lack of openness to the "requirements" of the situation — another key term of gestalt theory. Here is the common theme of Wertheimer's seemingly dispersed interests, his own explorations of perceptual structure as well as the research problems his disciples worked on at the New School. Of these, I will give three examples. One of his assistants, Solomon E. Asch, developed a social psychology intended to replace the dichotomy of individual and group with an integrated view of the social interaction and its intrinsic dynamics. A Chinese student, Miss Gwan-Yuen Li, explored the Taoist concept of non-willing (*wu-wei*) as a philosophical doctrine of how man may accord himself with the powers inherent in the cosmos and society. A third disciple, Abraham S. Luchins, showed in an experimental study on rigidity how a pre-established mental set prevents a person from searching a problem situation freely for a solution suggested by the particular given conditions.

Wertheimer himself devoted several of his last papers to philosophical discussions of ethics, value, freedom, and democracy, pointing in each case to the difference between wilful, personal preference and the objective requirements of the situation. These objective components of the situation, however, are not to be sought only outside, in the physical world, but also in the physiological and mental functioning of the person himself. The nervous system and consciousness, as a part of man's world, make their own contributions and have their own needs — not to be confused with the merely subjective inclinations of the individual. For example, the way in which a certain visual pattern is seen depends (a) on the stimulus configuration and (b) on the formative tendencies of the nervous system, as distinguished from the effects of the particular observer's interest, past experience, or capricious choice. One senses here an impatience with individual differences, which is indeed characteristic of gestalt psychologists. This brought forth no protest from behaviorists, but it tended to disappoint those American psychologists who concentrated on the genetic, social, and clinical aspects of the human personality with a strong practical emphasis on the character and needs of the individual person. Gestalt psychology was largely concerned with "human nature" — man as he perceives, man as he grows, man as he comprehends. Wertheimer approached psychology as a pure scientist, interested in the laws of general functioning, and at the same time with the attitude of the poet, who speaks of mankind.

It will be seen that the primary impulse of Wertheimer's psychology was a respect for nature, human as well as organic and inanimate. From this respect derived the protest against the "atomistic" method, that is, the dissection of integrated entities and against the pretension of rebuilding a whole by the summation of its elements. Only when these neat and convenient methods of analysis were put aside, did the entities of nature reveal that they were not amorphous, but possessed a structure of their own, inherent dynamic tendencies, and indeed an objective beauty. Thus the "law of the good gestalt" was formulated by Wertheimer in opposition to the doctrine of subjective association.

The gestalt law describes a striving, inherent in physical and psychical entities, toward the simplest, most regular, most symmetrical structure attainable in the given situation. This tendency has been demonstrated most clearly in visual perception, but it also shows up as the drive toward tension reduction in motivation. In the thinking of gestalt psychologists, this fundamental bent of the mind reflects the identical tendency operative in the nervous system. It holds in the field processes of physics, as Köhler has pointed out. Historically it relates to the law of entropy in thermodynamics, although this affinity is not apparent when the gestalt law is described as a tendency towards order and the entropy principle as one towards disorder.

As a law of nature, the striving towards a "good gestalt" was simply a matter of observed fact. It involved no evalution, expressed no preference. However, there were distinct advantages to the state of maximum order in a system. For example, in visual perception, once the simplest version of a pattern was apprehended, it appeared more stable, made more sense, could be better handled; and a state of balanced order made for better functioning in a human mind, a team, a society. It was this sort of value to which Max Wertheimer as a person was passionately attached. He found the tendency toward balance, order, goodness in nature. He found it in the basic impulses of man, wherever they were not disturbed by culturally inflicted distortions and by unproductive cerebral complications. Man was basically well organized and therefore good (i.e., in proper shape for adequate functioning) because good organization was the state to which all natural systems aspired. For this reason, Wertheimer disliked persons who relished the trickeries and intricacies of sophisticated brains, and he bitterly inveighed against those philosophers and psychologists who proclaimed that selfish indulgence and destructiveness were the mainsprings of human nature. His aversion for psychoanalysis was clearly imbued with personal feelings, although it may be said that basically Freud and Wertheimer pursued similar goals, the one wishing to straighten out the deflections of instinctual resources in order to impose a realm of reason, the other endeavouring to restore in his fellow men their innate, but badly mismanaged sense of harmonious functioning.

Wertheimer's pronouncements as a psychologist, then, were inspired by an attitude of optimism and trust, adopted as a creed and constantly present in his teaching. He insisted that the things of this world are basically the way they appear, that outside and inside, surface and core, correspond to each other, and that therefore the senses can be relied upon to report the truth, if only the weeds of secondary complication and distortion are cleared away. Hence his love for music and art, where the wisdom of the senses rules by definition.

There was implicit in Wertheimer's thinking the image of an ideal human being, a type familiar to us from the European literary tradition of Parsifal, Simplicissimus, Candide, Prince Myshkin, the good soldier Schweik — an unassuming hero whose childlike and spontaneous innocence penetrates the crust, reveals the core, embarrasses, amuses, and appeals to a hidden decency. In an essay on the nature of freedom Wertheimer wrote:

What differences! In the way a man faces a counterargument, faces new facts! There are men who face them freely, open-mindedly, frankly, dealing honestly with them, taking them duly into account. Others are not able to do so at all: they somehow remain blind, rigid; they stick to their axioms, unable to face the arguments, the facts; or, if they do, it is to avoid or to get rid of them by some means — they are incapable of looking them squarely in the face. They cannot deal with them as free men; they are narrowed and enslaved by their position.

Inevitably there were those who reacted to his message as did Dostoevsky's Aglaia Ivanovna when she filed Prince Myshkin's letter in her copy of *Don Quixote*.

And yet, Max Wertheimer was anything but a dreamer. His spiritual ancestors were Spinoza and Goethe. Spinozistic was the notion that order and wisdom are not laid upon nature from without but are inherent in nature itself; of great influence also was Spinoza's idea that mental and physical existence are aspects of one and the same reality and therefore reflections of each other. With Goethe, Wertheimer shared the belief in the unity of percept and concept, of observation and idea, of poetical insight and scientific scrutiny, and like Goethe he prided himself on his devotion to tireless experimentation.

He wrote *more geometrico,* in Spinoza's geometrical manner; he liked algebraic formulæ, and he filled his study with piles of notes intended to be reduced to the sparest expression. The responsibility of the final wording kept him in agony, and the one comprehensive book he published, *Productive Thinking,* was finished after some twenty years of preparation in a sudden outburst of initiative during the few weeks before his death in 1943. Although his constant references to the richness and beauty of the things of nature seemed to promise a respite from scientific rigor to the lazy, he was severe to the point of cruelty with those among his professional colleagues who glossed over problems and neglected verification in favor of a soft-minded, pseudo-poetical eloquence. He drove himself hard and settled for nothing less in his students.

Wertheimer loved America. A son of ancient Prague, he found in the young culture of the new world the unspoiled freshness he preached. He liked the spontaneous ingenuity of the young men and the naive imagination of the girls. And he was forever indignant with selfish politics and social injustice because these flaws tarnished not only the country that had given him a home but also the image to which he was committed as a scientist and a man.

On Hannah Arendt
Politics: As It Is, Was, Might Be

BY GEORGE MC KENNA

> "Our citizens attend both to public and private duties, and do
> not allow absorption in their own various affairs to interfere
> with their knowledge of the city's. We differ from other states
> in regarding the man who holds aloof from public life not as
> 'quiet' but as useless. . . ."
>
> —Pericles, *Funeral Oration.*

WHEN HELEN and Robert Lynd visited Muncie, Indiana — "Middletown" — in 1925 they were told by one of its citizens that "no good man will go into politics here. Why should he? Politics is dirty."[1] Ten years later when they returned they were greeted with this observation from another Middletown resident: "Whatever changes you may find elsewhere in Middletown, you will find that our politics and government are the same crooked shell game."[2] Great changes have swept Middletown since 1937: urbanization, industrialization and enough education and sophistication to escape the parochialism once attached to being a "Hoosier." But what remains constant, defying all these social changes, is Middletown's fundamentally negative attitude toward politics. A recent survey by *The New York Times* sampled the reading habits of contemporary Middletonians.[3] Certainly they read more than they did in the 1920's and 1930's; the libraries are well used now, and new bookstores have opened to a flourishing business.[4] But what do they read? High on the list of best sellers in 1966 were *Peyton Place, Valley of the Dolls* and Dr. Spock's baby book — but nothing even remotely touching on the political life or the political involvements of this nation. Not a single book on Vietnam could be found on the bookstore racks. Measured over a period of months, the most consistent best seller was one entitled, *Flying Saucers — Serious Business.*[5]

[1] *Middletown* (New York: Harcourt, Brace & Co., 1929), 221.
[2] *Middletown in Transition* (New York: Harcourt, Brace & Co., 1937), 319.
[3] Richard R. Lingeman, "*Middletown Today,*" *The New York Times,* Special Paperback Supplement, February 26, 1967, VII, part 2.
[4] *Ibid.,* p. 1.
[5] *Ibid.,* p. 24.

It is not necessary to argue that Muncie is representative of America (although in many ways it is more so than New York City) to observe that its tendency to regard politics as something dirty is deeply embedded in the American mind. The clichés of Americans and the connotations they instinctively place upon words are unerring indicators of their feelings about politics: to "play politics" is to subordinate the public good to partisan advantage, a "politician" is a cynical, usually corrupt, manipulator, and a "political animal" is a ruthless, arrogant species ready to go any length to get into office. All too often, of course, this *is* the case, but only because our citizenry have abandoned politics to precisely that group of professionals who can hardly be expected to make of it anything more than a way of earning a living or assuaging their vanities. Thus the opprobrium which quite properly attaches to so many of its practitioners is carried back to the concept of politics, and the bias is reinforced.[6] What is needed is some way of breaking this circle, of impressing upon Americans the simple truth that politics — especially today, when its outcome can be so immediate and devastating — is too important to be left to the politicians.

Our nation's political scientists, on the whole, have done exactly the opposite. Instead of goading us with a model of politics as it might be, they have formulated a vast and sometimes arcane rationalization for politics as it is. Sometimes they adopt an attitude of stoic resignation: in 1960 Richard E. Neustadt saw no alternative to "emergencies in policy with politics as usual" in America; what we need, then, is a strong President who will hold the country together in the course of seeking his own personal power.[7] Sometimes they cele-

[6] There are exceptions to the general mood of political apathy, exceptions so important as to be models for understanding what Arendt means by political action, namely, the peace and civil rights movements of the past decade. But it must be remembered that they are composed of a small minority who are regarded with bewilderment, sometimes with horror, by the overwhelming bulk of their fellow citizens who wish only for a return to normalcy. What is more to the point of this essay, there is at this time virtually no support or even understanding of what they are doing from the social science community. Like the teachers of astronomy who would not look through Galileo's telescope, our teachers of political science in the nation's universities continue to talk to one another aided by graphs and charts and then write books on "the governmental process" without really noticing what is going on under their windows. The great danger is that, without being incorporated into a secure intellectual tradition, our contemporary movements may degenerate into mindless fanaticism or trail off into some kind of "campy" merriment. If so, they will be consigned to infamy or oblivion without ever having been understood.

[7] Richard E. Neustadt, *Presidential Power* (Science Editions: New York: John Wiley & Sons, Inc., 1962.) In 1964 Neustadt was hopeful that he had gotten

brate: at the end of the 1950's, Daniel Bell and Seymour Martin Lipset proclaimed "the end of ideology" in the West for the simple reason, in Lipset's words, "that the fundamental political problems of the industrial revolution have been solved." [8] Nothing remains, then, but to bring our blessings to the less fortunate countries of the world and "accept the fact that serious ideological controversies have ended at home." [9] The end of ideology thus emerges as an ideology of acceptance. This is the sociologists' counterpart to "pluralism," the ideology *par excellence* of political science professors since the early 1950's. The emergence of pluralism as a school of analysis was an intellectual expression of the end of the New and Fair Deals, the consequent decline of political competition and the re-emergence of bi-partisan "consensus" politics. But the pluralism as an analysis became pluralism as a doctrine when those who expended so much to explain how a politics of general stagnation "works" acquired a vested interest in showing that it *does* work. Hence, a whole philosophy of man and his capabilities, a trifle cynical perhaps, but in keeping with the tough-minded, debunking posture of those who take pride in being, not mere political thinkers but political scientists:

> It would clear the air of a good deal of cant if instead of assuming that politics is a normal and natural concern of human beings, one were to make the contrary assumption that whatever lip service citizens may pay to conventional attitudes, politics is a remote, alien, and unrewarding activity. [10]

More is involved here than a questionable empirical statement; it is clear that Robert Dahl believes the citizenry at large *should* stay out of politics. When the people at large get involved, "emotion rises and reasoned discussion declines." [11] What political science textbook does not cite some study or another suggesting that a little apathy is a good thing and a high voter turnout is a sure sign of "extremism"? The chief characteristic of the pluralistic school is this patroniz-

---

his man: "He *[Lyndon Johnson]* began as a New Deal Democrat and he was a member of the Kennedy Administration, and he has been a foremost professional politician. I take it he savors the use of power as well as its possession, and wants to move things in terms of policy." Interview in *U. S. News and World Report,* LVII (August 10, 1964), 35.

[8] Seymour Martin Lipset, *Political Man* (Anchor Books Edition; Garden City, New York: Doubleday & Company, Inc., 1963), p. 442. For Bell, see *The End of Ideology* (New York: The Free Press, 1964), pp. 369-75.

[9] Lipset, p. 455.

[10] Robert A. Dahl, *Who Governs?* (A Yale Paperbound; New Haven and London: Yale University Press, 1961), p. 279.

[11] *Ibid.,* p. 322.

ing attitude toward the public. Government becomes a matter for professional brokers who mediate among pressure groups. The rest of the citizenry are dissolved into an abstraction called "the common man," [12] a separate species of animal from Yale professors, who is to be studied, probed and above all apologized for. If he is apathetic, then apathy is the price we pay for democracy. [13] If he is primarily absorbed with accumulation — getting things — rather than in political participation, then the social scientists will obligingly construct their models of politics upon the question of "who gets what, when, how." For "in liberal societies, politics is a sideshow in the great circus of life." [14] This is the way we do things here, mister.

It is against this background of apology for mass apathy and oligarchic control that the political thought of Hannah Arendt stands in sharp relief. In a land where politics is a sideshow and flying saucers are serious business, something more is needed than bland description of how the system works: what is needed is a political discipline which asks, broadly, about the ends toward which the system works, which undertakes a critical analysis of those ends, and, if they are wanting, which provides alternatives that are viable and attainable, or at least worth striving for. Arendt's political thought, taken as a whole, is an important step toward such a reconstruction. Her unique contribution is an attempt to recapture the meaning of political action as it was understood by the actual participants in great political enterprises, and, using them as a guide, to measure the areas where politics has declined or altogether collapsed in today's world. What emerges is a radical critique of all those aspects of the modern world which either result from or contribute to the political environment in which most of us live. It is radical in the sense that it attempts to go to the roots of the problem by tracing it to its historical origins; it is a critique because it makes no attempt to treat phenomena such as totalitarianism in a "value free" manner: Arendt is convinced that to describe, say, concentration camps *sine ira*, "is not to be 'objective,' but to condone them." [15]

---

[12] See, for example, Robert E. Lane, *Political Ideology; Why the American Common Man Believes What He Does* (New York: The Free Press, 1962). Lane represents the best example of professorial condescension. One of his interviewees, who turned out to be "overeducated," became insulted at Lane's line of questioning. His "presence . . . in our sample is, on balance, unfortunate." *Ibid.*, pp. 7, 49.

[13] *Ibid.*, p. 477. Cf., *Ibid.*, p. 33: "But the social reward for [the] sense of disengagement from government is the capacity to bear an internalized *political* conflict without excessive pain. Perhaps it should be said that the price of freedom is eternal vigilance for some and a modest disengagement for others."

[14] Dahl, p. 305.

[15] See infra.

It is fair to challenge any radical critic of the status quo to give some indication of the kind of political order he would substitute for it. A later chapter of the book I am writing outlines more fully Arendt's attempt to meet this challenge, but it is necessary, even at this stage, to see what Arendt means by political action if we are to understand what she has to say about its decline. In this essay, then, we shall be concerned only with Arendt's definition of politics, a definition which will serve as a normative standard throughout the book. However, normative or not, a definition cannot simply be concocted out of fancy. Arendt, herself, contends that, outside the purely formal disciplines such as mathematics, we are not at liberty to define terms as we wish, that the price paid for such a form of "liberalism" is the destruction of intelligible communication.[16] From what experiences, then, does she derive her definition of politics?

First and foremost, the source is ancient Greece, when man was defined as a *zoon politikon*, "an animal who lives in a *polis*." What kind of animal, then, used to live in a *polis*, and what is a *polis*? To answer this, she turns, not to the philosophy of the Greeks and Romans (which was, after all, born during the decay of their political life), but to their experiences, many of which may have been forgotten or misunderstood in the tradition of political philosophy. Hannah Arendt, then, is not another "neo-classical" philosopher. She is not, like Leo Strauss,[17] criticising modern thought for its loss of Aristotelian rigor, nor, like Eric Voegelin,[18] asserting that Platonism provides a key to understanding our present perplexities. Quite the contrary. Arendt contends that Plato and Aristole actually misunderstood the real nature of politics, got it mixed up with other activities not really political and passed this very fundamental misunderstanding down to subsequent generations of philosophers and into the Western tradition of political philosophy. This does not prevent her from citing them with approval when they have, as she sees it, accurately recorded Greek *experiences* undistorted by the apolitical cast of their thought. But more important than Greek philosophy as texts for Greek political experience are the works of Herodotus, Homer, Thucydides and the dramatists, and Arendt makes free use of them. Nor, in trying to recapture the essential meaning of the *polis* and in its dwellers, is her debt exclusively to the Greeks. Its

[16] *The Human Condition.*
[17] Leo Strauss, *Natural Right and History* (Chicago: University of Chicago Press, 1953).
[18] Eric Voeglin, *A New Science of Politics* (Chicago: University of Chicago Press, 1953).

spirit, she believes, transcends any particular time or place. It can be found at times in the Romans, among the revolutionists of the past two centuries, in the resistance fighters of World War II and the Israeli *Kibbutz*. All of these political experiences are the mortar from which Arendt constructs a definition of politics as it might be.

The best way to begin studying her definition of politics is to note this observation which she makes of it in *The Human Condition*:

> Action [i.e., political action], the only activity that goes on directly between men without the intermediary of things or matter, corresponds to the human condition of plurality, to the fact that men, not Man, live on the earth and inhabit the world.[19]

In other words, politics has three characteristics: First, it does not require the intermediary of things or matter but goes on directly between man and man. Second, because of this fact, it cannot be performed in solitude and always requires the presence of others. Third, and following from the first and second, it corresponds to the plurality of men. Her meaning here ought to be explained.

What sets men apart from animals, in Arendt's thoroughly secular philosophy, is not the presence of an immortal soul or even a rational faculty, but the fact that men are mortals whereas animals have, in a sense, an eternal life.[20] This seems to be the exact opposite of the Christian understanding. What she means is that animals have eternal life because they are properly viewed, not as individuals, but as parts of their encompassing species; and the species "dog," for example, will go on living indefinitely, whatever may befall individual dogs. Of course, the same is also true in the case of the species "mankind." But the difference, for Arendt, is that man admits of more than *en masse* classification. Man, properly understood, is really individual *men*: each member possesses his own life, a *"bios,* with a recognizable life-story from birth to death,"[21] rising out of the eternal cycle of biological life or zoe. In short, "men are 'the mortals,' the only mortal things there are, for animals exist only as members of their species and not as individuals."[22] Anyone who has owned pets might object to this line of reasoning. Her elaboration of it makes it more defensible while bringing it closer to the Christian understanding. Very simply, what she has in mind is the unique-

[19] *The Human Condition*, p. 9.
[20] *Between Past and Future*, p. 42.
[21] *Ibid.*
[22] *Ibid.*

ness of the human person. All things, including even inanimate objects, possess the quality of *alteritas,* "otherness."[23] But only individual men are able, actively, to express their distinctive qualities and not merely, passively, to be considered distinct. Each man, in other words, is able to "communicate himself," to reveal himself as a "who" rather than a "what."[24]

Political action corresponds to this human plurality — the fact that men, not Man, live in this world — because it is the means by which men are able to communicate their distinctness without recourse to anything other than themselves. Painters and poets also communicate themselves, but they must perform their works in solitude and require the intermediary of things — if only pen and ink — to express themselves. Political action is the most completely human of activities.

Politics, as Arendt understands it, is indissolubly bound up with speech. A whine or growl might communicate anger or hunger, the use of mathematical symbols might communicate certain concepts, a computer can analyze and communicate data with superhuman accuracy, but only human speech can communicate man's distinctness as a person, can reveal him as a "who" and not simply a "what."

"Action and speech are so closely related because the primordial and specifically human act must at the same time contain the answer to the question asked of every newcomer: 'Who are you?'"[25] Aristotle, she believes, "only formulated the current opinion of the *polis* about man and the political way of life"[26] when he defined him as both a "political animal" (*zoon politikon*) and a "live creature capable of speech" *(zoon logon ekhon),* for both these activities were integrally connected in the life of the *polis.* It is no accident to Arendt that the Greeks, who loved nothing so much as a good argument, were the most political of peoples. In contrast, a glance at the *Congressional Record* should be sufficient to disclose something of the attitude which professional politicians today have toward focused debate. At any rate, she is convinced that without the accompaniment of speech action would be meaningless and subjectless.

> Without the accompaniment of speech . . . action would not only lose its revelatory character but, and by the same token, it would lose its subject, as it were; not acting men but performing

[23] *The Human Condition,* p. 156.
[24] *Ibid.*
[25] *The Human Condition,* p. 158.
[26] *Ibid.,* p. 26.

robots would achieve what, humanly speaking, would remain incomprehensible. Speechless action would no longer be action because there would no longer be an actor, and the actor, the doer of deeds is possible only if he is at the same time the speaker of words. The action he begins is humanly disclosed by the word, and though his deed can be perceived in its brute physical appearance without verbal accompaniment, it becomes relevant only through the spoken word in which he identifies himself as the actor announcing what he does, has done, and intends to do.[27]

For Arendt, "speechless action" is a contradiction in terms, for action without speech is no longer politics but violence. Because of the contemporary confusion between political power and violence, this point is particularly relevant today, and I will return to it presently.

"The *raison d'être* of politics is freedom. . . ."[28] Although Arendt claims to be stating but a truism,[29] it would be disputed by a number of premodern and modern political thinkers from Hobbes to Reinhold Niebuhr. The latter has made these observations:

> It is our common assumption that political freedom is a simple *summom bonum*. It is not. Freedom must always be related to community and justice. Every community seeks consciously and unconsciously to make social peace and order the first goal of its life. It may pay a very high price in the restriction of freedom so as to establish order; but order is the first desideratum for the simple reason that chaos means non-existence.[30]

Yes, Arendt might reply, it is quite true that communities — except during times of revolution — seldom make freedom the first order of business. But this anthropological fact does not negate the principle of the primacy of freedom. (All communities also have some form of ritualized cruelty, but this is hardly a justification for it.) Political life might well be impossible without order, but it would be, she believes, meaningless without freedom.[31] Niebuhr's observation, moreover, assumes an antithesis between freedom and order which Arendt would not accept. Freedom, Arendt believes, produces its own order, an order not imposed from without but growing out

---

[27] *Ibid.*, pp. 158-59.
[28] "Freedom and Politics: A Lecture," *Chicago Review,* XIV (Spring, 1960), 28.
[29] *Ibid.*, p. 32.
[30] Reinhold Niebuhr, "Reflections on Democracy as an Alternative to Communism," *Columbia University Forum,* IV (Summer, 1961), 10.
[31] *Chicago Review,* XIV, 28.

of mutual agreement. In Niebuhr's frame of reference, Arendt would almost certainly be classified among the "foolish children of light," for she goes the length of identifying politics with freedom. "Men are free, as distinguished from possessing the gift for freedom, as long as they act, neither before nor after, for to be free and act are the same."[32] Arendt acknowledges a debt to Martin Heidegger and other *existenz* philosophers,[33] and her own writings emphasize the concrete and the existential. She would not be put in the position of saying that man is "essentially" free for the same reason that she will not discuss an absolute, unchanging "human nature"; fixed essences have no place in her thinking about man and his activities.[34] Man, she believes, is as he acts and "the appearance of freedom, like the manifestations of principles coincides with the performing act."[35] She is interested in freedom as a phenomenon, a "demonstrable fact"[36] rather than a metaphysical category. She compares the appearance of freedom to the actions of the performing artist: it exists *only* in the moment of performance It is, therefore, unrealizable in an environment from which politics is excluded — in tribal societies, in the privacy of the household, or in "despotically ruled communities which banish their subjects into the narrowness of the home and thus prevent the rise of a public realm."[37] When she says that freedom needs

---

[32] *Ibid.*, p. 33.
[33] See her article, "What is Existenz Philosophy," *Partisan Review*, XIII (Winter, 1946), 34-56. In this article she praised the philosophy of another *existenz* philosopher, Karl Jaspers, while rejecting that of Heidegger. In a recent interview, however, she looked back on her 1946 essay as one affected by her personal dislike for Heidegger because of his Nazi leanings. In retrospect, she admitted, she had been strongly affected by Heidegger, especially for his addition of the historical dimension to the phenomenology of Husserl, i. e., Heidegger's insight that before you can say what a things *is*, you must say what it *was*. This historical approach is obvious in her treatment of totalitarianism. As she explains:
"What I did—and what I might have done anyway because of my previous training and the way of my thinking—was to discover the chief elements of totalitarianism and to analyze them in historical terms, tracing these elements back in history as far as I deemed proper and necessary. That is, I did not write a history of totalitarianism but *an analysis in terms of history [*emphasis added*] . . . .*" "A Reply *[*to Eric Voegelin's review of *The Origins of Totalitarianism].*" *The Review of Politics*, XV (February, 1933), 77-78.
[34] She doubts the possibility of man ever being able to define himself. It is highly unlikely that we, who can know, determine, and define the natural essences of all things surrounding us, which we are not, should ever be able to do the same for ourselves—this would be like jumping over our own shadows. Moreover, nothing entitles us to assume that man has a nature or essence in the same sense as other things. *The Human Condition*, p. 12.
An answer to the question "What is man?" can only be given by God—it can be settled only "within the framework of a divinely revealed answer." Here she claims to follow Augustine. *Ibid.*, footnote No. 2, p. 302.
[35] *Chicago Review*, XIV, 33.
[36] *Between Past and Future*, p. 149.
[37] *Ibid.*, p. 148.

a "worldly space" to make its appearance, we might put it again in terms of the performing arts and say that freedom needs a stage or platform to be seen in public.

Politics, as she understands it, does not depend upon any particular physical location. When she says that it requires a "public space" or "space of appearances," she uses these expressions in a figurative or social, rather than a literal, physical sense. The ancient *polis*, for example, was not the city-state as a geographical entity, but an organization of people that was, ultimately, independent of material factors; hence, the watchword, "Wherever you go, you will be a *polis*." The space of appearances is therefore to be interpreted in the widest sense of the word as "the space where I appear to others as others appear to me, where men exist not merely like other living or inanimate things but make their appearance explicitly." It is a space that "comes into being wherever men are together in the manner of speech and action," hence speech and action provide their own public realm and are not dependent upon buildings or even constitutions.[38] Arendt is simply taking note of the fact that one need not go to Washington or City Hall to take part in politics and that the real centers of political action may be far removed from the formal centers, from the "paraphernalia of officialdom." [39] A letter to an individual or newspaper can be a supremely political act. *The Federalist* papers and the letters of Thomas Jefferson (who spent the better part of his life at his writing desk in Monticello) are examples of how independent of location the "space of appearances" may be.

Political action, in Arendt's analysis, can appear in unlikely places because it goes on directly between man and man, without the intermediary of things. Wherever men gather it is found potentially; but, she emphasizes, only potentially. The rise and fall of civilizations is to be explained, not by material things or their absence, but the actualization and loss of *power*. Power, elusive and intangible as it is, plays a key role in Arendt's notion of politics.

> What first undermines and then kills political communities is loss of power and final impotence; and power cannot be stored up and kept in reserve for emergencies, like the instruments of violence, but exists only in its actualization. Where power is not actualized, it passes away, and history is full of examples that

[38] *The Human Condition*, p. 105.
[39] *Between Past and Future*, p. 3.

the greatest material riches cannot compensate for this loss.[40]
Power, as its etymological roots reveal, always has a potential character. In order for it to be actualized, it is not sufficient for men to be gathered together. They could be collected together like slaves, or inmates in a concentration camp or passengers on a bus. It is only actualized when men undertake joint action. And since action, as she understands it, always involves speech, her concept of power must be distinguished from another term frequently used as a synonym: violence. (One hears "black power" invoked by those who mean "black violence" and "power politics" used when "politics through violence" is really meant.) The hallmark of power is speech combined with creative action.

> Power is actualized only where word and deed have not parted company, where words are not empty and deeds not brutal, where words are not used to veil intentions but to disclose realities, and deeds are not used to violate and destroy but to establish relations and create new realities.[41]

Violence by itself is capable only of producing "an array of impotent forces that spend themselves, often spectacularly and vehemently but in utter futility, leaving behind neither monuments nor stories, hardly enough memory to enter into history at all."[42] Impotent while armed to the teeth: as examples Arendt could point to the last years of Rome, the Court of Louis XVI, the Romanoffs, the succession of petty tyrants in South Vietnam since 1954, our own Southern sheriffs of whom the freedom song prophesies: "All their dogs will lie there rottin'/All their lives will be forgotten." What she does use to illustrate a confrontation between impotent violence and non-violent power is the example of the Danish refusal to cooperate with the Nazis during World War II in the matter of deporting the Jews. So determined were the Danes to protect the Jews and so concerted were their efforts that they succeeded, even converting some high-ranking Nazis to their side.[43] "One is tempted to recommend the story as required reading in political science for all students who wish to learn something about the enormous power potential inherent in non-violent action and in resistance to an opponent possessing vastly superior means of violence."[44] This does not mean that Arendt is a pacifist.

[40] *The Human Condition*, p. 178.
[41] *Ibid.*, pp. 178-179.
[42] *Ibid.*, p. 181.
[43] *Eichmann in Jerusalem*, p. 155.
[44] *Ibid.*, p. 154.

Indeed, her model of political action is derived in large part from the revolutions of the past two centuries, and the Resistance movement during World War II, none of which could have succeeded without violence of some sort. But that is the point. Organized violence — warfare — may be necessary to *protect* the operation of the political process but it must not be *confused* with it. Arendt's approach to politics is thus sharply at variance with that school of realpolitik which proceeds on the maxim that "war is the continuation of politics by other means." The adoption of this principle might have the effect of limiting war (although this has hardly been demonstrated by the events of the last few years), but it also destroys the distinction between politics and violence by making politics the continuation of war by other means. And, far from being simply the attitude of a Prussian military officer, the maxim of Clausewitz is really a concise summary of the whole modern world's confusion between politics and violence, persuasion and force, debate and mute savagery. The United States policy, pursued with utter futility for three years, of bombing another country to "persuade" its leaders to negotiate only serves to underscore the danger in these confusions. Politics, for Hannah Arendt, comprises both word and deed. When men fall silent and turn to their weapons, politics comes to an end: "for man, to the extent that he is a political being, is endowed with the power of speech." [45]

By sharply distinguishing between power and violence, Arendt is also freeing power from all the negative connotations attributed to it by the classical liberals — that power corrupts, that the state is an instrument of oppression or at best a necessary evil, a badge of lost innocence and so on.

On the contrary, power, in Arendt's view is essential to the freedom of man and the survival of the body politic. "Power is what keeps the public realm, the potential space of appearance between acting and speaking, men in existence." [46]

Let us pause to consider the implications of Arendt's notion of politics and its connection with freedom. What she is saying is that no man can be free unless he participates in the political life of his community. It is important to keep in mind that Arendt considers politics in terms of active participation, not simply passive acceptance. Hence, the expression "government by consent of the governed" is, for Arendt, misleading if it is meant to imply that the governed are

[45] *On Revolution,* p. 9.
[46] *The Human Condition,* p. 179.

thereby taking part in politics. Consent alone does not constitute political activity. Government by consent, whether that consent be expressed in terms of periodic elections, referenda, plebiscites or whatever, is not government by the people but government by an elite which occasionally gets the approval of the people. Perhaps she would consider the act of voting itself as political (Arendt is not clear on this question), but when the voter returns to his private life for another year or two or (most usually) four, he is no more free than the subject of an oriental despot, though he may be treated more decently. This should hardly fail to provoke a number of questions. Is it not possible for activities other than political participation to be considered free? And what is freedom after all — does it not ultimately depend upon whether one *thinks* he is free, regardless of his political status? Is not free will and freedom from neurosis a much more fundamental measure of freedom than political freedom, which is, after all, only a matter of externals?

To the first question her answer here would seem to be a somewhat equivocal "no."

She admits that there is such a thing as freedom *from* politics, understood at various periods of history as the freedom to spend one's time in philosophic or religious contemplation, the freedom to make money without state interference, the freedom to go to work or play without worrying about the burden of political participation. But it is clear from the context in which she discusses freedom from politics that she does not regard this negative freedom very highly.[47] Such an understanding of freedom, which she considers either Platonic or Christian in origin, seems to her more an obstacle to the enjoyment of political freedom than anything that could be called a positive contribution.

But what of the activities themselves? Cannot man find freedom in the pursuit of monetary gain, visions of Truth, the joy of labor, or simply diversion? She would deny that any of these activities are, properly speaking, free acts. Contemplation is not even, as she understands it, an activity but a motionless state of wonder. Contemplation is "an experience of the eternal," a confrontation with Being, or perhaps The Being, which rules all of the universe with iron laws. Far from being an experience of freedom, it is a surrender to necessity: the philosopher can only gaze in helpless awe at a universe "where no beginning and no end exist and where all natural things

[47] *Chicago Review,* XIV (Spring, 1960), 30-32, Cf., *On Revolution,* p. 284.

swing in changeless, deathless repetition."[48] As for labor, business and play, since they serve nature's life processes (they are meant to feed the demands of the body which requires both food and rest), they are as much ruled by necessity as the "changeless, deathless" universe which surrounds and encloses all life. Hence, Arendt would probably agree that the prototype American, whose major preoccupations are his job, his golf and his home workshop, and who takes no part in political life, is not a free man. This is not to say that he is not, in his own way, happy. The Negroes in the antebellum South may also have been happier than those trying to liberate themselves today.

All of this underscores the difficulty of defining freedom as a state of mind. If freedom ultimately depends upon whether a man *thinks* he is free, then the term ceases to have meaning, for even a slave can be led to think he is free. (Arendt considers it more than a coincidence that "free will" originated with Epictetus, the slave-philosopher.) We are plunged into a sea of subjectivity with one man's feelings as valid as another's with no commonly identifiable landmarks. Thus, she is suspicious of "free will" for the same reason that she distrusts psychiatry: "the human heart, as we all know, is a very dark place and whatever goes on in its obscurity can hardly be called a demonstrable fact."[49] Arendt's concept of freedom is political freedom, which is not a phenomenon of the will—or heart, or psyche—but a "worldly, tangible reality."[50]

Let us summarize Arendt's definition of politics. Politics is that activity, involving both action and speech, by which men jointly participate in a common endeavor. To put it in terms of a familiar allegory, if six primitive men, never having moved a heavy log before, gathered together, discussed the problem and decided to lift it together, that—and not any formal contract or compact—would put an end to the state of nature, for it would be a political act. Politics is independent of location or any material thing. It requires no apparatus, machinery, buildings. Above all, it requires no weaponry, for it operates through persuasion rather than force or fear. Politics consists, not in the giving and obeying of orders, but in *mutual* action and common participation.

Politics, as she understands it, is concerned with the extraordinary; a political act is to that extent an extraordinary act. To Americans

<hr>

[48] *The Human Condition,* p. 84.
[49] *Chicago Review,* XIV, 30.
[50] *Between Past and Future,* pp. 148, 151.

who are used to thinking of politics as anything but extraordinary—
"politics as usual"—Arendt's assertion needs to be explained.

Since she considers politics as the most human activity, it is necessary, even at the expense of some repetition, to reflect on the meaning
of man's mortality. "This is mortality: to move along a rectilinear line
in a universe where everything, if it moves at all, moves in a cyclical
order."[51] What she means is that, while every creature exclusively
natural is bound to nature's cycle of eternal recurrence and is incapable of beginning anything new, man alone is able to move forward
in a straight line, i.e., to have a history.

Arendt's cosmology is postmedieval but pre-Darwinian. The medi-
evalists lived in a universe in which natural bodies and forces had
appetites for certain things while abhorring others—a human universe
not always friendly but at least on speaking terms with man. The
effect of Galilean science was to divest nature of these traits. Yet
Darwin's discoveries opened up the possibility that the medieval
view, purged of its naiveté, could be restored on an even better
footing. The opportunity was not lost on Pierre Teilhard de Chardin,
the Jesuit paleontologist whose posthumous writings have already been
enormously influential not only upon scientific thought but on secular
and religious attempts to find a place for man in what otherwise
seems a hostile and alien universe. The starting point for Teilhard's
cosmic humanism is Darwin's key discovery: that nature does not
go round and round, it goes forward. Toward what? Toward Parousia,
the consummation and end of the world, but not before man somehow
raises himself, evolves, to a spiritual level.

Teilhard, then, restores a teleological universe, not, however, a
teleological universe of iron determinism but one shot through with
human qualities. Even inorganic substances have something within
them akin to free will or at least to human intelligence, and Teilhard
makes use of the discoveries of Einstein, Max Planck, Werner Heisen-
berg and others to suggest that matter, the very stuff of the universe,
has a "within." Even protein molecules possess "deep down in
themselves, some sort of rudimentary psyche."[52] Teilhard strips
Darwinism of its Galilean-Newtonian residue of determinism and
finds a new home for man in a universe which is both teleological
and anthropomorphic.

Arendt's view is directly opposite. From the standpoint of man,

[51] *Ibid.*, p. 42.
[52] Pierre Teilhard de Chardin, *The Phenomenon of Man,* trans. Bernard Wall
(New York: Harper and Brothers, 1959), p. 77.

or more accurately *men,* living in the here and now, nature is not progress but circularity: the change of seasons, the cycle of birth, growth, reproduction, death, and so on and on again. Teilhard measures a time not our time: million-year units are for scientists and mystics to contemplate, but they are too vast for acting men. The progress of nature is a scientific hypothesis without political relevance; it has no meaning for this generation, or the next, or even a hundred succeeding ones. In the long run nature may move forward, but in the long run we are dead.

As for Teilhard's attempt to find human qualities in nature, it must be remembered that the analogy cuts both ways. On the one hand it can be taken to mean that the universe is permeated with some form of intelligence which, like that of humans, strives toward a goal. On the other hand the analogy between man and nature could mean that man is becoming more like the rest of nature, that nature can be compared to man only because man is losing the very qualities which once set him apart. What for Teilhard is an exhilarating revelation concerning nature is for Arendt a depressing fact about modern man.[53]

The present essay, however, does not deal with Arendt's view of man's plight but with her model of his capacities. If Teilhard's man is thoroughly at home in the universe, Arendt's man uneasily coexists with it. When Arendt describes political action as a straight line in a universe of circularity, the line must not be taken as a path (either upward or downward) marked out by nature but as a sword thrust into nature. Human activity is not in and through nature but against it and in spite of it; it is not the smooth process of natural evolution but the sudden intrusion into nature of something unexplainable by any natural laws, Newtonian or post-Newtonian. Since man is the only surprise in a universe of calculables, it follows that human action consists in reasserting and augmenting man's unpredictability, his unnaturalness, his insistence upon *not* being a phenomenon.

If man did nothing but his housework, he would, from the standpoint of what he left behind for future generations, be no different from the birds who work industriously, even "intelligently," but begin nothing new. The extraordinary act, then, is that which runs counter to nature's circular pattern of birth, procreation, death. What sets men apart from beasts is their capacity to defy nature by starting something new in a universe otherwise bound to a

[53] *See infra.*

cycle of eternal recurrence. What makes politics extraordinary is
that men leave the privacy of the household, meet together in public,
and decide to undertake something new, something which then
enters into history. When those first primitive men decided to move
the log, they cleared a path for human history to begin. Politics,
Arendt would agree, is "mundane," for by "world" she means
"the human artifice," the works of man which create a culture in
which subsequent generations may be nourished and to which they
in turn will contribute.

It is here that Arendt's philosophy becomes concerned with the
problem of the perishability or "futility" of politics. The danger, as
Arendt sees it, is that unless someone is around to see and record the
extraordinary deeds of man, they will sink into oblivion without a
trace. Speeches and deeds, considered by themselves, "lack not only
the tangibility of other things, but are even less durable and more
futile than the things which we produce for consumption." [54] Politics
is "as futile as life itself." [55] Human greatness, seen in terms of man's
extraordinary words and deeds, requires some means of preservation.
Arendt suggests two: "The whole factual world of human affairs
depends for its reality and its continued existence, first, upon the
presence of others who have seen and heard and will remember, and,
second, on the transformation of the intangible into the tangibility
of things." [56] The first condition assumes a body politic which will
not only be witness but have sufficient durability to pass from generation to generation the record of human greatness. This was the role
assumed by the ancient *polis* which was supposed to "offer a remedy
for the futility of action and speech." [57]

> The *polis* — if we trust the famous words of Pericles in the
> Funeral Oration — gives a guaranty that those who forced every
> sea and land to become the scene of their daring will not remain
> without witness . . .; without assistance from others, those who
> acted will be able to establish together the everlasting remem-

[54] *The Human Condition*, p. 82.

[55] *Ibid.*, p. 93. It would appear that Arendt is contradicting what she said about
politics in comparing it with violence (*supra*); there she suggests that what makes
politics different from violence is that politics is *not* futile. What she means,
however, is that politics has the *potential* of being remembered, for there is something for the historian to remember, whereas violence can never escape futility
bcause by itself it is nothing but destruction. But even though all great deeds have
the potential of not being forgotten, this does not mean that they will be remembered. We remember Achilles and Pericles, but how many other great men have
been lost to history for want of a chronicler?

[56] *Ibid.*, p. 83.

[57] *Ibid.*, p. 176.

brance of their good and bad deeds, to inspire admiration in the present and future ages.[58]

But the *polis* itself did not endure, nor did Rome, and the whole record of human greatness would have been lost were it not for a group of men whose activities have not yet been discussed: the artists, writers, and other makers of things whom she classifies together as *homo faber*.

The task of the fabricator is to transfer the intangible "into the tangibility of things." In this connection she considers the role of historians, poets, sculptors, architects and the like, who "reify" or make into things the memory of human greatness. *Zoon politikon*, by himself, produces nothing; if his words and deeds are to be remembered, they must be recorded. "Acting and speaking men need the help of *homo faber* in his highest capacity, that is, the help of the artists, of poets and historiographers, of monument-builders or writers, because without them the only product of their activity, the story they enact and tell, would not survive at all." [59] The task of poets and historiographers thus "consists in making something lasting out of remembrance. They do this by translating *praxis* and *lexis,* action and speech, into that kind of *poeisis* or fabrication which eventually becomes the written word." [60] Fabrication in its "purest" form is a handmaiden or auxiliary to politics. When things are made not for use[61] but to endure and commemorate the great words and deeds of man, they put the stamp of immortality upon the activities of mortal men.

This brings us to the role which Hannah Arendt has assumed. Arendt is convinced that for a number of reasons, the meaning of politics as the ancients understood it — the meaning of politics explored in this essay — has become lost or obscured over the past nineteen centuries since the decline of Rome. It is this "lost treasure" which Arendt attempts to unearth, not simply for the sake of scholarly curiosity, but with the hope that modern man may derive lessons from it. In other words, Arendt herself has undertaken the role of "*homo faber* in his highest capacity": in being a philosopher of politics, she must also be an historian commemorating what other-

---

[58] *Ibid.*

[59] *Ibid.*, p. 153.

[60] *The Review of Politics,* XX, 573-574.

[61] "Use-objects," chairs, tables, etc. differ from art objects in that their primary function is not to be seen but to serve the daily purposes of Man. They are less durable than art objects for they can be worn out or rendered obsolete. However, both art objects and use objects are much more durable than consumer goods. Cf., *infra.*

wise might be forgotten. Whether or not "all historiography is necessarily salvation,"[62] it is clear that hers is.

But it is not only the "lost treasures" of the past that she would have us remember as a means of understanding and perhaps even beginning to resolve our predicament. We need also to remember how we got into the predicament in the first place. Some of the forgotten fragments of the past such as those which set the stage for the appearance of modern alienation, mass society and totalitarianism also have to be recalled so as to "free" ourselves from their "burden," for the past presses upon the present[63] and shapes it. "Not even oblivion and confusion, which can cover up so efficiently the origin and responsibility for every single deed, are able to undo a deed or prevent its consequences."[64] In her study of totalitarianism, for example, she attempts to isolate those events of the past two centuries which became the chief elements of present-day crisis. These events, or at least their connection with totalitarianism, have become obscure. Nevertheless, this "subterranean stream," as she calls it in her preface to *The Origins of Totalitarianism,* "has finally come to the surface and usurped the dignity of our tradition."[65] To find the source of this stream and to survey its course before it broke the surface — in less metaphorical language, to find the hidden connections between events in our past and the crises of our own times — is not an easy task, and in many ways it is painful both to writer and reader because it raises the question of what might have been. Nevertheless, Arendt believes that the "tears of remembrance" are cathartic and essential to understanding our present predicament.

> The scene where Ulysses listens to the story of his own life is paradigmatic for both history and poetry; the "reconciliation with reality," the catharsis, which, according to Aristotle, was the essence of tragedy, and, according to Hegel, was the ultimate purpose of history, came about through remembrance.[66]

The task which Hannah Arendt has set for herself as political philosopher and historian is to bring the forgotten past to our attention — not only its "lost treasures" but also its "subterranean streams."

[62] *The Review of Politics,* XV, p. 77.
[63] *Between Past and Future,* pp. 10-11.
[64] *The Human Condition,* p. 209.
[65] *The Origins of Totalitarianism,* p. xi.
[66] *Between Past and Future,* p. 45.

The Heritage of Socialist Humanism

BY GEORGE L. MOSSE

EXILES ARE apt to be left behind by the times, forgotten in the countries they fled and ignored by those in which they found a home. For many years it seemed as if German refugee intellectuals would share this fate. To be sure, the contributions of eminent scientists and scholars were often appreciated by their hosts, for they managed to become part of the establishment, contributing to its success and survival. The wave of German refugee intellectuals who fled from National Socialism included not only such men and women, but also a sizable group who remained outsiders in exile, as they had been outside the establishment in the Weimar Republic. Their contribution as critics of that Republic had come to public notice, but once in exile they seemed to live apart, withdrawn into their own circle of like-minded friends. These left-wing intellectuals were writers or critics, and though some of them found positions abroad they still constituted a fairly well defined group within the general emigration.

In 1954, when Alfred Kantorowicz wrote about one of the most famous of this group, the novelist Lion Feuchtwanger, he lamented the obscurity into which this celebrated author had fallen — perhaps the generation reaching maturity in the year 2000 might once more appreciate such a writer and the principles for which he stood.[1] However, it is precisely the ideals represented by Feuchtwanger and his friends which have a relevance to our times denied to the writings of many who moved so easily from the establishment of the German Republic to the establishments of other European nations and of the United States. When the young generation of the 1960s looks

[1] Alfred Kantorowicz, *Deutsche Schicksale* (Wien, 1964), p. 153. The most helpful discussions of literature in exile for my purposes are Matthias Wegner, *Exil und Literatur* (Frankfort, 1967) and Hans-Albert Walter, "Literatur im Exil" (Mimeographed MS. Suddeutscher Rundfunk, 3. April, 1964).

back to the "golden twenties" of Germany, they focus upon the hopes and fears which these left-wing intellectuals had expressed. Even when living in isolation at the French resort of Sanay or, later, in southern California, they were destined to provide a bridge between some of the most fertile thought of the 1920s and the search for a new society which has preoccupied youth in our own decade.

In as much as they believed in the abolition of capitalist society, these left wing intellectuals were socialists. That society was corrupt and oppressive; its political institutions, such as parliaments, merely served to disguise the suppression of human freedom and of man's potential for development. And although they believed that war and violence were an outgrowth of capitalist society, they did not accept the full implications of a Marxist social analysis. The working of society was seen as part of the operations of autonomous reason, in the belief that thinking man can grasp what is true, good and right. Above and beyond any social or economic analysis of the present, there was a categorical imperative centered upon man's dignity and his ability to control his own destiny. Man must never be made the means but always the end of all social and political action.

From these propositions it followed that violence must never be used against men, and that all human institutions which restricted his freedom must be abolished. This included the discipline a political party might enforce and the violence which might occur in a revolutionary situation. Their attitude towards political, economic or social power is summed up in a phrase from Heinrich Mann's novel, *Man of Straw (Der Untertan*, 1911): "The use of power which is not filled with goodness and kindness will not last."[2] There can be no compromise with political parties or systems which use power differently, nor can any revolutionary strategy be tolerated which uses oppressive or violent means to bring about the socialist society. Small wonder that these intellectuals were outsiders both within organized revolutionary movements and in society as a whole.

We cannot follow in detail the thought and fate of all the men and women involved, but must confine ourselves to certain outstanding examples. Lion Feuchtwanger, Heinrich Mann, Leonhard Frank and Alfred Döblin will guide our discussion. It would have been easier to deal with these left-wing intellectuals as a group in the Weimar Republic, at a time when several journals expressed their

---

[2] Heinrich Mann, *Der Untertan* (Leipzig, 1918), p. 490.

point of view, in particular the *Weltbühne* and the *Tagebuch*.[3] However, after 1933, the *Weltbühne* as the *Neue Weltbuhne* came under
communist influence, and the *Tagebuch* as the *Neue Tagebuch* moved
perceptibly to the right. We are left, therefore, with a loose-knit
group of men, writers for the most part, who shared an outlook on
the world but no common journal or institutional framework.

The idealism they shared was expressed in Leonhard Frank's phrase
that the "path to socialism is humanism."[4] This humanism was
founded upon a belief in the traditions of the French Enlightenment.
Heinrich Mann was a leader among this group, and his whole life
had been committed to that tradition. When Leonhard Frank wrote
the short stories published under the title *Man is Good* (1919), he
meant that man is good if he is left free to develop his own potential, or, to put it in contemporary terms, is able to control his own
destiny.

Appealing as his combination of socialism and humanism is, it
had to confront the realities of the world in which these men lived
and worked; the "objective situation" as Marxists would describe it.
This is the crux of the problem, for such men wanted to change
society and thought not merely as writers but as doers as well. Should
force be used against counter-revolutionary elements? What about
the relationship of socialism to the aspirations of the working class?
And were Marxists correct to see in that class the true harbinger of
the future? Moreover, a socialist society was supposedly in being in
the Soviet Union: could this society serve as example? These questions were asked under the pressure of the Nazi seizure of power
and the collapse of a Republic towards which such men had been
critical long before the Nazi menace became a reality. How they
dealt with these problems gives some indication of the viability of
socialist humanism in the twentieth century world.

In his earliest novel, *Thomas Wendt* (1919), Lion Feuchtwanger
had already posed the problem arising from the confrontation of the
revolution with force. The hero becomes the leader of a revolution
meant to bring about a new society of freedom, but fails to carry
through the revolutionary impetus. Thomas Wendt cannot compromise the respect he feels for every individual, the very goal of the
revolution, in order to defeat those who oppose the socialist society.
He is told by a friend: "You will always have to use force against

[3] i.e. George L. Mosse, "Left Wing Intellectuals and the Weimar Republic,"
Germans and Jews (New York, 1969) discusses this group up to 1933.
[4] Leonhard Frank, *Links ist wo das Herz ist* (Munich, 1952), p. 66.

men if you want to eradicate their ideas. You must be unjust, Thomas
Wendt, for the sake of justice."[5] But Wendt cannot accept such
advice. This thread of humanism runs throughout the works of men
like Leonhard Franck, Heinrich Mann, Alfred Döblin and many
others. To be sure, in 1923 Mann called for a "dictatorship of reason"[6]
which would force men to shed the prejudices which they had imbibed
during the long darkness of Wilhelmian rule. But after this moment
of despair he counselled patience, for eventually reason would prevail and the existing social system would then be changed peacefully.

Lion Feuchtwanger's most famous novel, *The Jewish War* (1932),
which treats of the victory of the Romans over the Jews, is one song
of praise for reason amidst the passions and violence of the age.
Flavius Josephus, who was to write the history of that war, starts
the conflict under the influence of overwhelming passion. He has
abandoned reason, for the war can never be won by the Jews, and
it ends with the destruction of the Jewish temple in which Josephus
had served as a priest. Justus, his enemy, is correct in believing that
reason must triumph if war in which all truth collapses is to be
avoided. In the end Josephus himself is converted to this truth, and
opposes both the barbarism of Rome and the fanaticism of the Jewish
warlords.

The Nazi triumph and his own exile did not at first markedly
change Feuchtwanger's outlook upon the world. In *The Oppermanns*
(1933) he describes the fate of a Jewish family in the face of the
National Socialist seizure of power. The hero, Gustav Oppenheimer,
lives within the world of the Enlightenment and cannot understand
the political flood tide which is about to engulf him. However, the
Nazi terror awakens him to the reality of the situation and the
"unpolitical" man, who had spent his time writing a book about
Lessing, throws himself into the political struggle. He continues the
struggle against fascism in Nazi Germany until he is put into a concentration camp and dies as the result of ill-treatment there. He
comes to see that "one cannot remain silent when truth is falsified."[7]
This truth is the rationality of man which is linked with freedom
and tolerance. To be sure, there will be setbacks in the struggle for
these ideals, but as Gustav Oppenheimer had written: "We are
enjoined to labour, but it is not granted to complete our labours."

[5] quoted in *Lion Feuchtwanger,* ed. Kollektiv fuer Literaturgeschichte (Berlin,
1960), p. 12.
[6] Heinrich Mann, *Diktatur der Vernunft* (Berlin, 1923), passim.
[7] Lion Feuchtwanger, *The Oppermanns* (London, 1933), p. 384.

It is startling to what extent the humanism of such men survived the Nazi experience. Leonhard Frank provides another example. After a life which had meant exile both in the first world war and under National Socialism, he reiterates his belief in humanity. Victory over capitalism and oppression can be won without violating the life and sanctity of the individual. But it is also typical for this ideology that he brushes aside the specific means for accomplishing this task: to work this out is asking too much of one man.[8] But because none of these men paid attention to the mechanism of change, their ideology, abstracted from reality, was bound to suffer. Reading their works before and after the Nazi catastrophe one receives the impression that the new rational man would, by himself, solve all remaining problems. Their longing for spontaneity brings them close to many of the young rebels of the sixties, whose Utopia is also based on an optimistic view of human nature which tends to ignore the problems produced by revolution and the necessary use of power.

The fact that none of these intellectuals found their way into an existing political party should not astonish us. For parties, however far to the left, stifled the human spirit by their dogmatism, and encroached on man's control of his own destiny through the discipline which they enforced. When, in 1933, a young man asked Alfred Döblin if it were not time to join a socialist party in order to fight the Nazis, he received a negative answer. More important than any specific political commitment was the necessity to fight for humanism and justice in the world.[9] What, then, about the Nazis, who had triumphed over all such considerations in their march to power?

Germany, so the *Neue Tagebuch* wrote in 1933, was "occupied" by the Nazis and love for Germany meant hatred of the occupation.[10] This, indeed, was the crux of their attitude: the oppressive social sytem had finally shown its true face and had taken over the nation against the real wishes and interests of the people. Hugenberg, the big industrialist, von Papen, the leader of the junker class, had combined to sell the nation to Hitler. All these left-wing intellectuals denied that National Socialism was a popular movement; they could not conceive that Nazi ideology was accepted by man as they had defined him. For Heinrich Mann the meaning of exile consisted in the example which German intellectuals provided for their

---

[8] Leonhard Frank, *op. cit.*, p. 182.
[9] *Tagebuch* Jahrg. II, Heft 27 (July 5, 1930), pp. 1069-1070.
[10] *Das Neue Tagebuch*, I. Jahrg. (1. Juli, 1933), p. 3.

people. Through the patient proclamation of reason and justice they would keep alive the truth and recall Germans to their proper destiny. Feuchtwanger in his earlier works had been skeptical of the people's use of power; Thomas Wendt was the victim, not only of his own high principles, but also of the masses who did not understand them. But in *The Oppermanns* he emphasizes that the "people are good," and draws a sharp dividing line between the German masses and their fascist rulers.

This optimism may have been necessary for the self-esteem of these writers, it kept them going and gave a purpose to their lives. But it grew out of attitudes which predated the Nazi seizure of power, and is also reflected in the work of intellectuals who, being closer to Marxist orthodoxy, tried to see the German catastrophe in the light of social analysis rather than merely through the spectacles of a humanistic and rational spirit. There too, in spite of the concern with facts and figures, a preconceived socialist humanism comes through loud and clear.

Franz Neumann's *Behemoth* (1942), a book which has vitally influenced western views of National Socialism, set this belief in human rationality upon a different foundation. Starting from the sociological tradition inherited from Max Weber, he wrote that the rationalization of the labour process, essential to any industrial society, must in the end lead to rational thought and to the denial of violence. The masses in Germany had behind them a long tradition imbued with the critical spirit, which sooner or later would make them aware of the antagonism between an economy that can produce in abundance for welfare but does so only for destruction. The class struggle would continue and triumph over the forces now oppressing the nation.[11] This analysis provided the facts which, as Neumann saw it, must be kept separate from the ideological framework within which National Socialism operated. He was fully conscious that liberalism had failed Germany, for injustice lurked behind the slogans of political freedom. Democratic ideals like the self-determination of peoples had consistently been betrayed by those who professed them. Ideology is defined as the verbalization of aims and goals. It is absent when events move in a direction quite different from professed aims. Thus the Nazis may be promoting cultural activities through the "Strength through Joy" movement, but as culture can exist only in freedom, no garrison state can create a

[11] Franz Neumann, *Behemoth* (Toronto, New York, London, 1942), pp. 464ff also for discussion which follows.

demand for a genuine culture. This is the genesis of his belief that National Socialism had no ideology; it was a system which would sharpen the antagonisms of society and prepare for its own downfall. Terror was the cement of the regime, and all these intellectuals believed that by its very nature Hitler's movement could have no other cohesive force. Already during the Republic, some left wing intellectuals had asserted that Nazism could not last because it lacked genuine contact with the true course of human aspirations.[12]

For all his social analysis, influenced by Weber and Marxism, Neumann put a concept of freedom into the very center as a prerequisite for all political thought and action. Men can determine their own destinies, and it is a perverted society, rather than some basic fault of human nature, which prevents them from doing so. Neumann was a social democrat, but while in exile he came to see the faults of that movement; he never made contact with communism. A true democracy must be maintained whenever possible, and this democracy he defined as putting an end to political alienation: genuine participation by all in the making of society. But this end to alienation entails basic changes in society, indeed a socialist organization of the state. However, the final cement of such a democracy is a moral impetus — be it freedom or justice.[13] This ideal which he reiterated at the end of his life (1953) puts him on the same wavelength as the left-wing intellectuals we have discussed. Here also we have the humanism, the belief in the inevitable triumph of rationality, and the stress upon the overriding principles of self determination, freedom and justice, even if such ideals were combined with a social analysis foreign to most of the writers in exile.

In the hands of these intellectuals National Socialism became an aberration of history which would, sooner or later, right itself again. The "occupiers" could not succeed against the people. From this point of view they contested the prominence given to the persecution of the Jews in anti-fascist propaganda. As one writer put it: "The emigration is not merely an outgrowth of the Jewish question." Heinrich Mann wrote that hatred of the Jew took second place in National Socialism to the hatred of human freedom. He criticized, in 1933, the dominance which the persecution of the Jews exercised over all

[12] *Der Nationalsozialismus* (3 articles of the *Tagebuch*) (n.p. 1930), p. 5, p. 15.
[13] Franz Neumann, *Demokratischer und autoritärer Staat*, eingeleitet, Helge Pross (Wien, 1967), p. 17, pp. 100ff. See also H. Stuart Hughes, "Franz Neumann between Marxism and Democracy," *Perspectives in American History*, Vol. II (1968), 446-462. It may have been Neumann's dedication to "unmasking" reality which made him badly underestimate the power of ideology and myth in modern mass movements like Nazism.

anti-Nazi mass meetings.[14] Humanity was an integral whole, and all of it was menaced by fascism. Even Lion Feuchtwanger, many of whose novels deal with specifically Jewish themes, always connected these to the whole of mankind; the Jews were for him symbols of the travail of liberty. As he wrote in *The Oppermanns,* Jews never gave up the belief in their eventual freedom.[15]

The men whose ideals we have analyzed stood outside all political groupings and parties. But, in the end, not even their optimism about humanity could overcome their feeling of rootlessness now compounded by exile. During the Weimar Republic such intellectuals had tried to reach out to the people and to involve themselves in some kind of political action. Some had supported the USPD (independent socialists) at the beginning of the Republic, others the various socialist splinter movements. There was in 1932 some talk of running Heinrich Mann for the presidency. None of this amounted to a great deal, but in exile not even this kind of activity was possible, and the attempt (in which Heinrich Mann played a leading part) to found a popular front of all exiled political groupings came to nothing. The result of this dilemma was a heightened urge to anchor their beliefs in some sort of political reality, to find a positive force which could be used to defeat the fascist menace. For as time wore on the "occupiers" of Germany grew stronger, while much of the western world seemed to support their cause.

The confrontation of these men with reality took many different forms and we can only choose some examples in order to illustrate the problem. The intellectual evolution of Alfred Döblin presents one extreme. The man who had advised, as late as 1933, that one could fight for a humanistic socialism outside all established political parties began to lose faith in the socialist ideal. Later, he was to write that where he had looked for human brotherhood he found political bosses and parties. The small socialist splinter groups with which he had associated during the Republic were sects whose activities ended in disillusionment and dehumanization.[16] Döblin's socialism had been vigorously opposed to existing society and his most famous work, *Berlin-Alexanderplatz* (1929) demonstrated how in the big city, the ultimate product of capitalism, no hard and fast line could be drawn between the criminal and the non-criminal world. However, the positive side of his socialism was confused and stressed

[14] *Die Neue Weltbühne,* 2. Halbjahr (1933), p. 1154, p. 1560.
[15] Lion Feuchtwanger, *The Oppermanns,* p. 382.
[16] Alfred Döblin, *Schicksalsreise* (Frankfurt, 1949), p. 165.

the necessity of personal conversion to a truly humane and decent life. If necessary man must sacrifice himself in order to bear witness against the injustice of the present system. Shortly before the triumph of the Nazis he asserted that only a "new humanity" which had cut its ties with all nations could proclaim the eternal law of justice.[17]

In his earlier works, like *Berlin-Alexanderplatz*, Döblin's attitude towards the masses was ambivalent, but later he becomes more precise. In order to rouse the masses to recapture their own humanity a leader is needed: one who by his life and sacrifice provides an example. But here, as in the works of Heinrich Mann, Leonhard Frank, or Lion Feuchtwanger, it is the human posture of the leader which counts and any analysis of the objective conditions in the making of a revolution is omitted from the picture. Döblin shows the full weakness of this noble if ill-defined socialism. For under the stress of exile it collapsed rapidly in the search for more concrete roots. First, he sought refuge in a new realization of his Jewishness, in the arms of a Jewish Volk. Döblin became an impassioned territorialist, part of that movement which wanted to settle the Jews on the land but was indifferent to Palestine as the place where this should be accomplished. "More important than the land is the Volk." Ideas of class struggle cannot apply to Jews who are eternal foreigners within the society where such a struggle prevails. The Jews have to normalize themselves as a *Volk* and gain a new security.[18]

But in all this preoccupation with *Volk* and security something of his old posture remains. The Jews in their own exile have been victimized by priests and by those other Jews who had amassed worldly possessions. The settled *Volk* will change all this; now "freedom, the urge to build and responsibility" will take the place of a past marked by cowardice and humiliation. Religion will be the cement, and this is defined as strict morality culminating in justice. Döblin never shared fully the optimistic belief in human rationality. Now his hostility to technology and science (always for him a part of the evil City) culminates in an open denial of rationalism. The Volk and its morality are inspired by the simple and direct relationship between God and man. This relationship provides the cohesive force which creates a genuine community.[19]

But Döblin did not stop at this point. His relationship to the Jews

---

[17] i.e. Roland Links, *Alfred Döblin* (Berlin, 1965), p. 87, p. 101.

[18] Alfred Döblin, *Flucht und sammlung des Judenvolkes* (Amsterdam, 1935), pp. 130, 126, 125.

[19] Alfred Döblin, *Jüdische Erneuerung* (Amsterdam, 1933), pp. 45, 86, 87.

was idealistic, based upon the same idealism as his earlier socialist commitment. It proved no more lasting when confronted with the reality of political struggles among the Jews. His final conversion to Christianity took place within this context. Christ becomes the exemplification of justice and freedom, fighting to prevail in an evil world without recourse to force. The problem of revolution, force and power, which was to occupy so many of his fellow intellectuals, had been solved. Moreover, Döblin's Christianity also gave him roots, a resting place in his wanderings. For he joined the Catholic Church which provided him with a "halt" and a "harmonious, coordinated system." At the same time he castigated Jews who, after all their suffering, still clung to business as usual, while he seemed to have recaptured his old idealism within a more settled and traditional form.[20]

Döblin's evolution cannot be duplicated by others, but it shows how vague socialist humanism became under stress. The precedence given to the individual over society within this socialism proved an inadequate device against both the feeling of rootlessness and the escalating fight against fascism. However, his fellow intellectuals looked to a different east from that marking the cradle of Christianity. The Soviet Union seemed at times to be the only power willing to stand up to Hitler. On the other hand, these intellectuals had a long history of skepticism towards the Soviet Union behind them, and Heinrich Mann was only one of many writers who had signed protests against the violations of justice in that state. Moreover, they had opposed the German Communist party as merely another oppressive institution. The growing Nazi menace had made little dent in this attitude, even though, in the presidential election of 1932, the *Weltbühne* advised its readers to vote for the communist leader Thälmann, notwithstanding the oppressive nature of communism.[21] It was a counsel of despair. After 1933, with the despair heightened, the search for positive action against the Nazi state still focused attention on communism and the Soviet Union.

Lion Feuchtwanger can illustrate the problems which these socialists faced in their efforts to come to terms with communism. As we saw, in the first years of exile he continued, and indeed deepened, his older line of thought. He now interpreted his novel on the *Jewish War* as meaning that the traditional nationalism of the Jews must

[20] Alfred Döblin, *Schicksalsreise*, pp. 359, 360.
[21] *Die Weltbühne*, 28. Jahrg. Nr. 9 (1932), passim.

be subordinated to a broader socialism which embraced concern for one's neighbors as well as for one's own people. The Jews symbolized commitment to an ethical principle hostile to the use of force or, indeed, to territorial and racial nationalism.[22] To be sure, the two subsequent volumes of the Josephus trilogy, which were written later in exile, seem to contradict this outlook. Josephus discards his cosmopolitanism, his rootlessness, and finds his way back to the Jewish *Volk* in its revolt against the Romans. At the end of the last volume, however, Feuchtwanger writes that Joseph "searched for the new world prematurely. Therefore he merely found his nation."[23] Patience and self-discipline were needed in the long endeavor to create a new world (a cry Heinrich Mann was to utter as well).

However, side by side with this stress on reason, patience and self-discipline, Feuchtwanger strikes a contradictory note. Subdued at first, this could well provide a bridge towards his later commitment to communism. Already in *The Oppermanns* he believed that arguments based upon the preservation of true humanity and civilization were insufficient to rouse the world against the German barbarians. The democracies feared bolshevism more than the Nazis, and were benefitting from the rearmament industry. Feuchtwanger fully accepted the Marxist interpretation of the victory of National Socialism. One of the characters in *The Oppermanns* accuses a German capitalist: "I know the only way you could save your rotten economic system was by calling in that lousy gang to help you."[24]

This interpretation of the Nazi seizure of power was reinforced by the belief that Germany was filled with anti-Nazis whom one could not leave in the lurch. Gustav Oppenheimer reiterates that the majority of Germans were decent people and that reason must triumph in the end.[25] Other left-wing intellectuals in exile shared this Marxist analysis of the success of National Socialism, not because they had devoted any scholarship to its investigation, but because it explained how the "occupiers" could succeed despite that rationality and goodness which Germans shared with the rest of humanity. In face of capitalist corruption, the indifference of the democracies, something more forceful than arguments based on humanity and civilization was needed. Communism and the Soviet Union lay ready at hand to fill this void.

---

[22] Lion Feuchtwanger, Arnold Zweig, *Die Aufgabe des Judentums* (Paris, 1933), pp. 27ff.

[23] quoted in Jurgen Rühle, *Literatur und Revolution* (Koln-Berlin, 1960), p. 211.

[24] Lion Feuchtwanger, *The Oppermanns*, pp. 354, 383.

[25] Lion Feuchtwanger, *The Oppermanns*, p. 141.

By the time Feuchtwanger wrote his novel, *Exile* (1940), communism is seen as the logical commitment of the intellectual emigration. For Feuchtwanger the turning point came with his journey to Moscow in 1937. The book which followed is filled with praise and admiration for the Stalin regime. This praise is consistent with an attitude which had, indeed, been exemplified in many of his earlier works: that world history is an unending battle between a minority devoted to reason and an unthinking majority which, however, could be redeemed through a new society. The conformism which he had opposed throughout his life, but which he did find in the Soviet Union, was brushed aside for it was based upon a justified commitment to the principles of communism, love for the Soviet State, and the hope that the Soviet Union might become the happiest and richest land on earth. What, then, about the oppression which accompanied such hopes and beliefs? The Stalinist purges are taken at face value — after all the accused had always been conspirators and could not be expected to have changed their life style.

Typically enough, his only criticism concerned censorship over literature. He could not believe that the enforcement of a "heroic optimism" was good for literary endeavor, for a novelist must be free to write what he himself feels and believes. But this is a minor drawback when compared with the building of a "practical socialism."[26] It is quite clear that this practical socialism does not always coincide with the ethical imperative, but it now becomes the *prerequisite* for the establishment of humanistic socialism. Feuchtwanger seemed to have found solid ground to which he could anchor his hopes for the future. But his commitment to the new Soviet society soon became ambivalent again. He was convinced that the future belonged to the socialism practiced in the Soviet Union. His humanistic socialism had not proved capable of dealing with the political realities, had not become a "practical socialism." But in his novel *Exile* he was unwilling to give it up altogether. "All I can do is to learn new theory but not new practice," says one of the chief characters.[27] The fundamental lines of communist policy might be correct, but heart and feeling could not "affirm them."

It can be said that the change was due to a failure of nerve, a refusal to practice that patience which he had counselled in his earlier works. However, at the end of the war he returned to his earlier

[26] Lion Feuchtwanger, *Moskau 1937* (Amsterdam, 1937), pp. 8, 48, 105, 9.
[27] quoted in Matthias Wegner, *Exil und Literatur*, p. 209.

self. In *Arms for America* (1947) he reaffirmed his belief in the "slow, very slow, yet certain growth of human reason between the last ice age and that which is to come."[28] After the war Feuchtwanger did not contemplate settling in communist East Germany. Once again he stood between all fronts, a position similar to Leonhard Frank's, who lived out his last years in Munich, almost forgotten and at war with the world. Heinrich Mann was preparing to settle in East Germany when he died, but almost against his better judgment and with a reluctance which meant a constant postponement of the journey.

Heinrich Mann has been claimed by the communist world with greater certainty than Feuchtwanger or Frank. Thus it has been asserted that his conversion to a communist outlook was deeper and more lasting, that eventually he saw in the struggles of the working classes the only hope for the future.[29] To be sure, Mann was politically active from the very first year of exile. He attempted to form a united front which the Communist Party was supposed to join. Moreover, he supported all anti-Nazi efforts. Did he, then, also depart from his ideal of reason and humanism under the pressure of events?

Mann attempted to take a leading part in the anti-fascist struggle wherever it was to be found. The Popular Front over which he presided was supposed to be a broad grouping which would take in not only the socialists and communists, but also Catholics and other democratic forces. As the leader of this front he wrote in communist journals and took part in communist-inspired organizations. Yet he continued to write for bourgeois liberal papers, like the *Pariser Tageblatt*, and his efforts to form a popular front were constantly sabotaged by Walter Ulbricht, the communist leader. Indeed, Heinrich Mann came to hate Ulbricht and the bureaucratic and oppressive movement which he represented.

To be sure, Mann believed that the bourgeois world was in decline and had to be liquidated. But he did not deduce from this that the working classes were the sole instruments for bringing about a socialist society. Like all these left-wing intellectuals, he rejected class analysis in favor of an organic humanism in which intellectuals would take the leading part. Typically enough, this point of view dominated a review which Mann wrote of the poetry of Johannes R. Becher, the communist writer. Becher wrote with humor, in an easy style with a broad popular appeal. Therefore what he called "class" must

---

[28] Lion Feuchtwanger, "introductory remarks" before start of the book, *Proud Destiny* (New York, 1947), The English translation of *Waffen für Amerika*.
[29] i.e. Klaus Jarmatz, *Literatur im Exil* (Berlin, 1966), passim.

refer to the people as a whole, to all Germans. However, Mann was careful to add that belief in the healing power of social and economic change constituted a reasonable doctrine.[30] Nevertheless, concern for the spirit and consciousness of humanity must have priority over all other considerations. This is illustrated by his greatest work of that period: the novels which deal with the French King Henry IV (1935-1938). Here all social analysis is subordinated to the ideals of reason, toleration, and peace. They sound a new note, not that of class but of a militancy which permits the use of force in order to bring about the good society. However, this force is exercised by a power (like the monarchy of Henry IV), not wedded to class but committed to goodness and reason. The basic ideal is still the same as that which he had put forward in *Der Untertan* many years before.

This does not exclude a criticism of bourgeois society. Heinrich Mann, Leonhard Frank and others anticipated in exile that rejection of American society which Herbert Marcuse was to put forward in his *One Dimensional Man* (1964). Marcuse, for all the social analysis involved, concentrates upon those cultural aspects of society which prevent man from controlling his own destiny. Earlier, Leonhard Frank had attacked the poverty of spirit *(Gefühlsarmut)* in America, putting this down to a consumer-orientated society which forces man into choices which he does not want to make.[31] We have already seen that the ideological outlook of the left wing intellectuals was shared by other critics of society notwithstanding their commitment to Marxist social analysis. The common heritage of German idealism which had filtered through Kant united such men in the priority which they gave to the autonomy of rational man over concern with the Marxist definition of objective reality.

Their leadership theory bears this out. The intelligentsia must lead society, it is the custodian of the categorical imperative. For intellectuals stand above all classes of the population, having their roots in none of them. This concept of leadership is not a product of exile, but goes back at least to the first world war. During the German revolution of 1918-19 Heinrich Mann presided over a "soviet of brain workers." This soviet was supposed to provide general guidance for the other soviets of workers and soldiers. It never amounted to much, but it does show how such intellectuals attempted to become relevant to society on their own terms. Intellectuals were supposed

[30] Heinrich Mann in *Pariser Tageblatt,* Nr. 684, 3. Jahrg. (27 Oktober, 1935), p. 3.
[31] Leonhard Frank, *Links ist wo das Herz ist* (Munich, 1952), pp. 228-229.

to have a heightened consciousness of what society needed, because they were "free floating" (to use Karl Mannheim's term) and because of their rational approach to life. This is what Feuchtwanger meant when he wrote that throughout world history an enlightened minority has always battled the stupidity common to most men.[32] Both Heinrich Mann in his *Lidice* (1943) and Alfred Döblin repeat the same ideas: intellectuals as fighters for righteousness confront the masses.[33] We are back once more with concepts deriving from the French Enlightenment: mankind is redeemable but it has to be enlightened by *philosophes* before it can properly enter the age of reason. Today, when the workers seem content and apathetic, men like Herbert Marcuse have once more transferred leadership to a revolutionary intelligentsia. Perhaps new experiments with a "soviet of brain workers" will follow and, in fact, something of this sort seemed to inspire some students during the university turmoil of the mid-sixties.

It might seem as if most of the men with whom we are concerned had been forgotten, their works scarcely read. But their obscurity is more apparent than real. These writers popularized an ideology which did seem to offer an alternative to social-democracy, communism, and capitalist society. To be sure, under the pressure of exile, they seemed to compromise their principles of humanistic socialism, but this did not last. By and large they carried their trend of thought through from the Weimar Republic to the post-war world. However, the wavering of some and the apostasy of others like Döblin do throw light upon the problems which their ideals involved. The intelligentsia on the one hand, and the people with their potential on the other, would build the "Republic of Reason," as Heinrich Mann called the socialist state of the future. The idea that such a change could come about through individual example rather than violence, the constant emphasis upon the dignity of man, are beguiling as a road to Utopia.

But would reason automatically solve all problems? Were the social and economic aspects of society merely mechanical problems, as Heinrich Mann believed?[34] Marxism entered into their thought, but as providing a critique of present society, rather than exemplifying the mechanism by which society must be overthrown. To the doctrine of class war these left-wing intellectuals opposed the ideal of the autonomy of human reason. They recognized the irrational

---

[32] Alfred Kantorowicz, *op. cit.*, p. 169. For a discussion of these "soviets," see George L. Mosse, *op. cit.*
[33] Roland Links, *op. cit.*, p. 103.
[34] Heinrich Mann, *Diktatur der Vernunft*, passim.

forces in human history. They fought irrationalism, but their true attitude towards it was once more rooted in the tradition of the French Enlightenment. Evil was something which existed, but it was best to brush it aside, for you could not build a new society by acknowledging its extent and its depth. Thus they never understood National Socialism, for they refused to believe that millions could find a congenial home in its irrational embrace.

Socialist humanists outside Germany showed greater realism in their approach to politics. The *Political Action Party* in Italy was founded on very similar presuppositions and became a leading and effective anti-fascist organization. The ideal of one of its founders, Carlo Roselli, that "the spiritual essence of liberalism can be preserved only within a socialist society," sums up the thought of the men we have discussed — provided that liberalism is connected to the tradition of the French Enlightenment and not to its evolution in Germany. Roselli also condemned communism but he did not posit the intelligentsia as the only true revolutionary force. A strong and united proletariat was the only mechanism by which fascism could be overthrown.[35] It is astonishing that the German exiles had so little contact with this Italian anti-fascist movement. In spite of their urge to save all of humanity they seem singularly Germanic in their orientation and in their pattern of thought.

We cannot here analyze the extent to which the socialist humanism of the German left-wing intellectuals once again appeals to a new generation. Many other factors enter into their search for an alternative to every part of the existing order, including the established socialist parties. But their ideal of democracy, of individuality and socialism, has many parallels with the ideas discussed. They also tend to be socialist humanists in the definition which we have given, though some of them are finding their way back towards more traditional Marxist attitudes. However that may be, the newly found love for the "golden twenties" in Germany does not focus upon Marxist orthodoxy but upon the ideas for which many of these left-wing intellectuals stood. The weakness of this socialism should be obvious and the so-called revolt of the younger generation has shown a similar disregard for objective reality, and for similar reasons. Socialist humanism is easily catapulted into the realm of abstract philosophy and instant Utopia. This heritage of German refugee intellectuals is of importance to our age. However, contrary to their own opinion,

[35] i.e. Emilio Lussu, *Sul Partito d'Azione e gli altri* (Milano, 1968), p. 40.

it does not belong to the mainstream of human history which has stubbornly refused to follow the guidance of reason as they understand it. Instead this "socialist humanism" belongs to the narrower and more constricted history of European intellectuals.

Introduction to T. W. Adorno

BY FREDRIC JAMESON

THE FOLLOWING essay of T. W. Adorno, in its density and scope, amounts to a complete course in the new Western Marxism (I'm tempted to call it a *post-industrial* Marxism), chiefly familiar to American readers through the works of Herbert Marcuse, and in particular *One Dimensional Man*. (For it is perfectly consistent with the spirit of Marxism that there should exist several Marxisms in the world today, each answering the specific needs and unique situation of its own economic system: thus, one corresponds to the industrial countries of the socialist block, another — a kind of peasant Marxism — to China and Cuba and the countries of the third world, while yet another tries to deal theoretically with the special problems posed by the monopoly capitalism of the Western countries and particularly of our own.)

The principal characteristic of this new Marxism is the feeling that Western society has somehow become a total system, and that what used to be held together by external constraint, by easily identifiable coercive forces and physical violence, has now been interiorized by means of general cultural conditioning, through advertising and the mass media. In an economy which has transcended physical need, but which depends for its functioning on the constant sale of new products, artificial needs must be stimulated and maintained: everyone reproduces the market system within himself like a conscience.

Thus the old model of class conflict, in which the force of the proletariat came in part from its *exclusion* from society, its resultant intellectual freedom from what oppressed it physically, seems increasingly unsuitable for our society, where such classes are drawn into the system itself and — in Eldridge Cleaver's expression — "programmed" for it. (Indeed, I believe that the metaphor of computer programming lies behind the whole theory of the total system like a nightmare image.)

All of which explains the premium placed on theory in Adorno's essay: in our present context, empirical thought and a common-sense viewpoint only serve to reinforce the existing institutions — not only because they lead us to imagine that such institutions are eminently natural and self-explanatory, somehow justified by human nature itself — but also, and primarily, because the only way to understand a fact which is part of a total system is to begin with an idea of the totality. This is what Adorno calls *speculative theory*: it is what we may also call dialectical thinking, thought which moves from the whole to the part back to the whole again. If the sentences in which such thinking is expressed sometimes strike the reader as being involved and overladen with abstractions, he should see the difficulty, not as a stylistic one, but as a measure of the unfamiliarity, in our society, of attempts to think the total system as a whole.

Characteristic also of this evaluation of speculative theory is the relatively intellectualistic note with which it ends. This temporary refusal of any practical commitment, of any speculation as to tactics or action, is certain to strike some people as an a-political tendency, or at best, a professional distortion, the overestimation by the intellectual specialist of his own particular type of work. Yet in the total system, all action risks being drawn into the system and absorbed, institutionalized, by the mass media; and it is only fair to point out that the student movement itself — in its tactics of the provocation of institutional violence, in the manner in which it attempts to force the latent but disguised oppression of the social structure to light — has to that degree a theoretical rather than a practical thrust, aims at articulating — on your television screen, in blood and clubs for everyone to see — a theoretical model, an anatomy lesson in the social structure.

A final word about the dialectical method itself: the difficulties of the present essay serve as a particularly striking illustration of dialectical thinking, which may be defined as an attempt to think self-consciously about our own thought while we are in the act of thinking about some object, to be both conscious and self-conscious at the same time. So here what for an older analytical thinking would have formed two different objects of two different disciplines — social theory, or the history of the ideas of society, and sociology, or the history of the forms of society itself — are here united as two levels of the same thought, and Adorno operates an incessant, sometimes bewildering passage back and forth between the two, in a kind of game of mirror reflexions which I will call the dialectical *pun*.

Thus, he defends a non-empirical, "speculative" notion of society by showing that in real life there are no "empirical" facts, that the peculiar structure of the speculative theory of society, undefinable at any given point yet omnipresent, corresponds precisely to the supra-individual control which "society" (this time, the thing itself) exerts over individuals: "While the notion of society may not be deduced from any individual facts, nor on the other hand be apprehended as an individual fact itself, there is nonetheless no social fact which is not determined by society as a whole."

In one sense, such thinking expresses the feeling that thoughts and thought processes, conceptual instruments, logic itself, are also historical: that their development in time corresponds to the development and enrichment of their objects in the "real world." For analytical thought there is something scandalous about time itself, something intolerable about the notion that certain economic laws, say, or certain concepts of society come into being along with the realities to which they correspond: it is more reassuring to think of them as having been there all along in limbo like mathematical truths, eternal but not yet revealed, simply waiting for the appearance of an adequate object on which to be demonstrated.

In another sense, of course, this temptation of the analytical is nothing more than the permanent danger of idealism which hangs over all consciousness as such. Dialectical thought lives in symbiosis with this danger, as a perpetual movement of de-idealization — the mental shock administered by its puns and sudden shifts in level and referment is designed to jar the smooth movement of our own static logical processes like the sickening dip of an airplane. The mind tends inevitably towards illusions of its own autonomy, if only because it is impossible to be self-conscious all the time, if only because thought inevitably tends to forget itself and to sink itself in its object. Then there comes into being an illusion of transparency, in which the mind looks like the world, and we stare at concepts as though they were things. The dialectic is designed to eject us from this illusory order, to project us in spite of ourselves outside our own concepts into the world of genuine realities to which those concepts were supposed to apply.

We cannot, of course, ever really get outside our own subjectivities: to think so is the error of scientism, of "objective" thought, of mechanical materialism: but, every time they begin to freeze over, to spring us outside our own hardened ideas into a new and more vivid apprehension of reality itself is the task of genuine dialectical thought.

Fredric Jameson

Society

BY T. W. ADORNO

THE IDEA of society confirms Nietzsche's insight that concepts "which are basically short-hand for process" elude verbal definition. For society is essentially process; its laws of movement tell more about it than whatever invariables might be deduced. Attempts to fix its limits end up with the same result. If one for instance defines society simply as mankind, including all the sub-groups into which it breaks down, out of which it is constructed, or if one, more simply still, calls it the totality of all human beings living in a given period, one misses thereby all the subtler implications of the concept. Such a formal definition presupposes that society is already a society of human beings, that society is itself already human, is immediately one with its subjects; as though the specifically social did not consist precisely in the imbalance of institutions over men, the latter coming little by little to be the incapacitated products of the former. In bygone ages, when things were perhaps different — in the stone age, for instance — the word society would scarcely have had the same meaning as it does under advanced capitalism. Over a century ago, the legal historian J. C. Bluntschli characterized "society" as a "concept of the third estate." It is that, and not only on account of the egalitarian tendencies which have worked their way down into it, distinguishing it from the feudal or absolutistic idea of "fine" or "high" society, but also because in its very structure this idea follows the model of middle-class society.

In particular it is not a classificatory concept, not for instance the highest abstraction of sociology under which all lesser social forms would be ranged. In this type of thinking one tends to confuse the current scientific ideal of a continuous and hierarchical ordering of categories with the very object of knowledge itself. The object meant by the concept society is not in itself rationally continuous. Nor is it to its elements as a universal to particulars; it is not merely a dynamic category, it is a functional one as well. And to this first, still quite abstract approximation, let us add a further qualification, namely the dependency of all individuals on the totality which they form. In such a totality, everyone is also dependent on everyone else. The whole survives only through the unity of the functions which its members fulfill. Each individual without exception must take some function on himself in order to prolong his existence; indeed, while his function lasts, he is taught to express his gratitude for it.

It is on account of this functional structure that the notion of society can not be grasped in any immediate fashion, nor is it susceptible of drastic verification, as are the laws of the natural sciences. Positivistic currents in sociology tend therefore to dismiss it as a mere philosophical survival. Yet such realism is itself unrealistic. For while the notion of society may not be deduced from any individual facts, nor on the other hand be apprehended as an individual fact itself, there is nonetheless no social fact which is not determined by society as a whole. Society appears as a whole behind each concrete social situation. Conflicts such as the characteristic ones between manager and employees are not some ultimate reality that is wholly comprehensible without reference to anything outside itself. They are rather the symptoms of deeper antagonisms. Yet one cannot subsume individual conflicts under those larger phenomena as the specific to the general. First and foremost, such antagonisms serve as the laws according to which such conflicts are located in time and space. Thus for example the so-called wage-satisfaction which is so popular in current management-sociology is only apparently related to the conditions in a given factory and in a given branch of production. In reality it depends on the whole price system as it is related to the specific branches; on the parallel forces which result in the price system in the first place and which far exceed the struggles between the various groups of entrepreneurs and workers, inasmuch as the latter have already been built into the system, and represent a voter potential that does not always correspond to their organizational affiliation. What is decisive, in the case of wage satisfaction as well as in all others, is the power structure, whether direct or indirect, the control by the entrepreneurs over the machinery of production. Without a concrete awareness of this fact, it is impossible adequately to understand any given individual situation without assigning to the part what really belongs to the whole. Just as social mediation cannot exist without that which is mediated, without its elements: individual human begins, institutions, situations; in the same way the latter cannot exist without the former's mediation. When details come to seem the strongest reality of all, on account of their tangible immediacy, they blind the eye to genuine perception.

Because society can neither be defined as a concept in the current logical sense, nor empirically demonstrated, while in the meantime social phenomena continue to call out for some kind of conceptualization, the proper organ of the latter is speculative *theory*. Only a thoroughgoing theory of society can tell us what society really is. Recently it has been objected that it is unscientific to insist on concepts such as that of society, inasmuch as truth and falsehood are characteristics of sentences alone, and not of ideas as a whole. Such an objection confuses a self-validation concept such as that of society with a traditional kind of definition. The former must develop as it is being understood, and cannot be fixed in arbitrary terminology to the benefit of some supposed mental tidiness.

The requirement that society must be defined through theory — a requirement, which is itself a theory of society — must further address itself to the suspicion that such theory lags far behind the model of the natural sciences, still tacitly assumed to binding on it. In the natural sciences theory represents a clear point of contact between well-defined concepts and repeatable experiments. A self-developing theory of society, however, need not concern itself with this intimidating model, given its enigmatic claim to mediation. For the objection measures the concept of society against the criterion of immediacy and presence, and if society is mediation, then these criteria have no validity for it. The next step is the ideal of knowledge of things from the inside: it is claimed that the theory of society entrenches itself behind such subjectivity. This would only serve to hinder progress in the sciences, so this argument runs, and in the most flourishing ones has been long since eliminated. Yet we must point out that society is both known and not known from the inside. Inasmuch as society remains a product of human activity, its living subjects are still able to recognize themselves in it, as from across a great distance, in a manner radically different than is the case for the objects of chemistry and physics. It is a fact that in middle-class society, rational action is objectively just as "comprehensible" as it is motivated. This was the great lesson of the generation of Max Weber and Dilthey. Yet their ideal of comprehension remained onesided, insofar as it precluded everything in society that resisted identification by the observer. This was the sense of Durkheim's rule that one should treat social facts like objects, should first and foremost renounce any effort to "understand" them. He was firmly persuaded that society meets each individual primarily as that which is alien and threatening, as constraint. Insofar as that is true, genuine reflection on the nature of society would begin precisely where "comprehension" ceased. The scientific method which Durkheim stands for thus registers that Hegelian "second nature" which society comes to form, against its living members. This antithesis to Max Weber remains just as partial as the latter's thesis, in that it cannot transcend the idea of society's basic incomprehensibility any more than Weber can transcend that of society's basic comprehensibility. Yet this resistance of society to rational comprehension should be understood first and foremost as the sign of relationships between men which have grown increasingly independent of them, opaque, now standing off against human beings like some different substance. It ought to be the task of sociology today to comprehend the incomprehensible, the advance of human beings into the inhuman.

Besides which, the anti-theoretical concepts of that older sociology which had emerged from philosophy are themselves fragments of forgotten or repressed theory. The early twentieth-century German notion of comprehension is a mere secularization of the Hegelian absolute spirit, of the notion of a totality to be grasped; only it limits itself to particular acts, to characteristic images, without any consideration of that totality of society from which the phenomenon to be understood alone derives its meaning. Enthusiasm for the incomprehensible, on the other hand, transforms chronic social antagonisms into *quaestiones facti*. The situation itself, unreconciled, is contemplated without theory, in a kind of mental asceticism, and what is accepted thus ultimately comes to be glorified: society as a mechanism of collective constraint.

In the same way, with equally significant consequences, the dominant categories of contemporary sociology are also fragments of theoretical relationships which it refuses to recognize as such on account of its positivistic leanings. The notion of a "role" has for instance frequently been offered in recent years as one of the keys to sociology and to the understanding of human action in general. This notion is derived from the pure being-for-others of individual men, from that which binds them together with one another in social constraint, unreconciled, each unidentical with himself. Human beings find their "roles" in that structural mechanism of society which trains them to pure self-conservation at the same time that it denies them conservation of their Selves. The all-powerful principle of identity itself, the abstract interchangeability of social tasks, works towards the extinction of their personal identities. It is no accident that the notion of "role" (a notion which claims to be value-free) is derived from the theater, where actors are not in fact the identities they play at being. This divergence is merely an expression of underlying social antagonisms. A genuine theory of society ought to be able to move from such immediate observation of phenomena towards an understanding of their deeper social causes: why human beings today are still sworn to the playing of roles. The Marxist notion of character-masks, which not only anticipates the later category but deduces and founds it socially, was able to account for this implicitly. But if the science of society continues to operate with such concepts, at the same time drawing back in terror from that theory which puts them in perspective and gives them their ultimate meaning, then it merely ends up in the service of ideology. The concept of role, lifted without analysis from the social facade, helps perpetuate the monstrosity of role-playing itself.

A notion of society which was not satisfied to remain at that level would be a *critical* one. It would go far beyond the trivial idea that everything is interrelated. The emptiness and abstractness of this idea is not so much the sign of feeble thinking as it is that of a shabby permanency in the constitution of society itself: that of the market system in modern-day society. The first, objective abstraction takes place, not so much in scientific thought, as in the universal development of the exchange system itself; which happens independently of the qualitative attitudes of producer and consumer, of the mode of production, even of need, which the social mechanism tends to satisfy as a kind of secondary by-product. Profit comes first. A humanity fashioned into a vast network of consumers, the human beings who actually have the needs, have been socially pre-formed beyond anything which one might naively imagine, and this not only by the level of industrial development but also by the economic relationships themselves into which they enter, even though this is far more difficult to observe empirically. Above and beyond all specific forms of social differentiation, the abstraction implicit in the market system represents the domination of the general over the particular, of society over its captive membership. It is not at all a socially neutral phenomenon, as the logistics of reduction, of uniformity of work time, might suggest. Behind the reduction of men to agents and bearers of exchange value lies the domination of men over men. This remains the basic fact, in spite of the difficulties with which from time to time many of the categories of political science are confronted. The form of the total system requires everyone to respect the law of exchange if he does not wish to be destroyed, irrespective of whether profit is his subjective motivation or not.

This universal law of the market system is not in the least invalidated by the survival of retrograde areas and archaic social forms in various parts of the world. The older theory of imperialism already pointed out the functional relationship between the economies of the advanced capitalistic countries and those of the non-capitalistic areas, as they were then called. The two were not merely juxtaposed, each maintained the other in existence. When old-fashioned colonialism was eliminated, all that was transformed into *political* interests and relationships. In this context, rational economic and developmental aid is scarcely a luxury. Within the exchange society, the pre-capitalistic remnants and enclaves are by no means something alien, mere relics of the past: they are vital necessities for the market system. Irrational institutions are useful to the stubborn irrationality of a society which is rational in its means but not in its ends. An institution such as the family, which finds its origins in nature and whose binary structure escapes regulation by the equivalency of exchange, owes its relative power of resistance to the fact that without its help, as an irrational component, certain specific modes of existence such as the small peasantry would hardly be able to survive, being themselves impossible to rationalize without the collapse of the entire middle-class edifice.

The process of increasing social rationalization, of universal extension of the market system, is not something that takes place beyond the specific social conflicts and antagonisms, or in spite of them. It works through those antagonisms themselves, the latter, at the same time tearing society apart in the process. For in the institution of exchange there is created and reproduced that antagonism which could at any time bring organized society to ultimate catastrophe and destroy it. The whole business keeps creaking and groaning on, at unspeakable human cost, only on account of the profit motive and the interiorization by individuals of the breach torn in society as a whole. Society remains class struggle, today just as in the period when that concept originated; the repression current in the eastern countries shows that things are no different there either. Although the prediction of increasing pauperization of the proletariat has not proved true over a long period of time, the disappearance of classes as such is mere illusion, epiphenomenon. It is quite possible that subjective class consciousness has weakened in the advanced countries; in America it was never very strong in the first place. But social theory is not supposed to be predicated on subjective awareness. And as society increasingly controls the very forms of consciousness itself, this is more and more the case. Even the oft-touted equilibrium between habits of consumption and possibilities for education is a subjective phenomenon, part of the consciousness of the individual member of society, rather than an objective social fact. And even from a subjective viewpoint the class relationship is not quite so easy to dismiss as the ruling ideology would have us believe. The most recent empirical sociological investigation has been able to distinguish essential differences in attitude between those assigned in a general statistical way to the upper and the lower classes. The lower classes have fewer illusions, are less "idealistic." The *happy few* hold such "materialism" against them. As in the past, workers today still see society as something split into an upper and a lower. It is well known that the formal possibility of equal education does not correspond in the least to the actual proportion of working class children in the schools and universities.

Screened from subjectivity, the difference between the classes grows objectively with the increasing concentration of capital. This plays a decisive part in the existence of individuals; if it were not so, the notion of class would merely be fetishization. Even though consumers' needs are growing more standardized - for the middle class, in contrast to the older feodality, has always been willing to moderate expenditures over intake, except in the first period of capitalist accumulation - the separation of social power from social helplessness has never been greater than it is now. Almost everyone knows from his own personal experience that his social existence can scarcely be said to have resulted from his own personal initiative; rather he has had to search for gaps, "openings," jobs from which to make a living, irrespective of what seem to him his own human possibilities or talents, should he indeed still have any kind of vague inkling of the latter. The profoundly social-darwinistic notion of adaptation, borrowed from biology and applied to the so-called sciences of man in a normative manner, expresses this and is indeed its ideology. Not to speak of the degree to which the class situation has been transposed onto the relationship between nations, between the technically developed and underdeveloped countries.

That even so society goes on as successfully as it does is to be attributed to its control over the relationship of basic social forces, which has long since been extended to all the countries of the globe. This control necessarily reinforces the totalitarian tendencies of the social order, and is a political equivalent for and adaptation to the total penetration by the market economy. With this control, however, the very danger increases which such controls are designed to prevent, at least on this side of the Soviet and Chinese empires. It is not the fault of technical development or industrialization as such. The latter is only the image of human productivity itself, cybernetics and computers merely being an extension of the human senses: technical advancement is therefore only a moment in the dialectic between the forces of production and the relationships of production, and not some third thing, demonically self-sufficient. In the established order, industrialization functions in a centralistic way; on its own, it could function differently. Where people think they are closest to things, as with television, delivered into their very living room, nearness is itself mediated through social distance, through great concentration of power. Nothing offers a more striking symbol for the fact that people's lives, what they hold for the closest to them and the greatest reality, personal, maintained in being by them, actually receive their concrete content in large measure from above. Private life is, more than we can even imagine, mere re-privatization; the realities to which men hold have become unreal. "Life itself is a lifeless thing."

A rational and genuinely free society could do without administration as little as it could do without the division of labor itself. But all over the globe, administrations have tended under constraint towards a greater self-sufficiency and independence from their administered subjects, reducing the latter to objects of abstractly normed behavior. As Max Weber saw, such a tendency points back to the ultimate means-ends rationality of the economy itself. Because the latter is indifferent to its end, namely that of a rational society, and as long as it remains indifferent to such an end, for so long will it be irrational for its own subjects. The Expert is the rational form that such irrationality takes. His rationality is founded on specialization in technical and other processes, but has its ideological side as well. The ever smaller units into which the work process is divided begin to resemble each other again, once more losing their need for specialized qualifications.

Inasmuch as these massive social forces and institutions were once human ones, are essentially the reified work of living human beings, this appearance of self-sufficiency and independence in them would seem to be something ideological, a socially necessary mirage which one ought to be able to break through, to change. Yet such pure appearance is the *ens realissimum* in the immediate life of men. The force of gravity of social relationships serves only to strengthen that appearance more and more. In sharp contrast to the period around 1848, when the class struggle revealed itself as a conflict between a group immanent to society, the middle class, and one which was half outside it, the proletariat, Spencer's notion of integration, the very ground law of increasing social rationalization itself, has begun to seize on the very minds of those who are to be integrated into society. Both automatically and deliberately, subjects are hindered from coming to consciouness of themselves as subjects. The supply of goods that floods across them has that result, as does the industry of culture and countless other direct and indirect mechanisms of intellectual control. The culture industry sprang from the profit-making tendency of capital. It developed under the law of the market, the obligation to adapt your consumers to your goods, and then, by a dialectical reversal, ended up having the result of solidifying the existing forms of consciousness and the intellectual status quo. Society needs this tireless intellectual reduplication of everything that is, because without this praise of the monotonously alike and with waning efforts to justify that which exists on the grounds of its mere existence, men would ultimately do away with this state of things in impatience.

Integration goes even further than this. That adaptation of men to social relationships and processes which constitutes history and without which it would have been difficult for the human race to survive has left its mark on them such that the very possibility of breaking free without terrible instinctual conflicts — even breaking free mentally — has come to seem a feeble and a distant one. Men have come to be — triumph of integration! — identified in their innermost behavior patterns with their fate in modern society. In a mockery of all the hopes of philosophy, subject and object have attained ultimate reconciliation. The process is fed by the fact that men owe their life to what is being done to them. The affective rearrangement of industry, the mass appeal of sports, the fetishization of consumers' goods, are all symptoms of this trend. The cement which once ideologies supplied is now furnished by these phenomena, which hold the massive social institutions together on the one hand, the psychological constitution of human beings on the other. If we were looking for an ideological justification of a situation in which men are little better than cogs to their own machines, we might claim without much exaggeration that present-day human beings serve as such an ideology in their own existence, for they seek of their own free will to perpetuate what is obviously a perversion of real life. So we come full circle. Men must act in order to change the present petrified conditions of existence, but the latter have left their mark so deeply on people, have deprived them of so much of their life and individuation, that they scarcely seem capable of the spontaneity necessary to do so. From this, apologists for the existing order draw new power for their argument that humanity is not yet ripe. Even to point the vicious circle out breaks a taboo of the integral society. Just as it hardly tolerates anything radically different, so also it keeps an eye out to make sure that anything which is thought or said serves some specific change or has, as they put it, something positive to offer. Thought is subjected to the subtlest censorship of the *terminus ad quem:* whenever it appears critically, it has to indicate the positive steps desired. If such positive goals turn out to be inaccessible to present thinking, why then thought itself ought to come across resigned and tired, as though such obstruction were its own fault and not the signature of the thing itself. That is the point at which society can be recognized as a universal block, both within men and outside them at the same time. Concrete and positive suggestions for change merely strengthen this hindrance, either as ways of administrating the unadministrable, or by calling down repression from the monstrous totality itself. The concept and the theory of society are legitimate only when they do not allow themselves to be attracted by either of these solutions, when they merely hold in negative fashion to the basic possibility inherent in them: that of expressing the fact that such possibility is threatened with suffocation. Such awareness, without any preconceptions as to where it might lead, would be the first condition for an ultimate break in society's omnipotence.

Translated by F. R. Jameson

After Karl Kraus

BY THOMAS W. SIMONS, JR.

IN A COLLECTION devoted to the legacy of the last generation of Central
European intellectuals, it is well to recall a man who was its enemy
and who will have no successors. The stylist and moralist Karl Kraus
(1874-1936) can be situated within his generation in many interesting ways: as a writer of exceptional German; as a critic of literature
and culture; as a publicist; as a Viennese; as a Jew. But this historical
mode of appreciation is incapable of rendering for men of a later time
what it was that he sought to achieve and what he in fact achieved.
Karl Kraus is more likely than any other writer of that generation to
remain irreducibly peculiar, perpetually novel and perpetually inaccessible.

This prospective isolation has little to do with his historical situation. Many sensitive spirits of that time felt isolated, felt themselves
to be everywhere outside: outside Vienna because they came from
Bohemia, outside Austria because they were Jewish, outside Germany
because they were Austrian. The most typical response to this feeling
was however a flight into a larger context, a desperate search for
universal validity, in science, in politics, in language. Kafka is trans-
lucent even in translation. Karl Kraus also wrote for eternity, and
indeed the subject of his work was always and only the German
language, the possibilities inherent in it and its deep internal logic.
But the objects upon which his language caught fire, the stuff around
and upon which it played, consisted almost entirely in the most
transient and ephemeral language of his contemporaries, the journalists of the daily press and the journeyman members of the German
literary *gens* of the early 20th Century. Wishing to serve eternity by
satirizing the loathsome or merely second-rate German of the day,
he will be forever associated with the mortal remains of those he
flayed.

Karl Kraus' isolation likewise has little to do with any special difficulty of language. He has the reputation of being untranslatable. It is true that his work is long: more than eight hundred numbers of his journal, *Die Fackel*, between 1899 and his death, and more than twenty books. It is also true that his language is demanding of the reader. But the work is more accessible than that of some other major writers — it is currently being reprinted — and the language is not more trying or obscure than that of lesser writers translated every year.

Karl Kraus' isolation in posterity is in part a reflection of the isolation he enjoyed, in which he gloried, while he lived. He was the sworn enemy of most of the major trends and achievements which this collection celebrates: he hated the emigrant generation with a passion which was called uncharitable and picayune at the time and which seems positively callous in retrospect. Although he discovered and defended some of the great names of modern literature — Strindberg, Wedekind, Brecht — his enemies were the staff of life to him, and they were legion, for they were in every camp, of every tendency, under every throne. The satirist attacks only the weak, he said, because for him the strong do not exist. A man's intentions did him no good if his language fell short of the eternal standards which Karl Kraus set for himself. In the great age of ideologies there was scarcely a German writer who did not fall victim during most of his waking hours to the urge to categorize and serve some cause. All categories were hateful to Karl Kraus, so that he was the enemy of all the causes and all their flag-bearers. From the most prominent — Stefan George, Franz Werfel, Moritz Benedikt of the Vienna *Neue Freie Presse*, Max Reinhardt — through the master-sergeants — Alfred Kerr, Maximilien Harden — to the infantry, now justly forgotten — Moissi, Schalek, Unruh: for Karl Kraus they were merely dreadful puppets in a world-historical panorama of decay, all equally representative, all equally disastrous. All the classifications into which the historian can fit him were anathema to him: publicists, German writers, Viennese, Jews. The legacy of that generation is theirs, and not his, and it is unseemly to include him in it.

But what truly sets Karl Kraus apart from his contemporaries and from us is a uniquely personal combination of ethical absolutism and of form. He sought to create a monumental tribute to an eternal ideal of language by patient satirical examination of every unsightly departure from it. He saw himself as an artist with a holy mission, a witness to the ethical foundation of language in a world torn loose from its origins, where the tear has been stuffed with phrases. These origins are not historical. They pre-exist us, and exist outside us and time. They are not, therefore, to be sought in time, in a past golden age like the Biedermeier, which was fashionable in his day, or the Old Vienna of Freud, Hofmannsthal, and Karl Kraus. They exist now, in the moment and forever, and are accessible to each of us through the mediation of language, in the ethical discipline which service to language expressing them can give to every man.

Everything created remains as it was before it was created. The artist brings it down ready-made from heaven. Eternity is without beginning. Lyric or wit: the creation lies between the assumed and the definitive. Dawn is always breaking. It was already there and gathers itself again from the spectrum. Science is spectral analysis; art is light synthesis. The thought is in the world, but man does not have it. It is scattered through the prism of material experience in elements of language; the artist brings them together into thought. Thought is something found, a rediscovery. And he who seeks it is an honest discoverer, it belongs to him, even though another had found it before him.

Not only is this gift, this privilege of contact with essential being, accessible to all, but it is entirely adequate. Language can express everything; there is nothing of which it is not capable; its harmonies are emanations of the essential harmony which is the foundation of the world. The fleeting glimpses of this pre-existent harmony which are revealed to us by service to it in language are sweet beyond the sweetness of any other human experience. Nothing else is useful. But the search may not seek utility: to subordinate it to the attainment of any (other) worldly good is perversion, a sublimation which makes us incapable of contact with reality. Deprived of expression, reality — the reality of basic urges which the new science of psychoanalysis was seeking to define with terrible inadequacy, according to Karl Kraus — would revenge itself unto the third and fourth generations. And this perversion, for him, was historical, had happened within historical time, just as its consequences were historical and palpable in every contemporary crime, however minor. Language had become the handmaiden of the useful, rather than the bride of being. By making it into a means of communication, for whatever end, rather than an expression, a medium in which eternity touches us, men make themselves the whores of contingency, unable to doubt and thus to make ethical judgments, and condemned to follow every plausible phrasemaker.

(A) surety of moral gain lies in the spiritual discipline which establishes the highest measure of responsibility toward the one thing which may be wounded without sanction, language, and which is more than any other apt to teach respect for every other value of life . . . Doubt, the greatest moral gift which man could owe to language, a gift he has despised till now, could be the salutary check on a progress which is leading with total certainty to the end of a civilization it claims to serve. And it is as if that portion of mankind which believes it speaks German were being punished for being blessed with the language richest in thought by the curse of living outside her, of thinking after it had spoken, of acting before it had questioned her. Her speakers make no use of a language which has the advantage of consisting in all the doubts which stand in the space between its words. What a style of life could develop if the German obeyed no other ordonnance than that of language!

And since the German could not, he would obey every other ordonnance than that of his language. He was unable to hear the music of the spheres, the silence of eternity, in the interstices of a sentence. This was not true in the eye of eternity, in terms of present human possibility, but it was historically true: the German had become unused to trying, had forgotten what it meant to try, and was ripe, therefore, to be used by word-salesmen who would evoke the repressed and corrupted natural forces which swelled in isolation within him. The German was deaf to the harmony of being because he had forgotten the word. Karl Kraus, who had not, could hear whole worlds of venerable things collapsing into the gap between the phrases of his contemporaries and the original meaning of their words. In the present, in the concrete here-and-now, the artist could serve the word only by measuring this gap, by forcing the contemporary phrase up against original meaning, by descending into the jungle and showing every weed which called itself a rose for the weed it was, in the clear light of language. The artist, now trapped by history, was necessarily a satirist, because his material was necessarily the stuff of his times, the words of the men whose unwilling companion he was. Their existence, which stank in his nostrils, was his necessity. For their part they would necessarily be deaf to the miracles he recreated for them and would retain only the stuff which called him forth, and which he had to use. Every little treachery to language, every little debasement of expression into communication, had world-

historical significance for Karl Kraus. The fact condemned, whatever
the intention, and it had only to be reprinted to prove guilt. The
essence of art, then, was mimicry, but the artist would thereby always
be misunderstood. He must mimic the categories into which language
had been degraded in order to recall the origin, when language expressed reality, and mankind, which had become deaf to such recall,
would categorize him.

> The satirical artist stands at the end of a development which
> forsakes art. He is its product and its hopeless counterpart. He
> organizes the flight of mind before mankind. After him the
> deluge.

This absolutism wrapped in satire, embracing the most transitory
phenomena of a dead age the better to destroy them, makes any other
approach to Karl Kraus than the historical extremely difficult, but at
the same time ensures that the historical approach will be unsuccessful. Biographers and literary historians are appearing, and he is faring
poorly in their hands. A French critic striving for strict impartiality
brackets him with the Nazis, as a "language totalitarian," where he
merely found that the Nazis did their spiritual predecessors of the
German literary world too much honor by driving them from the
country.[1] In Austria, his latest biographer concludes that "he was
ours."[2] For us, favor of Mr. Frank Field's *The Last Days of Mankind*,
he is a historical figurine. Mr. Field's reductionism is of the psychological mode, and by that process of Hugo von Hofmannsthal's which
Karl Kraus described as stripping the hide from venerable cadavers
in order to stuff them with questionable corpses, he finds that "all
this reveals in a most striking way the neurotic character both of the
satirist and of the society which nurtured him." Elsewhere Karl
Kraus' moral fanaticism borders on the pathological for Mr. Field.[3]

[1] Pierre Missac, "Karl Kraus," *Critique*, No. 246 (November 1967), p. 924.
This is a review of several recent works, including Werner Kraft's *Karl Kraus*
(Salzburg, Otto Müller, 1956), Caroline Kohn's *Karl Kraus* (Paris, Didier, 1962),
and Paul Schick's *Karl Kraus in Selbstzeugnissen und Dokumenten* (Hamburg,
Rowohlt, 1965,) the best short introduction. Missac also mentions J. P. Stern's
"Karl Kraus' Vision of Language," *Modern Language Review*, 1966, No. 1.

[2] Hans Weigel, *Karl Kraus oder die Macht der Ohnmacht* (Vienna-Frankfurt-
Zurich, Fritz Molden, 1968), pp. 339-42. The best of several recent *Germanistik*
dissertations is Joachim Stephan, *Satire und Sprache. Zu dem Werk von Karl Kraus*
[Munich, Pustet, 1964 (Freiburg im Breisgau dissertation 1962)].

[3] Frank Field, *The Last Days of Mankind. Karl Kraus and his Vienna* (London,
Macmillan-St. Martins, 1967), pp. 31, 13. Another historical treatment is to be
found in Hans Kohn, *Karl Kraus. Arthur Schnitzler. Otto Weininger. Aus dem
jüdischen Wien der Jahrhundertwende* (Vol. 6 of "Schriftenreihe wissenschaftlichen
Abhandlungen des Leo Baeck Institute of Jews from Germany") (Tübingen, J. C. B.
Mohn [Paul Siebeck], 1962). Schnitzler comes off best.

The most faithful images of Karl Kraus are thus to be found in the appreciations of two contemporaries, Walter Benjamin and Theodor Adorno.[4] For all their intellectual infidelity to the essence which Karl Kraus served, they are able, when they surrender to the language which expressed it, to distinguish the judgment from the brass of the trumpet. These images are distorted, surely, since expository prose cannot give back the complexity and irony of a language creation like Karl Kraus', and since both authors refract Karl Kraus through the prisms not only of their sense but of their convictions. Both, in their ways, are Marxians, and are preoccupied to show what true things, from their vantage point, Karl Kraus revealed, as a phenomenon and from his vantage point, about modern society. What they say about Karl Kraus as a witness of the age is not false, nor uninteresting, but it reflects their interest in the material, the historical, the corrupt, whose faithful pursuer Karl Kraus was, rather than the timeless harmony which he sought to recreate. Expository prose itself is a diminishment appropriate to communication, rather than expression, and Karl Kraus' image fades as the description sharpens. Still, use of such prose is a guarantee of comprehensibility for readers who prefer not to read Karl Kraus themselves, and in addition the two articles smuggle in a benefit, all unexpected, worthy of the subject himself. By a kind of language miracle, in certain passages a reflection rather than a refraction of Karl Kraus' own language can emerge. While it is true that every time either author pauses to tell us what Karl Kraus represented we learn mainly what Benjamin or Adorno thinks, it is also true that these writers devoted to process, to dialectical thinking, have been better able than writers who merely possess principles and standards to apprehend in words the meaning of a work based on the immutability of order.

This is so partly because the commentators were contemporaries, because they lived in the same linguistic and intellectual atmosphere, in the same history, as Karl Kraus. If this were all they would surely be consigned with him to the lumber-room of history, as representatives of another era. But this contemporaneity of lived experience does not account in more than small measure for their successes in translating a vision which was not theirs for readers who share nothing with

[4] Walter Benjamin, "Karl Kraus," *Illuminationen. Ausgewahlte Schriften* (Frankfurt a/M, Suhrkamp, 1961), pp. 374-408; Theodor W. Adorno, "Sittlichkeit und Kriminalität," in *Noten zur Literatur III* (Frankfurt a/M, Suhrkamp, 1965) (originally a short notice in *Der Spiegel,* August 3, 1964). The most comparable treatment in English is Erich Heller's Nachruf in *The Disinherited Mind. Essays in Modern German Literature and Thought* (Philadelphia, Dufour and Saifer, 1952).

Karl Kraus. More basic is a shared respect for language as an expression of something real, the conviction that language, as nothing else, is the path to and from the concrete, that words are things and have to do with things, and that they may be used lightheartedly, perhaps — neither Benjamin nor Adorno will ever pass for a humorist — but never frivolously, as slogans, or, what differs only in degree from slogans, as propaganda, which actually kills. This respect for the real, and its expression in language, is not of course surprising in Marxian thinkers. But that they should be led to mimic a man whose whole work was itself mimicry, and that this process should validate, for them, the view that what is usually taken by mankind for reality is in reality a hodgepodge of phantasms, says something important about them and about Karl Kraus.

Marxists have perhaps become less Marxian as they have drawn away from the hidden god of the dialectic and have transformed it, too, into a phrase, an instrument, a justification of past acts. Conversely, there is a secret place, in language, where dialectical thinking and satire, as Karl Kraus conceived it, greet each other as comrades-in-arms. Both serve eternal laws, but these are laws of process, and both are bound to the historical, the current, the mortal. Contingency is essential to both. Karl Kraus' subjects — or rather objects, for language is his only subject — were the phrases of his contemporaries; every minute blasphemy, every self-serving pomposity, every cybernetic excrescence had only to be crammed into the original structure of the German language to be shown for the monstrosity it was, and to show the monstrosity it served. This structure had to be recreated constantly, instantly, nightly, however — Karl Kraus slept through the day and wrote at night — and it was only via this adventure, this process, that purity would show forth in the images of its corruption. In like manner dialectical thinking seeks to apprehend a process of which it is itself a part, through language. Contingency, for Karl Kraus, was an evidence of corruption, the sign that the artist was forced to be a satirist, to take the low road, whereas dialectical thinkers manfully accept it as a virtue. But this discord has not prevented them from seeing, and showing, Karl Kraus' work as language in process, a comment of language upon itself in motion, which yet succeeds in defining what is and predicting what will be.

Thus it was Benjamin who best described the inactuality, the intemporality, rooted in moral legalism, of Karl Kraus, and pointed out at the same time how Karl Kraus, like Nestroy, could "open heaven over a grocery store."

He stands on the threshold of the Day of Judgment. As in the masterpieces of Baroque altar-painting, where saints, forced to the very edge, stretch out their hands in defense against the breathtakingly entwined extremities of the angels, the blessed, and the damned which swim before them, so Kraus forces the whole history of the world into the extremities of a single local news item, a single phrase, a single advertisement. This is the legacy which came down to him from the sermons of Abraham a Sancta Clara . . . Kraus is no historical genius. He does not stand on the threshold of a new age. When he turns his back on creation, when, complaining, he breaks contact, it is only to accuse before the judgment seat. Nothing can be understood of this man so long as we do not recognize that for him everything, absolutely everything, cause and language both, necessarily takes place in the sphere of law . . . His "language message" is incomprehensible if it is not understood as evidence in the proces-verbal, if we do not understand someone else's words in his mouth only as corpus delicti and his own as the word of judgment. Kraus knows no system. Every thought has its own cell. But every cell can, in an instant, and because of an apparent triviality, become a chamber, a courtroom, in which language sits in judgment.

This is the desperate legalism with which Hannah Arendt condemned Eichmann: Thou shalt hang, not for crimes against the Jewish nation incarnate *ex post facto* in the state of Israel, but because thou hast broken the moral law, Whatever thy intentions. For Karl Kraus the moral law had been broken the instant, and every instant, that living language was made to serve the mortal intention, any intention, except that of language itself. And it is Adorno who catches something of this voracious moralism, endlessly exigent of himself, of every line of his work, of every reader:

He has not been overtaken by the worst, because he recognized the worst in the moderate, and revealed it when he reflected it. In the meantime the moderate has declared itself to be the worst, John Doe as Eichmann, the teacher who tempers the steel of youth as Boger. What repels those who would like to ward off Kraus not because he is inactual but because he is actual is linked to his irresistibility. Like Kafka he makes every reader potentially guilty, namely when he has not read every word of Kraus. For only the totality of his words produces the space in which he

speaks through silence. He who lacks the courage to plunge into
this circle of Hell is thrust mercilessly from the charmed circle
around it; only he can achieve freedom from Kraus who has
delivered himself freely into his dominion.

II.

Karl Kraus must therefore be judged on his own terms, those of
language, to be judged at all. He is inaccessible to those who do not
read German, since no translation can adequately render the evolution
of his sentences, the specific weight of the words continually turning
in upon themselves, the brilliance of the spark they throw as they
clash and roll on. He is inaccessible to historical judgment, which
can only capture the dead phrases he dragged screaming before the
judgment seat of language. He is inaccessible to the casual reader of
German, since his work is a totality, and long: any anthology muti-
lates this work, places its real content somewhere between and outside
the chosen passages. He is inaccessible to ethical relativism: relativists
only trespass on his work, and perjure themselves by their admiration.

Karl Kraus can be shown to have shared this guilt only if infidelity
to the German language can be proved. But this is to make him the
slave of every reader's taste in German, and every philistine who
reads German is capable of such a tour de force. The charge that
he did not live up to his own standards is unanswerable, since he is
dead. Adorno saw this too:

> The element of mythical irresistibility makes the objections to
> Kraus ripen as forcefully now as thirty years ago, when he was
> still alive; more bravely, because he died. Those who criticize
> him with priggish superiority need no longer be afraid that they
> will read themselves in *Die Fackel*.

And Karl Kraus would have cherished this final barrier best of all.
It is the seal on his own forehead of the satirist's destiny which he
ascribed to Nestroy: "He stands wedged in among the full-bellied
men of all vocations, holds monologues, and laughs metaphysically."

He is thus totally inaccessible. As a final proof, let me give a few
samples from these monologues, not as a measure of the man, but for
the pleasure that is in it.

Public Enemy Number One was first and always the daily press,
merely epitomized by the *Neue Freie Presse*. "Woe unto thee, that
thou art the descendant of a longtime reader of the *Neue Freie Presse!*"
Nature would revenge itself for the silence to which it had been driven

by the newspaper, "which thinks itself the brain of the world and is only its screaming larynx." The little earthquake of 1908, which filled the columns of the *Neue Freie Presse* with subscribers' impressions but caused no other damage, was a sign for Karl Kraus that this revenge had begun.

As the first shock came, not a single metaphysical thought troubled the purity of their affective lives. A people of cardplayers did not look up as destiny announced the ultimate. The need to communicate, which even in days without earthquakes babbles up to the rooftops, merely waxed to gigantic proportions. Not to go under unless others learned of it! Behold my last remains — but it has to be in the newspapers. This was not a telluric earthquake, it was a cosmic earthquake: this was stupidity! And it was a rehearsal for how the Viennese will act at the end of the world, which will surely come this year. It could be lovely. Once again we shall conduct ourselves so badly that we shall be ashamed in front of foreigners. A *Schlamperei* like nothing ever seen before will resign. The waters will stand still too late and the earth will not open on the time. And they will all want to be with it.

Since everything confirmed the imminence of catastrophe, the press play of the discovery of the North Pole did too.

The press, the goiter of the world, swells with the lust of discovery, explodes with achievements which happen every day . . . Progress, its head below and its legs above, kicks about in the sky and assures all creeping spirits that it rules nature. It burdens nature and says it has conquered her. It has discovered morality and the machine to drive nature and man out of nature and feels secure in a construct of the world held together by hysteria and comfort. Progress celebrates Pyrrhic victories over nature. Progress makes wallets out of human skin. When man travelled by stagecoach the world was better off than when salesmen fly through the air. What good is velocity when the brain leaked out on the way? How will we instruct the descendants of this age in the simplest manual operations needed to start the most complicated machines? Nature can count on progress: it already revenges her for the outrages it committed on her. But she will not wait, and shows that she has volcanoes to free herself from burdensome conquerors. She couples their women with the mortal enemies

of civilization, sets lust alight with morality, and stokes the fire
with racial fear into a universal conflagration. Man takes comfort and conquers the North Pole.

This driving of nature out of culture, and its replacement by a public
morality which created private immorality by sticking its nose, the
press and the police, into private, natural matters, was the major
theme of Karl Kraus' first decade, embodied in *Sittlichkeit und
Kriminalität* and *Die chinesische Mauer*. The title essay of the latter
work took fire on the murder of a *dame de charité* by a Chinese waiter,
her lover.

> With the thought of China, in the face of the magical individual-
> ity of this Mongol mass, every white man becomes a cuckold.
> The yellow peril has approached the life-nerve of Christian
> culture from a direction toward which the peoples of Europe never
> peeped. If they wish to keep their holiest goods, the purity of the
> wife and the virginity of the daughter, they had better watch
> out. The Chinese values neither, but he will conquer both
> without striking a blow. All resistance is hopeless against a race
> which does not load its natural necessities with the baggage of
> conscience. A people which need not fritter itself away in the
> civil war of morals versus nature takes the field at full strength.
> When they come, the women will deliver themselves up; and the
> men, long since become women, will not resist for long. A
> nation which detests virginity and consecrates its newborn
> daughters to their future vocation by an operation is the legit-
> imate heir to the province of a dispatched civilization. Of a
> civilization which in progress stepped on its own feet, because
> it could not venture out with morality; which builds dread-
> noughts but dances around the fetish of the hymen. Asia will
> discover savage peoples, electrically lighted barbarians . . . And
> chaos be welcome, for order has failed!

And it will not be the literary and intellectual world which will
reestablish this order. It has other things to do.

> Wildgans congratulates Tressler, and whoever congratulates
> Tressler can count on having Schneiderhahn and Seitz alongside;
> for all of them there is an official and an unofficial celebration,
> which however must also be reported and get fat headlines; it's
> all in the papers, whether they are being congratulated or whether
> they are congratulating, they change places, Jannings and Veidt

are also there, because they are after all there . . . for one is not sixty every day, but since every day someone is sixty, they just have to congratulate, let it fall as it may, day in, day out, congratulations all day long, so that it's hard to tell where the people in Vienna get the free time to do whatever it is they continually congratulate themselves for.

And even the artist will be unable to reestablish order, precisely because those who should serve culture have these other things to do.

God have pity on this development! Better that he let artists stay unborn than be born with the consolation that if they arrive at posterity, posterity will be better off. *This* posterity! . . . For the technicians have broken the bridges, and the future is what automatically connects. This velocity does not know that its achievement serves it only to escape from itself. Present in body, repugnant to the mind, and perfect as it is, this age hopes that the next will take it over and that the children which sport has produced with the machine and which the newspaper nourishes will be able to laugh even better. Anxiety is unwanted; if a mind knocks at the door it is told that the house is full. Science is given the task of guaranteeing hermetic isolation from anything otherworldly. What calls itself the world, because it can travel around itself in fifty days, is finished when it can count itself up. For it comfortably to face the question "What then?" there remains the confidence that it has also finished with the unaccountable. It is grateful to the authors who take the problem off its hands, as a pastime or as a dispute. But it must curse those, living or dead, whom it meets as admonishers or killjoys on the path between business and success. And when there is not enough left for a curse — for a curse requires devotion — there is enough for oblivion. And the brain scarcely reflects that the dawn of the day of iron has broken. Then the last organ is silent, but the last machine still roars, until it also is still, because the machinist has forgotten the word. Because reason did not understand that in drawing away from mind it might grow within a generation but lost the capacity to reproduce itself. If two times two is really four, this is due to the fact that Goethe wrote the poem *Meeresstille*. But now the product of two times two is so well known that in a hundred years no one will be able to figure it out. Something must have come into the world which never was before. A devil's masterpiece of humanity.

No one can reestablish order. The artist can only reestablish chaos, by chronicling what the world calls order.

The World War was not the beginning of a new age, or even the end of an old: it was simply a continuation, a consequence of the progress of the phrase. It began with phrases, pursued its awful course with phrases over mountains of bodies, and lived on in phrases after all the men were dead. The bullet, in Karl Kraus' language, went in humanity's one ear and out the other. Already in December 1914, before the universal huzzas had echoed away, alone in an orgy of jubilation, Karl Kraus evoked the war, that other war, thus:

> In this great age, which I knew already when it was so small; which will become small again if it has time; and which — since in the province of organic growth such a transformation is not possible — we should rather call a fat age and verily also a heavy age; in this age, in which the very thing happens which could not be imagined, and in which what can no longer be imagined must happen — for if it could be imagined it would not happen —; in this earnest age, which laughed itself to death at the possibility that it could become earnest; surprised by its tragedy, it longs for diversion, and catching itself in the act it looks for words; in this loud age, which roars with the frightful symphony of deeds brought forth by newspaper reports and of newspaper reports which commit deeds: in this age you may expect no word of mine from me. Beyond this one, which preserves silence from miscomprehension. Awe before immutability, subordination of language to misfortune, is too deep-seated. In the realms of poverty in phantasy, where man dies of starvation of the soul without feeling hunger of the soul, where pens dip in blood and swords in ink, that which is not thought must be done, but what is only thought must be unspeakable. Expect no word of mine from me.

And so, during the war, Karl Kraus wrote little himself; he had only to reprint what others wrote, without commentary, to have it censored from *Die Fackel*. And his next great work, begun during the war, which grew with the war, *Die Letzten Tage der Menschheit*, is in reality a compendium of what humanity wrote and said it was doing as it marched resolutely to the stake. In this play, eight hundred pages long, unproducable, inimitable, written to be seen from Mars, as he wrote, Karl Kraus had only to call his generation to judgment against itself, in its own words. He incorporated himself in it, in the role of the Grumbler, and shared its guilt, as the satirist always does:

And if the ages will not hear, then may a Being who stands above them hear! I have done nothing but abbreviate this deadly quantity which appeals, because it is immeasurable, to the transcience of time and the newspaper. All its blood was only ink — now what is written will be written in blood! The World War is this. This is my manifesto. I have maturely considered everything. I have taken onto myself the tragedy which disintegrates into the images of a disintegrating humanity, so that Mind may hear them, which takes pity on the victims though it forswear connection with the human ear for all eternity. May it accept the keynote of this age, the echo of my bloody folly, through which I too am guilty for these sounds. May it be counted toward redemption!

This work was brought forth by Karl Kraus' elemental outrage at the victimization of so many innocent men, betrayed and bled by meaningless words. And Karl Kraus, although he hoped, knew that it would have served nothing.

In this war, today's war, culture does not rejuvenate itself; it only saves itself from the executioner by suicide. It was more than a sin: it was a lie, a daily lie, from which printer's ink flowed like blood, one nourishing the other and flowing from each other, a delta before the great ocean of madness. This war of today is nothing but an outbreak of peace, and is not to be ended by peace, but only by a war of the cosmos against this rabid planet . . . (This war) was not played out on the surface of life; it raged in life itself. The front grew up in the rear. It will stay there. And the old state of mind will accompany life transformed, if there still is one. The world is coming to an end, and no one will know it. They will forget what yesterday was, they will not see what today is, they will not fear what will come tomorrow. They will forget that the war was begun, forget that it was begun, forget that it was waged. Therefore it will not stop.

Karl Kraus did not wish it so. *Die Letzten Tage der Menschheit* ends with the voice of God crying into chaos: "I did not want this!" "Not that you die," he wrote, "no, that you had to go through *this* makes every future sleep and every death in bed a sin. Not your death but your experience have I sought to revenge on those who loosed it on you."

This war, this other war, and this revenge, this old revenge, continued through the 1920's, and reached their culmination for Karl Kraus in *Die Dritte Walpurgisnacht,*, his last helpless, hopeless testimony to the magnificence of the German language before the monstrosity into which Germany was transmuted in 1933. This work consists in three hundred pages of holy silence — it was not published, even, until 1952 — within the cacophony of that terrible time. Mr. Frank Field has found a redeeming word to describe this language: gnomic: it is language driven underground by the experience it sought to apprehend, it writhes in the labyrinth beneath the world, out of sight of The Day. Unhappily the historian in Mr. Field soon reasserts itself:

> The picture which Kraus presents of the Third Reich in *Die Dritte Walpurgisnacht* is certainly open to some criticism. The events that he was documenting belonged to that particular period of confusion immediately after the accession of Hitler to power, a period in which rival groups within the Nazi movement fought for ultimate control and in which the process of Gleichschaltung was far from complete.[5]

Nothing could be more false. Nothing which the Nazi movement was and was to become escaped Karl Kraus, is absent from this book. The Gleichschaltung which was in process in 1933 was always in process; it was omnivorous; it was insatiable; only the names and the number of victims changed. Confusion was the essence of this movement; it was an old confusion; the only difference was that the trickle of blood visible in 1933 would swell to an ocean. Never was Karl Kraus' claim to foresee the funeral pyre of the universe in the rubbing together of two twigs more heroically put forward and more irrefutably validated than in this book. "I know that this civilization has its terrors even without the possibility that a blood-drunken rabble will administer its wares; and sensitive as I am to symptoms, I can infer war and hunger from the use to which the press puts language, from the reversal of sense and value, from the emptying and degradation of every concept and every content." Nazism was never anything more than just such convulsion of senses and sentences, and Karl Kraus' first, most famous word: Zu Hitler fäult mir nichts ein — About and beyond Hitler, nothing occurs to me — is a more accurate definition of Nazism than the last word in scholarship.

Karl Kraus had fallen silent as Germany awoke, and the blacklisted

[5] Field, *op. cit.*, pp. 196, 211.

intellectuals in emigration whom he had combatted all his life chose to take this silence for satisfaction at their blacklisting. He thought the supposition worthy of them.

That all the agents "from Reinhardt to Kerr" are deprived of power may be gratifying as a result; but, quite aside from the fact that I take no gifts from the dirty stupidity which brought it about, it will soon appear that my loss is greater than the loss to the world of culture . . . For I must lament a loss which is unfortunately not irretrievable and which I should not lament if it were. I cannot lament that many phenomena of the cultural world were lost, because I cannot honestly say I did not wish it. But I must still complain, because I wished it essentially otherwise and above all maturely considered everything. Especially because, as noted, a satirist from his very disposition cannot be completely agreeable to the diminution of his inventory, since for him it is not a question of dispatching the isolated case but on the contrary of preserving the example as a possibility of presenting the evil of the genus, a task he will never finish nor wish to finish . . . Thus it appears beyond any dilemma that I cannot enjoy the gain. For the simple reason that it is not a gain. It seems difficult to penetrate to the heart of this matter, and it may be remarked how cautiously I skirmish with the apocalyptic via the journalistic, in order to reach the medias res of something nonexistent which will stand in the annals of German cultural history on empty pages sticky with blood. The positive which has been achieved is first of all recognizable in that the basic decision to destroy living values has helped the worthlessness which has been shunted aside to an undeserved martyrdom or to an otherwise unattainable reputation abroad, where naturally every victim of German proscription tends to be mistaken for a talent or even for a man of character . . . The demand of the literati that the representatives of cultural Germany protest against the mishandling of their colleagues springs from an overvaluation of the ethical importance of literature and an undervaluation of a disaster whose smallest effect is its invasion of the book market. What was needed were words or acts against what was done to man, not against what was done to writers.

So, in this twilight work, Karl Kraus undertook a pursuit of the hunter which stalked Germany that year, following its every bloody footstep, meeting it every time it turned a corner into a new argument, a new sophism, a new lie. Set off against the witness of the German language, the mortal present over against the immortal stanzas of Goethe's own Walpurgis Night, it is all there: from the apparatus of denial that atrocities were committed to the press reports, with pictures, of atrocities; from the assertions that concentration camps held so and so many people, for rest and rehabilitation, to the claims of Ministers-President that their provincial camps together held more than the number given for the whole Reich; from the aryanization of the Oberammergau Passion Play, moderated so as not to keep the tourists away, to the poisoned Jewish druggists; from the paeans to Germany's rebirth through the shaven-headed girls led between laughing crowds to the aged men pumped full of castor oil and left for days in gunny-sacks with their own urine, excrement, and vomit; from the "unforced interviews with prisoners," all well treated, on the radio, to Gottfried Benn's celebration of a new era of humanity, with its own new style of art. Gottfried Benn may now be considered to have been confused; Karl Kraus was not confused about Gottfried Benn:

> We may perhaps recall one thing to Herr Benn: architectonic development may have been influenced, like every living thing, by revolution, war, and pestilence, and where there are ruins there may also be new life blossoming among them; but it is just as certain that an architectural style of the future, which even now makes the genius of mankind cover its eyes, is bought at too dear a price in so many valuable human lives — and I know of some.

As with the war, it was not only that they died which was so horrible, but the lies that killed them. The true picture of that age is not the one the regime projected, and which historians counterfeit by studying the regime: it is the image of chaos which Karl Kraus projected in his living struggle to wrest the language from the masters of the phrase:

> Strained and shaken, the world, which still thinks in formal concepts, follows this competition of words with deeds, of deeds with words, waiting for the end. If it gives more credence to the words and their warlike sense, it will be told that Germany must be judged by its deeds; if it points to the latter, speeches in the Reichstag are quoted. If it appeals to contradictions, these are mere side-effects which have nothing to do with the kernel of

the revolution, which came to power legally; furthermore an evolution is in store, for the revolution is over and its powerful successes demand veneration, but it is (also) just beginning, and what has happened till now is mere child's play, the commissioners must be gotten rid of, and if irresponsible elements intervene, watch out, or we'll take care of you and take the full responsibility for it. In such circumstances the world again prefers to give credence to the words and is content, in order to be adequately informed about atrocity propaganda, with the various declarations and especially with the assurance that the Party has hitherto been generous, which its enemies have only taken for a sign of weakness. The deeds which then follow are only the understandable reaction to the world's concern about the deeds. New misunderstandings are thereby produced, which call forth confusion but which nevertheless permit a certain overview, all the more easily since daily directions are issued. This proceeds from the confirmation that everything which happened happened to secure Germany from the Communists, beginning with the Reichstag fire, which they made to happen. Warnings follow against individual acts, which the leadership disavows, which it admits it incited, and which are undertaken by the enemies.

And everyone's conscience was clear, since everyone's good faith was beyond dispute.

Mere mortals are unjust when they respond to what is happening in their midst with skepticism . . . Must there be a cause for what is itself cause? This people amazes the world: no wonder the world amazes this people. If it confronts the doers with their deeds they are astonished, like the wolf listening to the fairy-tale about the wolf. For they did the evil that they did with such good intentions and cannot understand how they are so bitterly misunderstood . . . It was a lie, but now it is true. Certainly there must have been a misunderstanding, and it can perhaps be set aright by the recognition that here a state of being is openly proclaiming itself which is not naturally bad, but only does and is responsible for what it does with certain sensory equipment. The fact that the brother-in-blood does not believe things he heard about may be explained by the isolation evidently required by the takeoff of all life-relationships. But the fact that he does not believe the things he sees, or even those he does; that he does not know what he does, and therefore reveals himself in doing them, testifies to a guileless temperament, which men who are differently fashioned may wish to avoid, but which they cannot mistrust.

For once it was all beyond satire, beyond art, beyond the possibility of apprehension. No words could describe, define, reflect the terror of the unleashed, the corrupted phrase, the phrase become action.

It remains unimaginable; but since it happened, the word is no longer usable. For instance: to get off cheap — "to come out with one blue eye." In the unreal sense not all were able to do so; in the real sense there were many. It was a metaphor. But it was only a metaphor when the other eye was lost; or then it was a metaphor no longer. And something which fit like a glove, and when then went beyond the measure of humankind, is again an apparition, for the gloved fist has struck the eye so often that it no longer signifies anything inappropriate. The rhetorical flourish comes alive and dies away. In every area of social and cultural rejuvenation we remark this outbreak of the phrase into the deed. Contrary to the direction of technical progress it lived through a world war in which the sword was drawn to fight to the knife with gas. It will not outlive the losses of this revolution.

For Karl Kraus, National Socialism was only the triumphant executor of the press' legacy.

The notion that I could perceive this victory as my own is as pitiable as the spiritual being from which it descends and whose perorating cannot prevent me from rejecting it along with the presumptive helpers. I do so with a sense of greater responsibility and am capable of a perception which embraces both evils. For National Socialism has not annihilated the press; the press created National Socialism. Apparently only as a reaction, really as fulfillment. Beyond any question of what humbug they feed the masses — they are journalists. Editorial writers who write with blood; babblers of the deed. Troglodytes to be sure, but they have only moved into the caves which the printed word had made of human phantasy; the fact that they do without ornament or are incapable of clumsily imitating ornament indicates a certain cultural headstart. The deed has extricated itself from the phrase, and if the phrase is now turned against it, this is without significance, it is only grotesque. The phrase can do nothing more to *Geist*.

And Karl Kraus chose silence. When the reality of the satirist becomes reality, his work is done. *Die Dritte Walpurgisnacht* was not published in his lifetime. Only a few issues of *Die Fackel* appeared in the years before his death in 1936: a long piece on why *Die Fackel* did not appear, a funeral oration for his friend Adolf Loos, a poem — ten lines of silence —, a Shakespeare adaptation. *Die Fackel* was nearly bankrupt in any case; had he not died, it would have died before him. He had emigrated long ago; "faithful hater of the fatherland," he had stayed behind only to testify against its faithless adulators. Even that fatherland is dead. His work died with them. The phrase did not survive that revolution, and with it he belongs to our history.

Thomas Mann and America

BY HENRY HATFIELD

I.

THE EMIGRANTS from central Europe who came to the United States from 1933 to about 1940 formed perhaps the most brilliant group ever to reach these shores. Einstein, the Manns, Brecht, Bruno Walter, Broch, scholars like Werner Jaeger and Erwin Panofsky — these were only the most prominent among hundreds if not thousands of highly gifted persons, distinguished in the arts and professions. Undoubtedly Thomas Mann was the most prominent, indeed the dominant figure among them. This was due not only to his genius and reputation — Einstein was at least equally renowned — but to the fact that he was willing and able to engage in political activity, in speeches, polemics, and public appeals, and equally willing to devote untold hours to helping refugees escape from Europe, raising money for them, finding them teaching positions, fellowships, or publishers. Not all of his efforts were successful, of course.

Yet there are some who feel that Mann was wrong to divert so much energy from his creative work. Apparently he was sensitive on this point; he wrote to Agnes Meyer in 1941, emphasizing that he had produced *Joseph in Egypt, Lotte in Weimar,* and *The Transposed Heads* — "works of freedom, of serene gaiety" — during his exile, rather than letting himself be paralyzed by hatred. His friends should see a sign of strength in his political involvement. There is a clear and persuasive implication that if Mann had not had the outlet provided by his activity as a polemicist, he might have become artistically sterile.

A few even questioned Mann's motives. During the war, some observers found that he was still a nationalistic German, subtly camouflaged; while not a few of the other emigrants and some German-Americans believed that he had betrayed the "fatherland." As his comments on American life and policy, after 1945, became increasingly critical, he was subjected to attacks, even to denunciation. Thus the whole theme of Thomas Mann in America is, as they say, "controversial." The matter is further complicated by Mann's pervasive ambivalence. He can appear a bitter anti-American in one letter and a defender of this country in another, written a few days later. A courteous person, he often adapted his views, within limits, to those of his correspondent; and clearly he could be influenced by strong-willed persons like Agnes Meyer, on the whole a champion of the United States, or Erika Mann, who took, on the whole, the opposite position.

There is comparable if much less bitter controversy about the impact of Mann's stay in America and of the role he played here upon his literary work. It may seem axiomatic that separation from his native country, his language, and his public, would gravely harm a writer. Some critics find the fourth volume of *Joseph* and *Doctor Faustus,* for instance, clearly inferior to the major works which preceded them. Yet such exile need not harm a writer, as Joyce's novels and the poems Heine wrote in Paris attest. It has been claimed that the years spent in Princeton and Southern California corrupted his style; that he tended, like most emigrants from Germany, to mix the languages in an unlovely way. While he did make a few inadvertent slips, like using *aufgebracht* (excited) as if it meant "brought up," Mann often combined the languages deliberately, humoristically, for parodistic effect. Also his use of a polyglot idiom reflected his belief that the age of nationalism, and hence of hermetically separated national idioms, was over. "It is far from sure what language I'm writing, whether Latin, French, German, or Anglo-Saxon," says Brother Clemens in *The Holy Sinner.* "Above all languages is Language."

The ultimate question, "Did the experience of emigration change the character of Mann's work in an essential way?" is not easy to answer. Doubtless the confrontation with absolute evil in the form of Nazism was, to use Gundolf's term, a primal experience for Mann: it affected his inmost existence. Mann became more radical in a moral sense; for once ambivalence played no significant part. He testified that the years of the struggle against Hitler were a "morally good epoch" for him. *Doctor Faustus,* his most powerful, harrowing work, abandons ambiguous playfulness completely. Yet it would seem that it was the experience of Germany not of America, or rather, of Hitler not of Roosevelt, which caused this existential alteration in the novelist. Granting that exile as such was an integral part of this "primal experience," one wonders if it would have made any profound difference if Mann had spent the war years in Mexico or Brazil instead of the United States. Still, his reactions to America and Americans seem to me fascinating and important in themselves. What follows is a brief account of the impact of the American scene on Mann's politics and his literary work.

II.

To judge by Mann's early works, he neither knew nor cared a great deal about the United States before he actually visited it in the Thirties. It appears in the background as a semi-barbarous country producing types who are at best uncultured, at worst brutal. The billionaire Spoelmann, in *Royal Highness,* must flee the vulgar curiosity and hostility of his fellow citizens. Nor is Mann's praise of Whitman, in his political manifesto "On the German Republic," to be taken literally; as he admitted, it was intended as well-meant propaganda, designed to strengthen the Weimar Republic;[1] it is not evidence that he had embraced Whitman's ideal. Yet Mann was pleased and flattered by the success of his books in America. The word that Harvard planned to award him an honorary degree, which reached him in 1935 during the first phase of his Swiss exile, apparently did much to restore his spirits.

Mann had considered America as a possible refuge ever since leaving Germany in February, 1933. The annexation of Austria in March, 1938 made him decide to go to the States "for the time being." A letter of that year, written after his arrival, to his old friend Erich von Kahler, describes Americans as "well-meaning through and through, incorrigibly confiding; I think you could breathe freely among them, be touched by them, be happy." It is clear that Mann is pleased to be in the United States; that he finds its people naive but agreeable. In a graceful speech delivered at Princeton in 1938 Mann summed up his reactions on coming to America:

> The magnificently broad scope of things, a free atmosphere, the life of a powerful nation disposed to place its power in the service of decency, appealed to me very much. . . .[2]

[1] *Thomas Mann an Ernst Bertram* (Pfullingen, 1960), pp. 115ff.
[2] Quoted in Herbert Lehnert, "Thomas Mann in Princeton," *Germanic Review,* XXXIX (1964), pp. 25ff.

Before long Mann took on countless chores, many of which involved helping emigrés and would-be emigrés; others concerned Americans who had written him. The many letters of recommendation and encouragement show that he was generous with his money as well as with his time. Three letters written in the fall of 1939 attest in an almost comic way to this generosity. A polite letter to one Mervyn Rathbone is apologetic: the novelist feels unable to sponsor a committee to defend the rights of American telegraph boys; a month later, he helps to obtain a Guggenheim Fellowship for Hermann Broch; still later, a hospitable note to three West Point cadets grants their request to call on him after the Army-Princeton game. All this is done in addition to his creative work, not instead of it. At this point Mann appears completely admirable. It has been charged that he helped people because this made him feel important. Obviously there is some egotism in everything anyone does; one could wish that this type of egotism were more common.

Mann soon became acquainted with various leading American liberals: Archibald MacLeish, Eugene and Agnes Meyer, Edward R. Murrow, Henry Wallace, even Franklin and Eleanor Roosevelt. His image of Roosevelt was of decisive importance to his relations to the United States. (The part it plays in his fiction—Roosevelt as Joseph —is discussed below.) Increasingly the President appeared to him as a mythical figure, somewhat devious at times but mighty and benevolent, almost a god. It was a fascinating way of viewing a contemporary statesman but a somewhat risky one.

Roosevelt seemed to Mann to be not only "the politician of the good"—which he undoubtedly was—but a "Hermes nature," willing to use all his wiles and charm to gain his goals. Roosevelt's famous or notorious "shrewdness" appears as a virtue.[3] Typically, Mann stresses the antithetical quality of his appeal: like Caesar, he was a rich aristocrat whom the people loved. Not interested in the arts, he was himself an aesthetic phenomenon. Above all, he was not only a favorite of the gods but a genuine hero, who had overcome seemingly insuperable obstacles. "He could not walk, and he walked; he could not stand up, and he stood."

As Mann's nephew Klaus H. Pringsheim has observed, Roosevelt became almost an idol.[4] Since Hitler was utterly evil, his most powerful opponent appears as almost perfect. Mann's mythicizing

---

[3] Thomas Mann, *Gesammelte Werke* (Frankfurt a. M., 1960), XII, pp. 941-944.
[4] Klaus H. Pringsheim, "Thomas Mann in Amerika," *Neue deutsche Hefte,* XIII (1966), p. 29.

of politics does not stop here: Churchill in turn is stylized as the brave but reactionary warrior. When the President died, Mann was psychologically unable to give his successor the benefit of any doubt. Similarly, when Joseph McCarthy emerged, his repulsive figure was mythically magnified into a sort of Hitler Redivivus. Earlier, during the war, Mann wrote of "*Gauleiter* Lindbergh." (Obviously there is a great deal of truth in some of these simplistic constructions, but the difference between the mythical and the pragmatic view of politics is striking.)

The President's death marked the crucial turning point in Mann's relation to the United States. After describing his experiences on becoming an American citizen, in *The Story of a Novel,* Mann remarked that he was happy that this had happened during Roosevelt's life, adding rather darkly that he had better not expatiate on the subject. Of course he had realized, ever since coming to this country, that it had its full share of "difficulties, inadequacies, and human frailties."[5] A letter of 1943, to his son Klaus, counterpoints the Europeans, the powerless *"Graeculi"* of the coming postwar world, to the Americans—"the good-natured barbarians." Another letter of the same year, to Bruno Walter, complains that American faces are "curiously empty and amiably stereotyped." It is a note frequently struck by Europeans; Rilke actually proclaimed that an American apple was not an apple at all. Perhaps Mann was extrapolating rather rashly from observations made in southern California.

From about the year 1946, Mann evinced great concern about the political condition of the United States. Again and again he mentions the threat of fascism, which tends to become an obsession. His moods shift rapidly. In a letter of March, 1949 he writes that this is still "the best country in which to live," but a few months later he remarks that Americans will never forgive Roosevelt for having defeated Germany instead of Russia. It is this sort of heavy sarcasm, conveying at best a quarter-truth, which one resents. Even as early as 1946, he made the astonishing statement that since the "war against fascism was never seriously and wholeheartedly waged, it was never defeated. . . ." Perhaps, from the point of view of political perfectionism, there is some truth in this, but it is a gross if unintended insult to Mann's own hero, Franklin Roosevelt, and to millions of others. One is not surprised to find such hysterical exaggerations in, say, the *Nation* of those years, but one would have expected better from Thomas Mann. What is allowed to an ox is *not* necessarily allowed to Jove.

[5] Quoted by Lehnert, p. 27.

At times Mann's criticism is very well founded, as when he protests against the term "American century" or worries about the erosion of the Bill of Rights during the period of post-war reaction. He struggles between antithetical attitudes, writing to a Mr. Gray in 1947 that "America seems to have decided to buy the world rather than lead it" but affirming his belief, in the same letter, that "this great country is worthy of our love, our concern—and our trust." Even if the latter statement, coming after the sarcasm, seems mere rhetoric, one cannot doubt that Mann was genuinely torn. Klaus Pringsheim has attested that the decision to leave the United States for Switzerland was not an easy one. The novelist even said, perhaps jokingly, that if Stevenson were elected he would not return permanently to Switzerland, but that he feared that first Eisenhower, then McCarthy would become president.[6] (Apparently he saw Eisenhower as a "respectable" forerunner of fascism, a mythical repetition of Field Marshal Hindenburg.)

By the early Fifties, Mann's mood was black indeed. The political and cultural climate was not the only factor; he was disappointed in the reception of *Doctor Faustus;* many of his old friends had died; he lost both his son Klaus and his two brothers within a year. A letter of 1950 is almost paranoiac: "Everyone who opposes the *destruction of democracy* [Mann's italics] is about to become a martyr." In the same year he writes Theodor Adorno that he is seriously thinking of leaving the country, remarking that he would never have considered this three years earlier. The following year elicits grim prophecies: "Nothing more will come. Barbarism is descending upon us, a long night perhaps and a deep forgetting." It is the mood of *The Black Swan* and of Professor Kuckuck's philosophising in *Felix Krull.* In 1953, writing of an invitation to lecture before certain Quaker colleges in the United States, he remarks that he is not "stupid" enough to accept it. Erika Mann observes in a note that Mann feared that his American passport would be taken from him if he returned. (He had left the United States permanently in June, 1952.)

What is regrettable here are not Mann's polemical comments; however bitter, they are often just. The sad thing is that he totally failed to see those aspects of American policy which were farsighted, like the Marshall Plan or the Fulbright program. (Possibly there is unpublished material in which a more judicious view prevails.) Of course Mann was annoyed and harassed by stupid, sometimes vicious charges that he was a "fellow-traveler." And it was all too natural

[6] Pringsheim, p. 42ff.

for him to assume that the German pattern would be repeated: that reaction would lead to dictatorship, concentration camps, and total war. Still, this chapter of Mann's career was in both senses an unhappy one. As in the days when he was writing the *Reflections of a Non-Political Man,* Mann too often misused his formidable mind to speculate about matters on which he was badly informed. Thus he concluded that Eisenhower was made president of Columbia to prevent him from having a political career.[7] The truth, apparently, is precisely the opposite.

An article published in *Comprendre,* in 1953, partially redresses the balance. Mann now writes much more calmly, viewing American developments in perspective. On the one hand he gives an eloquent summing-up of the defects of contemporary life in the United States:

> Compulsion to conformity, called "loyalty"; spying out people's opinions, mistrust, training people to denounce others, refusing passports to respected scholars who are out of favor, . . . the cruel banishment of the unorthodox into the economic desert—. . . .

He nevertheless speaks of the national character as "basically good and generous" and foresees a gloomy future for McCarthy and McCarran. Yet Europeans are, he feels, more perceptive and therefore less hysterical about political matters. They are wrong to look down on the United States in cultural matters, but at least equally wrong to be subservient to American policy. He is himself not politically neutral, Mann insists—not for the first time—but a Westerner.

Once or twice the tone is downright hostile. Thus the account in a letter to Erika Mann of a humiliating American defeat in Korea, in a battle allegedly staged "before invited guests, with printed programs" [!], is suffused with *Schadenfreude.* This seems much less characteristic than a certain condescension towards Anglo-Saxons, especially Americans. (This is still extremely common in central Europe, not only in Germany; again, I am not reproaching but describing Mann.) He writes his brother Heinrich that his Nietzsche essay of 1947 went down well in London, Washington, and New York, but his Zurich audience will note that it was written for "ignorant Anglo-Saxons." (Actually, Mann's audiences in New York and elsewhere were composed largely of emigrés from Germany and Austria.) The description of America and Russia as two good-natured but very

[7] *Gesammelte Werke,* XI, pp. 228ff.

primitive giants, in the autobiographical piece "Meine Zeit,"* annoyed many Americans—and perhaps many Russians as well.

While Mann's attitude towards the United States was shifting and complicated, his concept of democracy is clear-cut. In a letter of 1942 he admitted to Agnes Meyer, who apparently was his mentor in things American, that he was a rather shaky democrat: by nature he tended to an individualistic [and aristocratic] belief in culture, rather than in the community. Intellectually he accepted democracy, but it ran contrary to his own essential character. This is strikingly honest; Mann was moving towards a Jeffersonian concept of democracy but would never have accepted a Jacksonian one, nor have claimed to believe that all men are created literally equal. His political ideal, as mirrored in *Joseph*, is anything but egalitarian; he provides for the common people because of humanity, "friendliness" as Brecht called it, not because of solidarity. Similarly, Mann described his *Royal Highness* as a democratic novel because the prince is friendly and amiable; but everything is done *for* the populace, from above.

Mann's idea of democracy from above is best illustrated by a passage in an essay of 1944:

> I don't primarily understand democracy as a claim for equality raised from *below*, but as kindness, justice, and sympathy from *above*. I don't consider it democratic if Mr. Smith or little Mr. Johnson slaps Beethoven on the back and calls out "How are you, old man?" But when Beethoven sings: "Seid umschlungen, Millionen, diesen Kuss der ganzen Welt!" *that* is democracy.[8] (Emphasis Mann's.)

This is a faithful translation of the German original. When the essay appeared in English, the first part of this passage was altered, presumably at the suggestion of the translator, to read:

> Democracy is of course in the first line a claim, a demand of the majority for justice and equal rights. It is a justified demand from below. But in my eyes it is even more beautiful if it is good will, generosity and love coming from the top down.[9]

Whereas the original passage is Goethean in tone, the revision represents a somewhat precarious compromise between two very different points of view.

* Translated in part as "The Years of My Life," *Harper's*, October, 1950.
[8] Translated from *Gesammelte Werke*, XII, p. 933.
[9] Thomas Mann, *The War and the Future* (Washington, D. C., 1943), p. 18.

Mann was disarmingly aware of a certain inner weakness in his political writings: aimed at a broad public, they generally conveyed only a part of what he believed. To have revealed his inmost doubts and reservations might have given "aid and comfort" to the enemy. He implied that his American interviews were unduly optimistic and conceded that his political excursuses were "a sort of higher propaganda, polemical and pedagogic in nature." In 1952, admitting that the spring flowering of his "democratic optimism" had passed, he accepted Philip Toynbee's characterization of his political position as "almost too good to be true":

> He is right, my democratic stance is not strictly speaking true *(nicht recht wahr);* it is only an irritated reaction to German "irrationalism" and the German profundity-swindle. . . . Clearly, these admissions do not show that Mann was "insincere."

Rather he was, in his own words, a man of balance who, when the boat tipped too far, instinctively leaned to the other side. Politics, as Klaus Pringsheim put it, "was not Thomas Mann's strongest side. There is no reason that it should have been."[10]

III.

Turning then to Mann's strongest side, we find images of America, or rather of the American, in *Joseph the Provider* and in *The Black Swan.* In the former, the symbolically American protagonist is admirable; in the latter, Ken Keaton, literally an American, is well-meaning but rather pathetic. *Joseph the Provider* appeared in 1943, when Mann's sympathy for the United States was at its height; *The Black Swan* ten years later, under radically different circumstances. While *Joseph* is one of Mann's most genial works, *The Black Swan* (literally "The Woman Deceived") is, with the possible exception of *The Blood of the Walsungs,* his darkest.

As has often been pointed out, Mann's Joseph is modeled in part after Franklin Roosevelt. Most of what Mann wrote about the President applies equally to Joseph, who is genial, brilliant, charismatic — and very wily, a "Hermes-nature." Quite capable of deceiving people, of playing tricks on them, he is basically benevolent; his tricks are those a "politician of the good" would tend to play. Roosevelt and his country were, in European eyes, the "providers" of the epoch, the only refuge. When Mann wrote: "in all of Egypt, and only here,

[10] Pringsheim, p. 46.

there was bread: in the hand of the state, in the hand of Joseph," he was doubtless thinking of the American scene as well.

Similarly, Joseph's reformist schemes appear in the tetralogy as a Biblical anticipation of the New Deal. They are effective but never violent; the rich Egyptian barons lose most of their power but continue to live comfortably; a "roguish" compromise between capitalism and socialism is worked out. The poor are given free food, partly out of sheer humanity, partly to strengthen the power of the central government. When Mann refers to Egyptian peasants as farmers, calls Jacob "the old chief," [11] or reminds us of Henry Wallace's ever-normal granary, his own roguishness is evident.

It is perhaps less obvious that Mann himself is reflected in his picaresque hero. He often saw his own role, like that of Joseph and of Roosevelt, as one of mediating between extremes. He too was a "provider" or "nourisher" for hundreds of emigrés; he was himself a brilliant exile driven from his home by hostile brethren but ready in due time to forgive them — or to forgive them as far as was psychologically possible. (Moses, in *The Tables of the Law,* plays a similar part.) In a sense, Mann was "standing before Pharaoh" when he visited Roosevelt in the White House.

While the combination of American and Biblical elements is in part aesthetic play for its own sake, it makes a serious point. The (ideal) American appears as benevolent and powerful. Further, it seems appropriate that Joseph is not the "inspired lamb" Pharaoh expected to meet but a very practical person, an administrator, indeed an "operator." The religious blessing goes not to him but to his brother Judah. Finally, whereas Joseph is admirable, many things about Egypt are absurd — Mann can thus hint at disagreeable or ridiculous aspects of American life as well as the attractive ones. Not that *Joseph the Provider* is primarily an allegory about the United States; the political level is secondary. The image of America as conveyed in the *Joseph* stories is more nuanced and balanced than are most of Mann's direct statements about the United States in speeches and letters. As Bernhard Blume has remarked, often a writer's creative writings have a higher "truth content" than do his non-fictional statements.

For reasons already discussed, Mann's frame of mind was a very different one when he came to write *The Black Swan.* It is one of

[11] See Jürgen Scharfschwerdt, *Thomas Mann und der deutsche Bildungsroman* (Stuttgart, 1967), p. 212.

the least successful of his stories, but of interest as political allegory: young Ken Keaton, a voluntary expatriate, is presented as a representative American. (It may be recalled that Keaton, in his twenties, unwillingly arouses the love of Rosalie von Tümmler, a widow who has passed the menopause. Her vital functions seem to be restored by her passion, but she has been cruelly deceived; what she has thought a sign of rejuvenation is a symptom of cancer. Keaton is the innocent occasion of her death.)

Attractive if unremarkable, Keaton shares the typical American feeling of inferiority vis-à-vis Europe:

> "He didn't care for America," he thought nothing of the country, finding it actually horrible in its dollar chasing and churchgoing, its cult of success and overwhelming averageness, above all its lack of historical atmosphere. Naturally it had a story but that wasn't "history," but just a short, shallow success story.

As Ken points out, one can speak of *das heilige Köln,* but not of "Holy Kansas City." Ken is more attractive than Rosalie's children, but aside from an amiable disposition and a good physique he has little to offer. Rosalie's daughter has doubts even about his well-meaningness and his robustness. Most revealingly, when the infatuated heroine speaks of the "great democratic spirit of his spacious homeland — one is reminded of some of Mann's political addresses — her sharp-tongued daughter replies: "He doesn't like his country at all." Alas, the last American in Mann's fiction reminds us of Robinson's Miniver Cheevy.

IV.

Despite the some fourteen years he spent in America, Thomas Mann remained a European, a cultivated German of the patrician class, in many ways a conservative. (His Russophilia, when it was political, stemmed primarily, I think, from "leaning to the other side of the boat" to balance the hostilities of the cold war.) His favorite city, after all, was not Paris, certainly not East Berlin, but — Zurich. To paraphrase Pringsheim, why should Mann *not* have remained a conservative European? Once the anomalous situation created by Nazism no longer obtained, he was inevitably attracted to Europe. His disillusion with the United States, while genuine, was probably a secondary motive in his decision to return to Switzerland. Even if Stevenson, or for that matter Henry Wallace, had become president, the good European would not have really belonged in California or even in Princeton.

The American chapter in Mann's career remains an episode, though an important one. In some ways the story is disappointing and unhappy. Yet Mann put his American experiences to creative use; *Joseph the Provider* is the happiest product of his exile. Certainly the United States contributed a great deal to his political education. After his exposure to the atmosphere of the Roosevelt era, he never again underrated the importance of economic and social factors. Never a materialist, he tried characteristically to balance justly the demands of the spirit and the flesh.

From this point of view his return to Zurich seems symbolically right: rejecting both Los Angeles and Munich, he finished his life in an atmosphere combining democracy with the European cultural tradition. Without the latter, he was always an exile.

The Epochal Innovations in Hermann Broch's Narrative

BY ERICH KAHLER

THE ARTISTIC rank of an author cannot be established without considering his innovative contributions, that is, the extent to which he advanced the development of forms of art relevant to his time. The innovative quality of a work of art is intimately connected with the artist's ability to grasp the ever new, ever changing reality of the human condition, to give it original, precisely adequate expression, and to create a new style for this new reality. Truth is always new.

Hermann Broch's first literary work, *Die Schlafwandler* published in 1931-32 (English translation, *The Sleepwalkers* by Willa and Edwin Muir, paperback Universal Library Edition, 1964) consists of three novels: "Pasenow or Romanticism," "Esch or Anarchy," and "Huguenau or Factuality." The trilogy describes an entire era, and with it the unfolding of a universal social and psychic crisis. This, however, is not its actual innovation; such description had been undertaken before by various great authors of the 19th century, most prominently by Balzac and Zola. But what had not been done before was to use different narrative styles for each of the three phases of the crisis, and this without losing the specific author's original quality.

The first novel takes place in 1888; it is Broch's version of a novel by Theodor Fontane — an organized, coherently progressing action in the narrative style of the 19th century, but without a trace of parody, depicting the atmosphere of a period already undermined by destructive forces. The second novel describes the situation in the year 1903 when the established life structures were visibly crumbling; the style used here is naturalistically abrupt. The third novel finally illustrating the year 1918, shows the completely disintegrated, chaotic condition after World War I, that uncontrolled mixture of fragmented rational and irrational behavior, of cynically business-like factuality and brutal emotionality. It shows the disruption of all intrinsic communication among people, and the psychic, even physical derangement of the self. As a further innovation, the third novel in its entirety is interspersed with historical and philosophical interpretations of this universal process of dissolution, a "disintegration of values."

In Broch's last book, *Die Schuldlosen* (1950, *The Guiltless*), a collection of loosely connected stories, the accent is shifted to one of radical morality. The *Sleepwalkers* who are not yet aware of the great crisis in which they are involved, who are its objects, turn into the hypocritically *Guiltless* who shun the responsibility for what is happening — a responsibility to themselves as well as to their fellow men. They evade this responsibility with indifference, and eventually meet their judgment.

The three novels written by Broch between his first and his last work, carry out this transformation in which a process of human nature becomes a trial at the day of reckoning. In the center of this development at the crossroads of human responsibility stands his main work: *Der Tod des Vergil* (*The Death of Vergil*). In this extraordinary work, one of the greatest though most difficult works of world literature, it is impossible to point to individual innovations; in its entirety it is unprecedented and original. In it we find the universal crisis in which and with which Broch has grown up, turning inward, from an external objective of observation into an issue of personal destiny. This crucial experience is carried to such depth that it touches upon the ultimate question and innermost problem of human existence: the affinity of life and death.

People become aware of this problem particularly in times of great crisis. What is death but a transformation of life and what is a great crisis, a world crisis such as ours, but an immense transformation of life. There is much dying in such crises. Human beings perish in vast numbers, but so do values, institutions, life structures, whether we admit it or not. Thus, during the Thirty-Years'-War, Baroque literature was obsessed and preoccupied with the idea of dying, with premonitions of death and the futility of temporal existence; all of life was viewed and taught solely as a preparation for dying. Consequently, it is not incidental when by the end of the 19th century the death motif again begins to figure predominantly in literature and philosophy. Not in the same manner, to be sure, as in the religiously inclined Baroque period where the individual soul, being spiritually prepared for death, was assured of eternal life. At the "fin de siècle" — which encompasses more than just the end of a century — there is no spiritual solace any more, death emerges undisguised, as a fact of life, indeed, as an elucidating element of temporal existence itself. The "fin de siècle" begins with Schopenhauer, Richard Wagner, Kierkegaard. It dawns in the writings of some French symbolists, in their wooing of death. In his great story, "The Death of Ivan Iljitsch" Tolstoi for the first time describes death as the key to earthly life, as illuminating true existence. The same experience then emerges in the writings of the young Hofmannsthal — in "Der Tor unt der Tod" ("Death and the Fool"), "Terzinen über Vergänglichkeit" ("Terze Rime on Transience"), "Das Märchen der 672 Nacht" ("The Tale of 672nd Night") — in Beer Hofmann's "Der Tod George" ("The Death of George") and Andrian's "Garten der Erkenntnis" ("The Garden of Knowledge"), it was indeed prevalent in the mood of that whole Viennese circle. Rilke was totally preoccupied with the problem of death. "Everybody," he says in "Malte Laurids Brigge," "carries his death in himself, as a fruit carries its seed." Thomas Mann, finally, in "Death in Venice," *The Magic Mountain,* and *Doctor Faustus* deals with death as being intimately linked with life.

But none of these authors, above all nobody who loved life as much as Hermann Broch did, went so far in his inquiry, in his blasphemous curiosity, indeed in his love of life, as this writer who tried to descend to death in the midst of life, who tried to *live* death by means of an imagination that went up to and almost beyond the limits of the humanly conceivable. Living through the great crisis, which is still with us today, contemplating profoundly the nature of the crisis and within it the meaning of his own death which he felt approaching, Broch was thrust into the conception of this work. He followed the Orpheic descent to the shadows with a relentless realism, far beyond the realm of individual humanity into a cosmic sphere, into a community of all creatures, to arrive at the source of all being where death becomes transformation of life and creation.

Experiencing the descent into one's innermost self, descent to the point of transcending oneself, onto the borderline where extinction becomes regeneration — this kind of experience has been the core of all mysteries and mysticism. With Broch, however, the old mystic experience took a new turn and reached a new scope in that it is not a communion with God any longer. Where is God, who is God? He has become neutral, nonparticipant, the Unknowable, the Unexperiencable, the one who cannot be approached and whose messages never reach us; this is the way Kafka endured and expressed it in many parables. God is the one who does not answer us, "whose response is silence" "der uns anschweigt," as Rilke once burst out in bitterness; who ignores our prayers, as Broch himself has God declare in a poem at the end of his novel *The Guiltless*: "No prayer should be addressed to Me, as I don't hear it. Be pious for My sake even without access to Me, let this be your propriety, your proud humility which makes you a human being. . . . For as far as I am, and as far as I am existing for you, I implanted into you the nonpresence of my nature, the extremest exterior into your innermost being."

Indeed, for Broch there is no communion with God any more. The mystic union takes place between the individual and his innermost, deepest self, his *id* which merges with the basic elements of life that are universal and common to all. Here, in Broch's crucial experience, psychoanalysis has become a mystical process. The ego transcends to the id, indeed, to a deeper, a transpersonal stratum of the id, that is, to its unfathomable cosmic sources. Vergil, on his deathbed, is striving for an awareness and clarification of the common nature of life, and hence he comes to realize that in the pursuit of artistic perfection he has missed the principal duty of the human being, the care of the good of his fellowmen.

This specific quality of Broch's vision, the mystic penetration of death and the tracing of individual existence into the generic id, results in a very unusual quality of his style: His characters speak a vigorous, robust language, very much corresponding to their personalities and their social status, be they servants, peasants, or businessmen; often they speak almost in dialect. Broch is a master when it comes to specific characterizations. But then, suddenly the narrative reaches a culmination point where a character will express not only his ego but his self, not only what he is aware of but the essence of his personality. Without break or caesura the id begins to express itself. Along with this transformation, however, the tone is changed and raised imperceptibly to a heightened diction, without losing the naturalness and spontaneity of expression. This is how unintentionally the lyricism of Broch's prose develops. There is an effortless interchange between the simplest, everyday idiom and the most sublime, poetical language.

Actually, *The Death of Vergil* is a long poem. It became a poem because its lyricisms flow naturally from the state of mind of the dying poet, Vergil. The book describes the last eighteen hours of Vergil, beginning with his return from Greece and arrival in Brundisium with the fleet of Emperor Augustus, and ending with Vergil's death in the imperial palace on the following day. It describes these final hours by means of an inner monologue: all events are seen from Vergil's inner experience, even factual occurences, as when Vergil is carried through the streets of the harbor, when the odors from the docks, the storehouses, and the shacks come upon him, when the crowd closes in on him, and the women yell down to him from their windows — even then everything appears as it is perceived by the most delicate sensorium of the ailing poet. His feverish condition is used in an ingenious way to show how reality was momentarily sharpened and intensified for him and at the same time preserves a lasting transcendence. In a delirious state the border-line between hyperacute reality and phantasmagoria is blurred. Factual phenomena alternately appear and disappear, coming much closer to such heightened sensibility than under normal conditions. The outer world presents itself to the consciousness with such extreme, obscene nakedness that it is constantly on the point of falling apart, of dissolving a multitude of hallucinations, memories, premonitions, dream waves, and vanishing into the unfathomable. Inner and outer life are turbulently mixed. The new analysis of the disintegration of self, started by Broch in *The Sleepwalkers*, is continued here in his description of the condition of fever: erosion of consciousness, of perception of bodily consistency. The world of appearances is in perpetual flux and particular limbs develop an independent life of their own. Interspersed between, however, there are moments of lucid clarity such as normal consciousness can never attain. His whole life, the failure of his life, is made transparent in a flash. This is the condition of the ailing Vergil, and it is under these ever-changing and intensified aspects that the narrative unfolds. The inner monologue is presented in the third person; this facilitates the transition from the self to the id, and it is only through this device that the process of dying could be finally pursued to the cosmic sphere.

But the man who is dying here is not an ordinary man, he is a poet, and a poet living in a world shaken by great crisis, in an era of fundamental transformation of life similar to ours; tending in the opposite direction though, in that it saw the decline of paganism and the rise of Christianity, while today Christianity seems to disintegrate into a variety of pagan movements. He is a poet moreover who had come to the painful realization that, having spent himself in the service of art, he has neglected the essential duty of his age which was human and moral.

The fulfillment of this task was Broch's most urgent problem, which beclouded his last years and caused him much suffering. Paradoxically, his greatest book, to which he applied his most accomplished artistry, proclaimed the end of art as a salvation of humanity. After the completion of this work he intended to renounce any artistic effort and to devote himself exclusively to science, whose strict discipline and verifiable results he expected to exert a convincing power. He was, however, not allowed to conclude his tragic career the way he wanted to, as a scientist. Apparent circumstances aiding an innermost necessity forced him to round out his artistic work, thus giving it its organic end and moral apotheosis: *The Guiltless*.

In Vergil's last hours, in this hardly controllable state of delirium, when it takes the greatest effort to hold his ego together, yet when a sudden awareness of himself and his world overwhelms him as never before, in this condition Vergil takes stock of himself and of his relations to the figures in his life, among them the ruler of the world, his sovereign and closest friend, the Caesar Augustus. The climax of this inner reckoning, the point where it reaches out once more into the outer world, is the great discussion with Augustus, who visits him and with whom he argues about the work of his life even as he strives for a clarification of man's significance and obligation in this era of change. He wants to destroy the "Aeneid" because he deems it invalid and meaningless — not artistically but humanly meaningless — when measured against what he should have done with his life. He wants to destroy it as an act of atonement for the neglect of his human obligation, as anticipatory death, as an act of submersion into anonymity. But Augustus finally wrests the work from him; Vergil relinquishes it — as a last gift of friendship, of love between man and man.

What is happening here at last, in the mirror of this book, is a threefold transformation: transformation of the world, of the soul, and of the body, which is death. But death is here experienced in such local intensity that it rises beyond individual and physical death into a sphere of cosmic transformation: it has become an oversized model of the process of dying. The disintegration of consciousness, and with it the disintegration of the human body, takes the form of a reversal of the biblical process of creation: the mind, the self, the body sinks gradually back, passing through the animal, the vegetable, the mineral, and the cosmically material spheres, reuniting with all of them and, after looking back once more, like Orpheus, spanning the entire range of creation with a single, simultaneous glance, it slips away from him into the realm of the divine logos, the humanly inexpressible.

Translated from the German by Gisela E. Bahr.

A Note In Tribute To Erich Kahler

BY GEORGE STEINER

A GENIUS OF place inhabits Erich Kahler's sitting-room in Princeton. The book-lined walls, the tables covered with books, the pictures in the room, argue a high and specific legacy. Even if only this book-crowded space survived, the historian of ideas and feelings could, in some measure, reconstruct a lost world. It is that world of Central European humanism which Nazism and Stalinism have all but obliterated, and of which Erich Kahler is one of the distinctive, vitalizing survivors.

The roots of that lost world lie in the emancipation of European Jewry at the time of the French Revolution and the Napoleonic wars. Erich Kahler came of age during that complex, often brilliant interaction between Austrian-German and liberal Jewish energies to which our own culture still owes so much of its nervous, eclectic dynamism. His was the landscape of Hofmannsthal and of Freud, of Kafka and of Wittgenstein. From the outset, Kahler was both a thinker in his own right and a man the warmth of whose temper, the generous excitement of whose sensibility brought him into personal contact with the masters. He was at Rilke's side in Munich when the first world war was ending; Einstein was to be a frequent guest; without Kahler's guardian presence, Hermann Broch would, most likely, not have written *The Death of Virgil*. In short, his life is not only rich in itself, but is at work in the genius of others.

To read his books, to hear him teach, is to be in immediate reach of that lineage of humanistic hope which extends from Erasmus to Goethe. Underlying the manifold of Goethe's work we experience the conviction — profoundly rational yet animate beyond reason — that certain harmonic structures initiate and energize the seeming chaos of sensible and historical life. Both the arts and the sciences are, to Goethe, complementary aspects of a unity which the philosopher, the religious leader and the poet perceive, are wholly mastered by, in moments of illumination. Civilization itself is a paradigm, inside the condition of secular, historical fact, of that primordial unity. In seeking to destroy civilization, barbarism would uproot in man the 'memories', the intimations and premonitions of a transcendent dimension. Hence the key problem, in the humanistic stance, of a 'politics of civilized life.'

This problem, in the particular idiom of a 're-valuation of values' after Nietzsche's *Umwertung*, has formed the core of Erich Kahler's lifework. Earlier than most, he sensed in the catastrophe of 1914-19 far more than a crisis in international mores and European primacy. He perceived, as did Broch in *The Sleepwalkers* and Hofmannsthal in that extraordinary play *Der Schwierige,* that the war had brought on a fundamental collapse of humane possibility. A new dark ages was beginning. What could be salvaged of the past? More crucially, could the concept of civilization itself be so re-thought as to make less probable future crises of self-destruction? Whatever the object of his inquiry — the philosophy of history, the philosophy of art, formal ethics, the comparative study of poetics and literary genres — Kahler is seeking to clarify, to re-construct those indispensable concordances between politics and morality which have haunted the human imagination since Plato. The lunatic ravage of the culture in which he grew up, the pressures of loss and of exile that have marked his own life, give to Kahler's discourse its urgency and grandeur.

One need not agree with every skein in his argument (being himself so generous, so vivid a dialectician, he would not expect one to do so). In particular, it has seemed to me that Kahler's almost ontological optimism, the classic strength of his faith in man, have inhibited his analyses from proceeding to an extreme but necessary question. The barbarism of our time did not spring out of the steppe or the jungle. It arose in the very heartland of high civilization. Men tortured and gassed in the very neighborhood of the museums, schools, concert-halls, libraries which constitute the anatomy of humanism. Neither Bach nor Goethe, neither Pushkin nor Cervantes, proved any barrier to the actual inhuman. It is not enough to assert that those who committed these bestialities or condoned them through active indifference were, in some manner, outside their own culture, that universal education and an unprecedented degree of literacy had passed them by. The facts won't allow such evasion. We must, therefore, formulate as precisely as we can, and press home, a much more disturbing question: were there powerful elements inside humanism, within civilization, that not only failed to oppose barbarism but helped produce it? Is the notion of 'civilization' itself flawed or tragically implicated in the coming of bestiality? Do the habits of mental abstraction, of fictional conceptualization which liberal humanism placed at the centre of its educational process, in some way incapacitate man's more immediate political reflexes? Is it conceivable that the humanities 'de-humanize' or at least do very little to make of man — however learned, however much a custodian of the art and thought of the past — *ein Mensch?* I see no escape from this question; it gives to the novels of Broch and to Mann's *Doktor Faustus* their obsessive force. I am not certain that Erich Kahler's books have posed it with sufficient nakedness.

But perhaps it is his genius for hope that is needed most. One leaves his presence literally augmented. By his sheer learning, by his proud respect for the play of thought and language, by his candid fascination with what is new and exacting in the life of the mind. Generous to others far beyond the measure of their own, often niggardly response, harried by history yet entranced by its unfolding riddle, Erich Kahler has no rancour in him; few men in the intellectual current of the age have been freer of the vice of disdain. That is the secret of his vitality. The term "ancient" seems absurdly unsuitable. But in other regards, in respect of sagacity and of music, of the long journey and of the delight and hope he has brought to so many, Erich Kahler will, I trust, allow one to invoke those thoughtful magicians out of Yeats, those sages whose "ancient glittering eyes are gay."

Marcuse and the Freudian Model: Energy, Information, and *Phantasie*

BY ANTHONY WILDEN

> Man is perfectly human
> only when he plays.
> SCHILLER

MARCUSE'S *Eros and Civilization*[1] is a curious book. Although Marcuse's critical attack on the Freudian concepts liberated us from so much in Freud—notably from Freud's implicit scarcity economics—the liberation and the final synthesis were paid for in a questionable currency of doubtful assumptions and unrecognized problems—especially Marcuse's acceptance of the energy economics of Freud's theory of the "instincts" and his failure to trace back the problem of *Phantasie* to its source in the relationship of child and Other.

These remarks are criticisms of Marcuse only in the sense that the time has come to criticize, not in the sense that Marcuse somehow blundered in producing one of the truly seminal attempts to integrate Freud into a progressive framework. By virtue of the hindsight that a whole series of critical and theoretical developments (I hesitate to say advances) have given us since the 1950's, it is clearly necessary now to re-evaluate the whole of Freud's energy economics and, eventually, to dismantle the theory of the "instincts" in order to show that both are uncritically based on models derived from the nineteenth-century scientific consciousness. It is also necessary to ask some very hard questions about what *Phantasie* might mean in Freud, to say nothing of what it may mean in life. But much of this critical thinking about Freud would in fact be impossible without the insights into Freud that Marcuse himself gave us. It is important also to stress the characteristic depth of Freud's work, the result of which is that no

[1] New York: Vintage Books, 1955.

"re-evaluation" ever amounts in effect to "refutation." The problems of the traditional mechanical and energy models employed by Freud must be exposed, and it seems very clear now that communications models must replace them. But in a discipline founded on intercourse and exchange, in a theory concerned to understand psychic organization and the ever-renewed restructuring of the mind and memory "after the event" *(nachträglich)*, in a therapeutic process dependent on communication, in a theory of man based on the mediation of human relationships by transference and by "otherness," in a psychology elaborated on and around the translation, transformation, and restructuring of *messages* in a dialectical process—in this discipline and in Freud's works the communications-information model is already there. It is not as explicit as the energy model, of course, and it is in clear contradiction with it—which is precisely the reason why we can no longer read Freud in the way Marcuse once read him. Significantly enough, this re-reading in a communicational context will in the long run show that Marcuse was often right about the wrong Freud and—with some reservations—that no "refutation" of Marcuse is necessarily involved. The new reading tends to confirm, elucidate, and give a more solid theoretical base to the optimism of *Eros and Civilization*, and at the same time it implies an equally powerful confirmation of the pessimism of *One Dimensional Man*.

There is some difficulty in asking the reader to address himself to the contemporary possibility of reading Freud, because any one aspect of it involves all the others, and it is simply not possible in a limited space to give him all the information he may well need in order to assess the theoretical pedigrees of this approach. Nor can it be extensively shown here, as I have shown in a much longer version of this paper to be published elsewhere, just how the details and the vocabulary of Freud's works, as well as the very experience of Freud himself, support the theoretical statements I shall make in this essay. In any event, a contemporary reading of Freud must, I believe, depend very heavily on the not very well known work of the French psychoanalyst Jacques Lacan, on some of the prerequisites and the assertions of the structural anthropology of Claude Lévi-Strauss, on developments in the theory of communication, especially as it has been applied by Gregory Bateson and others to human relationships in psychotherapy, and—eventually—on the *general theory of systems* first elucidated by Ludwig von Bertalanffy in the 1930's, and recently applied with radical results to the models (the metaphysics) of sociology by

Walter Buckley.[2] The views of these authors are all offshoots of and
contributions to what we know as the "cybernetic revolution," whose
theoretical attack on our epistemology and our ontology has been
especially powerful since the (unfortunate) impetus given the theory
of communication and the theory of systems by the engineering developments of the Second World War.

II

> Why, goddamit, did they insist
> upon confusing the class struggle
> with the ass struggle?
>
> RALPH ELLISON

One of the greatest stumbling blocks to *Eros and Civilization* is the
traditional Freudian vocabulary it employs. One's constant reaction
is in effect "Yes, that's right, but it can't be said that way any longer."
This vocabulary of itself brings with it a whole series of faulty
Freudian models, with the result that one is impelled to want to
rewrite the book in another idiom in order to be able to understand
it. I have dealt with the lexical difficulties in some detail in the longer
essay of which this is a part, and I shall only touch on these problems
here.[3] But before doing so, I think it important to think about the
climate in which *Eros and Civilization* appeared, if only because it
appeared on the other side of a watershed, on the other side of a
revolution in our thinking about men in society.

It is not surprising that a man who is a Hegelian, a Romantic, a
dialectical rationalist, and a Marxist should have turned to Freud,
for Freud lies in a long line of dialectical thinkers, and Freud has
surely to be dealt with in some way or other by any responsible analyst
of society. What is surprising, however, is the particular Freud,
the "biological" Freud, to whom Marcuse turned, and to a lesser
extent, the time at which he turned to him. If we look at *Eros and
Civilization* in the context of the fifties, one can recognize that
amongst liberal intellectuals, a number of things, especially the

---

[2] See, for example: The yearbook of the Society for General Systems Research;
Walter Buckley, ed., *Modern Systems Research for the Behavorial Scientist* (Chi-
cago: Aldine, 1968); Gregory Bateson and Jurgen Ruesch, *Communication: The
Social Matrix of Psychiatry* (New York: W. W. Norton, 1951); Paul Watzlawick,
Janet Beavin, and Don Jackson, *The Pragmatics of Human Communication* (New
York: W. W. Norton, 1967); Walter Buckley, *Sociology and Modern Systems
Theory* (Englewood Cliffs, N. J.: Prentice-Hall, 1967).

[3] This essay is extracted from an as yet unfinished excursus on a series of
interrelated problems in Freud, Marx, and Marcuse, sparked by the utopian challenge of *Eros and Civilization*. It is necessarily tentative and incomplete.

fear of Stalinism, the aftermath of war, Soviet dogmatism, the successful responses of capitalism to the Depression and the American cold war, had all contributed to a feeling of *déjà vu* with the "orthodox" Marx. At the same time as the return to the so-called humanistic Marx was getting underway through the dissemination of the *Manuscripts of 1844* (available since 1930), there was a concomitant rejection of the "orthodox" Freud, and a resurgence of interest in "another" Freud. These tendencies were curiously contradictory in many respects, but as Marcuse points out in his critique of the neo-Freudians (he was not aware, of course, of the "neo-Freudianism" of Jacques Lacan in France) the essential motive force involved was what can be called, for want of a better epithet, a liberal-democratic attempt to defuse both Marx and Freud. A curious reaction, when one thinks of it, to a world situation which seemed to prove both of them fundamentally right, but an understandable reaction of the historical consciousness, particularly in America, in defense against what the war had shown: capitalism warring with itself for *Lebensraum*—called the defense of freedom—and man's perverse inhumanity to man.

There was in the fifties a rejection of the "old" Freud and "old" Marx—people who should have known better became extremely busy writing obituaries—but there was also a return either to a "new" Freud and Marx or perhaps to something touted as the "real" Freud and the "real" Marx. Both had proved somehow disappointing—and yet, certainly in the United States and England, the return to Freud exemplified by the publication of the *Standard Edition* and the spate of biographies and critiques of Freud was clearly in opposition to a return to Marx, who still remains much less well understood in the English-speaking world than does Freud (and what passes for understanding there is nothing to be especially proud of). It is only recently that one undercurrent of the fifties (in France) has been revealed: the radical *reading* of Freud by conservative (Lacan), influencing a new reading of Marx by an "anti-humanist" (Louis Althusser). The permanent contributions of this movement in France—directly related to Lévi-Straussian "structuralism"—have yet to be assessed, but in a very important sense this movement was part of a whole revolution in thinking about man and about *les sciences de l'homme*, a revolution related to the rise of communications theory and cybernetics.

Some sort of new totality was being built in the world of thought —intimately related by its origins and in many other respects to what had been destroyed and what was being built in the world of

alienation, exploitation, and manipulation—ready to come to a still
unforeseen detotalization which has yet to mark its passage into a new
totality. It is curious to try to fit the elements of this totality together.
On the one hand, the "to the things themselves" of phenomenology,
the "behaviorism," the rats, and the "here and now" of psychology,
and particularly the networks and the communications circuits of the
engineers, seemed to militate against any concern for the unconscious
of the Freudian theory. In spite of the experiments in perception as
reduction, "reductionism" was one of the most common of the attacks
against the notion of an unconscious infrastructure, whether in society
or in the individual. Sartrean existentialism had attacked the Freudian
unconscious, and the Heideggerean quest for the Being of being or the
Jungian excursus on archetypes were certainly a great deal less
emmerdant. But Heidegger's concern for the *discourse (Rede)* in *Sein
und Zeit* (1927) and the existential Sartre's turning of Heidegger's
"I am what I say" into "I am what I do" had a profound internal
relationship: being-in-the world, acting in the world, are both problems of *communication*. In the midst of Husserlian *cogito*-thinking,
which like all theories of consciousness as primary is doomed to the
solipsism of the subject in a world of objects, there appeared the Other,
a scandal, says Sartre. Behind the rediscovery of the Other lay the
Hegel of the *Phenomenology*, and behind Sartre (and Lacan) lay
Alexandre Kojève's extremely influential lectures on the *Phenomenology* in the 1930's (published in 1947). The existentialist and Heideggerean Hegel of Kojève, the notion of the *Ich* as desire, the definition
of human desire as corresponding to a lack, as corresponding to the
desire of the Other, the renewed consciousness of the master-slave
dialectic as an *anthropogenic* process (outside its Marxist validity)—
these notions can all be seen in retrospect as militating, consciously
or unconsciously, against the essentially atomistic individual which
had been the pride of the bourgeoisie, and which is still, again consciously or unconsciously, the *point de prise* of thinkers scandalized
by their discovery of otherness. "Intersubjectivity" appeared in the
fifties, or rather a new emphasis on it, for it was not the intersubjectivity of logical positivism in the sense of what is accepted or
agreed on by the collectivity of subjects, but rather the intersubjectivity
of a supposed reciprocal relationship between subjects, which the
Sartrean view of relationships as eternally sado-masochistic had
seemed to deny. Now intersubjecivity means nothing if it does not
mean communication, and communication, at least in the special sense
of *human* communication in *open* systems, means language or dis-

course. It was at this point that we discovered from Lacan that psychoanalysis, besides being many other things, was "the talking cure," that it was an epistemology of discourse, that it was concerned with the communication and relationship between *subjects* (with the Other as a third term)—rather than simply that between analysts and patients—and that the interpretation of dreams, all in all, meant the interpretation of discourse, for the dream was above all a *translation* and a *message*.

We had read Freud, but not this Freud. It would be too extensive a task to go into the somewhat tortuous details of the Lacanian reading here; one can only suggest that the reader go to the available texts.[4] The point is this, that if one could see in the fifties a regressive, somewhat narcissistic, and deathly emphasis on philosophies of individualism or philosophies of the subject (Kierkegaard, Dostoevsky, the Husserl of the *Cartesian Meditations*, Kojève's existentialism, the early Sartre, Camus, Mounier's personalism, Being-towards-death, the "autonomous ego" of the neo-Freudians), a regression which was clearly one of many symptoms of the temporary destruction by Stalinist Russia of idealist hopes for the community, there was at the same time a new movement towards dispensing with the subject altogether.

There are two interlinked facets of this movement. Advances in scientific structural linguistics in the thirties, notably by Roman Jakobson and Troubetzkoy on the phonology of the binominal opposition, formed the touchstone of Claude Lévi-Strauss' structural anthropology, which uses language in the widest sense, but without a *speaker*, as a model for societies and their myths. The rise of structural linguistics as a model paralleled Sartre's involuntary destruction of *cogito*-thinking, Merleau-Ponty's "behaviorism," and his discovery of "the body as speech." The Lévi-Straussian conception of structure as lacking a center or anchoring point has had an as yet unfathomed effect upon psychoanalysis (Lacan), literary criticism (Barthes), philosophy (Althusser, Foucault, Derrida). The rediscovery of the work of Ferdinand de Saussure by those outside linguistics proper, with, amongst other things, his view of the speech circuit as between a sender and receiver, was not unexpectedly contemporary with the

[4] Jacques Lacan, *Ecrits* (Paris: Editions du Seuil, 1966). Three of Lacan's articles are available in English: "Some Reflections on the Ego," *International Journal of Psycho-Analysis,* XXXIV (1953), 11-17; "L'Instance de la lettre dans l'inconscient," tr. Jan Miel, *Yale French Studies,* No. 36-37 (October, 1966), pp. 112-147; "Fonction et champ de la parole et du langage en psychanalyse," in: *The Language of the Self: The Function of Language in Psychoanalysis,* by Jacques Lacan, translated, with notes and commentary, by Anthony Wilden (Baltimore: The Johns Hopkins Press, 1968), pp. 1-87.

rise of communications theory, with its "codes" and "messages"—
categories most unlike our naive understanding of code and message.
And at the same time as Lévi-Strauss's concern for the symbolic function of exchange in society and for the structure "beneath" or "within"
the phenomena (depending upon how you interpret him) was gen-
erating in France the realization that not only the Other but now
the unconscious had become a scandal, the other facet of this dis-
pensation with the (autonomous) subject, the theory of communication, was beginning to affect theories of human relationships in the
English-speaking world, appearing in its most provocative and influential form in the "double bind" theory of (some types of)
schizophrenia published by Bateson, Jackson, Haley, and Weakland
in the fifties.[5] If one might call Lévi-Strauss's theory of myth the
rediscovery and the *restatement* of Freud's "archaic heritage"—the
past that speaks to us—one might equally well call the negation of
the scandal of the Other by communicationally oriented psychother-
apists, the rediscovery and, once again, the *restatement* of the Freudian
concept of the superego—the Other who commands us.

Given that these restatements have been particularly fertile in many
respects, we might still wonder why they are necessary—the question
behind William James's remark that all radically "new" theories are
greeted by unmitigated hostility and denigration, along with suggestions of moral turpitude on the part of their advocates, to be
followed (once the theory has become seriously accepted) by lengthy
proof that it had all been said before, that everybody knew it all along
—if one did not understand the difference between cognition and
recognition in Freud and Hegel (emphasized by Marcuse), the power
of negation or denial *(Verneinung)* in the social and in the psychic,
and the dialectical process of totalization in the later Sartre. The
dialectical process of the *Aufhebung* which (like the psychic *Verneinung)* suppresses and conserves, is simply the necessary step once a
certain level of contradiction has been reached—whether in society
or in thought—if it were not, it would be difficult to conceive how
man or knowledge could be possible. Restatement is part of *metacommunication* and metacommunication is impossible without (dialectical) *negation*.

But there is more to the changes in the intellectual climate than
the fortuitous piling up of supposed "intellectual influences" or "concomitant ideas." It is certain that the tensions of the cold-war in-

<hr/>

[5] "Toward a Theory of Schizophrenia," *Behavioral Science* (1956), I: pp. 251-
264.

duced by the economic designs of the United States on Europe and the resulting period of McCarthyism had a great deal to do with the interest, in the United States, in one pole of the misconstrued polarity between Marx and Freud. But the rebuilding of Europe into the American marketplace after the concrete, visible dehumanization and massacre of millions of human beings had other, if less visibly paranoid effects on the intellectual market. Liberalism, as both conservatives and radicals knew, was dying the slow death which the individualistic reaction against the "determinisms" of Freud, of Marx, and of science (at the very point when this last determinism was failing) had been trying to stave off. It is hardly surprising that a philosophy and a theology which spoke of discourse, of authentic dialogue, of "I" and "thou" in a world of "Its," or a viewpoint which rejected "intellectual systems" in favor of the solitary individual in the face of God or death or the Other (Buber, Kierkegaard, Camus, Heidegger, the early Sartre, for instance) should become fashionable at the very moment when both socialism and capitalism were discovering the merits (at least for the system as system) of the regulated economy and the enormous potentials of control invested in the simple propagation, laissez-faire or otherwise, of inauthentic communication. It seems that somewhere along the line we entered the phase of what Marcuse would term super-alienation, to which many intellectuals responded by the simplistic libertarian humanism denounced by Marcuse in the neo-Freudians. We cannot but recognize that the accompanying liberal rationale is a curious kind of cowardice; as sublimated, negated acceptance of unprovoked violence, it is dedicated to the ideal principle of letting every flower bloom in a society devoted to defoliation.

The contemporary manipulation of alienation seems to be new in scope, if not in essence. Managed economy, media, communication, projected image, regulation—it was not for nothing that the new engineering which sprang out of the Second World War was labelled *cybernetics,* the science of control. This word brings us to one of the central problems in this introduction to the problems of Marcuse's Freud. For just as the new developments in anthropology, psychoanalysis, "structuralism," and even to some extent in the *nouveau roman,* seemed to celebrate the final dethronement of the ideal of the regulation of men by men in favor of regulation of men by objects or by regulation itself, the rise of behaviorism, operationalism, and communications engineering, the spread of television, the conversion of Business Administration into Management Science, the metamorphosis of the computer from slave to master (whether by accident, logistics, or essence), game theory, decision theory, and attempts to use *systematism or systematization* as ends in themselves, without regard for value, direction, or purpose, all seemed to announce a general embourgeoisement, a depoliticization, a disengagement, a further step in the neutralization of thought in the favor of a status quo governed by the *Realpolitik* of "freedom" and "democracy."

One might consider especially symptomatic of this tendency the influence of Talcott Parsons in the United States, whose "equilibrium" sociology expressed the prevailing ideology by equating an ideal of "balance" with "socially normative" and with "institutionalized order" at the very point in time that the American, the generational, and the racial "consensus" was beginning to show its true colors. On the other side of the Atlantic, somewhat later, structuralism in France seemed clearly to be contributing to this neutralization by de-emphasizing history (at the very moment that the Third World was beginning to rewrite it), and the idealistic concern of the young for some ill-defined "relevance," for the here and now, for their own thing, seemed intended to cut off our relation to the past as process (as opposed to the past as honkie history or as systematic lie). "Change," "diachrony," and "process" seemed at least temporarily to have been replaced by words implying stasis, synchrony, controlled fluctuation, "tuning," structure, or steady states. Theoretical concerns seemed circular, centripetal, morphostatic—"morphogenesis" as the label corresponding to a non-Marxist theory of social change had yet to be seriously invented by American sociologists.

III

> Often we had to force ourselves by a conscious act of will to realize that Joey was a child. . . . Entering the dining room for example, he would string an imaginary wire from his "energy source" . . . to the table. There he "insulated" himself with paper napkins and finally plugged himself in . . . for he firmly believed that the "current" ran his ingestive apparatus. . . . Children and members of our staff spontaneously avoided stepping on the "wires" for fear of interrupting what seemed the source of his very life.
>
> BETTELHEIM: "Joey: A Mechanical Boy"

I have dealt somewhat cursorily with the climate in which *Eros and Civilization* appeared. In retrospect, Marcuse's "biological" Freud is a surprising choice of possible approaches to Freud. Given the widespread rejection of the so-called "death instinct," the apparent impossibility of giving it a biological basis, and the anti-libertarian consequences of accepting it, Marcuse performed a *tour de force* in integrating this "regressive" concept into a "progressive" view of Freud. However, even though this essentially metaphysical notion had received independent philosophical support from Heidegger's promotion of Being-towards-death, and in spite of its interesting parallel with the theory of entropy, the death instinct and the language that goes with it seem curious to anyone introduced to Freud by Lacan. A curious language, but not necessarily wrong. The notion of fundamental binary oppositions has been in the air very much since Jakobson, Wallon, Lévi-Strauss, and Lacan, and one was driven to wonder to what extent it was simply the *vocabulary*—notably the word "instinct"—besides the *model*, which caused difficulties over the binary opposition between Eros and Thanatos in Marcuse's interpretation of Freud.

At another level, Marcuse's use of *Phantasie* as a principle of liberation raised other difficulties, partly because of Freud's deliberate ambiguities in the use of the word, but especially because of the apparently regressive nature of the *Urphantasie* discovered by psychoanalysis. And again, Marcuse's concern for the "real" privacy of the individual[6]—which is after all the implicit privileged point (structural or historical) necessary to the concept of alienation—seemed to fit badly with professional and theoretical acceptance of the fact that the individual could not be considered to be discrete, that he depended upon the Other for his humanity and his existence, that all human relationships were networks of communication whose elements were senders and receivers—"black boxes," but not atoms—in open systems characterized by special relationships of feedback. Crucial to this question are the new ideas about the possible or potential isomorphy

---

[6] Cf. the following problematic statement in the preface to *Eros and Civilization:*

> This essay employs psychological categories because they have become political categories. . . . Formerly autonomous and identifiable psychical processes are being absorbed by the function of the individual in the state—by his public existence. . . . Psychology could be elaborated and practiced as a special discipline as long as the psyche could sustain itself against the public power, as long as privacy was real, really desired, and self-shaped. . . .

Cf. also *One Dimensional Man* (Boston: Beacon Press, 1964): "Solitude, the very condition which sustained the individual against and beyond his society, has become technically impossible" (p. 71). But the critique of repressive alienation and the desire for solitude appear only in times of trouble—for it seems that no man can actually divest himself of the alienating Other short of death, as Montaigne, or Hegel, or the early Christian hermits, or the most everyday schizophrenic could tell us. In Utopia, "Fay ton faict et te cognoy" (Montaigne) could presumably be neither demanded nor obeyed.

of models, along with recognition of the defectiveness of certain types of models that have been applied to human behavior in the past.

It is true nevertheless that some of these points of view seem to contain a built-in pessimism about man in society. If we go back to the thirties, for instance, to the recognition of statistical causality in physics, when some saw the discovery of indeterminacy for the individual electron as an analog statement about human free will (and it is because that was said that we must comment on it), we can see that what it would actually tell us, if anything, is not so much that the individual electron can do what it likes, but rather that the "free will" of the individual human being—that is, his freedom outside of the determining forces of biology, childhood, and cultural environment—is of no consequence whatsoever in the system, because of the statistical properties of the system itself. While such an analogy might be a point in favor of Hegel's "cunning of reason" or orthodox Marxist dialectical materialism, it does not, unfortunately, any more than some of the theories used here, say anything about the *direction,* statistical or otherwise, the system is assumed to be taking.

As another example, the "double bind" theory of schizophrenia—insofar as schizophrenia may justifiably be viewed in a phenomenological sense as a disease of communication—automatically leads us to some rather gloomy predictions about the double binds of daily life. Their paradoxical injunctions (injunctions logically equivalent to "Do not read this") which can be neither obeyed nor disobeyed, come to us as commands both from the powers that be and seemingly from the very conditions of existence itself (the human condition of separation from being).[7] The problem is to know to what extent the pessimism induced by this type of analysis is intrinsic to theoretical or empirical necessities (and there is no doubt whatsoever that they fit the field of experience to which they have been applied) and to what extent these theories simply reflect a stage of the historical consciousness or themselves serve the same function of control as did,

---

[7] Cf. *One-Dimensional Man,* p. 101: "The closed language [Roland Barthes] does not demonstrate and explain—it communicates decision, dictum, command." Bateson has pointed out that all propositions contain both a report aspect and a command aspect (we add that the interlocutor in the communication between the social order and the person being "socialized" is the Other—defined as the rest of the system or subsystem in which the subject is involved), and it would seem that there has perhaps been a progressive, historically discoverable, emphasis on the latter rather than on the former. But it was to the demand of the Other that Socrates responded, as did, at another time, the seekers of the Holy Grail.

As for the existential double bind, Montaigne's *Essays* are clearly an oscillating, Pyrrhonic response to what he himself calls that *commande paradoxe:* "Know thyself." See my "Montaigne's *Essays* in the Context of Communication," *Tri-Quarterly* (forthcoming, 1969).

for example, the theological justifications of the double-binding doctrines of the medieval church—an (Arian) God who says, like the
father to his son, "Be (like) me so long as you are not (like) me,
for you cannot be (like) me." (And the Reformation, far from taking
the road to the cure of the double bind, which is to be allowed to
metacommunicate, to communicate a*bout* it, simply managed to in-
ternalize it, producing the unhappy consciousness of the internalized
master-slave dialectic, at that very time in history when changes in
the economic infrastructure required an ideology of personal freedom
which would also be a mechanism of control.)

But there are important levels of difference between the analysis
of a mechanism of control and the control itself. The neutralization
of language which leads, for example, to the public acceptance of
blatant paradox and contradiction in words ("the clean bomb"), in
deeds (destroying a university in order to save it), and perhaps
especially in the puerile and irrational plots of television espionage
shows (which, like current foreign policy, cannot be read backwards)
—these are qualitatively and existentially different from the contradictions and paradoxes of *Oedipus Rex* or the paradox of a Montaigne
who declared that in his quest to know himself and do his thing he
often contradicted himself but never contradicted the truth.

The confusion of logical types which allows double binds in language ("I am lying"), and which, moreover, seems to be essential to human language and relationships, is as old as and older than the Cretan
or Epimenidean paradox itself. Yet the fact that it is the paradoxical
commands of the Other which drive men mad when they are prevented
from metacommunicating about them, and the corollary, that such
confusions are the distinguishing marks of schizophrenic language itself, would seem to indicate no more than that schizophrenia becomes
epidemic in certain conditions of alienation. On the other hand, it
seems that much of Marcuse's pessimism about fundamental social
change stems directly from his implicit recognition of the controlling
power of the double bind, of which the "sweet reason" of the liberal
rationale is an excellent example. The "vacillation between contradictory hypotheses" of *One Dimensional Man* (p. xv) is—unfortunately—typical of the oscillating schizophrenic response to the double
bind.[8] ("Unfortunately," not because the discourse of a penetrating
and vehement critic in a schizophrenogenic society could be anything

---

[8] Without the avenue of metacommunication, "the paradoxical injunction . . .
bankrupts choice itself, nothing is possible, and a self-perpetuating oscillating
series is set in motion" (Watzlawick et al., The *Pragmatics of Human Communication,* p. 217).

but schizophrenic, but rather because of the paradoxes of some double binds, *there may be no other answer.)* Similarly discouraging, as I have already indicated, are recent interpretations of the primordial phantasies discovered by psychoanalysis. As we shall see, the phantasy seems to reinforce the domination of the Other by (perhaps) binding us to repetition itself—which is not a "working" category of *Eros and Civilization.*

IV

> History is nothing but the activity
> of men pursuing their purposes.
>
> KARL MARX

For one of the possible Freuds in the text of Freud, man appears to be a neurotic steam-engine fluctuating between quiesence and runaway activity, with two conflicting *kybernetai,* Eros and Thanatos, at the controls, each haggling with the other over what is to be done with the daily delivery of coal. In so far as this machinery seems sometimes to be regulated by some sort of governor seeking to maintain a constant level of available energy in the system (the Freudian "principle of constancy"), another Freud presents us with man as a self-regulated homeostatic system. (Homeostasis was the term employed by Cannon in the 1930's to describe the regulation of the temperature of the blood.) For another Freud, man is a mechanical system striving for equilibrium. For yet another, man is a thermodynamic system condemned to the entropy of the "death instinct" (the Freudian "principle of inertia"), or else he is a biological system regulated by unelaborated "biological" principles (the "desire inherent in organic life to restore an earlier state of things," the inorganic state). The mind—brain or psyche—appears here as an anatomy, there as a neural network, elsewhere as a system of writing, and yet elsewhere as a nation containing individual provinces or agencies *(Instanzen),* ruled by organismic Id or Ego—or by that totally different *principe,* Superego (who is not an organism, but an environment)—an Austro-Hungarian empire grooving with the Tsar. Sometimes it is a question of topology or topography *(Topik),* sometimes a question of primary and secondary systems, sometimes that of the dynamics of repression, sometimes that of thermodynamics and the ideology of psychic economics. Here, for instance, the libido is a vast hydraulic system, elsewhere, not unnaturally it is electrical, and sometimes it simply seems to be the negative of entropy (that is to say, a principle of organization opposed to Thanatos, the principle of disorganization). The neuronal energy of the early works becomes psychic energy, without any fundamental changes in the modular metaphors, and the neuronal network seems clearly to be a foreshadowing of contemporary models of the brain (and man) as an information-processing system. The mind is a camera, a telescope, a city under archeological excavation, a network of traces *(Spuren)*, a "mystic writing pad," a system of *layers of signs (Zeichen)* —waiting to be *trans-lated (Um-setzung:* transformed, restructured, communicated at another level of communication) or simply *read* (inevitably *nachträglich).* Psychological resistance is described in terms of a theory of warfare, and repression in terms of a Department of Immigration—refusing entry to political, cultural, and pigmental undesirables. Repression produces a conscious discourse full of holes *(lückerhaft),* like a Russian newspaper at the hands of the Austrian censor. The superego is sometimes a kind of fearful political oppressor, sometimes a kindly commissar, and energy (labor) is invariably considered in terms of *price*—a viewpoint not unconnected with "working through" *(durcharbeiten)* at 20 marks an hour.

One could multiply these examples almost indefinitely, for Freud was surely one of the most metaphorical men that ever wrote. But there is more to the question than simple metaphors, and quite apart from the fascinating problems of the way Freud used the models he inherited from the nineteenth-century, the *metaphor as such* is Freud's profoundest paradigm. By metaphor in this sense I mean a category of the discourse as these categories have been developed by Roman Jakobson in linguistics, by Jacques Lacan in Freudian psychoanalysis, by Gregory Bateson in the application of communications theory to psychotherapy, and exactly as the principle of explanation in cybernetics corresponds to what Bateson calls "rigorous metaphor." I do not therefore mean "figure of speech," nor am I necessarily referring to the particular illustrative figures and analogies employed by Freud, but rather to metaphor as a label for what goes into the construction of a figure of speech—or into a psychological symptom, a slip of the tongue or pen, a dream, an ideology—that is to say, *metacommunication.* The metaphor becomes a paradigm for the relationship between the conscious and the unconscious discourse, for the relationship between the "phenomenon" (the symptom, the ideology) as a signifier in a discourse and what it signifies, because the metaphor involves a communication about a communication (a message about a message) or simply communication about communication, period. Roman Jakobson's distinction between the metaphoric (paradigmatic, selective) pole of the discourse and its metonymic (syntagmatic, substitutive) pole has a significant bearing on the polarity (and the coalescence) between condensation and displacement in Freud's epistemology of dreams, jokes, and paralogisms—the epistemology of the symptom.[9] In a word, it can be said, in complete faithfulness to both the neuro-physiological and the psychoanalytical Freud (and with almost equal faithfulness to Marx) that *a symptom (an ideology) is an overdetermined statement in a metalanguage about some relationship or other in an object language.* (If there is indeed one primary object language, the question arises as to whether the primary language is the erotic/aggressive relationship of self and Other bound by the lost object as in Freud, or the "language of real life," the "material communication *(Verkehr)* of men," as in Marx. Since the primary function in both these discourses is *goal-seeking exchange,* and since both are overdetermined, they are not necessarily exclusive. This problem is discussed from the point of view of general systems theory in the complete version of this paper.)

1. *The Concept of System*

To put it another way, in cybernetic terms, the symptom (the ideology) is a mapping or a transform of some other statement—and no aspect of behavior can in fact be excluded from the logical, information-processing model that cybernetics employs. *All behavior is communication.* That is to say, behavior involves the passage of messages bearing information along mediated and unmediated channels disturbed by "noise." Information in this sense is technically defined as "mapping between sets of structured variety," and the message may be heat, for instance, or an electrical impulse, or a word, a gesture, the flash of a knife. The channel similarly may be the air, light, sound, a wire, the imagination, society—depending upon the particular definition of the mode of communication being examined.

All behavior is communication, but not all communication is at the same level. Metacommunication occurs within many systems of communication, particularly (and most obviously)in language ("This message is in English"), but the *systemic* model I shall use must also insist that whatever the *scope* or *degree* of the complexity of communication within any one system, systems themselves can be distinguished by increasing *orders* of complexity. The scope of a system of communication may be viewed as increasing by a process of *aggregation,*

---

[9] See: R. Jakobson and M. Halle, *Fundamentals of Language* (The Hague: Mouton and Co., 1956); J. Lacan, *Ecrits,* especially pp. 493-528; and A. Wilden, *The Language of the Self,* pp. 238-49.

whereas the (evolutionary) passage from a lower-order to a higher-order system (from system to metasystem) may be viewed as occurring through *emergence,* in exactly the sense that the concept is used in Engels' *Dialectics of Nature.* And somewhere between the low order of systemic complexity or communication involved when two billiard balls strike each other and the very high order of complexity when men, nations, and ideas collide, we pass from the realm of *closed systems* to that of *open systems.* Somewhere along the line we pass from the inorganic to the organic, and, within the life sciences themselves, somewhere we pass from nature to culture, from biological "man" to man as a discursive (sociocultural) animal.

A closed system is one which does not interact or which is defined as not interacting with its environment. Any feedback relationships between variables are strictly internal (the feedback involved is called "pseudo-feedback" by some theorists), and the variables may indeed be isolated or varied one at a time in order to conduct experiments on the system. In quantum physics, for example, this amounts to the necessary limitation of all problems to two-body problems.

An open system, on the other hand, is in *essential* interaction with the super-system which is its environment (the two are not necessarily *distinct,* however), to which it is related by feedback. That is to say, the input received from the environment will be used to modify the output communicated to the environment and vice-versa. Feedback is in general either negative (deviation reducing) or positive (deviation amplifying).

All organisms are open systems of a higher or lower order. The open system may well involve the deterministic, reversible, linear causality (causal continuity) of chemistry or physics at some level or other, but the primary mode of causality in open systems involves non-linear, discontinuous, and irreversible sequences of transformation. The open system does not involve the transfer or the transformation of energy or matter as a primary principle; it is modelled more nearly on stimulus-response (requiring the *transfer of information* between sender and receiver) rather than on thermodynamics or mechanics. Insofar as the messages which occur depend on a stochastic or recursive process (the generation of possibly infinite sequences out of finite sets of elements), the non-linear causality of an open system can never be predictive in the classically determinist sense, but it is nevertheless possible, in theory at least, to discover a *grammar* or set of applicable morphological *rules,* just as we attempt to do for the particular open system we call language or as Marx and Engels set out to do for history. "Non-linear" is thus synonymous with "equifinality" or "multifinality" in biology and in general systems theory, whereby the same final state may be reached from different initial conditions and by different paths or the same initial conditions may produce different final states. Equifinality in the organism or in the system corresponds exactly to the *overdetermination* of the symptom in Freud.

The distinction between closed systems in general and a whole series of orders of open systems is crucial to any understanding of communication and exchange in the individual or in society. It is the lack of any such explicit distinction in either Marcuse or in Freud that makes the Freudian sociology and the Marcusean interpretation so disturbing. There is in Freud a constant contradiction between closed-system thinking and open-system thinking, on the one hand, and a characteristic confusion between various *orders of systemic complexity*, on the other. When Freud imposes his physical thermo-dynamics on the life of man, for instance, or when he fails to distinguish between the biological and the sociocultural individual, or when he implies that the mind is really no more than an anatomy of the brain, the charge of reductionism is apposite—to say nothing of the theoretical chaos which results. Fortunately, however, Freud makes none of these "errors" systematically. The pressure of psychic and social reality constantly makes itself felt, and the Freudian text never remains closed to new readings.

Let me make these distinctions as clear as possible. Since anything involving life or culture—organisms, nations, societies, traditions, *and the theories we construct*—invariably exist in a context of *selection* (not necessarily "natural selection," of course—but lack of space prevents me from including the discussion of Social Darwinism which follows this in the longer text), any such systems must necessarily be both goal-seeking (teleological) and adaptive (capable of learning or reacting at some level or other). Of all goal-seeking adaptive systems the sociocultural system is the most complex and the most adaptive. Unlike the inorganic world, which tends to inertia (entropy), and unlike the world of the individual organism, which tends to constancy (homeostasis), society is characterized by *emergent evolution* (negative entropy)—the constant tendency to higher and higher levels of organization—which implies a very high order of *morphogenesis:* the ability to elaborate and change structure (which is beyond any *individual* organism). These concepts, derived primarily from the application of general systems theory to psychology and sociology, are obviously essential to any contemporary understanding of Freud (or Marx)—because both are concerned above all with communication, exchange, and goals (not always explicitly of course) and because the Marxist dialectic is in fact a general theory of goal-seeking, adaptive, morphogenic systems. The consistent failure of many intelligent people to understand the nature of communication, and above all their inability to comprehend dialectic is, in its essence, a simple lack of information about the kinds of distinctions elaborated in this paragraph. And once we realize that Freud's energy models and the orthodox theory of the so-called instincts are primarily derived from theories of closed systems, once it becomes clear how much of his instinctual perspective is an attempt to impose a closed system upon an open one, we can begin finally to understand the impressiveness of Freud's own contradictions—for behind the energy model and behind the closed system, there lurks in Freud's very words the theory of an information-processing, metacommunicative, adaptive, open system. It is surely necessary only to understand that in Freud *Trieb* does not mean "instinct," it means "drive"—and that the theory of the drives is no more and no less than an attempt to elaborate a teleological view of man as driven by his past and drawn by his future. From the vantage point of general systems theory, such a "teleology of efficient causes" is indeed scientifically respectable. And within the "instinct" theory itself, it is very clear that we can view the "drives" as an over-determined metastatement *at the level of culture* about the "instincts" *at the level of nature,* in exactly the same way as we can view the psychological symptom as an overdetermined metastatement about the particular language of self and Other in which any man is involved.

Behind the introduction of the concepts of communication, meta-communication, and system lies the necessity of re-reading Marcuse and Freud in the terms of this methodological distinction between nature and culture employed by Claude Lévi-Strauss and the similar distinction between animal and human language made by Jacques Lacan, if only because this point of view provides a far more sophisticated analysis of the relationship between the instincts and man than is possible without it. For this we need the notions of system, regulation, goal, (hierarchical) order of complexity, degree of complexity, emergence, and metasystem, because we need to know *where* that methodological break may have been abridged if we are to understand the relationship between the instincts (necessity) and phantasy (possible freedom) in Freud. The importance of the notion of *regulation* goes without saying, and Marcuse rightly emphasizes it when he notes the change in the theory of the instincts which came about when Freud ceased defining them in terms of origin or organic function, but rather in terms of determining forces giving a direction *(Richtung)* to the life processes. "The notions *instinct, principle, regulation* are being assimilated" *(Eros,* p. 25). Here the underlying principle for Freud seems to be a movement from unity towards unity, since it appears impossible, says Freud, wavering in his determined dualism, to point to any drives other than the libidinal ones: *All "instinctual" impulses* (Triebregungen) *seem to be derivatives of Eros.* As will be clear later, this is very probably the case.

We agree with Aristotle and Heidegger that man is a creature and a creation of discourse, and if we assume a methodological discontinuity between human language and animal communication, this is not to deny the possibility of continuity, any more than we would deny that human desire and animal need are interrelated. But, as we shall see with Lacan's theory of unconscious desire, desire can be related to need through language and is thus phylogenetically and ontogenetically a problem of *emergence* (the quantum jump from one level of organization to a higher one), intimately related to the problem of the emergence of language itself and its relationship to phantasy.

2. *Emergence, Metacommunication, and Play*

Especially relevant here to the methodological use of the concept of metalanguage and object language is the theoretical background provided for it by Gregory Bateson, and particularly in his theory of play and phantasy (which, as we shall see, is immediately applicable to the Freudian analysis of phantasy and repetition).[10] Bateson is concerned with the fact that play and combat amongst animals are indistinguishable except that in play the tooth does not bite, and claw does not rend. Somehow it is communicated that this bite is not going to be what it is (a bite), but something identical-but-different (a playful nip). A message, "This is play," is communicated about the normal communication involved in "bite." "This is play" is a metacommunication: it is a message of a higher order of communication (and therefore of a higher order of sophistication or abstraction). What Bateson calls the *moodsign* "bite" has become what he calls

[10] "A Theory of Play and Phantasy," *Psychiatric Research Reports* (1955), 2: 39-51.

the *signal* "this is not a bite." (Others would prefer to call the mood-sign a signal and the signal a sign). We can say that moodsigns are related univocally to what they represent (as in the "wagging dance" of bees) and that no notions like truth-value can be assigned to them; they simply are, or are not. Signals (our signs) provide the possibility of ambiguity and deceit, however, and therefore the possibility of truth—which is itself a metacommunicative concept. Truth, we may say, is contextual, *intersubjective* (no other bee can repeat to another bee the first bee's dance, without first undergoing exactly the same experience that produced the dance in the first place), as Emile Benveniste, Lacan, and others have pointed out. But "This is play" does introduce something akin to human subjectivity (the message *has* to be perceived correctly and accepted or rejected by a receiver). Bateson therefore sees play as a significant possible stepping stone in the emergence of language and humanity:

> If we speculate about the evolution of communication, it is evident that a very important stage in this evolution occurs when the organism gradually ceases to respond quite "automatically" to the moodsigns of another and becomes able to recognize the sign as a signal: that is, to recognize that the other individual's and its own signals are only signals, which can be trusted, distrusted, falsified, denied, amplified, corrected, and so forth. . . . Not only the characteristically human invention of language can then follow, but also all the complexities of empathy, identification, projection, and so on (p. 40).

Threat, histrionics, and deceit are all observed in animals. Bluff, teasing play in response to threat, gambling, risk, spectatorship, self-pity, ritual, phantasy—in the world of human communication, these all involve metacommunication of the type of "This is play" (p. 42). But what is not observed in animals, as Lacan has pointed out, is the *pretence of deceit,* which is essentially human, a communication of a higher order than "This is play" ("This is/is not play"). (Cf. Freud on jokes, *Standard Edition,* VIII, 115).

It is clear that Freud cannot be properly read today without the methodological concept of object and metalanguage. I spent some time in the fuller version of this paper remarking on the status of models in Freud because I was seeking to provide some of them with a new language, and yet we know from the neurological models of

the *Project for a Scientific Psychology* (1895) that Freud has somehow preceded us. The paraphrasing *(Umschrift)*, the re-structuring
(Umordnung), the (new) registrations *(Niederschriften)*, and the
translation *(Uebersetzung)* of various *layers* of signs in Freud's neurological model is only another statement, in ontogenetic terms, of the
relationships between levels of language established by Carnap, Russell, Goedel and others in philosophy, which the communicationally
oriented therapists of the Bateson school have appropriated for their
own discipline.

As for the status of the theory itself, the concept of metalanguage
clearly avoids the gratuitous or implicit "reductionism" so often evident
in psychoanalytical and Marxist thinking. A metalanguage or commentary cannot in any respect be reduced to its object language or
text (any more than a metaphor is reducible), and it is not related
to it by the dubious notion of reflection *(Widerspiegelung)*. Moreover, and in a truly dialectical sense, the object language may in fact
be of a "higher" (more abstract) order than its supposed metalanguage. In literary criticism, for example, all great texts include all
possible commentaries—just as we see Freud's text including our
commentaries. In the wider relationship of language to experience,
furthermore, it is not possible to define in any absolute or analytical
fashion which is the metalanguage and which the object language,
except for more or less arbitrary methodological purposes. In other
words, the responsibility for *punctuation* is ours, and it is not inherent
in the "facts." In the specific instance of perception—if we assume
that the Gestaltists are correct in saying that we perceive relations
which we then codify into objects—we cannot decide on any final
priority of "realness" between the images of the viewing subject (the
transforms) and what is viewed (what we assume to be transformed).
"Objectivity" requires a touchstone, and the touchstone is always an
ideology or its conscious equivalent, a hypothesis.

3. *Nature and Culture*

Hopefully the necessity of the distinction between animal communication and human language has been made fairly clear. It should
also be obvious that the analog language of the primary process (which
knows no truth and never says no) is related to the (primarily) digital
language of the secondary process in exactly the same way as Bateson
would relate the "moodsign" (signal) to the metacommunicative

"signal" (the sign).[11] And since the primal phantasies are unconscious, they are in Freud's own system "thing-presentations" which
we know are meaningless (or too full of meaning) until they are
intentionalized or "bound" by the secondary system, where they appear
in *representative* forms, exactly as the "instincts" are "represented"
by that curious entity in Freud, the *Triebrepräsentanz*. The relationship of the primal phantasy to consciousness can only be the same as
that between the thing presentations (images) of the dream and the
word presentations of the dream text: the "regression through the *Ucs.*
to perception" in the dreamwork forces the thing presentations to
undergo condensation and displacement as if they were word presentations in language. The relationship, requiring intentionality (cathexis, *Besetzung*), is once again that between object and metalanguage.

This distinction between animal and human language, the passage
from the analog to the digital, from the primary process to the secondary process, is enormously significant. If we agree with Lévi-Strauss
that nature becomes culture at the emergence of the prohibition of
incest—the emergence of the positive injunction which makes the
nuclear "family" into society by saying "Give your sister your daughter
to another man outside your family," and provides for the kinship
system which results, through the fourth term of the originally tri-
partite family (often the mother's brother, the brother-in-law, the
maternal uncle)—then we must agree with him that language also
appeared "in one fell swoop," as he says, at that same magic moment,
simply because the prohibition of incest is a primal law which must
be *communicated*. This in addition to the rather obvious fact that in

---

[11] The distinction between the digital and the analog in communication rests on
the distinction between the analog computer, where quantities (of potential, for
example) are analogs of other quantities, and the digital computer, where the
representation depends on the articulation of binary oppositions which represent
a conventional mathematical code. Both means of representation could be said to
"reflect" something, but they are distinct in themselves in that the first operates
on a *continuous* (logarithmic) scale with no zero, whereas the second operates
discontinuously (digitally) and is unthinkable without zero. Moreover, the digital
computer depends upon the *position* of its symbols (syntax), whereas the analog
is richer semantically than it is syntactically. The distinction is valuable for
distinguishing between the primary and the secondary process. Negation *(Verneinung)* in the secondary process is analogous to zero in that (1) it is a function
of an infinite stochastic or recursive process like language or the series of integers,
(2) it involves a higher level of communication than what it denies (zero is not
on the same level as the other numbers), and (3) it always involves propositions
(order, place, syntax) or their equivalent (it is not a simple absence). From
another point of view, if we follow Frege, it is zero which generates the integers,
just as we may say that it is the metacommunicative possibility of negation (and
therefore of complex levels of deceit) which distinguishes human language from
the analog, finite, and univocal signals of animal communication. And we never
find a "No" coming from the unconscious, insists Freud.

order to know whom to marry and not to marry, you must be capable of naming, and naming, as Wittgenstein and others have remarked, is an abstract operation within language requiring the whole context of language before it can take place. Naming involves metalanguage, as Bateson points out in the article on play and phantasy:

> Denotative communication as it occurs at the human level is only possible *after* the evolution of a complex set of meta-linguistic (but not verbalized) rules which govern how words and sentences shall be related to objects and events (pp. 41-42).

If we now reconsider the instinct theory from the communications point of view, should there be any difficulty over that aspect of *Trieb* which seems clearly to be considered by Freud as instinctual (organic) in the traditional sense—such as the instinct for self-preservation *(Selbsterhaltungstrieb)*, the reproductive instinct, hunger and love— it is Lacan's distinction between need, desire, and demand and their metacommunicative relationship that will enable us to escape it. This simple lexical distinction alone allows us to comprehend Freud's difficulty in the following passage:

> The sexual drives are noticeable to us for their plasticity, their capacity for altering their aims, their replaceability . . . and their readiness for being deferred. . . . We should be glad to deny these characteristics to the self-preservative drives, and to say of them that they are inflexible, admit of no delay, are imperative in a very different sense and have a quite other relationship to repression and to anxiety. But a little reflection tells us that this exceptional position applies, not to all the ego-drives, but only to hunger and thirst, and is evidently based on a peculiar character of the sources of these drives. *(New Introductory Lectures* [1933], *Standard Edition,* XXII, 97).

It seems immediately clear that the lack of symmetry between the two types of drives lies simply in their absolute dissimilarity: the sexual drives—by their very plasticity and mutability—are unconscious *desires,* whereas hunger and thirst—by their instinctual rigidity—are *needs,* and thus do not belong in the category of psychic drives at all. Sexual needs are similarly immutable and non-psychic. This distinction is further confirmed by the difficulty Freud faced when he tried to assimilate the "aggressive" self preservative instincts, also called the ego-instincts, with the death drive, or Thanatos, in order to balance the assimilation of sexual needs (as well as desires) under the life drive, or Eros. He was forced to conclude that the ego instincts belonged with Eros as well—but he could as easily have been perturbed over the fact that sexual need (the reproductive instinct) is the manifestation of the *life of the species* over the *death of the individual:* whether in biology, where reproduction is often the end of the life-cycle of the individual, or in the wider sense of Hegel's aphorism that the birth of the child is the death of the parents.

If we consider *Trieb* as a psychic metastatement about the primary binary oppositions which went into the formulation of the "instincts" in Freud, and which lie behind the Freudian oppositions, life/death, inner/outer, union/destruction, introjection/expulsion, affirmation/negation, sadism/masochism, reproduction/decay, tension/inertia, potential/constancy, identification/projection, we can see how this human communicative code differs from, say, the genetic code of DNA. The code is relatively fixed, whereas the representative of the drive is mutable. We know that when Freud employs the term *Instinkt,* he uses it in the sense of an aspect of animal behavior which is fixed by heredity, characteristic of a species, and in general tied to a specific objective. He employs it without exception in speaking of animal instincts.[12] It is at this point that the distinction between *Instinkt* and *Trieb* becomes especially important, for, in the case so objectionably called the case of the "Wolf Man" (1918 [1914]), Freud uses the notion of what he calls "instinctive [*instinktiv*] animal knowledge" as an analogy to explain the existence of *primal (unconscious) phantasies* in human beings. He goes on:

> This instinctive [*instinktiv*] factor would then be the nucleus of the unconscious, a primitive kind of mental activity, which would later he dethroned and *overlaid* by human reason . . . but which in some people, perhaps in every one, would retain the power of drawing down to it [through the attraction of the "fixated" primal repression] the higher mental processes. Repression would be the return to this instinctive stage. . . . *(Standard Edition,* XVII, 120. Emphasis added.).

The significance of these remarks is that the notion of animal

[12] Lack of space prevents me from including the full discussion of what *Trieb* might possibly mean for Freud. There is a constant contradiction between passages which make the drives biological or truly instinctual (in which cases Freud tends to refer to the *Triebrepräsentanz* and not to *Trieb)* and passages which make them psychic. And in fact in one passage about the conservative nature of the drives, Freud uses the word *Instinkt* in one clause of a sentence (referring to animals) and the word *Trieb* in the next (referring to man), almost as if he had not noted the lexical change *(Standard Edition,* XXII, 106).

instinct is presented as analogy to the domain of phantasy, whereas the concept of *Trieb* is presented as an empirical construct. This is to further support the idea that whatever Freud says explicitly about the drives, they are always implicitly conceived as human rather than as animal. In following Freud on this point, it is not necessary for us to worry about the notion of inherited phantasies, since the work of Melanie Klein, Winnicott, and other English analysts has clearly demonstrated their ontogenetic origins in the universals of human experience. Nor is it necessary to become entangled in the mysticism of a Jungian collective unconscious which would seek to account for these archetypal phantasies, since as Freud had already said and as Lacan has repeatedly emphasized, the unconscious is collective anyhow.

Given Freud's contradictions, it is clear that Marcuse's use of the "orthodox" Freudian theory of the instincts puts him on very shaky ground, if only because the confusion in Freud between the animal and the human world is so great. It is also significant that in *Eros and Civilization* Marcuse seems to be unaware or unmindful of this confusion at the same time as he is seeking an escape from the Freudian thesis of the conservatism of the instincts: "the compulsion to restore an earlier state of things." This he himself confuses with the *recherche du temps perdu* — which is quite another matter, since this has to do with the articulation of unconscious *desire* in the metaphorical language of *demand*. This last distinction is crucial because, as we shall see, it will enable us to escape the implicit atomism in Freud's instinctual conception of the individual. By atomism, I mean that although Freud's thinking on the subject is typically subtle and complex, and although the Other is always there in some form or other (even in Freud's neuropsychology) neither Freud nor Marcuse ever really provide an acceptable way of passing from the instinctual level to the level of society — which is precisely the most significant of the problems to be explicated. In other words, there seems to be a clear confusion between the biological, skin-bound organism (called the individual), whose biological instincts are said to be "subjugated" by the reality principle and by the archaic heritage, and which supposedly evolves or is transformed into a social being through a *historical process* of agglomeration in the primal horde *(Eros,* pp. 11-14, 54-63, 120-126), and the actual status of the individual as a sociocultural subsystem *created* through *emergence* by a process of *organization* within a wider system. I recognize that I am forced to oversimplify Marcuse's careful argumentation at this point, but I think it important to point to what seems to me to be its essential weaknesses. It is true that Marcuse understands the necessity of an organizing principle (the primal father, p. 56), but he does not recognize the value of this myth as a statement not about reality or history (or even about evolution), but rather as a statement about the *symbolic* function of the father once the relation between parents and young has evolved to the point where a father can be a function (i.e. to the status of society with a primal law, the prohibition of incest). It is also true that he sometimes speaks, as Freud does, about the subjugation of the instincts and sometimes about a rather different process, their total transformation (pp. 11-12). But it is this very ambiguity which leaves an implication which is particularly difficult to accept: that individual men are the prerequisite of society rather than the other way around (as Marx would have it, for example). Moreover the notion that repression — and not simply surplus repression — is a historical process (pp. 118-126) shakes our faith in what we thought was history. History can be undone, evolution cannot. The morphogenic restructuring which produced society is simply not in itself a sociological process, but the way Marcuse seeks to make a distinction between the phylogenetic-biological level and the sociological level (p. 120) implies that it is, because he assumes precisely what has to be proved: that man (which he calls "the animal man") is possible outside the social conditions which seem to be, not simply his environment, but actually the very condition of his being. There *is* a passage from nature to culture, and it is culture — language, law, exchange, kinship, symbols — which creates man. This is of course a statement and not an explanation, but it seeks to respond to the *methodological* necessities revealed by Marx and Lévi-Strauss, and now by systems sociology, which require us to put into parentheses the question of the *actual* process of the evolution of society in order to be able to ask the right questions about its results. As a matter of fact Marcuse touches on the central point in this context: the *exogenous* nature of the sources of "instinctual transformation." I would simply push that statement to its limit and say what Marcuse seems to be trying to say: that whatever the biological instincts (needs) require of the biological individual, the human drives (desire) are the *new products of organization* as such, and at another level. They are *discontinuous* with what went before or below; the drives are social by their very nature. They come to us, not from ourselves, but from our relation to the Other; they are not the simple continuous transformation or repression or subjugation of something else in us or in our past. And this quantum jump, this emergence of a new level of organization, is in no sense historical; only surplus repression (the organization of some aspects of domination and some aspects of scarcity) can be so regarded. The biological instincts will always be with us in the history of man, whereas the drives can be transformed by new levels of organization in society.

It seems true that for the instinctual perspective, the other (a specific human being) as reciprocal subject is lacking. Such a perspective in effect tends to deny the desire for dealienated human relationships which informs Marcuse's work. There are others in the instinctual world as objects for "I," there are others who make "me" an object, but there is no other there in an intersubjective dialectic, in a reciprocal recognition, in any interaction which goes beyond sado-masochism. On the one hand we must be prepared to recognize that this may in fact be the case, just as on the other hand we need not necessarily dismiss the "interinstinctuality" which is what Marcuse is demanding of man, but we might well complain that the instinctual perspective is surely the most difficult basis upon which to build a truly persuasive case for the liberation of man. This is not to say that the other as reciprocal subject does not appear at another level for Marcuse. He does, he has to, as the subject of Marcuse's own desire. Thus, we can say that there is a contradiction in Marcuse similar to that in Freud: reciprocal intersubjectivitiy is brought in by the back door into an instinct theory that cannot contain intersubjectivity, which is the antithesis of reification or "interobjectivity." Marcuse chose to liberate us from a certain Freud from whom we had already, in some sense been liberated. We needed no saving from the conservatism of the instincts, we needed to be saved from *repetition* — which is not of the domain of instinct, but rather belongs to the human world of *Phantasie*.

V

> All that is not information, not
> pattern, not redundancy, is *noise* — the
> only possible source of new patterns.
> GREGORY BATESON

But before we approach the problem of *Phantasie* and its relationship to repetition, it is important to understand the defects of the energy model to which these concepts are eventually related in Freud's work — through the death instinct — and upon which Marcuse relies very heavily in his interpretation of Freud.

We know that the writing model in Freud, the *Vorstellung* model, the notions of translation, repression, primary/secondary system, the representative of the drive, and other Freudian notions require for their interpretation some sort of unifying conception of system and metasystem related by something equivalent to that which relates commentary (metalanguage) and text (object language) or simply by what is implicit in the notions of metaphor, mapping, and abstraction in language itself. Thus on the one hand we require emergence in development and on the other, metacommunication in the theory. But we have nevertheless yet to deal with the energy model itself, with the "economic" view of the psyche.

Let me begin with a quotation from Marcuse:

Now the (more or less sublimated) transformation of destructive into socially useful aggressive (and thereby constructive) energy is, according to Freud (on whose instinct theory I base my interpretation) a normal and indispensable process. It is part of the same dynamic by which libido, erotic energy, is sublimated and made socially useful; the two opposite impulses are forced together and, united in this twofold transformation, they become the mental and organic vehicles of civilization. But no matter how close and effective the union, their respective quality remains unchanged and contrary: aggression activates destruction which "aims" at death, while libido seeks the preservation, protection, and amelioration of life. Therefore it is only as long as destruction works in the service of Eros that it serves civilization and the individual; if aggression becomes stronger than its erotic counterpart, the trend is reversed. Moreover, in the Freudian conception, destructive energy cannot become stronger without reducing erotic energy: the balance between the two primary impulses is a quantitative one; the instinctual dynamic is mechanistic, distributing an available quantum of energy between the two antagonists.[13]

In the last sentence of this quotation, Marcuse restates his acceptance of that aspect of Freud's quantitative energy model which involves the first law of thermodynamics, the conservation of energy. This model also involves a principle of constancy, a principle of

[13] "Aggressiveness in Advanced Industrial Society," in: *Negations* (Boston: Beacon Press, 1968), pp. 257-258.

inertia (the Nirvana principle), and a relationship between "free" and "bound" energy (related to the "binding" force of Eros); it is also a homeostatic-equilibrium model which is both organismic and mechanical. The sources of this model are especially significant in the sociological Freud, where Freud extrapolates on the "instincts" discovered in the individual (system) so as to extend their effect to the aggregation of the instincts in the societal or species-specific system. Here (notably in *Beyond the Pleasure Principle*) the apparently normative equilibrium of the *fusion* of Eros and Thanatos in the individual is converted into a degenerative model of the life of the species where the conservatism of the "instincts" — principally the death instinct — the omniscience of the Nirvana principle, and "the compulsion to restore an earlier state of things," appears on the one hand as entropy (loss of gradient, of organization) and, contradictorily, on the other, as repetition (steady state). Eros binds (organizes) and Thanatos destroys (disorganizes), both in *time,* but somehow in Freud's mind the retrogressive, temporal nature of actual return to a past (inorganic) state — the expression of a return to inertia or zero — is seen as synonymous with the synchronic constancy of repetition, or in other words, with the attempted refusal of time and diachrony in the phantastic compulsion to repeat met with in analysis and in the play of children.[14] The question of time is significant, for only in an open system can time, like truth, be an essential category.

The notion of a restricted "available quantum of energy" for the drives is one of Freud's earliest methodological assumptions, taken more or less directly from G. T. Fechner's "stability principle." (Fechner was concerned, amongst other things, to introduce the recently stated first law of thermodynamics into the theory of organisms). Freud quotes from one of Fechner's works (1873) in *Beyond the Pleasure Principle* (*Standard Edition,* XVIII, 8), in which Fechner relates pleasure and unpleasure to psychophysical stability and instability. Beyond a certain limit, pleasure is said to be proportional to the approximation of stability, and unpleasure similarly, to deviation from stability. This is essentially a mechanical equilibrium model, with pleasure (stability) as the norm, equivalent to the stable equilibrium of a ball in a cup. From this Freud goes on to enunciate the combined principle of constancy and inertia originally adumbrated

---

[14] See: Ernest Jones, *The Life and Work of Sigmund Freud* (London: The Hogarth Press, 1954-8), II, 291-292, and my "Death, Desire, and Repetition in Svevo's Zeno," *Modern Language Notes,* Vol. 84, No. 1 (January, 1969), 98-119.

in the *Project* of 1895: "the mental apparatus endeavours to keep the quality of [free] excitation present in it as low as possible [inertia] or at least to keep it constant [constancy]" (p. 9).

In the neurological model of 1895, however, inertia and constancy are distinguished more clearly. Inertia is posited as the *primary* principle — the principle of keeping the neuronic network free from *external stimulus* through motor discharge. But *endogenous stimuli*, that is to say the later "instincts" (here; "the major needs: hunger, respiration, sexuality"), cause a break in the principle of inertia. Motor discharge (for example, flight from external stimuli) cannot take place in response to *internal* needs, and a "specific action" is called for (e.g. eating) (*Standard Edition*, I, 296-7).

With the help of the articles on the three Freudian principles in Leclaire and Pontalis' invaluable *Vocabulaire de La Psychanalyse*,[15] we can see that in the *Project* of 1895 the principle of inertia regulates the *free* energy of the *primary* process, whose task it is through reflex or other action to keep itself free from external stimulus. The reactions of the primary process give rise to a *secondary* process ("imposed by the exigencies of life") which discovers certain other paths of discharge to be necessary. The primary process and its free energy thus corresponds to the pleasure principle, which is regulated by *inertia*, or reduction of tension to zero, whereas the secondary process, whose energy is "bound" *(gebundene)*, corresponds to the reality principle, which is regulated by *constancy*, or by the maintenance of enough tension (unpleasure) to deal with the exigencies of life.[16]

Freud's free and bound energy are exactly the opposite of the free and bound energy of thermodynamics. The bound energy of the *Ich* represents a higher level of organization (gradient) than the free energy of the primary process, whereas in thermodynamics, bound energy is equivalent to disorder, degradation, and disorganization; it is entropic energy from which no further work can be obtained. Freud's energy is not, however, the same kind of energy; it is rather the metaphor of *energeia* on which the energy of physics was origin-

[15] Paris: Presses Universitaires de France, 1967. Both authors are former students of Lacan.
[16] Note that although these exigencies are viewed here as the *internal* demands of the organism (e.g. hunger), they automatically involve its essential and open relation to its environment—and that in the child they are responsible for his domination by the Other. (Freud points this out even in his most "atomistic" writings, his neurophysiology).

ally modelled. His organismic energy begins in the *Project* as a "nervous" energy, metaphorically akin to electricity, and eventually becomes "psychic" energy in the later works, where it can generally be equated with "instinctual energy." It is important to note that the energy of the *Project* seems to be equivalent to the much later so-called "neutral" *(indifferent)* energy suggested by Freud, which can attach itself to either primary "instinct" *(Standard Edition,* XIV, 78 and XLX, 44. See the editor's remarks on Q, *Standard Edition,* I, 395).

These notions are crucial for the theory of the death instinct in *Beyond the Pleasure Principle* (1920), upon which Marcuse bases his critique of the instinct theory and his own modifications of it. Freud was driven by the realization that there are many instances of pleasurable tension to modify his earlier correlation, derived from Fechner, between the principle of inertia/constancy and the pleasure principle. We have already seen that the pleasure principle of 1895 is closer to mechanistic inertia than to organismic constancy, so that it is not surprising to find it equated with the Nirvana principle in *Beyond the Pleasure Principle* and in "Economic Problem of Masochism" (1924) — although he calls it there the principle of constancy — both principles being "in the service of the death instinct, whose aim is to conduct the restlessness of life into the stability [here meaning "inertia"] of the inorganic state." Freud then goes on in this article to characterize the pleasure principle as involving some sort of *qualitative* characteristics, which, he feels, may be related to "the rhythm, the temporal sequence of changes, rises and falls in the quantity of stimulus" — that is to say, in spite of the word "temporal," to something like *repetition.* Since repetition was the central empirical fact that led him to go "beyond the pleasure principle," and since he goes on to say that the Nirvana principle is modified into the pleasure principle *because* it belongs to the death instinct, it becomes impossible for us to see any difference whatsoever between the two principles and the death instinct: all represent an inertial equilibrium model in mechanics or an entropic equilibrium model in thermodynamics. It is clear that there is nothing in fact beyond the pleasure principle — except the libido, Eros, which "tames" the death instinct *(Standard Edition* XIX, 159-60, 164). But Eros was defined by Freud as the "restlessness of life" — or in other words as gradient, tension — as a type of *negative entropy* which is impossible in the type of closed system he is building (Eros does not "run down," it must, by the very definition of love and aggressivity in man remain in the battle to the very end.).

It is the *Project* once again which comes to our aid in trying to make sense of all this, for the distinction between free, primary-system energy and bound, secondary-system energy, as Laplanche and Pontalis point out, offers the possibility of a more subtle interpretation. If we recall Freud's discovery of displacement in hysteria, which involves the conversion of *statements* or *presentations (Vorstellungen)* into somatic symptoms because of the necessity of disposing of "excess" excitations through "associative thinking" or motor action, if we recall his view of the "casually associated" signs of the unconscious inscription (which we may interpret, in distinction from the "associations of simultaneity" of the perceptual system, as a relationship of contiguity), his suggestions that (secondary system) cathexis or intentionality *(Besetzung)* may be equivalent to signification *(Bedeutung)*, and his recognition that the dream (primary system) must become a dream-text (secondary system, translation) before it can be interpreted, we may suspect that the idea of *bound energy* is tied to *meaning*, and that of *free energy to meaning which has not yet been somehow "stabilized" or anchored within the system of relationships, the context, which makes meaning possible.* It has already been suggested that meaning, truth, and negation, all of which are synonymous here, are necessarily related to the transformation of analog signs or moodsigns into signifiers through metacommunication. (For Bateson, the moodsign is first *there* — the bite — then *simulated* — the nip — then *recognized* — "This is play.") Time also is purely human, and Alexandre Kojève, for one, has simply equated time with discourse (or rather suggested that Hegel did, in opposition to Kant). To put it another way, if we view the "free" primary system as an analog language, we know that meaning, truth, and negation cannot be attributed to the analog in itself (however pregnant with meaning it may be), but that it requires intentionalization in a context to be meaningful, time, truth, and negation being the "binding" properties of the essentially digital secondary system. Freud always insisted that there was no time, no negation, no meaning in the unconscious: in one of his several "points of view," the unconscious consists simply of unintentionalized (uncathected) object presentations — which for him explained why the schizophrenic, who speaks the language of the unconscious, "uses words like things." But this is the same as saying that the schizophrenic cannot distinguish the word from the thing, the signifier from what it signifies, the metaphoric from the literal, that, as Bateson has said, he has lost the power of metalanguage — which returns us to our starting point. These considerations would seem to give substance to the following statements by Laplanche and Pontalis under "Principe de Constance":

> In effect, what Freud makes the principle of inertia regulate is a type of process whose existence the very recent discovery of the unconscious had caused him to postulate: the primary process. This is described in the *Project* by a number of privileged examples, such as the dream and the formation of the symptom [whose formation is essentially identical, involving displacement and condensation], in particular their occurrence in the schizophrenic. The primary process is essentially characterized by an unimpeded flow, an "easy displacement" [*Origins*, p. 404]. At the level of psychological analysis it was realized that one presentation could come to be completely substituted for another, could come to take from it all its properties and its effects: "But the hysteric who is reduced to tears by [the symbol] A is unaware that this is because of the association A-B, and B itself plays no part whatever in his mental life. In this case [like that of the soldier who dies for a flag] the symbol has been completely substituted for the *"thing."* [Or as Bateson would say of the schizophrenic, it has become a *metaphor which is meant*]. The phenomenon of a total displacement of signification from one presentation to another and the clinical proof of the intensity and the efficacity presented by substitutive presentations, very naturally find their expression for Freud in the economic formulation of the principle of inertia. *The free circulation of meaning and the total flow of psychic energy to the point of complete evacuation* [inertia] *are synonyms for Freud.* The unconscious processes . . ., in the final analysis, suppose an indefinite flow or transposition of significations, or, in energy language, a totally free flow of the quantity of excitation. The secondary process, as it is defined in the conscious-preconscious system . . . supposes a binding [*Bindung*] of energy, this binding being regulated by a certain "form" [i.e. Gestalt] which tends to maintain and re-establish its boundaries and its energy level: the *Ich*. (Emphasis added).

(Laplanche and Pontalis feel that the Freudian ego can only be clearly interpreted as a Gestalt built upon the model of the organism, "or, if you wish, as a realized metaphor of the organism" — and the ego is of course precisely this type of open system for Freud, because the easy analogy with an organism allowed him to gloss over — by the vague notion of "growth" — those troublesome elements of his mechanistic views which, because they were derived from a closed system, could not handle "life." On the question of "binding," see also *Standard Edition* V, 598, 599).

This "semantic" interpretation allows us to better comprehend the usefulness of the terms analog and digital as they are applied to the primary and the secondary processes and leads us a step further in understanding the social process. The schizophrenic's speech, the "language of the unconscious," seems often to be at the mercy of "unbound," uncontrollable, "meaningless," binary oppositions, as Lacan and his students have pointed out. If the advanced schizophrenic employs words like "good" and "bad," for example, there may be no *logic* to their use beyond the logic of opposition in itself. One should not therefore confuse "digital" with "binary," for although the digital computer employs binary digits, its mathematical code could have a base other than two and, more important, these "bits" can simulate what the primary process cannot: the distinction between "some" and "all," for instance. It is the logic and the syntax which is lacking in the primary process, and precisely because the binary oppositions there are "unbound" or devoid of metacommunication or truth. They simply *are* or *are not* (all or nothing) — they cannot be negated, because negation *(Aufhenbung)* requires syntax. In this context one would reiterate that the intellectual negation *(Verneinung)* which is used by the patient to "suppress and conserve" the return of the repressed is applied by Freud only to neurosis, whereas for psychosis the terms are "rejection" or "disavowal." Lacan has interpreted rejection *(Verwerfung)* as a foreclusion of the "Symbolic order," with a resulting loss of "anchoring in reality" for the psychotic — to whom "the Symbolic is the Real." This notion of an essential symbolic anchoring of the concrete discourse has a special significance in the theory of exchange. What anchors the phallus as the object of exchange between partners and between generations in psychoanalytical theory is the "rejection" of the father (as a *function* which may well be divorced from that of the biological or actual father) from the system, his *symbolic* status as a privileged reference point (the one to whom the phallus is offered and from whom it is received: by definition then, the one in the system who valorizes and evaluates the exchanges of the others). Similarly, in kinship systems, the maternal uncle is often the point of reference for the exchange of women in the matrimonial dialogue (both he and the phallus are to be conceived of as "fourth terms" in what would be a purely triangular and endogenous relationship without them). And, of course, in the Marxian theory of exchange value, gold is the anchor without which the exchange of commodities would be a tautologous, circular, and theoretically infinite process in which a bushel of wheat would eventually turn out to be the equivalent of a bushel of wheat.[17] These remarks are all metastatements about the privileged concept which underlies the thinking in this essay: the primacy, in "the language of real life," of exchange or communication between men. Language itself, as Marx and Engels point out in *The German Ideology* (London: Lawrence and Wishart, 1965), is subordinate to this necessity:

> The production of concepts, presentations *[Vorstellungen]*, and consciousness is at first directly contextual with the material activity and the material communication *[Verkehr]* of men, the language of real life. Presentation and thought, the mental communication of men, still appear at this stage as the direct emergence *[Aufschluss]* of their material behavior. . . .
>
> Language is as old as consciousness, language *is* practical consciousness that exists also for other men, and for that reason alone it really exists for me personally as well; language, like consciousness, only arises from the need *[Bedurfnis]*, the necessity of communication with other men (p. 37, pp. 41-42. Translation modified).

Communication is clearly more primordial in society and in human relationships than language, the law of incest, the Oedipus complex, or the division of labor, for whether it is symbols, signs, women, or commodities that are involved, the law of exchange and the mediation of the Other holds for all. And it is in some sense this primacy that the schizophrenic is above all trying to reject by means of his totally analog language where meaning flows in all directions at once. The final response to the double binds of a pathological communicational context is the decision to become "unbound" from the process, the impossible schizophrenic attempt to cease communicating altogether, for even silence speaks. And yet this very act is in a very special sense

[17] See: J.-J. Goux, "Numismatiques (I)," *Tel Quel*, No. 35 (Fall, 1968), pp. 64-89.

the "security operation" which is itself a part of the cure. It is in effect an effort to communicate at another level, and it is through his entirely personal language that the schizophrenic paradoxically becomes the privileged point himself. In another context, of course, this process describes the situation of the culture critic, Marcuse, for example, since the Great Refusal is in effect a privileged return to the level of all or nothing.

VI

> Does not everything depend on our
> interpretation of the silence around
> us?
>
> LAWRENCE DURRELL

It can at once be seen that from the moment we view Freud's "energy" as "free" and "bound" *signification*, from the moment we are concerned with *signs* or *presentations*, it is possible to move towards an information or communications model from the text of Freud. For as Bateson made abundantly clear in *Communication: The Social Matrix of Psychiatry* (1951), the simplistic energy model is a disastrous one. One of the difficulties of course, was that there was no acceptable or operational definition of teleology that Freud could employ, whereas now cybernetics has defined for us the complex, adaptive, goal-seeking system which makes a teleology springing from efficient causes scientifically valid. For Freud the concept of psychic energy and drive was the only available answer — and *Trieb* the best available *word* — with which to make "motivation" scientific. But the Freudian notion of psychic energy as an indestructible substance, as necessarily transformed (not created, destroyed, or suppressed), and as limited in quantity is extremely difficult to maintain in the face of information theory. Information is not a substance, nor can it be "located" anywhere (although particular "bits" can be stored in repeating circuits). Negentropy, or order, or pattern, or improbability, or information, or redundancy (all these terms are operationally synonymous here) can be and is continually created and destroyed — either by purposive entities in the struggle, not for life, but for pattern or structure, or by "random" intrusive events (noise). But, for Freud, energy is independent in quantity and type from the purposes or state of mind of any organism — there is just so much available regardless of our desires or of our intake of information. Negentropy or information, on the other hand, if still a quantity, is nevertheless dependent upon the purposive entity which emits or ingests it. "Entropy is a statement of a relationship between a purposive entity and some set of objects or events" (pp. 248-250).

The critique of psychic energy has become considerably more sophisticated since 1951. Not that we can do without some concept of energy in a theory of open systems, but that the energy is subordinate to the "information" it carries, as Buckley remarks in his *Sociology and Modern Systems Theory*:

> Though "information" is dependent upon some physical base or energy flow, the energy component is entirely subordinate to the particular form or structure of variations that the physical base or flow may manifest . . . This structured variation — the marks of writing, the sounds of speech, the molecular arrangement of the genetic code DNA, etc. — is still only raw material or energy unless it "corresponds" to, or matches in some important way, the structure of variations of other components [i.e. "receivers"] to which it may thereby become dynamically related. A person speaking a language foreign to a companion is emitting only noise or vibrating energy as far as the latter is concerned, because there is no mapping of the structured variety of the vocal energy with the repertoire of meaningful sounds structured in the mind of the companion . . .
>
> Thus information is not a substance or concrete entity but rather a *relationship* between sets or ensembles of structured variety . . . (p. 47).

Buckley points out, as W. Ross Ashby has done, that this relationship of energy to information involves a much more complex view of relationships in general, since the minute amount of energy required for a sender to communicate the message "Look out!" may be capable of "triggering" a relatively enormous energy response in the receiver, just as the perception of an impending blow may do within the receiver's information processing system itself. The significance of this shift in emphasis is correlative to the understanding of the difference between lower-level and higher-level behavioral systems: higher-level systems have a vast potential of energy, internal or external, which may be triggered by information flow, without the necessity for the spatial or temporal *proximity* required in lower-level systems. (Which is precisely Bateson's point in distinguishing moodsign from signal). From what has already been said, we can at once see the relationship between this view of energy and information and Freud's undifferentiated *(indifferent)* energy. Moreover, the problems in the Freudian texts over the *Triebrepräsentanz*, the "representative of the drive," with its component *Vorstellung* and its component *Affektbetrag* (quota of affect), become more easily comprehensible if we view the *Vorstellung* in repression as the information born by the representative and the quota of affect as what may be "triggered" in various ways by it. What is important, also, is that from a systems perspective there is no *essential* difference between this type of internal triggering of energy and a man kicking a dog or a nation waging war —the differences lie only in the realm of higher or lower *orders* of structure and organization.

This viewpoint disposes of the nagging and possibly illogical suspicion that in the energy model the restricted available quantum of aggressive energy in the individual should somehow be viewed as related one-to-one to the actual amount of destruction he causes—or that the actual behavior of "ordnance delivery systems (closed, of course) in and over Vietnam is somehow directly related to the accumulated daily tonnage of aggression available in the White House, or in the Pentagon, or in American imperialism. . . .

More significant at this point is the semantics of the information model elaborated by D. M. Mackay, for we realize that it is *not the energy, but the information which organizes the work to be done* in matching the system's or the organism's relation to its environment (whether accurately or not). A truism perhaps—except that the energy model ignores it—for it is not the explosion but the direction of the explosion that counts. And the available energy in our present social system is organized and reorganized every day in response to the inauthentic information being communicated by the system to its subsystems in the interests of control (the enemy without, the enemy within, divide and rule. . . .). No "conspiracy theory" from either right or left is needed to explain what actually happens in a social system (which is both a system and an environment) in which certain groups control the flow of information (for it is not freedom of speech but *freedom of communication* which the radical seeks). The goal of any adaptive system is invariably control over its own deviations through the application of negative feedback, which in certain conditions of tension or contradiction may result in a dangerous kind of oscillation or "hunting" (between "freedom"—which may be a subtle mechanism of control—and "repression"—which may increase the deviations). When the oscillations become too great for the present structure of the systems, positive feedback takes over, and morpho-genesis—revolution—is the only viable response to the system's internal contradictions.

To return to the distinction between lower-order open systems which depend on proximity for communication, and the higher-order systems which overcome space and time through the use of symbols, we can conclude with Walter Buckley that "information" does in every real sense "represent" structure or organization, and thus can preserve it, transmit it over space and time, and change it. This representability is a function of the system's order of complexity:

> The evolution of levels leading up to the socio-cultural system shows greater and greater dependence on independent, arbitrary, or symbolic communication linkage of components and less and less on substantive and energy linkages, until at the sociocultural level the system is linked almost entirely by conventionalized information exchange, with *process* overshadowing any rigid substantial structure such as is found at organismic levels (p. 50).

And since the environment is *essential* to an open system (part of its "essence," as the Other is for man), the "intrusion" of the environment does not lead to dissolution, loss of organization, or simply to another level of equilibrium as it does for the typical natural or the closed system, but rather to a restructuring or an elaboration of structure, at a higher level. The reason is that environmental interchange is not a *random* or *unstructured* event, or does not long remain so (remain as "noise," that is), because of the mapping, or coding, or information processing capabilities of the open system—its adaptive-ness (pp. 50-51)—for the system is negentropic, tends to increase in gradient and order. Buckley goes on to speak of the necessary *tension* in open systems ("the inherent instability of protoplasm"—of which Freud speaks—"tension or stress in animals, and psychic energy or motive power in men")—and it is not for nothing that we immediately think of Freud's equation of *Trieb* with *Tendenz*, or of his definition of the pleasure/unpleasure principle in terms of release from tension. We can see at once that whatever the case may be for that lower-order relatively open system, *biological man*, for the higher-order open system, *sociocultural man*, release from tension (i.e. pleasure) is a myth. We know that it was *pleasurable tension* that caused Freud to seek to go beyond the pleasure principle—the tension of sexual *desire*, that is to say, *anticipation, projecting towards the future and towards the Other*—and we can now see why *Beyond the Pleasure Principle* is so full of internal contradictions. Equilibrium (constancy) and inertia, besides contradicting each other and besides being characteristic of closed systems, correspond to the fundamental error of the Freudian model, taken from Fechner, that tension is *deviant* or an environmental intrusion, *whereas in fact tension is one of the products of organization itself*. This is why the principle of Eros remains substantially correct: it is the principle of organization, the tension-producing force, the gradient-retaining input, the "exigencies of life," the "restlessness" of life, the "information" or negative entropy upon which life feeds. There is no "psychical inertia" in the higher-order system we call the psyche, no death instinct corresponding to the aggressivity produced by Eros in its command for viability by suitable feedback responses. Freud was correct in wavering over the possibility that, as Marcuse emphasizes, there may be no drives other than the libidinal (negentropic) ones, for it is clear that aggressivity is a derivative of the particular state of organization (the social order) of the system. And the system can be restructured. Natural death is not part of the *psychic* system as Freud would have it, it is an environmental intrusion from the lower-order biological system, for which no further possibility of restructuring exists. And if *sociocultural* systems can be said to die, it is by accident, not by any internal or external necessity.

VII

> Order—peaceful coexistence under
> conditions of scarcity—is one of the
> very first of the functional imperatives
> of *social systems*.
> TALCOTT PARSONS (1951)

The Problem of Phantasie

Marcuse seeks in *Eros and Civilization* to discover through *Phantasie* the hidden principle of liberation in Freud. But it is only Freud's characteristically ambiguous use of this term which in fact allows the sort of straightforward progressive interpretation which Marcuse provides. In reading the passage from Freud quoted below, one is immediately struck by the fact that Marcuse seizes on the notion of *daydreaming (das Phantasieren)* or fantasy without paying any attention at all to the problem veiled in the words which follow, "the game of children":

... Freud singles out phantasy as one mental activity that retains a high degree of freedom from the reality principle even in the sphere of the developed consciousness. We recall his description in the "Two Principles of Mental Functioning" [1911].

"With the introduction of the reality principle one mode of thought-activity was split off: it was kept free from reality-testing and remained subordinated to the pleasure principle alone. This is the act of phantasy-making *(das Phantasieren)*, which begins already with the game of children, and later, continued as *daydreaming*, abandons its dependence on real objects." *(Eros*, p. 126)

The point is that it was from the *repetitious* play of a child at the level of a primal phantasy *(Urphantasie)* that Freud set out to derive the death instinct. The fact that Freud's derivation depended in any case upon a faulty, closed-system, entropic model is not so important as the fact with which he began: the child's effort to master at the level of a repetitive phantasy the most crucial of all discoveries, the discovery of difference (in *Beyond the Pleasure Principle).*

What is more, Freud explicitly says that phantasy-making is subordinated to the pleasure principle, and, whatever its unfortunate name implies, *the pleasure principle as such is death*. It is not pleasure (inertia, Thanatos) with which we must be concerned, but rather the other side of the pleasure principle, *unpleasure* (tension, organization, Eros). In other words, if we follow Freud's own logic and assumptions, fantasy, phantasy-making, and daydreaming are controlled by the retrogressive timelessness, the entropic inertia, the *utopian attractiveness of zero,* whereas if we apply the systems model, we can, I believe, integrate the primal phantasy (as a moodsign), the infantile phantasy (as a first step in substitution or metacommunication), and fantasy (as a liberating dream) into a coherent, progressive, and dialectical view both of our diachronic development and our synchronic states.

The key point in such an integrated view, which I can do no more than outline here, is the significance of the *coding* of the information involved. It is in fact the question of coding the primal relationship of *presence* and *absence* which opens *Beyond the Pleasure Principle.* However, there is yet an important distinction to be made within the concept of "goal seeking," which, in emphasizing Freud's "undifferentiated" energy and the notion of principle or regulation, I have tried to correlate with the modular imperative of the word *Trieb* in Freud.

In an article on "The Nature of Instinct and the Physical Bases of Libido"[18] Robert L. Marcus points out that while directiveness and goal are an inherent aspect of the instinctual concept, a specific goal for any instinct is difficult to define—thus restating in effect the problem Freud faced by dropping the untenable notion of the "specific action" corresponding to an instinct (as this notion appears in the *Project*, for example) and substituting for it the concept of the "mobility of the libido" (p. 145). The point is to distinguish between "a process with a goal, a direction, or purpose" and a process "manifesting a need for a goal, directiveness, or purposefulness." Since goal-seeking is characteristic of any closed-loop or feedback-type central system (e.g. the thermostat), it seems clear that it is not the manifestation of goals or purposes which is specific to higher-order systems such as man, but rather the *"need for purposefulness" itself*.

This "need for purposefulness" is surely no less than the specifically human "Desire of the Other." (Interestingly enough, this Hegelian-Kojèvian-Lacanian-Girardian notion is given its operational definition as "Newcomb's A-B-X system" on pp. 113-116 of Buckley's *Sociology.)* With this we are back to the vaguely defined force or tension behind the human world of communication and exchange. I have defined *Eros,* in apparently complete opposition to Freud, as the "great organizing force of life" (i.e. as negentropy, whereas for Freud this organizing force was entropy). At once we begin to see the fatal contradiction within the concept of Eros itself. As that which maintains and generates structure and process by seeking relationships between men, Eros is an affirmative, gradient producing, differentiating principle. But as that which seeks the *identification* of self with other, under the commands of the Other, as that which Norman O. Brown sees as the great unifying principle, being-one-with-the-world uniting the notions of narcissism and object choice),[19] Eros is the principle of the *negation* of difference, the reduction of gradient; it is entropic in itself. This fundamental contradiction is, as we know from Hume, intimately connected with the contradiction in the notion of identity. Identity is on the one hand the principle of individuality, of not being other, and on the other hand the principle of modelling, of being identical to an other, of achieving an identity through a looking-glass relationship to another (Hegel, Marx, C. H. Cooley), through taking on the role of the other (G. H. Mead), through the

---

[18] "Part II: The Instinct Machine," *General Systems Yearbook* (1962), VII: 143-156.

[19] *Life Against Death* (New York: Vintage Books, 1959), p. 42. Cf. the early Hegel on love: "In love life finds itself, as a duplication of itself, and as its unity," which is, of course, simply an aphoristic statement of Freud's own theory of love.

stade du miroir (Lacan).[20] Eros *is* the desire of the Other; it is a double bind.

(The desire of the Other, in one of its senses, would be termed a "goal-gap ratio" by operationally-minded general systems theorists, and it is this goal-gap ratio which is described by G. G. Lamb as "the intensive factor or driving force in information energy" or the "amount of motivation felt by the goal-seeking animate systems."[21] This is merely jargon for the notion of *lack* or *absence* to be found in Sartre[22] or Lacan (or Freud), in other words a word for *desire* in the widest sense.)

Absence means difference, and with difference comes phantasy and the Other. Freud begins *Beyond the Pleasure Principle (Standard Edition,* XVIII, 14ff.) with a description of the play of his grandson, who would alternately throw away and draw back a toy on a string, uttering an "o-o-o" and a "da" as he did so. Freud interpreted these phonemes as representing the Germans word *Fort!* ("gone") and *Da!* ("here"). He describes this apparently unpleasurable compulsion to repeat as evidence of the child's learning to master his environment actively through speech, for the active repetition seemed clearly to replace the passivity of a situation where the child's mother was (inexplicably for him) alternately present and absent. The throwing away was eventually coupled with a "Go to the front" obviously addressed to his father (the mediator of his desire for his mother) who

[20] Compare the Renaissance theory of sympathy and antipathy in Porta's *Magie naturelle,* summarized by Michel Foucault in *Les Mots et les Choses* (Paris: Gallimard, 1966), pp. 39-40:

Sympathy is an instance of the *Same* so strong and pressing that it does not rest content with being one of the forms of the similar; it has the dangerous power of assimilation, of making things identical to each other, of mixing them together, of making them disappear in their individuality—thus sympathy has the power of making them alien to what they were. Sympathy transforms. It alters, but in the direction of the identical, in such a way that if its power were not counter-balanced, the world would be reduced to a point, to a homogeneous mass, to the mournful figure of the Same. All its parts would hold together and communicate with each other without rupture or distance, exactly like chains of metal pieces suspended by sympathy through the attraction of a single magnet.

Sympathy is counterbalanced by antipathy, which is why the world remains what it is, related internally by similitude (resemblance), *convenientia,* and analogy.

[21] "Engineering Concepts and the Behavioral Sciences," *General Systems Yearbook* (1968), XIII: 165-169.

[22] "For the *pour-soi* is described ontologically as *manque d'etre,* and the possible belongs to the *pour-soi* as what is lacking to it." "Liberty is the concrete mode of being of the lack of being. . . . Man is fundamentally desire of being . . . [since] desire is a lack. . . ." "And the being lacking to the *pour-soi* is the *en-soi (L'Etre et le Néant,* Paris: Gallimard, 1943, p. 652). See also Kojève's *Introduction à la lecture de Hegel* (Paris: Gallimard, 1947), Chapter 1.

was away fighting in World War I,[23] and it is clear that the opposition between presence and absence was the essential feature of the game, for by a mirror the child soon learned to make himself disappear in conjunction with the appropriate phoneme.

Much has been made of the binary phonemic opposition in phonology—stemming in part from Ferdinand de Saussure's notion of the "differential element"—since the discoveries of Roman Jakobson and Troubetzkoy in the thirties, and Jakobson (to whom Jacques Lacan is indebted for his theory of metaphor and metonymy) cites the work of Henri Wallon on the thought of the child to support his thesis concerning the primacy of the binominal "element":

> In reality, thought only exists insofar as it introduces structures into things—very elementary structures at first. What can be ascertained at the very beginning is the existence of coupled elements. . . . Duality has preceded unity. The couple or pair is anterior to the isolated element. Every term identifiable by thought, every thinkable term requires a complementary term in relation to which it will be differentiated and to which it can be opposed. Without this initial relationship of the couple, the whole later edifice of relationships would be impossible. . . . [The couple] is the act which unifies at the same time as it distinguishes, without at first being able to specify the nature of the relationship.[24]

Jakobson comments: "The binary opposition is the child's first logical operation. Both opposites arise simultaneously and force the infant to choose one and to suppress the other of the two alternative terms."[25] A great deal of further research has now been done in phonology, attempting to confirm or disconfirm the primacy of two, but new phonological discoveries would not invalidate an argument concerned with the primacy of two in *logical* operations (and of course the structural anthropology of Claude Levi-Strauss, formed around the notion of binary oppositions, has had an effect on anthropology which seems likely to be permanent)—even if we had to introduce a surreptitious third element (neither one nor two).

[23] This transition is enormously significant, because the child had clearly progressed from the black/white opposition of presence and absence (a message *simulating* a moodsign) in his play, to the metacommunicative level of *framing* his message as "This is play." Or in other words he is doing what the schizophrenic cannot do: labelling the metaphor, implicitly including the necessary "as if." See: Bateson, "A Theory of Play and Phantasy," *loc cit.*, pp. 48-49.

[24] *Les Origines de la pensée chez l'enfant* (Paris: Presses Universitaires de France, 1945), p. 41, pp. 130-131.

[25] R. Jakobson and M. Halle, *Fundamentals of Language* (The Hague: Mouton, 1956), p. 47.

It is to a large extent on this opposition between two phonemes that Jacques Lacan has formulated his speculations concerned with the distinction between need, demand, and desire, which now seems a distinction essential in any discipline concerned with instincts, social interaction, or with Freud himself (for whom unconscious desire is represented by *Wunsch, Begierde,* and, sometimes, by the *Lust* of the pleasure principle). For the a-subjective child, as yet unrelated to objects, which Freud describes in the terms of "primary narcissism" in the article on negation or denial in psychoanalysis—"Die Verneinung" (1923) *(Standard Edition* XIX, 159)—what is most crucial is the child's discovery of difference (between himself and the world), which stems from the alternating presence and absence of gratification in the child's "objectless" world. Lacan has used a mathematical model derived from Frege to describe this situation: the primordial "Oneness" of the child cannot be "One" at all, since one requires two. What this a-subjectivity, this nonrelationship can be, however, is *zero,* in the precise sense that Frege, in order to "save the truth," defined zero in his theory of integers as the "concept under which no object falls." All objects being defined as identical with themselves, zero is assigned to the concept "not identical with itself." Zero makes a lack (rather than a no-thing) visible and thus provides for the linearity of the integers. Whatever the final value of this metaphor, it provides us with a correlation between the theory of desire as corresponding to a lack, the concept of primary narcissism, and the notion of the "compulsion to restore an earlier state of things." For Lacan, it is this "Oneness" of zero which is the most profound element in unconscious desire; this is the *recherche du temps perdu,* the lost object. For the object to be discovered (as lost) by the child, it must be absent, and he must discover his difference from the Other. Lacan goes on to suggest that it is at this point (in a general genetic or structural sense, rather than in a historical one) that the child's needs, through the emergence of language—that is, in our perspective, through the *restructuring* at a higher level of the goal-seeking morphogenetic system represented by the child—become *demands,* and that it is this conversion which generates the inarticulable desire of the unconscious—"the discourse of the Other." (In the same sense that one would consider the ego as emerging from an undifferentiated ego-id). But this desire is condemned to be the Desire of the Other —in all the (im)possible senses of that aphoristic slogan. To put it another way, *words* replace needs; needs become governed by the laws of language. In "La Direction de la cure," Lacan states his views as follows:

> It is worth recalling that it is in the oldest demand of all that the primary identification is produced, the demand brought about by the all-powerful [status] of the mother [the real Other], or in other words, the identification which not only suspends the satisfaction of needs from the signifying apparatus, but also that which carves them up, filters them, and models them in relation to the defiles of the structure of the signifier *[signifiant]*.
>
> Needs become subordinate to the same conventional conditions as those of the signifier in its double register: the synchronic register of opposition between irreducible [binary, differential] elements and the diachronic register of substitution and combination [metaphor and metonymy], through which language, even if it obviously does not fulfill all functions, structures the whole of the relationship between humans (p. 181).

On p. 158, he describes this (Hegelian) *Moment* as "The point of the insemination of a Symbolic order [of discourse, communication, and exchange] which pre-exists in relation to the child and according to which it will be necessary for him to structure himself."[20]

The point is that this play involves phantasy. The child is intentionalizing (cathecting) by means of a binary phonemic opposition a phantasy of opposition between presence and absence. We recall that Freud described primal phantasies as *instinktiv;* we know that *all* primary phantasies are concerned with oppositions. They are directly related to introjection and expulsion, and in the 1923 article "Negation," introjection "into the ego" and expulsion "out of the ego" become the bases of affirmation and negation, of Eros and "the destructive instinct." Some analysts, Susan Isaacs of the Kleinian school, for example, would say that no instinctual impulse is not experienced as (derived from) an unconscious phantasy. R. D. Laing points out

[20] J. Lacan, "La Direction de la cure," *La Psychanalyse* (1961), VI: 149-206. The term *signifiant* is derived from Saussure's *Cours de linguistique générale* (1910), where it means "acoustic image," as opposed to the *signifié, usually* meaning "concept." In one of the senses of the term as used by Lacan, "signifier" means any object of exchange in a communicational context—between persons or between generations. Thus, in the Freudian theory, the phallus is a signifier, just as in the Lévi-Straussian terminology the woman is a "sign" in the "matrimonial dialogue" of kinship and marriage-ties. On this point, see E. and M.-C. Ortigues, *Oedipe africain* (Paris: Plon, 1966).

The reciprocity of the Symbolic order (derived from Lévi-Strauss) is opposed in the Lacanian theory to the paranoia, the aggressivity, and the identificatory alienation of the Imaginary order (dependent on the *stade du miroir),* where there operates what Lacan calls a *parole vide* or a *discours imaginaire.*

that unconscious phantasy is a basic mode of experience (but that not all unconscious experience is phantasy, nor all infantile memories phantasies), that it is not necessarily infantile, that phantasies involve issues of full/empty, good/bad, destruction/reparation, anxiety/security and so forth, that "they always involve the union, confusion, separation, splitting, destruction, and repairing of bodies and parts of bodies in relation." Phantasies confuse whatever distinctions between self and other one has succeeded in living with.[27]

The relationship between these binary oppositions and the opposition of the "instincts," and their further relationship to that between self and world, self and body, self and other are curious enough. But what is more curious and more important at this juncture is that in his use of the word *instinktiv*, Freud regards the *Urphantasie*—which we can probably speak of as a "pure" opposition, as form rather than as content—as more primordial than the drives themselves.[28] Laplanche and Pontalis point out in the article cited that Freud seems to have considered the *lost object* (which is at the basis of desire, of repetition) to be constituted only when the child becomes capable of *seeing as a whole*, the person who controls the gratification of his needs—a stage which Laplanche and Pontalis, as students of Lacan, relate at once to "demand." It is at this point, says Freud, that the drives become auto-erotic, that is to say that the child learns to *substitute* one thing (his thumb) for another thing (the breast). He is thus involved at a meta-level of communication with the Other, which fits rather clearly into the notion of the emergence or the restructuring of this purpose-seeking system. *The thing, by substitution, has become a sign, that is to say an articulated absence, exactly correlative to the metacommunicative "bite" in animal play, which is the sign of a bite, but not the bite itself* (it is no-thing). And when this communication becomes *discourse*, its essential nature as tension or *Tendenz*—its contradiction of the pleasure principle in any but the most generic sense—becomes all the more apparent. It expresses an essentially regressive, but by the very token of its impossible gratification, an actually progressive movement: discourse is project towards the future, *Tendenz* towards the Other; for Lacan the demands of the discourse are all "demands for love," seeking to express

---

[27] *The Self and Others* (London: Tavistock Publications, 1961), pp. 24-26.
[28] On this point see: J. Laplanche and J.-B. Pontalis, "Phantasme originaire, fantasme des origines, origine du phantasme," *Les Temps Modernes* (December, 1963), No. 215, pp. 1833-1868. The authors effectively refute Susan Isaacs' theory of phantasy—in part by pointing out that for her the primary phantasies are already subjectified ("*I* want to eat, expel. . . ." etc.).

an inarticulable unconscious desire, the desire to be the Other's desire.

Although we seem to be able to dispose fairly easily of the whole biological area of an inherited death instinct in Freud, it remains true that the notion of the primal phantasy and the lost object seems to lead to the gloomiest sort of predications about man. Out of the unavoidable conditions generated by the premature birth of the human child, his necessary domination by the Other, there seems to come a principle binding us to repetition, to an affirmative but, also to a destructive goal, and to a binding quest for a paradise lost. If we have perhaps managed to dispose of death "as the great organizing force of life" (Svevo) and if the notions of equilibrium and inertia seem to make no sense whatsoever in the discontinuities of the birth and death of a goal-seeking system which is of a higher order than the biological reality which sustains it, we seem nevertheless to have brought either anxiety or the death drive or both into the system as constituent elements through the back door. We have been forced to reject the notion of an available quantum of energy at the service of the instincts as a primary principle, because it is the processing and communication of information—signs—which defines the higher order system known as man, but the concept of the search for purposefulness itself seems nevertheless to do no more than repeat an old quest. To put it another way, this would be the quest to return to a lower level of the system when its purpose or goal was *innate* and inseparable from the organism as such (the domain of need). Moreover, if it is indeed imagination which promises liberation, it is also the Imaginary which enslaves us to the Other, to our vision of the Other in his totality, and to identity. The most primary of all oppositions seems in the end to be that between Self and Other. Even if one's self is in fact alienated, identified with an other—an "ideal" ego who is far from ideal—this is not a principle of unity, but a principle of contradiction, disjunction, and conflict. Both difference and identity are inseparable. "The *moi* is essentially paranoid," says Lacan.

Here, however, there may paradoxically lie the principle of liberation and de-alienation. If we have disposed of the "evils" of human *nature* by disposing of the instincts as such, and particularly by rejecting the death instinct as a principle separate from Eros, we do so only to come face to face with the problem of the human *situation* or the human *condition*. In order to demonstrate the possibility of real liberation and de-alienation, without positing any necessity of outside control of the aggressive component of human relationships apparently generated by the child's relation to the Other,[29] we have on the one hand to demonstrate that the paranoia of the ego, the love-hate of the master-slave dialectic between ego's in the Imaginary (the domain of re-semblance, the *stade du miroir,* identity, and identification with and against others),[30] and the inauthentic discourse which accompanies this struggle to the death, are all products of history and of specific economic organization, as Lacan apparently believes them to be. On the other hand, it must be shown that the child's relationship to difference and to the Other, whatever its structural and a-historical necessities, is no more than a primary relationship of opposition which can be morphogenically restructured. These are profound problems for detailed discussion elsewhere, but it does seem that these propo-sitions may be demonstrable. If we leave aside for the moment all pessimism about the nature of organization as such, the binding of socially-induced aggressivity by libidinal relationships *which would not bring identity into question* may actually be possible. Repetition (the quest of the lost object) is impossible in itself, just as the gratifica-tion of human desire is impossible, but all that the compulsion to repeat actually compels—outside its pathological manifestations in what Sartre rightly calls *êtres circulaires*—is constant and repeated meta-statement and communication in which the possible choices are not in the hands of the instinct or the phantasy, *but in the hands of man.* We live at a time, as Nietzsche said, when madness is rare in indi-viduals, "but in groups, parties, peoples, ages, the rule," and the pathology of a social order is open to far wider possibilities and more extensive curative techniques than is the individual.

[29] The point is that the kind of scarcity which operates here has nothing to do with the organized scarcity of our present economic system.
[30] One has only to read a few of the masters of literature, from Montaigne to Proust, for example, to be convinced, without a word from Freud or Lacan, of the significance of models, images, and vision in this *short-circuited dialectic*—where one becomes two or two become one because of their desire to be at one with themselves. In this world, all roads seem to lead to and from Narcissus and Pygmalion (the titles of two of the plays of that great eighteenth century paranoid-schizophrenic, Jean-Jacques Rousseau).

Marx rightly says that "for philosophers, relationship equals idea *[Idee]*. They know only the relationship of 'Man' to himself and hence for them all real relation-ships become ideas" *(The German Ideology,* p. 79, marginal note). But his use of the word *Idee* is significant, for the problem of presentation and representation *(Vorstellung)* in relationships is not a question of ideas in the idealist sense, even if it certainly involves the *knowledge (eido)* of *idols.* It is rather a problem of communication in and about what seem to be the two most significant languages of real life: phantasy and economic relationships. These can perhaps be viewed as intimately connected in at least one area, insofar as the child represents an object of exchange (the phallus), from before his birth, both synchronically and diachronically, within the family and between generations. With the dissolution of the family, this exchange relationship could presumably disappear in its usual super-alienating forms, whereas it seems that the language of phantasy could not.

It should further be possible to show that Marcuse's view of *Phantasie* is an instance of Lacan's Symbolic order *(la parole pleine)* rather than an instance of the deadly world of the Imaginary *(la parole vide)*. And in the goal-seeking, self-regulating, structure-elaborating general system called history or society, the only question, as Adorno would say, is to know who is defining what goals, who is regulating what, and what future structures can be elaborated how and when. A large question, no doubt, but, for the sake of humanity, it had better not be an unanswerable one.

Bertolt Brecht and America

BY IRING FETSCHER

ON JUNE 18, 1920, Brecht noted in his diary: "How that Germany bores me! It is a good, medium country, with beautiful pastels and lovely planes, but what people! Degenerate peasants whose coarseness, though, does not give birth to fairytale monsters but to a quiet brutalization; an obese middle class; and a languid intelligentsia! What is left? America!"

America—that far-away land, large, vibrant, extravagant—fascinated the young Brecht. To him it was the land of technique and sports, and the land of the future. In America there still was hope; in Germany it seemed lost. In an early poem he expressed that same mood:

> Deutschland, du Blondes, Bleiches
> Wildwolkiges mit sanfter Stirn!
> Was ging vor in deinen lautlosen Himmeln?
> Nun bist du das Aasloch Europas . . .

and in the last stanza:

> O Aasland, Kümmernisloch!
> Scham würgt die Erinnerung
> Und in den Jungen, die du
> Nicht verdorben hast
> Erwacht Amerika! (1919)

Germany, fair one, pale one/clouded wildly with a friendly brow./What happened in your unruffled sky?/Now you are Europe's Carrionpit . . ./O land of carrion, hole of bitterness/Shame stifles memory/But in the young ones whom/You did not spoil/America awakens.

Clearly, America here stands for future, hope, spontaneity, the overcoming of mediocrity. In the word "America" there are overtones of nostalgia, romantic longing for far-away things, for new things, and at the same time Brecht's fascination with technique, with the big city, the outsize figures of big business.

Then, in the last poem of the "Hauspostille" (1926), "Of Poor BB," Brecht identifies with a people that has built "the long dwellings of Manhattan Island" "and the thin antennae that entertain the Atlantic Ocean." But the next stanza says:

Von diesen Häusern wird bleiben: der durch sie hindurchgeht der Wind.

Fröhlich machet das Haus den Esser: er leert es.

Wir wissen, dass wir Vorläufige sind

Und nach wird kommen: nichts Nennenswertes.

(Of these houses there will remain but the wind that blows through them./The house maketh the feaster merry: he drains it./We know that we are precursors/And after us there will be: nothing worth mentioning.)

We see here that coolly resigned nihilism toward which Brecht so often seemed to tend before he turned to Marxism. Thus, in the poems and early plays describing American episodes, fascination balances the impassive description of brutality, decay and chaos. Or rather, more to the point, brutality, decay and chaos are part of that fascination with America.

In a curious context Brecht for the first time publicly commented on America and on one of the literary sources to which he owed his image of America. On April 15, 1920, in the Augsburg daily "Volkswille," he reviewed a performance of Schiller's Don Carlos. But before taking up the subject, he had to convey the impression Upton Sinclair's *The Jungle* had made on him: "God knows that I have always loved Don Carlos. But these days I have been reading Sinclair's 'Jungle,' the story of a working man whom they starve to death in the Chicago stockyards. The story simply concerns hunger, cold, disease which undo a man as surely as if God himself had ordered it. At one time this man had a small vision of freedom; then he is beaten down with nightsticks. His freedom has nothing at all to do with Don Carlos' freedom; I know that. But I can no longer take Carlos' servitude too seriously. . . . But of course, Don Carlos is a fine opera."

We would expect that after taking up a source that is so clearly critical and even revolutionary, Brecht's writings on America would start out with a similar slant. However, Brecht's first play that is set in America, "In the Jungle of the Cities — The Struggle of Two Men in the Giant City of Chicago," is merely a highly gripping description, at once sober and baroque, of conditions that are shown only in their private and accidental aspects even where the context is social. In this play, on which he had been working from 1921 till 1924, Brecht tried to show "sheer martial fervor." But at the same time he exemplified most impressively "the unending isolation of man" in modern capitalist society and his inability to overcome this loneliness except at odd moments and on the level of mere physical contacts. The two protagonists, in their "metaphysical struggle" which sometimes is encoded in a Kafkaesque way, cannot let go of each other and yet never get to each other. Their faces are hidden from them and fade into indefiniteness. Buying and selling, blackmailing and seducing each other, they still remain strangers — intimate enemies. Without real human nearness, in different ways both protagonists strive for absolute freedom of their isolated egos, and they assume that they can realize this freedom by any means at all. Both fail. Their selfishness generates boundless hatred of family and humanity. Hating others, in the end they are no longer able to love themselves.

Not yet having an analytical tool to explain people's behavior by social conditions, Brecht did not go beyond the horrified and yet deliberately sober description of people's relations to each other. The brutality in their intercourse at the same time repelled him and fascinated him. Sports — especially boxing, in which America excelled so highly — attracted him in the same ambivalent way.

Only two poems or songs are known from another play that was to be set in Chicago, "Joe Fleischhacker in Chicago." The "Song of a Family from the Savannah" is about a family moving to San Francisco, Massachusetts, and finally Chicago, and sings of the roving little people's restlessness and discontent:

> 4. Wir haben kein Zimmer in Chicago
> Keinen Dollar und keine Aussicht, mein Gott
> Und: hier ist es schlecht, sagt jetzt Billy
> Aber nirgendwo wird es besser sein.
> Und wir hatten einst Geld und Aussichten
> Arbeit die Woche und frei am Samstag abend
> Und an allen Orten war es uns zu schlecht.

We have no room in Chicago/Not a cent and no prospects, oh Lord./It is bad here, says Billy/nowhere is it better./Once we had money and prospects/Work weekdays and free weekends/And we did not like it anywhere.

It was only by means of the Marxian method that Brecht transcended this impressionistic approach. A diary entry of Elisabeth Hauptmann's indicates that in July 1926 he started studying Marxist writings because in no other way could he comprehend the proceedings at the Chicago Wheat Exchange which he needed for the "Joe Fleischhacker" play. Twice later — in prose and in a poem — did Brecht discuss this connection between a theater problem and his Marx studies. Here is the poem:

Als ich vor Jahren bei dem Studium der Vorgänge auf
der Weizenbörse Chicagos
plötzlich begriff, wie sie dort das Getreide der
Welt verwalten
Und es zugleich auch nicht begriff und das Buch senkte
wusste ich gleich: du bist
In eine böse Sache geraten.

Kein Gefühl der Erbitterung war in mir, und nicht
das Unrecht
Schreckte mich da, nur der Gedanke
So geht das nicht, wie die's machen! erfüllte mich gänzlich.
Diese, sah ich, lebten vom Schaden
Den sie zufügten, anstatt vom Nutzen.
Dies war ein Zustand, sah ich, der nur durch Verbrechen
Aufrecht zu halten war, weil zu schlecht für die meisten.

So muss auch jede
Leistung der Vernunft, Erfindung oder Entdeckung
Nur zu noch grösserem Elend führen.

Solches und Aehnliches dacht' ich in diesem Augenblick
Fern von Zorn oder Jammer, als ich das Buch senkte
Mit der Beschreibung des Weizenmarkts und der Börse Chicagos.
Viel Mühe und Unrast
Erwarteten mich.

When, some years ago, in studying the/ways of the Chicago Products Exchange/ I suddenly understood how they manage the world's grain output/And simultaneously failed to understand/and put the book down./Then I knew: you have hit upon evil./There was no feeling of bitterness in me/nor was it injustice that frightened me/But the thought filled me: totally./The way they work it, it will not work./I saw that these people do not live/by the usefulness of their service/ but by the damage they are doing./This condition, I saw, can be maintained/only by crime. It is too vicious for most of us./Thus reason, invention and discovery/ must lead to more misery./These were my thoughts at that moment,/far from anger or pity when I put the book down./With the description of the products exchange/much effort and restlessness/were to be my fate.

Through Marxism, Brecht learned to comprehend the incomprehensible. And henceforth his image of the jungle of American cities and of American society changed fundamentally. At last he understood the chaos, and soon he was able to realize it artistically. As early as during his first Marx studies he wrote in one of the "Poems for City Dwellers":

Ich höre Sie sagen:
Er redet von Amerika
Er versteht nichts davon.
Er war nicht dort.
Aber glauben Sie mir
Sie verstehen mich sehr gut, wenn ich von Amerika rede.
Und das Beste an Amerika ist:
Das wir es verstehen.
Eine Keilschrift
Verstehen nur Sie
(Es ist natürlich eine tote Sache)
Aber sollen wir nicht von Leuten lernen
Die es verstanden haben
Verstanden zu werden?
Sie, Herr
Versteht man nicht.
Aber New York versteht man
Ich sage Ihnen:
Diese Leute verstehen, was sie tun
Darum versteht man sie.

I hear you say: he is talking about America/but he does not know it, he was not
there./Believe me, you understand me very well/when I talk about America./
The best thing about America is that we understand it./Cuneiform you alone
understand, it's a dead language, of course./But should we not learn from people/
who knew how to be known?/You, sir, one does not know./But New York can
be known./For I tell you/these people know what they/are doing and therefore
one knows them.

Now he understands America as the most typical and the most
developed capitalist country, which explains and at the same time
softens his fascination. Wieland Herzfelde tells of a conversation
in which Brecht showed this new understanding very clearly: "In a
group of politically interested people we were debating which country
was more modern: Germany or the United States. Brecht, joining
the group, was asked to be the arbiter. Without hesitation he
answered: 'America,' and he gave this reason: 'If Germany were
to continue her development along capitalistic lines, it would take
her decades to come down as low as America is now'." *(Erinnerungen
an Brecht*, Leipzig, Reclam, 1966, p. 133.)

But still Brecht was thrilled by the larger view, the generosity and
urbanity of Americans, which was manifest even in their business,
life, in contrast to German narrow-minded provinciality. Even later,
in his Californian exile, he wrote with reluctant respect:

"Now, in war, 'business as usual' is sometimes denounced (for that matter, everything here is pilloried, the pillar being nothing but a public bulletin board) as being bad for the war. But reform will merely mean 'business as unusual.' It is precisely this spirit of business that permits us to hope for Hitler's defeats — expensive defeats but eventually defeats nevertheless." (Feb. 18, 1942.)

In the showdown with the Fascist powers, Brecht sees greater chances for victory in the soberly calculating ways of capitalism. Even though the economic system of capitalism is irrational with respect to the solution of its inner conflicts, it seems comparatively rational when pitched against the Fascist system of ideocratic domination which has become completely irrational.

Marx' theory taught Brecht how to differentiate between people and the social roles they are forced to play in the capitalist system. Again and again he tried to demonstrate how the social character mask (to use Marx' term) can be lifted from the man. In the didactic plays set in America, this method had not yet been developed to the artistic heights he reached in *The Good Women of Sezuan* and in *The Caucasian Chalk Circle*. Still, in *St. Joan of the Stockyards* (1929/30), the third play set in Chicago, the capitalist anti-hero, Pierpont Mauler, confesses to the powerlessness of the individual (the enterpriser) against the total system, implying that the individual's power is only derivative. The enterpriser's power over the enterprisees (Brecht's name for the workers) does not rest on his, the individual's, superiority but on the advantages of the social role he has assumed and on the rules of the game, which guarantee that everything must turn out well for him.

  . . . Denn sieh, wenn ich
Der viel dagegen hat und schlecht schlaft, auch
Davon abgehen wollt, das war, als wenn eine Mücke davon ablässt,
    einen Bergrutsch aufzuhalten. Ich würd
Ein Nichts im selben Augenblick und über mich weg ging's weiter
Denn sonst müsst alles umgestürzt werden von Grund aus
Und verändert der Bauplan von Grund aus nach ganz anderer
Unerhörter neuer Einschatzung des Menschen, die ihr nicht wollt
Noch wir, denn dies geschahe ohne uns und Gott, der
Abgeschafft würd, weil ganz ohne Amt. Darum müsst ihr
Mitmachen, und wenn ihr schon nicht opfert, was
Wir auch nicht von euch wollen, so doch gutheissen die Opfer,
Kurz und gut: ihr müsst

Gott wieder aufrichten
Die einzige Rettung, und
für ihn die Trommel rühren, auf dass er
Fuss fasse in den Quartieren des Elends und seine
Stimme erschalle auf den Schlachthöfen.

Look, if I—who have a lot against it and sleep poorly—/were to cease now, it
would mean no more than a fly/desisting from stopping a landslide. I'd be a
nobody/at once and it would continue rolling over me./Or else everything would
have to be overthrown down to the ground/and a fundamentally new, unheard-
of notion of man/would prevail. That you/don't want, nor do we. It would make
us obsolete/and God unnecessary. You ought to cooperate/even if you don't wish
to sacrifice that which we/ anyhow don't want of you. You still might sanction/
the sacrifice. In a word:/Set up God once more. It's the only salvation./You must
beat the drum for him so that he/may gain a foothold once more in the slums/
and his voice be heard in the stockyards.

Pierpont Mauler, the industrialist-racketeer or racketeer-indus-
trialist presented by Brecht not without covert sympathy, does not
masquerade like Herr Puntila or the whore Shen-Te; his personality
is not split distinctly, and yet he admits more than a businessman
who supports the Salvation Army is usually aware of. Transcending
his social role he understands it as part of a complex system which
a religious ideology can help to preserve. He even hints that there
is "a lot to be said against it" and that he does "not sleep well." But
he does not see how the system could be improved, unless it were
abolished or changed as fundamentally as neither the Salvation Army
nor business could tolerate since they both would be made super-
fluous.

The higher insight Brecht endows Mauler with, however, tends to
damage his efforts, for it contributes to the revolutionary education
of Joan Dark, the Salvation Army girl. The most radical agitator
could not as effectively as Mauler himself reveal the connection
between business and religious solace in the slums. Mauler stands
beside himself, alienated as it were, and describes the role he is
playing without being split into person and role as are Shen-Te
and Puntila. He is not to be blamed for the cruelty of the economic
system. In this respect Brecht has followed more or less closely the
formulation of Karl Marx in the preface to *Das Kapital*:

"I paint the capitalist and the landlord in no sense *couleur de rose*.
But here individuals are dealt with only in so far as they are the
personifications of economic categories, embodiments of particular
class-relations and class interests. My standpoint, from which the
evolution of the economic formation of society is viewed as a process
of natural history, can less than any other make the individual

responsible for relations whose creature he socially remains, however much he may subjectively raise himself above them." (Preface to the First German Edition; translated from the third German edition by Samuel Moore and Edward Aveling. Foreign Languages Publishing House, Moscow 1961. Vol. I, 10.)

Thanks to his insight into the social conditions and the environmental determinism, Pierpont Mauler almost appears as a tragic character — much against the author's intentions. The Marxian theory of history, which forms the background, crowds out the bourgeois great tragedy, whose style is enlisted to achieve an ironic effect. Mauler sees clearly:

> So ohne alles, nur mit Kauf und Verkauf
> Mit kaltem Hautabziehen von Mensch zu Mensch
> Kann es nicht gehn; es sind zu viele, die
> Vor Jammer brüllen, und es werden mehr.
> Was da in unsere blutigen Keller fällt, fast
> Ist nicht mehr zu vertrösten, die
> Werden uns, wo sie uns fassen
> Auf die Pflaster schlagen
> Wie faulen Fisch. Wir alle hier, wir
> Sterben nicht mehr im Bett. Bevor wir
> So weit sind, wird man in Rudeln uns
> An Mauern stellen und diese Welt saubern
> Von uns und
> Unserm Anhang.

It won't work that way/with cold-blooded skinning/of man by man,/through buying and selling./There are too many/howling with pain/and more will follow./ Those who fell into our/bloody cellars are almost/beyond consolation./If they ever catch us/they are going to dash us to the pavement/like rotten fish. None of us here/will die in bed. Long before/we get there they'll put us up/against a wall and purge us from this world./Along with our minions

But precisely because Mauler recognizes the objectively revolutionary situation, and even though he has been moved by the Salvation Army girl's speeches "for it's being done in vain" and because "there is much to be said against it," he is prepared to use the harshest methods in order to save the system off which he lives:

> Denn nur durch
> Aeusserste Massnahmen, die hart erscheinen könnten
> Weil sie einige treffen, ziemlich, viele sogar
> Kurz: die meisten, beinah alle
> Kann jetzt gerettet werden dies System

Von Kauf und Verkauf, das wir nun einmal haben
Und das auch Schattenseiten hat.

For only the extremest measures will do. They may seem severe because they
strike some people, or even many; briefly: most or almost all. If only now we
can save this system of buying and selling which is the only one we have and
which admittedly has faults too.

His operations in the meat market and his simultaneous sponsor-
ing of the Salvation Army (vainly resisted by Joan Dark, who, dying
finally recognizes what purpose she was serving) point up what
Brecht means to say:

Diese Leute verstehen, was sie tun
Darum versteht man sie.

These people understand what they are doing./That is why we understand them.

Mauler understands his role as "personification of the economic
categorie," the capitalist. He knows: "Accumulate! Accumulate! That
is Moses and the prophets," as Marx once said pointedly, stating
the gospel truth.

The separation of the role from the person lifts from the individual's shoulders the moral responsibility for the system which,
as an individual, he is unable to change. But at the same time this
separation deprives the businessman of his alleged greatness. By
identifying crime and business, Brecht tried again and again to debunk
the idolatry of the rich and the successful. In the *Three Penny Opera,*
in *Mahagonny* and in *Arturo Ui* the gangsters appear as small, unsuccessful businessmen who try by breaking the rules to achieve what
the great achieve almost without trying by following the rules of
the game. When, however, good luck has permitted the criminal to
take off and to accumulate a respectable sum of money, then he
may pass over to the more reliable forms of profit-making — say,
from robbing a bank to founding one. It may not be an accident,
however, that the effect Brecht expected from this equalization failed
to materialize. In the *"Buch der Wendungen"* he says:

"Kin-jeh [Brecht's alter ego] had a soft spot for simple criminals
like thieves, murderers, counterfeiters and thugs. He said: When
they break the customs, they don't use the argument suggested by
the masters for breaking the customs, but they do so for the same
reason: because hunger prevails and profits are drawn from violence.
You might say: It is for profit that they sin against the profit system.
After all, they are breaking the bad laws and that is why the people

love them. . . . These criminals do not know how to solve the difficult problem, but they are asking for a solution. They are isolated and it only looks as if they were standing up to the community, i.e. against everybody else. Actually they stand against the few who know how to make believe that they are the community."

That "soft spot" indicates the anarchistic-individualistic trait that never quite disappeared from Brecht's image of man. While the profit motive manifesting itself in those criminals ought to be explained as the product of a social order founded on the competition of profit-seekers, and while the lack of solidarity should be interpreted as the individual's isolation from his class (and group), secretly Brecht still admires the power of the individual who by violent means manages to change circumstances in his favor or who at least has the guts to rebel against fate, even through criminal acts. In the last resort, Brecht respects vitality, willpower, and energy. This appreciation of unscrupulous toughness and irresponsible violence derives from the same source as his admiration for great sportsmen, holders of world records, and tycoons. We remember the outcry that preceded Brecht's first exaltation of America: his German contemporaries' impotence, literally down to sexual effeteness. A residue of this adulation of vitality Dionysiacally abounding in early plays like *Baal* lingers on in the characters of his late plays: in Puntila, in Azdak, in Galilei so perfectly incarnated by Charles Laughton. No doubt this fascination can hardly be justified in Marxist terms, despite Brecht's amusing apology in his "Buch der Wendung."

Another facet of this gap between the great role and the person is found in a poem from the "Lesebuch für Städtebewohner" (Reader for City Dwellers):

Ich will nicht behaupten, dass Rockefeller ein Dummkapf ist
Aber Sie müssen zugeben
Dass an der Standard Oil ein allgemeines Interesse bestand.
Was ein Mann hatte dazugehört
Das Zustandekommen der Standard Oil zu verhindern!
Ich behaupte
Solch ein Mann muss erst geboren werden . . .

I do not wish to say that Rockefeller is a blockhead./But you have to admit/That there was a public interest in having Standard Oil./What a man it would have taken/To prevent the occurrence of Standard Oil!/I assert/That such a man has not even been born yet.

In other words, the concentration of oil holdings was determined by objective economic trends, and Rockefeller happened to be its instrument. He did what anybody would have done. While free-market sociologists (like Alexander Rüstow) attribute the concentration of big enterprises to the mysterious individual "drives" of the individual, nay to subjective megalomania, Brecht in the spirit of Marx assumes the inevitability of the trend toward concentration, with the managers readily conniving.

Only a few years after Brecht had assimilated Marxism, the great depression set in. It had already provided the background for *St. Joan of the Stockyards*. But explicitly its disillusioning effect is shown in the great poem "Verschollener Ruhm der Riesenstadt New York" (The Past Glory of the Megalopolis New York). After twelve stanzas of "praise of the megalopolis New York" in the first decade after the great war, the thirteenth brings a sudden reversal:

Allerdings dauerte dieses Jahrhundert
Nur knapp acht Jahre.

Alas, this century/lasted barely eight years.

Denn eines Tages durchlief die Welt das Gerücht seltsamer
    Zusammenbrüche
Auf einem berühmten Kontinent, und seine noch gestern gehamsterten Geldscheine
Wurden wie faule, stinkende Fische mit Ekel weggewiesen.

For one day a rumor ran through the world of strange bankruptcies/on a famous continent and its shares, which only yesterday it had hoarded greedily,/now were being rejected disgustedly like rotten stinking fish.

Now, after the collapse, Europeans see the land of promise, the "country of unbounded opportunities," with a disillusioned eye:

Was ist das mit den Hochhausern?
Wir betrachten sie kühler.
Was für verachtliche Schuppen sind Hochhauser, die keine Miete
    mehr abwerfen!
So hoch hinauf voller Armut? Bis unter die Wolken voll von
    Schulden?

What about those sky-scrapers?/We cast a cool eye on them./What contemptible barracks are sky-scrapers that have stopped yielding rent!/Why climb this high toward poverty? With debts reaching to the clouds?

And so it goes with all the other glories the first twelve stanzas had praised. They all look different now: the hit records, the machines, the railroads, the young girls' make-up, the boxing matches.

Welch ein Bankrott! Wie ist da
Ein grosser Ruhm verschollen! Welch eine Entdeckung:
Dass ihr System des Gemeindelebens denselben
Jammerlichen Fehler aufwies wie das
Bescheidenerer Leute!

What bankruptcy! How/vanished a great pride! What a discovery!/Their system
of community life showed the same/Pitiful effect as that/Of humbler people.

Theoretically, the great depression has completely destroyed
America's magic — or so it seems at least. What began with Marxist
analysis has been completed by the economic debacle. And yet, there
is still that difference in scope. After as well as before his Marxist
conversion, Brecht continued to admire the gigantic, the powerful
and even the brutal facets of America. Even in crisis America is
great. Humility and the golden mean, in Brecht's mouth, are no
praise.

But America is not only the country of big business and boxers,
of depression and sky-scrapers. In a few poems Brecht also speaks
of the solidarity of the poor, the generosity and democratic spirit of
those who have made it. A little poem, "Das Nachtlager" (Shelter
for a Night), which seems to have been composed a few years after
St. Joan of the Stockyards, sounds like an antistrophe qualifying the
unconditional condemnation of the Salvation Army's eleemosynary
activities which obscure class-consciousness:

Ich höre, dass in New York
An der Ecke der 26. Strasse und des Broadway
Wahrend der Wintermonate jeden Abend ein Mann steht
Und den Obdachlosen, die sich ansammeln
Durch Bitten an Vorübergehende ein Nachtlager verschafft.

Die Welt wird dadurch nicht anders.
Die Beziehungen zwischen den Menschen bessern sich nicht.
Das Zeitalter der Ausbetung wird dadurch nicht verkürzt.
Aber einige Manner haben ein Nachtlager
Der Wind wird von ihnen eine Nacht abgehalten
Der ihnen zugedachte Schnee fällt auf die Strasse.
Leg das Buch nicht nieder, der du das liesest, Mensch.
Einige Menschen haben ein Nachtlager
Der Wind wird von ihnen eine Nacht lang abgehalten
Der ihnen zugedachte Schnee fällt auf die Strasse
Aber die Welt wird dadurch nicht anders

Die Beziehungen Zwischen den Menschen bessern sich dadurch nicht
Das Zeitalter der Ausbeutung wird dadurch nicht verkürzt.

I hear that in New York at the corner of Broadway and 26th street/every night
during the winter months a man/offers help to the paupers who gather/by asking
passers-by to give them shelter for a night./That does not change the world./
The relations between humans do not improve./The age of exploitation is not
being shortened./But a few men have a bed for the night./They will be sheltered
from the wind for a night./The snow which was meant to cover them falls down
on the pavement./Don't put the book down which you are reading, then,/a few
men have a bed for the night./The wind will not blow on them for the night./
The snow will fall on the pavement/but the world will not be different./The
relations between humans will not be better./The age of exploitation will not be
shortened.

Here the friendly gift is not rejected. But Brecht underlines its
significance by reversing the order of events in the last stanza: "Some
people do have a place to sleep." For these few at least, that is an
indubitable, absolutely positive fact. It is true that such a deed cannot "abbreviate the age of exploitation" and we dare praise it only
inasmuch as we disregard the illusion it might create: that it could
contribute to changing the world, improving the relations between
people, abolishing exploitation.

In a less ambivalent way Brecht celebrates the solidarity of workers among themselves. The poem "Coals for Mike" apparently was
composed as early as 1926 after Brecht read Sherwood Anderson's
"Poor White":

1. Ich habe gehört, dass in Ohio
   Zu Beginn dieses Jahrhunderts
   Ein Weib wohnte zu Bidwell
   Mary McCoy, Witwe eines Streckenwärters
   Mit Namen Mike McCoy, in Armut.
2. Aber jede Nacht von den donnernden Zügen der Wheeling
      Railroad
   Warfen die Bremser einen Kohlenklumpen
   Ueber die Zaunlatten in den Kartoffelgarten
   Mit rauher Stimme ausrufend in Eile:
   Für Mike!
3. Und jede Nacht, wenn der Kohlenklumpen für Mike
   An die Rückwand der
   Hütte schlug
   Erhob sich die Alte, kroch
   Schlaftrunken in den Rock und räumte zur Seite den Kohlen-
      klumpen

Geschenk der Bremser an Mike, den Gestorbenen, aber
Nicht Vergessenen.
4. Sie aber erhob sich so lange vor Morgengrauen und räumte
Ihre Geschenke aus den Augen der Welt, damit nicht
Die Bremser in Ungelegenheiten kämen
Bei der Wheeling Railroad.
5. Dieses Gedicht ist gewidmet den Kameraden
Des Bremsers Mike McCoy
(Gestorben wegen zu schwacher Lunge
Auf den Kohlenzügen Ohios)
Für Kameradschaft.

1. I have heard that in Ohio/At the beginning of this century/A woman lived
in Bidwell,/Mary McCoy, widow of a signal-man/named Mike McCoy, in poverty./
2. But every night, from the thundering trains of the Wheeling Railroad/the
brakemen dumped a lump of coal/over the fence pickets into the potato patch,/
shouting briefly in harsh voices:/For Mike!/
3. And each night, as the lump of coal for Mike/struck the rear wall of the
cottage,/the old woman got up, drowsy,/struggled into her gown and moved aside
the lump of coal,/gift of the brakemen for Mike, dead, but/not forgotten./
4. But she arose so long before daybreak and moved/her gifts out of the sight of
the world, lest/the brakemen get into trouble/with the Wheeling Railroad./
5. This poem is dedicated to the comrades/of the brakeman Mike McCoy/(dead
of a weak lung/on the coal trains of Ohio)/for comradeship.

Like the poem, "Shelter for a Night," this one starts with the statement "I heard." Without high-sounding words, but approvingly, the
poet reports a good deed — or, more specifically, two good deeds. Not
only do the brakemen remember their late colleague by providing
coal for his widow; Mary McCoy too shows comradeship by concealing
the lumps of coal so as to save the brakemen trouble. For such conduct Brecht later used the words "kindliness" and "courteousness"
in a sense no longer current.

A similar solidarity is referred to in a poem composed in California
which tells of the expulsion of Americans of Japanese descent:

Immer wieder in dem Gemetzel
Steht ein Mensch da und reisst sich vom Hemde
Die Streifen, zu verbinden den Mitmensch.
An der Küste, von ihren Heimen
Ziehen die Gelben in die kahlen Lager.
Von der Menge am Strassenrand
Kommt ein Ruf: Kopf hoch!
Es dauert nicht ewig . . .

Again and again in the midst of the slaughter/a man arises and tears his shirt/
into strips to bandage a fellow man./On the coast, from their homes,/yellow men
walk into the barren camps./Out of the crowd lining the road/a call: chin up./
It cannot last forever.

In the poem "The Democratic Judge," Brecht praised the kindness of a judge who "examines people who try to become citizens of the United States." An elderly Italian innkeeper has come before him several times but had only one answer to all questions about American history and constitution: the number 1492. After this had happened three times,

> erkannte der Richter, dem der Mann gefiel, dass er die neue Sprache
> Nicht lernen konnte, erkundigte sich
> Wie er lebte, und erfuhr: schwer arbeitend. Und so
> Legte ihm der Richter beim vierten Erscheinen die Frage vor:
> Wann wurde Amerika entdeckt? Und auf Grund seiner richtigen Antwort
> 1492, erhielt er die Bürgerschaft.

the judge, who liked the man, saw that he could not learn/the new language, inquired/How he lived, and was told: hard-working. And so,/At his fourth hearing, the judge asked him:/When was America discovered? And upon the correct answer,/1492, he granted him his citizenship.

Thus, a ruse reminiscent of Azdak in *The Caucasian Chalk Circle* — and for that matter of Schwejk — allowed the fulfillment and at the same time the circumvention of the law in the interest of justice for an immigrant disadvantaged by hard work, old age and origin. In the character of this wise and resourceful judge, Brecht has set a monument to one of the noblest traits of North Americans: their free hospitality.

It is much rarer that we find in Brecht's work examples of revolutionary resistance against the American social system. (With the exception of *The Mother* and *The Rifles of Mrs. Carrar* revolutionaries are not central in Brecht's plays, stories and poems.) In *St. Joan of the Stockyards,* the heroine is converted to revolutionary violence by the deeds and the fate of the revolutionary strike leaders rather than by their speeches. What Brecht shows is not the revolutionary person but the process that changes the compassionate religious fighter into an advocate of practical revolution. Several times the

> workers' chorus declares
> dass es nur durch Gewalt geht und
> wenn ihr es selber macht.

that only violence will work and/you have to do it yourselves.

Joan at first objects:
> Halt! Lernt nicht weiter.

Nicht in so kalter Weise!
Nicht durch Gewalt
Bekämpft Unordnung und Verwirrung . . .

Stop! Stop learning./Not like this in cold blood!/Do not use violence/To fight
disorder and confusion . . .

And eventually she says to herself:
Ich will weggehen. Es kann nicht
gut sein, was mit Gewalt gemacht word.
Ich gehöre nicht zu ihnen. Hätten mich
Als Kind der Tritt des Elends und der
Hunger Gewalt gelehrt, würde ich zu
Ihnen gehören und nichts fragen.
So aber muss ich weggehen.

I want to go away. It cannot be/good if it is done by violence./I do not belong
with them. If/As a child the boot of poverty and/Hunger had taught me violence,
I would/Belong with them and ask no questions./But as it is, I must go away.

It is also because she loathes violence that she keeps the strike
leaders' important letter, for "da steht doch nur wieder etwas Gewalt-
tätiges drin" (there would just be some more violent stuff in it).
Actually, the letter contained the news of a general strike in all
Chicago factories. Joan failed to pass the letter on, and the workers,
who could not wait any longer, went home. Joan's inaction therefore
permitted the employers to break the strike. The heroine is shown
not as an idealized and stylized, "ready-made" figure but as learning
from experience. Joan Dark, the Salvation Army girl from a middle-
class background, has learned her lesson and dies with this confession:

Eines hab ich gelernt und weiss es für euch selber sterbend:
Was soll das heissen, es ist etwas in euch und
Kommt nicht nach aussen! Was wisst ihr wissend
Was keine Folgen hat?
Ich zum Beispiel habe nichts getan.
Denn nichts werde gezählt als gut, und sehe es aus wie immer, als
   was
Wirklich hilft, und nichts gelte als ehrenhalft mehr, als was
Diese Welt endgültig andert: sie braucht es.
Wie gerufen kam ich den Unterdrückern!
O, folgenlose Güte! Unmerkliche Gesinnung!
Ich habe nichts geandert.
Schnell verschwindend aus dieser Welt ohne Furcht
Sage ich euch:

Sorgt doch, dass ihr die Welt verlassend
Nicht nur gut wart, sondern verlasst
Eine gute Welt!

One thing I learned, and dying I know it for you:/I guess something is inside you
that has not come out yet./What do you know that has no consequences?/I for
instance did nothing./Oh, let nothing pass for good, however good it may look,/
unless it has really helped some./And let nothing any longer be counted honorable
unless it has changed the world./It needs change. I came like an answer to/the
prayers of the oppressors! Oh goodness without/consequences! I have changed
nothing./Vanishing from this world quickly and without fear/I say to you: Take
care that when you leave the world/you not only were good but leave a good world.

And a little later she adds the sad insight:

Es hilft nur Gewalt, wo Gewalt herrscht, und
Es helfen nur Menschen, wo Menschen sind.

Where violence rules, only violence is the remedy, and/Only humans can help
where humans exist.

Not content with showing us the process of Joan Dark's political
education, Brecht sees to it that in the end its result is annulled. For
the speculator Slift and meat king Mauler contrive to have Joan
sainted. They figure that Mauler's harsh measures can be made
acceptable only through a credible religious ideology:

Slift: Das ist unsere Johanna. Sie kommt wie gerufen. Wir wollen
sie gross herausbringen, denn sie hat uns durch ihr menschen-
freundliches Wirken auf den Schlachthöfen . . . auch durch ihre
Reden gegen uns über schwierige Wochen hinweggeholfen. Sie
soll unsere Heilige Johanna der Schlachthöfe sein. Wir wollen
sie wie eine Heilige aufziehen und ihr keine Achtung versagen.
Im Gegenteil soll gerade, dass sie bei uns gezeigt wird, dafür
zum Beweis dienen, dass die Menschlichkeit bei uns einen hohen
Platz einnimmt.

Slift: This is our Joan. An answer to our prayer. We must boost her big. For
with her philanthropies in the stockyards . . . and also with the speeches she made
against us she helped us through difficult times. She must be our Saint Joan of
the Stockyards. Let us plug her as a saint and pay her all due respects. By promoting her we will prove that humanitarianism is honored in this place.

Dying, Joan is hardly able to defend herself against this exploitation.
We must assume that those not near her could not hear her last words
announcing her conversion to revolution. The economic system has
won a spiritual victory over the revolutionary fighter.

During his exile in the USA, since the summer of 1941, Brecht
apparently had hardly any contacts with revolutionary Marxists. "The
left-wing actors and script-writers in Hollywood, as it happened, were
followers of Stanislawsky's — who for Brecht was a red rag. Brecht's

theories on stage direction and the art of acting were the precise opposite of his." (Esslin, Brecht — Das Paradox des politischen Dichters, Frankfurt/Main, 1962, p. 115.) As we know, Brecht could not isolate his political views from his artistic methods. If his theatre was revolutionary, that is to say a theater that promoted revolution and "the great production," then Stanislawsky's theatre could only be reactionary. In his California diary he notes a visit with a left-wing writer, "who repeated the well-known thesis that the American worker rejects Marxism because he has been bribed through affluence (caused by the 'cultural imperialism of the bourgeoisie') — a reason why we should address ourselves to other strata of the population." The writer admitted that "we made the worker what he is through our films, newspapers, radio operas etc." Brecht notes critically: "I am interested in this 'we' of his tirade. At first he called it an 'editorial we' and then he said he wanted to put his complicity on the record. To my mind, it was a case of representing 'the nation'." (April 3, 1947.)

It seems that Brecht had little understanding for this line of argumentation and did not worry about the lack of revolutionary tendencies among the workers. In any case, he could not agree with the complaints about the decrease of physical suffering as voiced on another occasion by left-wing intellectuals:

"In Adorno's house the Frankfurt Institute [of Social Research; once in Frankfurt, then in Hollywood] started a seminar. Adorno, Horkheimer, Nürnberg, Eisler, Marcuse, Pollok. Horkheimer quotes, with a sort of alarm, a statement by Vice-President Henry Wallace that after this war every child in the world should get a pint of milk every day. . . . The Institute is already wondering whether it would not mean a gigantic danger for culture if capitalism served so much milk (and not just milk of human kindness) . . ." (June 16, 1942.)

Again, two months later he notes: "Horkheimer worries about some phenomena of modern times, especially the decrease of cultural demands. The more ice boxes, the less Huxley. When the needs of the body are too well satisfied, the needs of the spirit get the short end. Suffering created culture; apparently barbarism will follow if suffering is abolished." (August 13, 1942.)

Possibly Brecht misunderstood his friends' arguments. But it seems characteristic of his identification with the suffering and of his mentality, which always disregarded his personal situation, that he instinctively rejected an argument which seemed to rest on the incompatibility of culture with the satisfaction of physical needs and the reduction of bodily suffering.

On the other hand, even in face of American affluence, Brecht held on to Marx' pauperization theory. He refused to take note of Keynes' theory and of the practice of economic planning, which even in the most capitalistic countries guarantees stability through the constant improvement of regulatory instruments. He simply did not believe it:

"Dr. Pollock, the economist of the Institute for Social Research, is convinced that capitalism can escape the periodic depressions simply by organizing public works. Marx could not foresee that one day the governments could simply build highways! — Eisler [Hanns Eisler, composer of *Die Massnahme*] and I grew impatient and put ourselves in the wrong." (August 13, 1942.)

Acute as Brecht was in observing the cultural phenomena of his new environment, he was dogmatic in evaluating economic conditions. In his eyes apparently economists like Pollock were "Tuis" — his word for certain intellectuals whose role in German as well as in American society Brecht had begun to study in his Danish exile. "Tuis" are intellectuals, or more precisely small commodity producers, who specialize in the manufacture of arguments, excuses, rationalizations, in exchange for a suitable remuneration. For Brecht they were a most repulsive example of an alienated mode of production; even the producers of revolutionary theses are not immune from this kind of alienation. The play *Turanadot or the Whitewashers' Congress* and the fragmentary *Tui-Novel* (both published posthumously in 1967) are attempts to represent intellectual prostitution. In the California diary we find three entries concerning the Tui project; here are two of them:

"With Eisler at Horkheimer's for Lunch. After that, Eisler suggests for the Tui novel: the story of the Frankfurt Institute for Social Research. A wealthy old man [the wheat speculator Weill]* dies, worried over the suffering in the world, leaves in his will a substantial sum of money establishing an institute that shall search for the source of misery — which of course was he himself. The activities of the institute occur in an age where even the Emperor wishes to be told the source of misery, since the people's indignation is rising. The institute participates in the Council." (May 12, 1942.)

"Adorno here. This Frankfurt Institute is a gold-mine for the Tui novel. The 'Friends of the Armed Uprising' are the counterpart of the 'Disinterested Admirers of the Idea of Materialism.'" (Oct. 10, 1942.)

In an article which Brecht often quoted and used in his writings,

* Father of Felix Weill, the founder of the Institute.

Lenin dubbed "Friends of the Armed Uprising" the reformist Mensheviks, who counselled against revolutionary action because it might go badly and then shed crocodile tears when setbacks occurred. The "Disinterested Admirers of the Idea of Materialism" are, as it were, the radical reformists whose concern about critical dialectics was as unserious as the reformists' concern with practical revolution.

In an entry of December 18, 1944, Brecht refers to specific American conditions, especially the role of large and small foundations in financing the "Tuis." The entry deals with the substantial grant given by the American Jewish Committee to the Frankfurt Institute for a series of "Studies in Prejudice." Brecht complains that no attention is paid to the connection between capitalism and anti-Semitism and refers to Marx' "Jewish Question," of which Adorno said that it was obsolete, whereupon Brecht mischievously asks "whether in his opinion the New York crowd would finance the Marxist position [on the Jewish question] if Marx had *not* been wrong, or if the Institute could prove that he was right after all."

In a less aggressive way he alludes to a grant Hanns Eisler received in April 1942: "Eisler here. He has a grant from the Rockefeller Foundation (subject: film music), to describe fifteen kinds of rain. (Film reels with rain, for which austere music.) Perhaps my Tui novel is not quite . . .?" The trouble here is not the adjustment of political orientation to the sponsor's assumed intention but a revolutionary composer's flight into an area as unpolitical and as uncontroversial as rain music for films. Brecht's judgement here is milder because Eisler has not modified his political convictions but merely, in order to make a living, refrains from expressing them in his work for the grant. A few days later Brecht notes: "Eisler's record with the rain music. It is very beautiful, reminiscent of Chinese ink drawings." (April 24.)

The lyrical poetry of the playwright in exile also reflects his convictions. Rarely is he able to look at the California landscape without thinking of the social system, the poverty, the inequality, the commodity character of everything. Of course Brecht was not blind to California's beauties:

Die Landschaft des Exils

. . . Die Oeltürme und durstende Gärten von Los Angeles
Und die abendlichen Schluchten Kaliforniens und die Obsmärkte
Liessen auch den Boten des Unglücks

Nicht kalt.

The oil derricks and the thirsty gardens of Los Angeles/And California's ravines in the evening dusk and the fruit markets/Affected even the messenger of misfortune/Not a little.

The beautiful poem "Garden in Progress" about Charles Laughton's park garden in Santa Monica seems to him unfit for the "dark times" and he refuses to publish it. In a "Letter to a Grown-Up American" he describes his immediate California environment:

"The world is hungry and in ruins. How can one regret to be here? I saw no possibility until the idea came to me that these pretty villas [in Santa Monica] are built from the same material as the ruins over there; as though one and the same ill wind that tore down the buildings over there had taken all that dust and dirt and whirled it here together into villas. For one thing is true. We live in a time without dignity.

"It is hard to describe; I have often started and given up again. Of course the reason must be people. To begin with the neighbors, small people. They are friendly and not snoopy. They see a woman keeping the house and the garden in shape, a man at his typewriter; so they tell the police which inquires about us that we are 'hardworking people' who should be left in peace. They get figs from our garden and bring cake, and they don't have the pinched, neurotic disposition of German petty bourgeois nor their servility and arrogance. They move more freely, more gracefully and they don't nag. To be sure there is something empty and meaningless about them as in the characters of superficial, glib novelists. In school marks are given not only for zeal, literacy and intelligence but also for "popularity." One can hardly object: perhaps I object only because I was not popular myself nor did I wish to be. If the children are to learn how to adjust to society, one should ask first of all: To what kind of society?

"The newspapers, on the other hand, are full of violence among the lower classes: men shoot unfaithful wives, teen-agers axe drunken fathers who beat up mothers, and so on. . . . People change their place of work and even their trade incessantly and apparently without giving it a second thought and they move into districts or even into other cities that are easier of access; some move across the entire continent, and several times at that. So they hardly get to know their dwelling place; they have neither a fatherhouse nor a home. No friendships grow, but no hostile feelings either. As for opinions, the ideas of the ruling class rule almost unchecked. . . . Adjustment is a subject of instruction. The more intelligent man succeeds better in it, the reluctant one is a problem for doctors and psychologists. To hold one's job — it is always insecure — one has to be a 'regular guy,' that is to say normal. Never mind the qualifications; what matters is replaceability, the minimum. All this leaves little room for individuality."

The insecurity of existence and the vulnerability of most American families is described in the following passage:

"Apart from the great general crises, one is theatened by the small personal ones. Sickness of a single family member can rob the family of all its savings and of most of its plans for the future. Under these conditions the hidden, hardly ever mentioned, stinking prejudices of broad masses against Negroes, Jews and Mexicans assume a sinister significance."

"The great lack of security and independedence perverts the intellectuals and makes them superficial, fearful, and cynical. Yet, it is part of their contract as it were that they appear 'easy-going, cheerful and mentally balanced' [all three expressions given in English], which requirement they fulfill by smoking a pipe, keeping their hands in their pockets, and the like. In the Old World, intellectuals still take pride in the illusion that they work for something finer than their pay. Civil servants maintain public order, doctors heal, teachers spread knowledge, artists entertain, engineers produce. 'Of course' they get a remuneration, but that's only because they have to live; their work is important far beyond that."

In the United States this fiction is no longer valid and Marxism has lost one of the most sensational effects it had in Europe:

"By sensationally unveiling the deals of the bourgeois state, Marxism achieved an educational shock effect that is not possible here. Here you have to deal with a state directly managed by a bourgeoisie that is not for a moment ashamed of being bourgeois. The parliament here is more or less an agency and it acts and speaks as such. That can hardly be called corruption, for there is no illusion." (February 2, 1942.)

In conclusion, Brecht says: "No wonder everything affecting man's relations to man lacks nobility, decency and dignity. Utensils too, dwellings, furniture, even the landscape itself are mean, infamous and undignified."

In numerous poems and prose notes Brecht speaks of the lack of dignity of a commodity-producing society, and he opposes to it the great dignity of old products fashioned directly for use. In his diary he says:

"The elements of this way of life are ignoble. It must be the baseness of the production relations which makes everything banal. Here if anywhere it would be necessary to keep one's distance; but no one respects this desire. Eating, looking at a landscape, talking, writing a book, reading a book, business — all that has an ulterior purpose, one that does not smell quite right and is not quite dignified and satisfying in itself." (March 30, 1942.)

The higher dignity of artifacts belonging to past epochs has been celebrated in a poem from his pre-Marxian time:

Immer noch
Wenn schon der achte Autotyp
Auf dem alten Eisen des Fabrikhofs liegt
(R.I.P.)
Stehen die Bauernkarren aus der Lutherzeit
Fahrbereit unter dem Moosdach.
Ohne Makel . . .

Still,/when the eighth model of car/will be rotting in the iron yards/R.I.P.,/the peasant wagons from the Pilgrim's age/will be standing under the moss-covered roof/ready for use/without fault.

Not only their old age or their origin from pre-capitalist times — when products were not manufactured for the sake of profit but just for use — but long-established use also may lend dignity to the products of human labor:

Von allen Werken die liebsten
Sind mir die gebrauchten.
Die Kupfergefässe mit den Beulen und den abgeplatteten Rändern
Die Messer und Gabeln, deren Holzgriffe
Abgegriffen sind von vielen Händen: solche Forman
Schienen mir die edelsten. So auch die Steinfliesen um alte Häuser
Welche niedergetreten sind von vielen Füssen, abgeschliffen
Und zwischen denen Grasbüschel wachsen, das
Sind glückliche Werke.

Eingegangen in den Gebrauch der vielen
Oftmals verändert, verbessern sie ihre Gestalt und werden köstlich.

Of all things I like the best the used ones./Copper vessels with dents and flattened brims/Forks and knives with wooden handles handled by many hands/Such shapes are the noblest in my eyes. Flagstones around old houses/And with tufts of grass growing between them. These/are good things./Absorbed by the users/they have often changed, their shapes/have been improved, they are precious.

Objects of this kind are rare in the "New World," and Brecht appreciated it all the more highly when his son Stefan managed to find one for his Birthday:

> *Das Fischergerät*
> In meiner Kammer, an der getünchten Wand
> Hängt ein kurzer Bambusstock, schnurumwickelt
> Mit einem eisernen Haken, bestimmt
> Fischnetze aus dem Wasser zu raffen. Der Stock
> Ist erstanden in einem Trödlerladen in "Downtown."
> Mein Sohn
> Schenkte ihm mir zum Geburtstag. Er ist abgegriffen
> Im Salzwasser hat der Rost des Hakens die Hanfbindung
> durchdrungen.
> Diese Spuren des Gebrauchs und der Arbeit
> Verleihen dem Stock grosse Würde . . .
> *The Fisherman's Tool*

In my room, on the white-washed wall/a short bamboo stick, with a string wound around it,/and an iron hook made to gather in/the nets from the water. The stick/was brought from an antiques dealer downtown./My son gave it to me for my birthday./It looks well used. Saltwater has eroded the hook,/the rust has colored the hemp./These traces of use and work bestow great dignity on the stick . . .

Brecht read Walter Benjamin's essay on Baudelaire in Svensborg, and though he ridiculed it at the time he may have found some value in Benjamin's theory of the "loss of aura" as a historical interpretation of that depersonalization and loss of dignity in objects of daily use. Long before Marshall McLuhan and in a much more sophisticated way, Benjamin knew "that over great historical epochs the manner and character of perception changes along with the entire way of human communities." *(Schriften,* I, 273.) In the Baudelaire essay, this loss of aura is exemplified in photography: "What must have been resented in daguerrotypy as inhuman, not to say deadly, was the need to stare into a camera. For the camera receives the person's image without returning his glance. The eye expects a response from him to whom he gives himself. Where that expectation is fulfilled, . . . the experience of aura is received in its fullness. . . . The aura experience therefore is based on the transference of a form of reaction current in human society onto the relationship of inanimated objects or of nature to human beings." (ibid., p. 461.) In a footnote Benjamin adds that the ability to lift one's eye is the source of poetry, and one may conclude that poets are especially sensitive to the loss of aura.

Mass-produced goods in sanitary wrappers, offered without a trace of the work that made them or of previous use, lack aura. They are "virginal" both in the sense that their origin is invisible and that no hand has touched them. (A car, in contrast to a horse, need not be broken in.) In mass-produced goods individual traits as a rule are called defects. Inasmuch as modern production methods and the method of commodity production for the market have historically appeared as two sides of one phenomenon, it is not surprising that for all practical purposes the technological products cannot be distinguished from the system that maximizes profit. Brecht, sensitive to such experience, preferred the noble character of pre-capitalistic craftsmanship and its products. The revolutionary seems to turn into a romantic; yet he is only trying to use the example of old times to demonstrate what — on a far higher level of development — ought to be restored. To characterize his own activity, Brecht has used a term that corresponds to his evaluation of contemporary brand goods: he styled himself a craftsman of words, fashioning utensils for the tasks of a revolutionary class. Thus he tries to transcend the commodity-producing society both backward and forward.

Brecht's non-bourgeois mind also explains his disregard for private fame and private distinctiveness. He did not mind incorporating into his own poems gleanings from Villon, Rimbaud, Lucretius, Goethe, and he accepted collaborators in writing his plays. Like a medieval master, who humbly concealed his person behind the work, Brecht wants to be a useful comrade-in-arms in the fight for a better world. It is precisely this trait that has made Brecht so eminently original and his style so incisive.

To sum up Brecht's image of America in the context of his development: in the beginning there was the young man's obvious fascination with the greatness, generosity, the power and dynamism of North Americans. Enthusiasm for modern technology and its achievements (Lindbergh crossing the Atlantic, radio, sky-scrapers) and for boxing ("Memorial Plaque for Twelve World Champions," IV, p. 307 f.) blend with the image of a new continent that does not know Germany's tepid mediocrity and weakness. To be sure, at an early stage Brecht also utters esthetic skepticism against the *forms* of new utensils, the ugliness of which however he is willing for the moment to tolerate as inescapable. Nor is this fascination muted yet by the unspeakable misery he encounters in Upton Sinclair's novels. Not until he becomes familiar with Marxist theory in 1926 does his perspective change. Now America turns into the horrifying model of the capitalistic production form. The impressionistic description of total alienation in human relations which we have seen in the

Jungle of the Cities is (in *St. Joan of the Stockyards*) transformed into an allegorical stylization of class war and of the use of religion as an ideology designed to conceal increased exploitation.

The depression came at the right moment as it were to confirm Brecht's conversion to Marxism. America's image lost all glamor. In his Californian exile, Brecht discovered an aspect of American reality which the Marxist abstractions had previously prevented him from seeing: the life of the little man (the non-proletarian), his Lebensangst, his conformism — but also his greater freedom in comparison with the German philistine. The intellectuals' venality was not so much a new discovery as a second encounter, on a higher level, with a phenomenon he already had known back home.

Even so, Brecht's image of America was not devoid of kindlier hues. The poems "Coals for Mike" and "Shelter for a Night" bear witness, as does Joan Dark, the "middle-class girl" who progresses from a religious-eleemosynary engagement to a revolutionary one.

As to the American system of government, Brecht's entries in his diary are casual. He mentions the formalistic character of the American Constitution, which is ignorant of its own economic foundation (November 14, 1941). Nevertheless, he was not completely unmoved by the American democracy. On November 7, 1944, he notes: "Roosevelt reelected. Evenings with Laughton at Pascal's. . . . There (among others) Groucho Marx and Chaplin, Helli; I and Chaplin the only ones to listen to the radio." It seems that he was more interested in Roosevelt's election than most of the other guests. And on April 12, 1945, he notes: "Roosevelt dies. With the death of the enlightened Democrat the leadership of the democracies passes on to Churchill. W.'s friend reports that many of the women workers in her shop cried. Gandhi sends a telegram to Mrs. Roosevelt: condolences on her husband's death; congratulations that the man of peace did not live to see the murder of peace." There is no other political event in this eventful time between 1938 and 1946 to which Brecht paid so much attention in his diary.

On October 30, 1947, Brecht had to appear before the House Un-American Activities Committee to be questioned about his Communist activities. He had prepared a statement, which however the Committee refused to let him read (but which exists in the record).

It is a typically Brechtian way to speak the truth or his conviction and yet to use so much ruse that the audience cannot take offense. Brecht knows that there is free competition of ideas in the United States — or at least pride in the belief that it exists. In the spirit of

John Stuart Mill he argues that Marx' ideas should be admitted into this marketplace, and he concludes with a formulation which — though he may not have been aware of the allusion — is reminiscent of Schiller's intention in his "Essay on the Esthetic Education of Mankind." Schiller's wish, to be sure, was not to ennoble revolutionary ideas but to ennoble man and thus to make him capable of a nonviolent revolution.

© Copyright by Iring Fetscher, Frankfurt/Main
translated from the German by Henry and Hedwig Pachter

Karl Mannheim and the Sociology of Knowledge

BY EDWARD SAGARIN
AND ROBERT J. KELLY

I

WHEN, IN 1933, Karl Mannheim joined with many of Germany's great intellectuals to become refugees, it was for the forty-year-old sociologist already the second time in his life that he was to become an exile. The child of a Hungarian father and a German mother, he had been brought up in Hungary and had attended the University of Budapest, had been an enthusiastic supporter of the short-lived Communist regime that followed the defeat of the Central Powers in the First World War, and then, after the Hungarian Bolsheviks fell, he feared the course that the counter-revolutionary regime would lead.

Now, approximately one decade later, and already acclaimed as one of the most brilliant sociologists in Europe, Mannheim left the Germany to which he had only so recently come, this time to go to London. There he taught at the London School of Economics and turned out a prodigious amount of writing, and so great was the admiration of European scholarship for the man that following the end of Europe's second great holocaust and the downfall of Fascism Mannheim was invited to head the European UNESCO. It was an honor that he could not accept, for he was then ailing, and he died in 1947, only a few months after writing an introduction to a work dedicated to the concept of freedom in a planned society.

Almost a quarter of a century has passed since his death, and during this time Mannheim's renown has grown, and his work has become almost synonymous with the field of the sociology of knowledge. Although there is hardly a scholar who is not puzzled and does not object to some of the inherent paradoxes in his system of thought, it is possible that at least his best-known work, *Ideology and Utopia,* is as close to having become accepted as a classic in sociology as any work that has arrived on the scene since the First World War.

Mannheim devoted himself to demonstrating, in a manner that had not been done before, that ideas were products of their times and of the social statuses of their proponents, and that they had continuities from both previous ideas and from other social forces. If his position is valid, then Mannheim himself and the idea system that he created must be seen as spanning the years in which he lived; as being derived from and influenced by the vantage point of his being a Hungarian Jewish refugee, then a German refugee, of being intellectual, and of having found haven in a land that promised freedom without chaos, planning without dictatorship.

The influences on Mannheim were many, of schools and of individuals; it is difficult to mention a major name in European social science without noting what Mannheim borrowed, or what he rejected, for rejection is likewise an influence. For Mannheim's *Wissenssoziologie* was a stream into which flowed the confluential tributaries derived from Max Weber, Durkheim, Hegel, Marx, Thomas, Mead, Dewey, Husserl, Freud, Schlegel, and many more. But more than that, he was the product of the times of men whose names seldom appear in his works and even less frequently in commentaries and encomiums about him: of Henri Bergson, for example, and even more, of Albert Einstein.

II

Central to the work of Mannheim, most widely read, most controversial, most influential and perhaps most vulnerable, is *Ideology and Utopia,* but his other work, and particularly his output in England, can hardly be ignored. Actually, the bulk of what later came to be translated as *Ideology and Utopia* appeared in German in 1929; a section that was included in the English translation was also published in German, two years later in 1931; and Part I of the work was written expressly for the English translation, and first appeared in 1936. The major thesis of Mannheim's work, his search for the meaning of social reality, for the concept of truth, and for the role of the intellectual in discovering this truth, are already his concern in essays predating *Ideology.* Published in German in the 1920's, when he still had great hopes that democratic freedom in Germany would be saved by the efforts of the intellectuals, these essays were collected and translated, and they were published posthumously under the title, *Essays in the Sociology of Knowledge.*

One other book, that probably should follow *Ideology* in a Mannheim chronology, was written in the early thirties, shortly before the author fled from Germany. In 1956, this work was published in English under the title, *Essays on the Sociology of Culture.* Carrying an introduction by Ernest Manheim, and edited by him in cooperation with Paul Kecskemeti, the work is said to have undergone major revision after Mannheim reached England. It is like a postscript to *Ideology,* a bridge between Mannheim's concern with social reality and his later concern with democracy. If *Ideology* was concerned with reality, *Culture* focuses attention on the mind that perceives that reality; and both are concerned with the role of the intelligentsia.

Except for some introductory lectures that he delivered in 1934 and 1935, and that were published posthumously under the title *Systematic Sociology,* Mannheim's British output became more involved with social problems than with sociological problems. He was deeply dedicated to freedom, tolerance, dissent, but not to chaos; and he saw in England, and possibly in America and in the Scandinavian countries, the hope for a third way, where even intolerance would be tolerated, and where there would be a great moral commitment, of a quasi-religious (but not a supernatural) nature, to a faith in freedom. His work of this period bears a remarkable resemblance to that of Professor Hook, all the more interesting because their approach is from different vantage points, different disciplines. To those who would use this as an argument against Mannheim's relativism, one might answer that it is an argument in favor of his concept of the intellectual as being capable of transcending a position-based viewpoint in favor of truth.

III

The question, why does man behave differently in the framework of different social groups and class situations, is one of the fundamental problems Karl Mannheim sought to formulate and answer. The understanding of the psychological dynamics and elementary social processes which foster the "living together of man" was for Mannheim the crucial focus of the study of society.

Mannheim practiced what might be called macrosociology: his attention and interests centered around such topics as social stability, social groups and the psychic differentials corresponding to social status or class cleavages. What intrigued Mannheim was the role and function of the public vis-a-vis (in Mannheim's formulation) organized social groups. "The Public" as it is used by Mannheim testifies to the humanitarian-enlightenment ghettoes of the European intellectual heritage of which he was one of the most outstanding spokesmen. The democratic-socialist traditions and ideologies which provide the basis for his scientific humanism are not mere slogans cynically employed for purposes of power aggrandizement or mass exploitation. Rather they energize and sharpen the intellectual instruments by which the sociologist examines social conflict and disorder. The Public is a proud democratic abstraction. Timidly employed by Rousseau in the disguise of the General Will, it engendered a revolution, misused by the Bolsheviks and Social Darwinists. As The People it engendered pain, misery, and organized economic slavery; philosophical analysis led Plato to the justification of a totalitarian state so that the Republic (Public) could ensure the fulfillment of its mandates.

Mannheim's humanitarian impulses led him to a fresh conceptualization of the "public" in terms of its dynamics in the totality of society. "The public is the ever-present fluid element alongside the consolidated groupings," he wrote in *Systematic Sociology*.

In this sense the public as a viable sociopolitical category serves as the stage upon which a wide perspective of a society may be constructed. Not limited to insulated class structures or benighted by narrow vested interest groups, the public becomes the sociological mechanism through which opinion may be articulated, unfettered by class or group commitment. Recast in Durkheim's words, the public is a collective representation, an organic fusion of highly varied groups situated in a sprawling diverse social terrain. The public is the *sine qua non* of Freedom of Thought. "Freedom of thought, sociologically," Mannheim wrote, "means that a person can think not only in terms of his organized group patterns but also in terms of the flexible reactions to the more fluid integrations of various abstract publics. The abolition of the freedom of thought in modern dictatorial society consists not simply in forbidding people to think but in organizing and thereby making rigid, the public, which is in its essence an unorganized entity and can only function properly if it remains unorganized and fluid."

The public was for Mannheim a vital structural component in the life of a democratic society. Research conducted in Europe and the

United States confirmed Mannheim's fears that the trend toward total mobilization of society, the growing organizations and closure of opinion and communication for the sake of efficiency or whatever, invariably leads to the totalitarian nightmare. The democratic, humanistic goals espoused by many groups tend to be subverted toward oligarchic ends when the channels for dissent, reply and opposition are "organized." The public as a vocal instrument serves, dialectically, to chasten or clarify the actual tendencies of a society.

IV

Mannheim attempted to resolve the Marxian-Freudian dilemma which plagued European intellectual thought. It was perhaps the frank entertainment of contradiction that gave *Ideology and Utopia* its very special appeal. The intellectual legacies of both Marx and Freud had radically altered social thought. The emerging knowledge of human affairs, far from being helpful or useful, tended to undermine the easy and glib assurances of rationalist ideologies. No longer were European intellectuals optimistic about the human condition: the novels, poems and belles lettres of the period in which Mannheim's work first appeared were fraught with the pessimism of unresolve and ambiguity. The human dimension had been dramatically widened and prospects for its comprehension drastically reduced by the inheritors of Marx, as well as by Freud, Bergson, Sorel, and Pareto.

Marx's thesis that consciousness is inexorably tied to economic situations and that sociocultural perspectives cannot transcend one's class or group connection short-circuited permanently the rationalist-humanist tradition. In effect, conflict was a necessary consequence of collective life. Society by implication was indeed a Leviathan. The Freudian metaphysic "that every culture must be built up on coercion and instinctual renunciation" only deepened the human tragedy. *Civilization and Its Discontents,* with its social philosophy that the essence of civilization was predicated on pain and psychic warfare between the unfathomable depths of the Id and Ego, nourished the growing cult of irrationalism spreading over European social thought. Man was not only at war with his fellowman but struggling incessantly within himself.

Into this bleak and despairing universe of thought came *Ideology and Utopia.* Mannheim attempted to bind together in tense reconciliation a number of divergent philosophies and ideologies — to integrate into the rationalist tradition certain of the "irrationalist" tendencies circulating in his time. While most of the European intellectual camps floundered in their obsessions with the value-laden and culturally closed character of their *Weltanschauungen,* Mannheim confidently incorporated the contradictory and conflicting currents of these world-views into his works. To distinguish his works from relativism which he wished to transcend, he called the theoretical scheme "relationism":

"Relationism signifies merely that all of the elements of meaning in a given situation have reference to one another and derive their significance from this reciprocal interrelationship, in a given frame of thought. Such a system of meanings is possible and valid only in a given type of historical existence to which, for a time, it furnishes appropriate expression. When the social situation changes, the system of norms to which it had previously given birth ceases to be in harmony with it." And: "Every epoch has its fundamentally new approach and its characteristic point of view, and consequently sees the 'same' object from a new perspective."

As history conditions thought perspectives, so too social stratification "structures" perception and knowledge. One's class or group plays a major role in what one "sees," thinks and feels. Thought and knowledge for Mannheim are phenomenological in essence. What is entailed by the stratification of society is a differential system of reward and punishment — in a word, social inequality. Since inequality is institutionalized, since it is a structural feature of a society, the most reasonable procedure to adopt toward the eventual elimination of this social malaise fomenting frustration, poverty and war, would be, in Mannheim's view, to provide for the most articulate and knowledgeable representatives of each segment of a society to engage together in the formulation of policies and alternatives oriented toward change. The intellectuals of each group, classless intellectuals, would combine the diverse special knowledge relative to each class or segment of a society. Social continuity and consequently social stability rests largely in the hands of the intellectuals recruited from every segment of the society. By bringing their class or group-related knowledge together, the intellectuals can create the means by which society may meet the needs and fulfill the goals of all its component groups. To do otherwise, to either deny or betray this role, is to invite political, economic and social oppression. Totalitarianism and anti-intellectualism are rarely isolated phenomena. Democracy is the political entailment for such idealistic aspirations. Without the existence of egalitarian statuses shared by all, intellectual exchange becomes nothing less than a dreary vocalization of fantasies.

It was Mannheim's hope that the sheer variety of intellectual representation would tend to neutralize any one particular ideology and result in the development of a "detached perspective" not of the ivory tower but rather of a type at once deeply immersed in the depths of the society's experience and sensitive to all expressions of belief and knowledge. Thus the "common stock of knowledge" to which all members of a society would appeal and add would enhance rather than repress social life.

Mannheim anticipated the possibility underscored by Michels and others of the oligarchic tendencies in any group toward self-aggrandizement and self-perpetuation. The dangers of a class of "philosopher kings" was quite real to Mannheim. Such a possibility loses force, however, when we consider Mannheim's stipulation that the classless intellectual group be representative of all segments of a society — from the most oppressed and deprived to the most gifted and privileged. Moreover, the tendency toward oligarchy is present in those elites functioning in an exploitative milieu where one group benefits from the misery of others. In Mannheim's vision the function of the classless intellectual is to pursue a Utopian goal in which no class group is victimized by another. The mission of the intelligentsia, then, is the eradication of socially-induced deprivation and exploitation.

V

Karl Mannheim was caught in the cross-fire between skepticism and absolutism, and his view of the social universe was an attempt to reconcile the two. There is a reality, and though it may change with time and place, it is absolute in any given social setting. The partial and of necessity incomplete views that ideologically-positioned groups see of this reality do not preclude the existence of truth as an absolute, but merely the ability of a social movement (or those involved therein) to see this truth. The problem is not whether the thing is, but how to know what it is.

The position of Mannheim at this point almost coincides with that of Bergson, who finds that two people must look at the same table from different vantage points, no matter how slight this difference, and that it is impossible to attribute to the table any essences congruent with the experiences of all persons so viewing it. This ultra-phenomenological, neo-Berkleyan, and essentially solipsistic view would be rejected by Mannheim on many grounds, but immediately on his differentiation between the social universe and the physical universe. But despite the similarity of the approach of Bergson and Mannheim, they part company sharply in their conclusions: Bergson's that there is no universal truth of an absolute nature, even for physically existent phenomena; Mannheim's, that there is such truth but that we seldom perceive it, even for social phenomena.

Mannheim was himself too much a pragmatist — even an operationalist — not to see in his own position an insoluble paradox. For if there is a truth that cannot be determined, one that is not merely unknown but unknowable, then, as William James contended, it has no meaningful impact on human beings as truth. And Mannheim might have demonstrated that there is no reality other than the relativist position as observed by any group in a society. Or, finally, he might have contended that truth emerges from a synthesis of the relativist and positionist viewpoints of many observers: a viewpoint attributed to him by others, but one which he never himself espoused. There is a total and true reality, Mannheim asserts, but it cannot be achieved by merely adding all that is common in the ideological relationism of the various viewers. It is a reality that can be seen by the intellectual, although not by the intellectual who deserts his special position (in the world of what we have lately been calling academe) and attaches himself to the position of a given ideological group.

No single element in the sociology of knowledge that Mannheim creates is so crucial for his system, none so vulnerable, none so little understood. For, asserting that reality exists in only one form, and denying that each ideological position is true for that position and that no one truth exists, Mannheim would be at a dead end if he were unable to delineate a manner of arriving at the existing reality.

Hans Speier has criticized this aspect of the Mannheim thesis (in a paper devoted, incidentally, to Sorokin, not to Mannheim, but which deals with what Speier considers a common weakness in these two thinkers):

> Integral truth (of Sorokin) resembles the type of "synthetic" thinking which Karl Mannheim invented, in order to rid his "sociology of knowledge" of the epistemological difficulties arising from the "perspectivism" of "situationally determined" types of thinking. Both Sorokin and Mannheim speak of the relative and "partial" truth of the philosophies they reject, and then they

emerge from the welter of relativism with a pretentious claim of a "supertruth." Mannheim proposes that his "sociology of knowlege" may serve as a foundation of all social science . . . However, it is precisely the synthesizing of partial truths to arrive

at a supertruth (a word that Mannheim, of course, does not employ and which is used to suggest the pretentiously nonexistent) that Mannheim rejects. For it is not through synthesis that Mannheim arrives at knowing, not through a putting together of the partials. The intellectual becomes, Mannheim maintains, capable of understanding relativist distortion; through such understanding, he can remove the ideology from the perception. The intellectual alone can make an objective study of a situation, can dissociate from a perspectivist position, can analytically penetrate into the nature of the ideology, and thus can arrive at a non-biased view of reality. It is not a synthetic view, as has been imputed to Mannheim, so much as it is an analytic view. The social reality at which he arrives will be neither absolutist nor relativist; in a sense, perhaps, it will be both. Absolutist, in that it is inherent in the nature of the reality, and not phenomenologically induced by the viewer; relativist in that its truths are based in a social structure that is in flux, although also in balance, and hence the reality is time-centered and place-centered.

Many sociologists, including admirers of Mannheim, such as Merton and others, have taken exception to this view of the role of the intellectual, to Mannheim's exempting the intelligentsia from the pitfalls of ideology. Almost invariably, they catch Mannheim in a neat little paradox of his own making; namely, if all search for truth about social reality is distorted by the position from which this reality is viewed, then of necessity Mannheim's view of the sociology of knowledge is likewise distorted. He, too, is the banner-bearer of an ideology, namely, that of intellectualism.

It seems to the writer that the position of Mannheim is indeed vulnerable, but not for the reasons offered by his critics. The latter, it would appear, are asking the wrong question. In a system such as Mannheim's, his critics ask, can the intellectuals remain free from ideological bias? I should prefer to pose the question: Will they? — rather than: Can they?

What seems to be apparent here is the deification of the intellectual in order to get through the impasse that the author, by his own analysis, has created. That the intellectual can arrive at such truth, and that no one but the intellectual can do so, may be an empirically validatable and theoretically demonstrable fact (there is more of the latter, however, than the former, in Mannheim). But it is most unlikely that the intellectual will, or at least that he will in any great numbers, or if he does that his voice will be heard and that he will be effective. For the intellectual is psychologically motivated, it would seem, not only by class interests and social position, but by a fear of his own unreliability. Embracing, as he often does, a class position out of sentiment, rather than out of interest, he fears any deviation from that position that might mark him as an alien to it. He must be holier than the pope; he must be more distortionist than the ideologists whose views he is espousing.

Mannheim anticipated this objection (although he did not subject it to a psychological analysis of human behavior) by stressing that only the intellectual not assuming an ideological position is capable of viewing the absolute reality. Can such an intellectual be found? How long will he remain above the battle? What is wrong with his own motivations if he remains aloof from all ideology? And did not Mannheim himself, in the two decades from the writing of *Ideology and Utopia* until his death, strongly commit himself to an ideology: anti-totalitarianism, democratic freedom, planning, the Third Way? The contradiction is that the perspectivism from the position of the sidelines is as perspectivist as is the ideology from within the battle-lines. This is a difficulty which Mannheim (following in the tradition of Max Weber, who could not see the sociologist *qua* sociologist as a man of action) did not resolve, and yet the resolution of it can be found within the Mannheimian outlook.

VI

The position of the intellectual, as well as of other ideologists, is complicated by the concept of commitment. The group (or individual) that has taken a position, at which it may have arrived because of class interests (as stated by Marx) or economic origin (as contended by Brooks Adams and Beard), embraces an ideology, and then is committed by the dynamics of its position to continue to see reality in a manner dictated by that ideology. Thus, commitment is responsible for the self-perpetuation of ideology, and ideology becomes the support for commitment. The commitment acts as a caste-like barrier, structuring reality in a manner that fortifies, fixes, and redefines it, and this newly restructured reality then fortifies the commitment. It is cumulative, interactive, and continues on its own momentum.

The uncommitted scientist suffers from the isolation of being above the battle; the committed scientist from the prejudgments of involvement. The uncommitted scientist can never see the total reality because if he did, he would commit himself to social action; the committed scientist can never see the total reality because some area of it might shake his ideological orientation.

Is the situation hopeless? Can there be a sociology of knowledge? It is precisely in Mannheim's conceptualization that one can find the key to unlock this dilemma. The intellectual, as Mannheim contended, can indeed be the viewer of total social reality; he can see truth, and he alone can see it. The view of society taken by the intellectual is free of ideological distortion when it is consciously analytic and self-consciously self-analytic. It subjects each concept to study under its own microscope, to determine validity, to search out positional prejudice, to examine conscious and unconscious motivation for the view taken, to note cultural and societal determinants of a viewpoint, to make man the master and not the slave of his linguistic creation.

Such an intellectual must be committed, because having examined, he cannot refrain from a viewpoint, but his commitment to scientific analysis must take precedence over the commitment to an ideology, whose partial and inadequate view he has brought to the surface by his own awareness. His position is correct, not because it will be useful in arriving at an end which he finds desirable; but the position will aid in arriving at an end which is desirable because it is correct.

It is not in adding all that is common in diverse ideologies that the intellectual will arrive at the truth of social reality; it is by subjecting all such diverse ideologies to analytic techniques that he will arrive at a reality which is truth. In this manner, Mannheim offers to the modern thinker and doer a sociology of knowledge.

Otto Kirchheimer

BY JOHN H. HERZ

OTTO KIRCHHEIMER's life as a "German refugee intellectual" was perhaps typical, but also paradoxical in its impact. He came to the United States as one of a group of social scientists who were all deeply steeped in the neo-Marxian tradition of the Central European 'twenties, and with whom he shared the insights and the prejudices. He arrived at a time when Karl Marx, a bit belatedly, had likewise "arrived" in America, and so one might have assumed that his and his group's impact upon the intellectual life and even on the practical politics of the United States would have been considerable. In reality there was nothing of the sort. The practical effect that Marxism might have had was dissipated in the sectarian quarrels of the 'thirties, while in regard to theory the German group at first had to learn more from its American experience than it could contribute to it. What it did contribute at that time was understanding of what had happened in Germany. In this respect, Kirchheimer proved to be very close to Franz Neumann, who, in his *Behemoth*, provided the first, and still outstanding interpretation of the German version of fascism. Kirchheimer wrote searching analyses of the legal system and of social developments under Nazism. He had previously analyzed the Weimar system and the stages of its disintegration. At that time, already, his genius of understanding the typically "political," the peculiar constellation of social and political forces in its impact on system and structure of government, had been clearly revealed. With his Marxism he had combined the insights and methods of his principal teacher, Carl Schmitt, who, with his habit of always penetrating to the exceptional, extreme, "emergency" situation, had frequently been able to extract more understanding of the normal as well as the abnormal than the professional dissectors of the "typical" or "average" had been.

But in American social science the trend was away from the area in which the German intellectuals could make their contribution. It went in the direction of making social science more "scientific" in the quantifying and conceptualizing sense. That a group of Marxians would find itself outside the stream of a conceptualizing social science was certainly paradoxical. The reason was that their concepts did not fit those of the new American "scientists." They were too "sociological," derived as they were from tradition, from history, from philosophy, while those of the "modernizers" were adapted from engineering, mathematics, economics, and cybernetics. Hence "alienation" between them and the refugee scholars.

With the advent of the war came the practical problems of how best to serve the task of defeating fascism and rebuilding, or building, a democratic society in its stead. The "Central European Section" of OSS, where Otto Kirchheimer worked together with Franz Neumann, Herbert Marcuse, and others, of all places turned out to be the place where the left-Hegelian *Weltgeist* was to find its temporary abode. An interesting example of the convergence of theory and practice, this office served as crucible for German postwar revival as well as academe for an entire generation of younger American social scientists and historians who this way were saved from military service for intellectually more fruitful purpose. After the war Kirchheimer proved to be one of those whose efforts in the cause of German democratic reconstruction were tireless and unceasing. It was not their fault that in many areas "restoration" (that is, of pre-Nazi authoritarianism) rather than democratic or socialist reconstruction was the ultimate result.

The greatest paradox of Kirchheimer's career was that it began to bear its chief intellectual fruits toward its very end, that is, at a time when "social scientism" seemed victorious all over the place but when those in the forefront of intellectual endeavor came to realize its shortcomings and to accept the value of the approach and the insights of men like Otto Kirchheimer.[1] In the last decade and a half of his life Kirchheimer had concentrated on two topics, each vast but clearly defined, each particularly well suited to his background, training, and analytical power: the field of what he called, felicitously, "political justice," and the area of political parties and their impact on the political life of European postwar society.

His occupation with the first yielded his one major work, *Political Justice* (Princeton, 1961) (almost everything else he left scattered in periodical articles and the like, a vast agglomeration of writings

[1] Cf. following page.

only now to be collected and published in posthumous volumes).[2]
It constitutes a great intellectual achievement. The peculiar European
habit of training political scientists (who only in the postwar period
emerged as a professional group apart) in the law, which frequently
accounted for poverty of results and formalism of approach, in Kirchheimer's case meant that he was able to subject the law, that is, the
normative aspect of government and politics, to an encompassing and
penetrating political analysis. It served him to subject vast stretches
of the history of man, the most varied structures of political and legal
systems of past and present, of constitutionalism and democracy as
well as of authoritarianism and totalitarianism (in both its Commun-
ist-Stalinist and fascist versions), to questioning in regard to what
he defined as "political justice": the uses and abuses of legal procedure for political ends. Political crime, political criminal, political
trial here have found their classical treatment.

The second major area of his interest and research, that of party
developments, proved to be particularly rewarding because it happened to fall into an era of fundamental change, a transformation of
the structure and the functions of political parties which Kirchheimer,
with his almost uncanny sense for the new and coming and for the
specifically "political," forecast and analyzed in its essentials at the
earliest point of this development. He was the first to point out the
change of the ideological, class- or religion-oriented party of mass-
integration, and especially the leftist, workers-class-based party of
"opposition of principle," into the "catch-all" "people's" party, a type
of party which more and more tends to dominate the political landscape of Europe. With "moderation" and "deideologization" of parties
there goes hand in hand the development of a political system where
the classical "game of alternation" of government and opposition in
the traditional parliamentary fashion gives way to what Kirchheimer
called the "waning of opposition," the vanishing of the role-function
which "opposition of principle" or any other meaningful opposition
had played in the game of democratic politics. Kirchheimer discovered
and analyzed the first model of the new system in its Austrian version,
where "government by party cartel" had replaced the alternation of

[2] It is strange that he began to come into his own exactly at a time when his
friend and collaborator, Herbert Marcuse, suddenly began to achieve fame not
only as an author and scholar but, above all, as leader of the radical movement
of young people all over the world. Just now Kirchheimer, too, emerges posthumously as one of the intellectual beacons of the neo-socialist left, in particular in
Germany. The reason, perhaps, lies in the indebtedness of the group of which
Kirchheimer was a member to the young, "humanist," anti-alienation and anti-
establishment Marx, the Marx whose rediscovery in the 'Twenties had been one
of the lasting impressions that group had undergone.

rulers and opposition. He did not live to see, although he would not have been surprised by, the application of the model to West Germany under the "grand coalition" of the two major political groups. He did foresee the consequences of the new politics, such as the emergence of "extraparliamentary opposition," depolitization, anomie, conformism, but his criticism was by implication rather than by express deploration. There are situations which, as the saying goes, are "more easily deplored than described." Kirchheimer described.

Here he was, as usual, at the frontiers of knowledge, making it his business, as he once had put it, "to uncover the basic mechanisms of political order and disorder," making use of Marxism, no longer to build a utopia of things to come but still as "the best method of analyzing reality." "Opposition of principle" and "catch-all party," "game of alternation" and "waning of opposition," "political justice" and "judicial space" (the latter a term he coined for that realm of judicial discretion left to the judge in certain *Rechtsstaat* systems) — expressions like these not only testify to Kirchheimer's felicity in coining fitting terms but to a power of conceptualization infinitely more fruitful, because more "political," infinitely more pregnant with concrete significance than that of the input-output," "feedback," "civic culture" conceptualizers of the new "science" of politics. Kirchheimer's "political science," remaining in the great tradition of the Tocquevilles and the authors of the "Federalist," of Marx and Lorenz van Stein, of Georges Sorel and Carl Schmitt, is genuine "political" science rather than pseudo-political "science." As such it is beginning to influence the thought and approach of political scientists all over the world, and especially in this country. Kirchheimer, to be sure, was not a "systematic" thinker. He did not found a "school." He was above all an initiator, but his specific talent, his sensitivity to the historically relevant and to the uniquely political, taught many in many fields how to understand, analyze, and criticize political phenomena. Like his friend Franz Neumann he died too early, still pregnant with ideas and projects. We do not know to what kind and what areas of investigation they would have led him. What he contributed during his lifetime, however, constitutes a legacy which places him safely in the first rank of that group rich in talent and achievement which is the subject-matter of this issue of *Salmagundi*.

Felix Kaufman

BY REUBEN ABEL

IT WOULD be pleasant to be able to believe that ideas have lives and careers of their own — that they grow and flourish, or wither and die, on their own merits. Truth, crushed to earth, will rise again; in the free market-place of ideas, the truth will prevail; build a better mouse trap, etc. But the difficulty with this view is that it is pretty hard to determine what indeed is the truth; and there aren't any really free philosophical market-places. Rather, there are fads and fashions in ideas; and there are Berlin walls in the realm of the mind.

One such wall divides philosophy into two independent, and mutually unconcerned, armed camps. One camp (located chiefly in the English-speaking world, plus Scandinavia) works in the frameworks of naturalism, empiricism, positivism, pragmatism, philosophical analysis, logic, philosophy of science, and allied interests. The other camp (mainly in continental Europe — although Vienna was the birthplace of logical positivism) sees philosophy as largely consisting of metaphysics, existentialism, phenomenology, Marxism, Thomism, and varieties of philosophical anthropology. There is no conflict between these two views of what philosophy ought to be — would that there were! Rather, the attitude is one of pointed disinterest; of cultivated ignorance; of a rather edgy lack of concern. Philosophic debate now consists of certain pragmatists denouncing certain logicians; or of Marxists holding "dialogues" with Thomists; but these disputes are internecine: the participants are on the same side of the wall. As to what crosses the wall, it is often the loud accusation — and not altogether in jest! — that the other side isn't "doing philosophy" at all. This reciprocal incomprehension is due in part to a radical difference in temper of mind; in part to historical conditioning; in part to garden-variety narrow-mindedness. A British newspaper once carried the headline, when the English Channel was impassable because of heavy fog, "Continent isolated!"

Felix Kaufman was one of the very few remarkable individuals who traversed that intellectual fog bank. He grew in pre-Hitler Vienna, under influence of Edmund Husserl and Hans Kelson, two of the great figures in European thought. While still a young man, Kaufman did important and original work in jurisprudence, in philosophy, and on the concept of the infinite in mathematics. The famed "Vienna Circle" was meeting in those seething years between the two wars. In it there were gestated many of the revolutionary new ideas in philosophy, such as the verifiability theory of meaning, the tautological character of logic and mathematics, the attack on metaphysics, the view that the statements of ethics are expressions of emotion, and others. Kaufman was never a member of the Vienna Circle, but he attended many of its meetings. His own thinking then was dominated by the phenomenology of Husserl. He believed that there must exist objective structures of meaning in the world, and logical relations between them. The mind apprehends them directly, by an immediate intuition. This was the heritage of a powerful tradition of German idealism. Kaufman always considered that such objective certainties of meaning had to be taken for granted, or there would never be a foundation for any philosophy.

When Hitlerism came to Austria, Kaufman was one of the European intellectuals who were brought to this country by the efforts of Alvin Johnson, to join the "University in Exile" (now the Graduate Faculty of the New School). Those terrible years produced a great migration of ideas, as well as of men. After Kaufman arrived here, the single greatest influence on his thinking was that of John Dewey. Dewey believed, however, that it was meaningless to regard logic as existing objectively and independent of men; rather, logical relations between propositions emerge within a context of inquiry, in problematic situations which must be clarified by human beings on pain of suffering biological extinction. Kaufman did not see how so thorough-going a naturalism could be supported; he believed that logic, and the fixity of meanings, had to be presupposed in inquiry, and could not, like empirical knowledge and the sciences, emerge within inquiry; such presuppositions could not themselves be defined in naturalistic terms. Dewey, after reading a paper of Kaufman's on "Verification, Meaning, and Truth," wrote to Arthur Bentley (March 22, 1944) that Kaufman's

statements about logical grounds (and) methodological rules . . .
as not intrinsically related to scientific goals, are simply survi-
vals of Kant's *a priori* (that is, supplied by the mind) conditions
of knowledge, lugged in because of inability to forget.

And again (on March 18, 1945)

the difference between us springs from the fact that he thinks
that there are *antecedent* conditions and rules, and his "methodology" takes account of them, while I, of course, hold that it is
a matter of what takes place in ongoing, continued inquiry and
its consequences.

This basic issue was never resolved between them. Kaufman could
not account, to Dewey's satisfaction, for the source of the presupposed
logical and mathematical relations and meanings; and Dewey's quasi-
genetic explanation did not seem to Kaufman sufficiently sensitive
to the distinction between the rational and the empirical. But each
man studied the other's position, and each man grew accordingly.

Kaufman's *Methodology of the Social Sciences* appeared in 1944
(dedicated, incidently, to Alvin Johnson). In the preface, Kaufman wrote,

Shortly after the publication of my *Methodenlehre der Sozial-
wissenschaften* (Vienna, 1936), it was suggested that I write a
similar book in English, and I started to work on it. But gradually it became a very different book. This is largely due to my
study of Dewey's *Logic, the Theory of Inquiry*. While I was
strongly impressed by Dewey's analysis of scientific procedure,
I could not accept his theory of meaning. This led me to a
reconsideration of the problem how the logical analysis of scientific procedure (methodology) is related to deductive logic. I
came to the conclusion that methodology must be clearly distinguished from deductive logic and recognized as an autonomous
discipline . . .

Thus what came out of this remarkable meeting of minds was a
philosophic insight of great vitality and subtlety. It may be fairly
described as building on what is best in the two traditions. It leads
Kaufman to assert that there is nothing which is inherently unknowable, or incapable of precise statement. There is indeed a logical
skeleton inside our scientific and empirical knowledge, which must
be presupposed in any investigation, because without it nothing could

be investigated at all. But it would be gratuitous to make any further assumptions, metaphysical or otherwise, about this structure. There is no certainty in empirical knowledge, no "self-evident" truths, no reliance on an intuition into the nature of being, no synthetic *a priori*. Kaufman called this lack of finality in matters of fact, the Principle of Permanent Control. It is a close analogue to Dewey's view that science is essentially self-correcting.

It was a great loss to philosophy when Kaufman died, at the age of 54, on December 23, 1949.

Ernst Bloch—A Marxist Romantic

BY JURGEN HABERMAS

WERE I NOT scared by Ernst Bloch's generous use of mottoes — especially those citing the author himself — I might have picked the following: "Reason cannot flower without hope, hope cannot speak without reason, both in Marxist synthesis — other science has no future, other future has no science." This is one of the few epigrams of an epic thinker whose forte is not always the small gem, the aphorism, the parable. Bloch allows the abundant stream of his thought to expand into broad narrative. The voluminous compendium "Das Prinzip Hoffnung" (Hope as a principle), written in the United States, finished and edited in East Germany and published in West Germany (Frankfurt, 1959), is a mirror of a philosopher's wanderings and of his inner development — a mind's Odyssey in the spirit of Exodus. Like a knight errant, the thought wanders in quest of the dark source of being, as Jakob Boehme said: "Nothingness craves thingness, and hunger is desire expressed in the first verb: fiat (let there be.)" Bloch follows the same motif when he stresses hunger over Freudian libido as the fundamental drive. Ever-renewed hunger makes man run, widens self-preservation into self-expansion, and in its most enlightened development transforms itself into a force blowing up the prisons of need. Informed hunger, another form of *docta spes* (learned hope), unfolds into a resolution to abolish all conditions under which men vegetate as shipwrecked creatures. Hunger appears as the elemental energy of hope. The work itself which Bloch devotes to Hope betrays some of that hunger — a grandiose systematization of gleaned hopes into an intended system of conceptualized hope still in the making.

On hearing that reason cannot *flower* without hope, the positivist will object that reason ought to *comprehend*. Bloch however, in a singularly positive way, appropriates to himself that which the positivist seems to have unmasked as wrongly posed questions. Like the positivist he criticizes myths, religions and philosophies as shadows; but he takes them seriously as foreshadowing that which is to be created. Utilizing a distinction made in the modern logic of science, he retains the norm which, as it were, has been skimmed off the facts; but instead of conceiving of it as an ontological substratum, he understands it as an aura of intentional experiences transcending the existent. He does not object to previous philosophers' "courage to transcend" but to their false consciousness of it: to their mistaken belief that in transcending they get to know something that already has been there. This is how Aristotle understood essence as *fuisse;** and in the same way Heidegger still understands the absent presence of being as the expected return of something that already had existed in the beginning. Knowing, which from Plato's *anamnesis* down to Freud's analysis was understood as a return of memory, in fact refers to something expected, something that objectively is only potential. This defines the contours of a *vérité à faire,* of a truth to be realized, which "nowhere" is real, yet and to that extent is utopian. It is true that since the days when Thomas More gave Utopia its name, it has been able to unfold into a concrete utopia only to the extent that analysis of historical development and of its social motors has begun to unveil the conditions of its possible realization. Bloch does not deal with such analysis; he simply assumes it as accomplished through Historical Materialism. Yet he perceives a greater danger, namely that in his own camp the "regulars with their treasury of quotations" and the "know-it-all practitioners" would betray utopia for the business of its realization. To meet that danger, he calls for a more strenuous effort: to delineate the dimensions of utopia and to fix it inalienably for posterity.

What Bloch wants to preserve for socialism, which subsists on scorning tradition, is the tradition of the scorned. In contrast to the unhistorical procedure of Feuerbach's criticism of ideology, which deprived Hegel's "sublate" of half of its meaning (forgetting *elevare* and being satisfied with *tollere***), Bloch presses the ideologies to yield their ideas to him; he wants to save that which is true in false consciousness: "All great culture that existed hitherto has been the foreshadowing of an achievement, inasmuch as images and thoughts

---

* Translator's note: (lat.) *fuisse* the past tense of *esse,* to be.

** Translator's note: In fact Hegel's "sublate" has three meanings in one: to raise, to preserve, to abolish.

can be projected from the ages' summit into the far horizon of the future." Even the critique of religion, which Marx summarizes in his "Theses on Feuerbach*," is given a new-old interpretation. God is dead, but his locus has survived him. The place into which mankind has imagined God and the gods, after the decay of these hypotheses remains a hollow space. The measurements-in-depth of this vacuum, indeed atheism finally understood, sketch out the blueprint of a future kingdom of freedom.

Alluding to the amendment that Locke added to Leibniz, Bloch with tongue in cheek puts the economic determinism of official Soviet Marxism through the wringer to explain the "cultural surplus," the codified truth in mythology: there is nothing in the superstructure that was not inherent in the foundation — except the superstructure itself. A Solomonic orthodoxy, here as everywhere — yet not a return from Marx to Hegel as some might assume. Unlike the phenomenology of the mind, the phenomenology of hope does not pursue its former incarnations. In Bloch's opinion, rather, the mind's figurations derive the objectivity of their appearance from the "experimenting validation" of the innovation projected originally. So far, Philosophy has kept incognito her essence, the objective possibility of a kingdom of freedom: "In the final count, Platonic *anamnesis* has always smothered the dialectically open Eros; and all philosophy that existed hitherto, including Hegel's, has locked it up with contemplative-antiquarian devices" — "antiquarian" because it dresses the future up as the long-ago past; "contemplative" because of a double inversion whereby first the still-to-be-expected end is projected into the beginning and then this act of genesis is subjected to theoretical discussion instead of being achieved through responsible praxis after critical preparation.

Resistance to Utopia — literary and psychological

The odds against a boom in utopia are high. Ever since, decades ago, Karl Mannheim pronounced the utopian impulse moribund, the sociology of knowledge has accumulated further confirming symptoms. The more long-range military planning, the more hermetically the Western world is closing itself off from the future. In West Germany

* Ludwig Feuerbach: Marx's predecessor in the critique of alienation.

the aborted revolution from the right boasts posthumous literary triumphs over the revolution from the left: from Nietzsche it gains arguments against the wishful thinking of philosophical history; Hegel, whose strictures against mere opinions are well known, is seen as a promoter of progress, though only that progress in the consciousness of freedom that so easily is mere opinion.

In the campaign against utopia, two strategic approaches are discernible. On the one hand, a sort of direct negation of history — the essence of that anthropological Platonism which decrees constant yardsticks for the optimum conditions of survival. It is supplemented by an esthetic Platonism, which in a universe of pure forms promises eternity to the crystals formed by great individuals in felicitous moments. In both cases the stream of history turns into a stagnant swamp; instead of a meaning being realized, nature meaninglessly returns into itself.

But world history wants to be understood in terms of epochs. It does not recognize any allegedly immutable nature; nor does the dialectics of progressive rationalization permit us to deny the possibility of a meaning in history. Another line of argumentation, therefore, tries not to negate history but to overtake it. Eschatological thinking bets on the return of a mythological age, be it through pious evocation of destiny or through a botanizing philosophy of universal history. Philosophy of history has been outbid by metahistory, and a situation that has been defined by its place in history need no longer be subjected to a rational analysis of its objective possibilities. This thinking subjects history to the cycles of metahistory; it diverts the open historical process of possible self-determination back into the given proportions of natural events: the book of history is retranslated into the book of geological layers of world ages.

The conservative theorem of the preservation and equilibrium of energy, which provides a common denominator for physics and ethics, excludes innovation and progress toward improvement; it even forbids dreaming about it. Bloch, however, describes even the most evanescent wish-thoughts as elements of a great dream into the future, as the cell of a hope whose principle shall place humanity "back on its hinges." Ernst Jünger, who may represent an entire school of thought, dismisses such speculations: "Nowadays even philosophers may be heard to say: 'If this or that did not exist, everything would be all right.' Presumably if this or that did not exist, things might be even more ghastly — not to mention the fact that one horror usually follows the other. Such ideas feed on the habit of identifying reason with morality. The world is full of reasonable men who denounce each others' unreason. Nevertheless life goes on, though often in a direction different from what everybody intended." Bloch would recognize this as the language of doormen who once more shut out the openness of the world since it must be administered, must be a closed world. Against the new romanticists he could quote one of their respectable ancestors, Franz Baader: "A fundamental prejudice of people is the belief that what they call the future world is a thing created and perfected for men, like a house built without their doing and ready for them to move in, whereas the real world is a building that man only can erect for himself and that grows only with him." (Works 1851/61, vol. VII, p. 18).

Nietzsche re-invented the old idea of eternal return in order to sanctify "the moment." In the notion of amor fati, the will to power climbs the high mountain to the summit of high noon; this is the moment of full happiness for the disillusioned consciousness, because even in this most fragile moment of its restless striving it is guaranteed return and thereby eternity, meaningfulness and an equal value with all other moments. The effort of this ultimate will negates its projection into the future and takes the present as it is. In the same spirit Bloch says: "The ultimate will is to be truly in the present. Man finally wants to be here and now as himself; without delay and distance he wants his full life." But his redeeming word, hope, excludes the notion of eternal return. The darkness of the lived moment can only become more impenetrable through a mere reform of moral consciousness, through a revaluation that only refortifies that which has been revalued. Therefore the chain of eternal return must be broken; the exit into the virginal openness must be won in a utopian way: "The urge not only presses itself into the openness where there still are alternatives of choosing, discerning, seeking a way; besides that way there is in the objectively possible something that agrees with us and that promises to satisfy the urge." Carpe diem can be realized only when the seal of amor fati has been broken. The cover of Platonic anamnesis has been taken off the dialectically open Eros. This relationship to Nietzsche makes Bloch an antipode of the opponents of enlightenment who, in their own way, try to use Nietzsche to take the wind out of utopia's sails.

Disregarding for the moment such resistance, the reception of Bloch's work may also be handicapped by his mannerisms. The style of late expressionism made famous by Gottfried Benn* in literature and by Karl Schmidt-Rottluff in painting, is now represented in philosophy by Bloch. It is the style of the first decades of our century, which in its middle now has become antiquarian, though with signs of maturation and relaxation. There are erratic blocks of hyphenated terminology, luxuriant growths of pleonastic turns, the heaving of dithyrambic breath, a choice of metaphors that is reminiscent of Arnold Böcklin** rather than of Walter Benjamin. All this still shows forcefulness and greatness, but it has become obsolete.

Moreover, the utopian beam is broken into a spectrum of generational experiences that no longer are readily understood. The Youth Movement cannot be outmoded in the same respectable way as was Victorianism. We are a little tired today of breaking out into free nature, of nostalgia for a vagrant's life, of sentimentality for the circus and prostitution. There are traces of the *Wandervogel's* juvenile sociology even in the concept of hope. Present-day youth has been called skeptical for good reason; and the question arises whether all that Boy Scout romanticism did not reflect the experience of a past generation, whether new generational experiences may not clash if not with utopia then certainly with Bloch's initiation into utopia.

The Heritage of Jewish Mysticism

Bloch unexpectedly emerged in the Bonn latitudes and has wrought havoc among the accustomed topography.***

Wherever Marxism appropriates European philosophy without melting it in the heat of transcendent criticism, with Bloch's help it creates an amazing reconciliation of traditions that, especially in Germany, seem to have been separated along religious lines. The Jewish sensibility in Marxism brings to life certain perspectives that once were the province of cabbala and mysticism; likewise, it unearths the Pythagoreic and Hermetic traditions that often were cut off and rarely were refined to the level of official philosophy. The Christian philosophy of the Middle Ages never succeeded in unravelling the Hellenistic knot. Under the label of neo-Platonism, this tradition re-entered the German consciousness during the Renaissance. Start-

* Germany's greatest poet during the Hitler years; tried to pin expressionism on Hitler's coat-tails but was repudiated.

** Neo-romantic painter of the Wilhelminian era.

*** Bloch gave up his professorship in Leipzig, East Germany, and sought asylum in West Germany after the Hungarian revolution.

ing with Paracelsus and Jakob Boehme, handed down through the Swabian Pietists to Hegel, Schelling and Hölderlin, it crossed the threshold of high speculation with Schelling's "philosophy of nature" and his doctrine of the "ages of the world." The very names of this philosophy of nature and of the ages of the world indicate how his thinking was orbiting elliptically around the two centers of matter and historical progress. Marx himself alluded to this apocryphal tradition of historical materialism, specifically quoting Jakob Boehme, in connection with a polemic against the mechanical materialism in 17th century England and 18th century France. The passage, quoted by Adorno, can be found in "Die Heilige Familie." Bloch ties this thread into a knot and makes its development his business.

One must realize that in Germany philosophy is so thoroughly imbued with the Protestant spirit that Catholics who wish to philosophize must almost turn Protestant, while on the other hand Catholic thought has never emerged from the ivory tower of Thomism except in non-philosophical form. In this light, Bloch's philosophy (which incidentally interprets Christ, very much in the spirit of the Old Testament, as a prophet of a kingdom of *this* world) assumes interesting functions of mediating between traditional Protestant philosophies. Philosopy has been alienated from nature because its ears listened to the divine *logos* in history; Catholic thought has been alienated from history because its eye was turned exclusively to the appearance of the divine logos in nature. The tradition to which we have alluded, however, from its beginning embraces both ideas: the autonomous liberation of mankind through history, and the restoration of fallen nature. In Marx's *Paris Manuscripts* Bloch found the formula for a rational retrieval of this utopia still enmeshed in myth: socialism promises, along with the naturalizing of man, the humanizing of nature. Fully developed nature and definitively realized history lie together on the horizon of the future. "Therefore nature, which is never gone, and which always envelops us with so much brooding, indefiniteness and cipher, remains the vision of tomorrow, not of yesterday."

The overtones in this sentence of Bloch's point to the melody in Schelling's philosophy. Bloch's basic experience is darkness, the unresolved, the lived moment's nostalgia, that nothingness of the mystics which always craves thingness, the abstract reflection of which can still be seen in Hegel's logic. In this primeval hunger, the world knot longs to be untied; if not untied, it will throw back, unsolved, life into its origins. "Each lived moment therefore would, had it eyes, witness the beginning of the world which always recommences in it; each moment is undeveloped, the year zero, the beginning of the world." This determination might have been gleaned from Schelling's first fragment of *Ages of the World,* where he studied "time in its entirety." The same could be said of the subsequent sentence: "Nothingness as 'not yet' traverses 'having become' and beyond; hunger becomes a productive power at the brittle front of an unfinished world. Therefore the world as process is the gigantic proof of its saturated solution, that is to say, of the kingdom of its saturation." In Schelling's "System of Transcendental Idealism" the unconscious assumes the double meaning of an impulsive subconscious out of the "dark foundation of nature" and a winged superconsciousness out of the "voluntary favor of a higher nature"; likewise, Bloch separates the nightly dream's unconsciousness from the day dream's, the no-longer-conscious of memory from the not-yet-conscious of the future.* In this view, the romantic pathos of an antiquarian approach misses an entire sphere of ciphers, symbols, mythical elements which appear not only in legends but in viewing nature and art, in dreams and visions, in poetry and philosophy. Bloch subjects these elements to a "utopian treatment," trying to unravel their unredeemed nature and to interpret these emblems of the future. Into this anticipatory consciousness he even invites Carl Jung's "archetypes" and Ludwig Klages' diluvial "images," though turned upside down. He finds in this consciousness the kingdom of freedom where mankind is rid of self-alienation and directs its destiny in freedom. This can be achieved only by abolishing the domination of man over man, that is to say in a socialist way. Only then one man's fortune need no longer be another man's misfortune; only then the one need not be measured against the other.

Matter as soul of the world; technology without violence

However, any dream of a better life would be "limited to an inner, nay quite enigmatic world enclave" were there not a potential that was to meet its anticipation at least in history. Bloch skips the sociological-historical inquiry into the objective possibilities derived dialectically from the social process; instead he goes back immediately to the general substratum of the world process: to matter; for "real possibility is nothing but dialectical matter." This concept of potentiality, which already was subsumed in the Aristotelian conception of

* *Translator's note:* "bewusst means both "conscious" and "aware."

matter, had been enriched and fecundated in the subterranean streams of neo-Platonism until Schelling took it up again. Matter, or *natura naturans*, no longer needs the entelechies of form; it is the one and all; it creates, and gives birth to, the incarnations of its fertility. It is that which exists in potentiality, yet in such a way that the history of nature points to the history of mankind and "depends" on it. For mankind is charged with the ability to do or to do differently; in exchange with nature this ability frees an ability to become and an ability to become different. The subjective potential reacts to the objective potential, though it is not arbitrary but always mediated: first, through the objective tendencies of social development; then through that which nature, though not completed yet, makes possible or makes impossible. That which is authentic in the world is still in expectancy; it is waiting, "fearful of being frustrated, hopeful of success," to be realized through the labor of socialized men — literally through the work of their hands. Here is Schelling's doctrine of potentiality in a Marxist interpretation: "Subjective potentiality coincides not only with what is coming into existence but also with him who is realizing it in history; and these coincide the better, the more consciously men become creators of their history. Objective potentiality coincides not only with that which is changeable but also with that which can be realized in history; and these coincide the better, the more the independent environment is also increasingly mediated with man." In utopistically postulating the harmony of the unreified object with the manifest subject, the harmony of the unreified subject with the manifest object, this new philosophy hopes to decipher the echo of an old identity.

Bloch does not shrink from using the Kantian concept of judgment, as broadened by Schelling's philosophy of nature. Along with the alienation of socialized man, nature is "lost" and demands to be confronted with the aborted outline of its concealed "subject," to be interpreted as *natura naturans*, and to be led to its goal by the hand of man. The "mechanical" view, which leads to the technical management of the forces of nature, misses the concept of nature as needing to return to itself. Only when the "teleological" view comprehends the phenomena as extrapolations of themselves as it were, the subjective purposes of human endeavor will no longer be suspended in empty air but will find the connection with a purposefulness suggested by nature itself. Bloch takes up Goethe's quarrel with Newton and opposes to the science of nature a phenomenology of nature as a sympathetic configuration based on the profound heritage of Pythagorean number symbolism, cabbalistic teachings on signatures, Hermetic physiognomics, alchemy and astrology. But unfortunately, this Shellingian adumbration of a knowledge of beauty experienced in nature, of a knowledge of nature through art, but scantily conceals the embarrassing fact that there is no methodical direction for a "phenomenology of nature." For all previous attempts were based on an inapplicable simile, the analogy of microcosm and macrocosm, of man and universe.

To be sure, in these musings Bloch encounters the memorable problem of a "technology without violence." Scientific theories and their technological application are indeed "alien to nature." Both dispose of nature according to stated laws defining its behavior "for use." The functional relationships determined by these laws are indifferent to nature "per se" and productively ignorant of its "essence." Technology, which has to proceed according to such laws, lacks the relatedness to any favors of nature, to the "'old, natural world." Bloch criticizes this lack of relatedness to the earth, which is the source of the exaggerated artificiality of "the bourgeoisie's mechanical universe," its specific misery and its specific ugliness. The overworked epithet "bourgeoisie" appears in this place because, Bloch feels, in the framework of capitalistic production relations our technology has not only been developed but also been disfigured by them. Just as in the exchange of commodities the abstract relations of exchange values remain indifferent to the concrete use values, so in the natural sciences the abstract laws remain alien to the natural substratum. This analogy, touched upon by Lukacs some decades ago in *Geschichte und Klassenbewusstsein*, encourages Bloch to expect a new development in the technological production forces under socialism: they will shed their abstract form and adapt themselves to a concrete "cooperation with nature in production." The freedom won in social policies will be projected into natural policies: "As Marxism has discovered the subject of history — the worker concretely creating himself in man as a worker —; as Marxism expects the full discovery and realization of this subject under socialist conditions, so it is probable that Marxism will also, in its technology, penetrate into the subject of natural processes, not yet manifest per se: mediating men with the subject, the subject with men, itself with itself."

According to Marx's original conception the forces of production, including technology, remain the actual carriers of social wealth. When production relations that had become obsolete and narrow were revolutionized, these forces were merely liberated. It was even assumed that these production relations alone are responsible for the irrationality of an order that prevents objectively possible progress to reach a higher stage of development. Bloch, on the contrary, sees himself forced by certain experiences to question the production relations' innocence, which seems philosophically guaranteed. There are indications that in the East and in the West, in spite of their conflicts, social developments are tending towards a common denominator. Anyway, on both sides of the Iron Curtain we observe an increasing number of phenomena lending themselves to the sociological interpretation of the "industrial society." This aspect may have led some observers in the West to neglect, dangerously to neglect, the diverging trends that result from the different orders of property. But it seems to be true that the technological development per se produces an organizational framework that is less dependent on production relations than the Marxists had ever assumed. Moreover, the "power of alienation" produced by these institutions on the basis of technology is no smaller under socialism than under capitalism. Bloch preserves his utopia by prophesying a socialist resurrection not only for capitalism but also for the technology it has produced. The "capitalist" nature of technological means and their organizational framework which exists in the socialist countries could then be explained as a sort of "cultural lag."

Extravagance of utopia and melancholy of fulfillment

This idea should not be confused with the effect that accompanies it. The latter appears in resentful cultural criticism, in social romanticism almost in spite of our knowing better. Bloch betrays it in his polemics against Walter Gropius and Le Corbusier, against the engineers' art of steel furniture and flat roofs and concrete architecture; the curse of abstract technology is said to communicate itself to the lines of architecture: "They have an even more chilling effect as they allow no crannies but only kitsch lighting." In a general way, Bloch like Lukacs opposes modern art not merely from a feeling of duty: in his praise of "realism" he shows his affinity with classicist esthetics. Like Hegel he interprets art after the model of the symbol. The beautiful appearances reflect that appearance which things and forms project towards what they could be in the future: emerging matter instead of contoured ideas. This esthetic can be seen as a complement of Adorno's: art must not demonstrate its truth by referring to existing contradictions.

The esthetic problem takes us back to the political problem: Bloch is a citizen of a different republic.* His thinking addresses itself to a different audience, for instance when he tries to melt the dogmatism and empiricism of a frozen dialectic materialism under the sun of its utopian origins. His writing is beholden to different conventions. Thus, he fulfills his quota of jargon: he denounces Martin Heidegger's phenomenology as the experiences of a petty-bourgeois animal; he scoffs at Klages, the complete Tarzan philosopher; he dismisses D. H. Lawrence as a sentimental penis poet. The most obnoxious feature in all this is its lack of precision. Similar invectives against Jaspers may be explained as a defense against the fatuous phrase calling Bloch "the Jaspers of the East." The comparison is self-destructive; there is not one *tertium comparationis*. But on the whole Bloch's polemicisms use a coin in which many Western critics have paid him back. He feels no qualms about using, in his original version, the Stalin quotations which then were purged from the West German edition of his book but which our local anti-Communists** did not fail to hold against him.

But neither the political denunciation nor the complementary attempt to transform the gnostic Bloch into a distant theologian should prevent us from looking for the dimension in which his philosophy takes its political root. Bloch merely dresses his intimate relationship to Lenin's strategy of violence in Gothic rags: "Not without reason does Marxism include, besides the sort of tolerance that expresses itself in the kingdom of *freedom*, the cathedral-like vision that expresses itself in the *kingdom* of freedom, where freedom itself is conceived as a kingdom. Nor are the roads to that kingdom liberal: they are conquest of state power, discipline, authority, central planning, collectivization, orthodoxy . . . Total freedom precisely does not lose itself in hopscotch arbitrariness, which only leads to empty desperation; it can triumph only through its will to orthodoxy." These ideas are at one with deep traditions of German philosophy; and yet in the same breath that "vision of kingdom," that "essence of order" are being sanctified in a manner which, with due respect, borders on the totalitarian: "Order *in all kinds of fields* and spheres — from cleanliness and punctuality to the vista of all that is manly and masterly, from ritual to architectural style, from numerals to the philosophical system." The practical violence of the means transgresses the purpose even in the muddiness of its theoretical anticipation. To be sure,

---

* He came from East Germany.
** in West Germany.

Bloch knows very well about the "melancholy of fulfillment"; he speaks of "a measure of non-arrival even in the advent," of the bitter dregs in that which can be realized. For the realizer's deed cannot be separated from the act of realizing: in realizing his cause, he can realize himself only step by step. The circle posed by the problem of educating the educators returns on the level of utopia; but even for this, a tempting solution is suggested in the formula of the increasing self-mediation of man and nature.

A utopia that understands the dialectics of its own realization as utopian is not as concrete as it pretends it is. Perhaps the image of the kingdom of freedom owes its features, frozen in the "vision of kingdom," to the exuberance of its orginal project. This exuberance, in turn, may be based on the sort of speculative materialism that exempts materialism from speculation. In discussing his famous thesis that you cannot realize philosophy without abolishing it, Marx argues against the young-Hegelians' philosophy as follows: Their philosophy only considers its critical warfare against the world, but fails to recognize "that all philosophy *hitherto existing* belongs to this world and is its supplement, even if only in the idea." Bloch concludes that the negation of philosophy refers to "philosophy hitherto existing" and not to "every possible and future philosophy." Marx, however, unmistakably meant to say the opposite; for he continues: The young-Hegelians lack self-criticism, "for they start out from the preconditions of philosophy and stop with its given results . . . even though on the contrary the latter (assuming their justification) can be obtained only through the preconditions of the philosophy that existed hitherto, of *philosophy as philosophy*." (MEGA I, I, I, p. 613.) Awareness of its autonomy belongs to the preconditions of philosophy: philosophical reason must be able to give its own reason. A philosophy, however, that is critical of its own preconditions and has become critique itself is aware of being part of that which it criticizes; it is an expression of alienation — and its transcendence. Not before it abolishes itself and thereby realizes itself will philosophy be able to stand next to itself and make possible that knowledge which speculation always imagined it owned.

Bloch's error here is more than one of interpretation: he crosses out the merely experimental validity of utopia, thus leaving unclarified the relationship of philosophical criticism to the sciences. The same is true of other representatives of dialectical materialism. If utopia wishes theoretically to understand the practical need for abolishing existing conflicts, then it will have to scientifically legitimatize its interest in knowledge in two ways: as a really objective need and as objectively capable of fulfillment. The hypothetical humility of utopian thinking is different from the awareness of being autonomous held by speculative thinking. The first feels that a philosophical concept can be disproved by science analyzing the conditions of its realization; but it does not expect its truth ever to be proved for good. For revolutionary praxis transcends even anticipatory theory. Speculative thought, on the other hand, believes that it can continue philosophy through research, that the latter can only prove, never disprove it.

Bloch attempts a third alternative: he wants to retain speculation and to vary it in a utopian way. The guaranty of salvation is lost; but the anticipation of salvation retains its certainty: it must work out either this way or not at all. It can achieve all — or nothing; hope finally fulfilled according to the anticipated image of fulfillment — or chaos.

If utopia draws the power of its consciousness from the experience that in history seemingly natural limits have proved to be transcendable, then it ought just as sternly to develop a consciousness of its own kingdom's limits. Certainly a dialectical analysis that functions not in merely approaching totalities but in anticipating them cannot meaningfully be lowered to the level of differential analysis; the utopia concept must not be demeaned into contents of regulative ideas. Just the same, it must keep aware of the possibility of such changes, which without warning might devour even utopia. In realizing itself, utopia could precipitate itself into a situation that categorically is concealed from utopian prevision: new obstructions, new difficulties, new unbalances might appear which, altogether truly different from all previous ones, might be so incompatible with the structure of problems conceivable at present that, even from the horizon of perfectly utopian awareness, they could not have been anticipated as problems. Utopia, realized, would be "different." This awareness of a limit certainly does not suspend its consciousness, nor would it justify a renunciation of utopia by militants of the counter-enlightenment. The propaganda against the Jacobin results utopian beginnings may lead to, the hypocritical preachments against the terror of morality only increase the dangers to which they blind us.

Bloch's materialism remains speculative. His dialectics of the enlightenment transcends dialectics and reaches a doctrine of potentiality. Metaphorically speaking (and utopia always retains a measure of metaphor), Bloch's thought processes are derived from the development of a pregnancy of the world which is generally assumed rather than attempting to free us from the societal immobility of existing contradictions. Philosophy of nature here turns into the nature of his philosophy.

The philosophers of a surviving European tradition, squeezed between Anglo-Saxon positivism and Soviet materialism, can only note the irritating fact that on the opposite banks of the Elbe River a philosophy has been created which — having skipped Kant as it were and with a pre-critical approach — is just the same inspired by the great breath of German idealism. Thought is spreading its wings — as it must, even if the time of the Augurs is gone.

NOTE: The preceding essay first appeared in German in 1960, and is translated here by Henry and Hedwig Pachter.

NOTES ON CONTRIBUTORS

REUBEN ABEL is professor of philosophy at The New School's Graduate Faculty and author of *The Pragmatic Humanism of F.C.S. Schiller* • T. W. ADORNO is the late German philosopher, music critic, and man of letters; Director of the Institute for Social Research in Frankfurt am Main, and author of many volumes including *The Authoritarian Personality* and *The Philosophy of the New Music* • RUDOLF ARNHEIM is professor of psychology at Harvard and author of many works including *Film as Art* and *Towards a Psychology of Art* • IRING FETSCHER is professor of literature in Frankfurt • JURGEN HABERMAS is one of Germany's most distinguished younger social scientists, a professor in Frankfurt am Main • HENRY HATFIELD is professor of comparative literature at Harvard and author of books on Thomas Mann and others • JOHN H. HERZ is professor of political science at City College of New York and author of *International Politics in the Atomic Age* • FREDRIC JAMESON is professor of literature at the University of California, San Diego, and author of *Sartre: Origins of a Style* • ERICH KAHLER was professor of philosophy at Princeton, and is author of many books including *Man the Measure, The Tower and the Abyss*, and *The Disintegration of Form in Art* • WALTER KAUFMANN is professor of philosophy at Princeton and author of many distinguished volumes, including works on Nietzsche and Hegel. A recent book is entitled *Tragedy And Philosophy**• GEORGE McKENNA is professor of political science at City College of New York and author of a forthcoming study of Hannah Arendt • GEORGE L. MOSSE is professor of history at University of Wisconsin and author of many volumes, including *The Crisis of German Ideology: Intellectual Origins of the Third Reich*. He is an editor of the journal *Survey* • HENRY PACHTER is visiting professor of political science at City College of New York and a former Dean of The New School for Social Research. He is UN correspondent for *Weltwoche* (Zurich) and author of many volumes including *Magic into Science, Nazi Deutsch*, and *Collision Course*. He is a regular contributor to *Salmagundi* • EDWARD SAGARIN is professor of sociology at City College of New York and an editor of *Salmagundi*. He is author of the recent volume *Odd Man in: Societies of Deviants in America* • THOMAS W. SIMONS, JR. is a foreign service officer working for the United States in Poland. He has published articles in the field of Austrian history and culture • GEORGE STEINER is the distinguished author and critic whose many volumes include *Tolstoy or Dostoyevski, The Death of Tragedy*, and *Language and Silence* • ANTHONY WILDEN is professor of French at University of California, San Diego, and author of a volume on Jacques Lacan entitled *The Language of the Self*. His study of questions associated with the work of Herbert Marcuse, appearing in this issue, is part of an extensive work on Marcuse, and a slightly altered version of the present piece will appear in the French journal *Les Temps Modernes*.

---

*Walter Kaufmann's "The Reception of Existentialism in the United States" appeared originally in the Summer 1968 issue of *Midway*, and is published with permission of the author and The University of Chicago Press.